# Julia Margaret Cameron's 'fancy subjects'

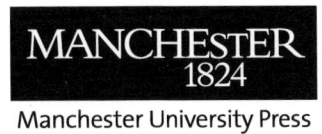

MANCHESTER
1824

Manchester University Press

# Julia Margaret Cameron's 'fancy subjects'

## Photographic allegories of Victorian identity and empire

JEFF ROSEN

Manchester University Press

Published by Manchester University Press
Altrincham Street, Manchester M1 7JA
www.manchesteruniversitypress.co.uk

British Library Cataloguing-in-Publication Data
A catalogue record for this book is available from the British Library

Library of Congress Cataloging-in-Publication Data applied for

ISBN    978 1 7849 9317 7    *hardback*

First published 2016

Typeset in Monotype Dante by
Koinonia, Manchester
Printed in Great Britain by
TJ International Ltd, Padstow

For Lynn

# Contents

# List of figures and tables

## Figures

## Tables

# Acknowledgements

In the spring of 1985, I took a break from my research in the French national archives and joined my dissertation advisors Susan Siegfried and Rick Brettell at the Centre National de la Photographie to view an extraordinary photography exhibition, Mike Weaver's seminal retrospective, *Julia Margaret Cameron 1815–1879*. I'm grateful to Rick and Susan for introducing me to the possibilities of studying Cameron's work and would also like to thank David Van Zanten, Larry Silver, and Holly Clayson for their support during those years. For memorable conversations about allegory, symbolism, and Victorian photography, I would also like to thank Leonard Barkan, Joel Snyder, Anne McCauley, Julie Codell, Debra Mancoff, George Dimock, and Jerry Mead.

Many curators opened their collections to me, and I would like to acknowledge: David Travis and Sylvia Wolf, formerly of the Art Institute of Chicago; David Wooters, Rachel Stuhlman, and the late Robert Sobieszek of the International Museum of Photography at the George Eastman House; Maria Morris Hambourg of the Metropolitan Museum of Art; Weston Naef and Gordon Baldwin of the J. Paul Getty Museum; Roy Flukinger and Linda Briscoe of the Harry Ransom Humanities Research Center at the University of Texas at Austin; Pam Roberts of the Royal Photographic Society, Bath; and Mark Haworth-Booth, formerly of the Victoria and Albert Museum.

Research leave, fellowship support, and travel grants came from numerous sources for which I am extremely grateful. I would like to acknowledge the Samuel Kress Foundation, the Art Institute of Chicago Old Masters Society, and the Center for Advanced Study in the Visual Arts of the National Gallery of Art, which made my early research possible. I am also grateful for a sabbatical leave and several professional development grants from Columbia College Chicago; a Fanny Knapp Allen Post-Doctoral Fellowship at the University of Rochester; several grants from the National Endowment for the Humanities Travel to Collections program; and a Fleur Cowles Fellowship from the Harry Ransom Humanities Research Center at the University of Texas at Austin.

The book is entirely written anew, although an earlier version of Chapter 5 was published as 'Cameron's Photographic Double Takes', in Julie Codell and Dianne Sachko Macleod, eds., *Orientalism Transposed: The Impact of the Colonies on British Culture* (London: Ashgate, 1998), and an earlier version of Chapter 7 appeared as 'Cameron's Colonized Eden: Picturesque Politics at the Edge of the Empire', in Jordana Pomeroy, ed., *Intrepid Women: Victorian Women Artists Travel* (London: Ashgate, 2005). 'Classical Cameron' was presented as a paper at the annual meeting of the College Art Association in 2005, and grew into Chapter 2, and 'Julia Margaret Cameron's Orientalism', a presentation at the annual meeting of the Association of Art Historians in 1995 in London, is the foundation for Chapter 4. In 2000, I presented an earlier version of Chapter 6 to the North American Conference on British Studies. I am grateful for the feedback of friends and colleagues who shared their thoughts after these presentations, and indebted to earlier published studies of Cameron by Julian Cox and Colin Ford, Mike Weaver, Joanne Lukitsh, Victoria Olsen, and Amanda Hopkinson. All opinions, and any errors contained in this book are of course my own.

Almost thirty years ago, after viewing Cameron's photography on the Trocadéro, Rick, Susan, and I went to a nearby oyster bar to talk about the exhibition. They might not remember the darkness of that night or the chill in the air, but I still do.

# Note to the reader

Like many artists before her, Julia Margaret Cameron used evocative titles to identify the subjects of her imagery. But sometimes these references are obscure and she left many photographs untitled. *Julia Margaret Cameron's 'fancy subjects'* examines Cameron's pictorial allegories, and the titles that she assigned to her photographs help identify each subject. But precise identification can be complicated because she frequently used the same title for different prints, or gave multiple titles to the same image, or returned years later to some photographs to reprint and retitle them yet again.

For example, she titled several photographs *Sappho* to refer to the ancient Greek poet. She registered one *Sappho* for copyright on 19 May 1865; she registered another *Sappho*, using the same model but in a different composition, on 11 November 1865; and she registered a third image on 18 June 1866, using a different model but containing the traditional iconography used to represent Sappho.

To clarify the pictorial references in the text, this book draws upon the *catalogue raisonné* of Cameron's photographs produced in 2003 by the J. Paul Getty Museum and edited by Julian Cox and Colin Ford. The *catalogue raisonné* contains a reproduction of every photograph produced by the artist. The digital edition of this publication is available electronically to all from the Getty Publications Virtual Library; the permanent URL is: http://d2aohiyo3d3idm.cloudfront.net/publications/virtuallibrary/0892366818.pdf. Accordingly, references to Cameron's photographs within this book follow the citation style (Cox no.) to refer readers to the *catalogue raisonné* number in this publication. In this particular example, the *Sappho* registered on 19 May 1865 is (Cox 252); the *Sappho* registered on 11 November 1865 is (Cox 253); and the photograph registered on 18 June 1866 that depicts a woman in an ancient Greek head dress, representing *Sappho*, is (Cox 340).

# Introduction

Mrs Cameron is making endless Madonnas and May Queens and Foolish Virgins and Wise Virgins and I know not what besides. It is really wonderful how she puts her spirit into people. (Letter from Emily Tennyson to Edward Lear, 1865)[1]

## 'Fancy subjects'

When Julia Margaret Cameron took up photography in 1864, she passionately embraced allegory as her preferred artistic impulse and arranged her sitters in poses taken from classical literature, the Bible, contemporary poetry, and recent history. She called these photographs her 'fancy subjects', borrowing the term from the tradition of academic painting practised by her friend and mentor, George Frederic Watts. Working methodically, she carefully noted the textual sources that inspired her most valued pictures and gave evocative titles to each photograph she produced for public exhibition, mass production, or inclusion in a photographic album. Cameron's avid pursuit of photography apparently won her much esteem from friends and neighbours, but her seemingly arbitrary choice of subjects bewildered even some of her most fervent admirers. Emily Tennyson, for example, was clearly confused by the wellspring of her friend's imagination and the purpose of her activities.

This book argues that an organizing principle informed Cameron's choice of 'fancy subjects' and that they were not chosen randomly or without design. During a decade of activity that started in the mid-1860s, when the medium itself was still young, Cameron created allegories in photography as part of a sustained effort to represent the country's national heritage and cultural identity. To nineteenth-century Britain, this was a complex inheritance that traced its National Church to ancient Rome and its parliamentary government to ancient Greece. It based its moral guideposts on the heroic legends and chivalric code of medieval England and established domestic norms upon the familial bonds celebrated in biblical tales. It justified its territorial expansion across the globe as part of a 'civilizing mission' that would spread these very ideas and narratives to new lands and peoples in the colonies. And it was through allegorical storytelling, whether by means of poetry, fiction, theatre, or visual art, that it broadcast these ideas.[2]

Cameron was among the earliest to bring allegory to photography, but the model of the 'fancy picture' had its roots in eighteenth-century English painting. This visual form emerged from its origins in Dutch and French genre painting, and was associated with Sir Joshua Reynolds, George Romney, and Thomas Gainsborough.[3] Pictures containing 'fancy subjects' were inherently sentimental, often theatrical, and always contained a narrative element; they included scenes of everyday life that featured individuals or small groups as well as picturesque subjects extracted from a broad sweep of well-known historical, mythological, religious, and literary stories. They could be sugary, nostalgic, or erotic, but they were typically invested with romantic or idealistic thoughts about the human condition and often embodied pretensions to the 'nobility' of high art. By the mid-1850s, the 'fancy picture' became a catchall term for paintings that framed isolated subjects in a momentary suspension of activity, capturing quiet contemplation, religious devotion, or sentimental feelings.

In photography, men as diverse as Oscar Gustave Rejlander, Lewis Carroll, and Roger Fenton embraced this approach, and called it 'pictorial photography'. Rejlander's photograph, *Poor Jo*, is a typical example, the subject taken from the fictional street urchin created by Dickens in *Bleak House* (1850). In order to focus attention on the pathos of the sick and impoverished child, Rejlander clothed his model in rags and darkened his bare feet with charcoal, all within a controlled studio setting. Importantly, this aesthetic did not frown on artificiality, nor did it elevate naturalism. Cameron often echoed its romantic motives, claiming she sought inspiration in Romantic or Renaissance painting more so than she did in other contemporary visual forms that surrounded her, like book illustrations or graphic art. As she wrote to her friend Sir John Herschel: 'My aspirations are to ennoble Photography and to secure for it the character and uses of High Art by combining the real & Ideal & sacrificing nothing of Truth by all possible devotion to Poetry & beauty.'[4] She combined the real and ideal successfully only by carefully understanding her narrative sources and applying their allegorical references wisely when she titled her photographs.

The first meaning of each image derives from its assigned title. These titles were chosen directly from well-known texts in order to identify specific sources and subjects of each photograph, but occasionally her titles also possessed more than one meaning. Sometimes, she borrowed titles from contemporary poems or excerpted lines directly from them; at other times she gave her sitter a new identity entirely: Sir Henry Taylor, for example, became *King David*; her personal maid, Mary Hillier, became *Maud by Moonlight*; a village boy became *Young Endymion*. Cameron's titles are preserved on the prints themselves, in the lists she made to accompany albums and exhibitions (see Figure 1 for an example), and in the

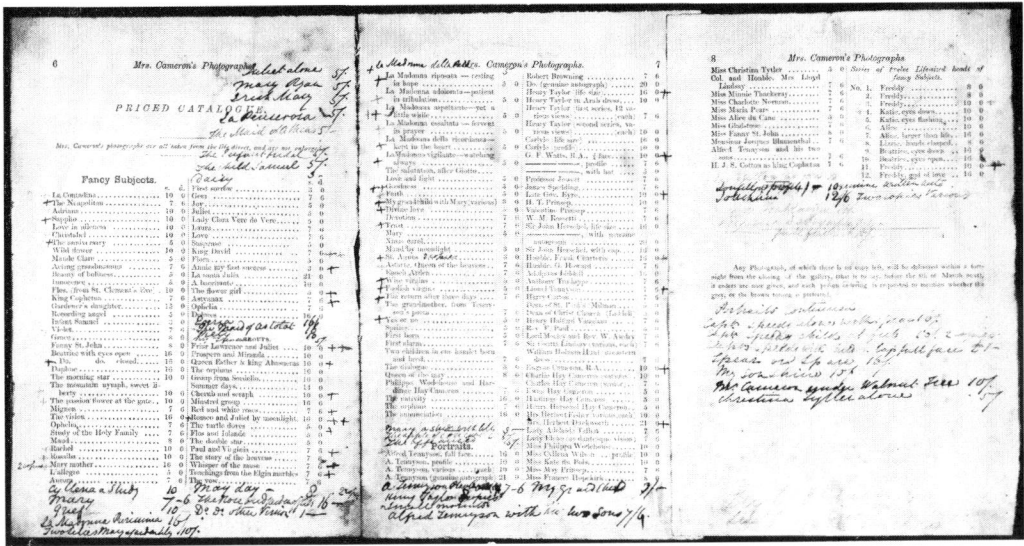

*Mrs Cameron's Photographs. Priced Catalogue*, 1868. Pamphlet, 22.3 x 41.6 cm. 1

copyright registrations she filed in order to preserve her exclusive right to reproduce these works. The entries describe her models' poses and notes their gestures and use of any props or unique costume, itemize the number of individuals used in each composition, and very often record the title she chose for the photograph.

During Cameron's time, copyright registers protected artists by recording such details, making it difficult for anyone other than the true owner to claim authorship and reproduce the same imagery. Because they listed new records chronologically, the registers help historians recreate the events of a given day or period. For example, a brief selection of sequential entries made for 4 November and 12 December 1864 helps to support Emily Tennyson's observation that Cameron was simultaneously pursuing a wide range of symbolic, mythological, and biblical subjects:

> 90. St. Agnes (Mary Hillier) eyes down, hands together, with moon in background, draped figure
>
> 91. May Queen (Mary Ryan & Caroline Hawkins), one figure in bed ¾ face, the other Profile
>
> 92. Madonna almost profile, child full face on lap
>
> 93. The Water Babies. Two Children seated as if floating, both nearly full face, nearly naked,
>
> 94. Mary Hillier, full face, with shawl over chest, star on brow, eyes upraised
>
> 95. Photograph entitled 'Gentleness' with two children. Mother ¾ face looking up child on one side standing on the other side kneeling naked figure ¾ face on Mother's shoulder[5]

Julia Margaret Cameron has been inscribed as a pioneer in the history of photography for more than a century, but many gaps still exist in our understanding of why she pursued certain subjects and not others, and of what forces drove her ambitions. For example, the *catalogue raisonné* of Cameron's photographs produced by the J. Paul Getty Museum in 2003 identifies more than 1,200 of the known photographs she produced.[6] Nevertheless, the nineteenth-century copyright registers record little more than 500 of her photographs, and even today, scholars have matched up only about half of those written descriptions with the actual photographs. In some cases, too, the copyright registers mention sitters for which no surviving prints exist. But the registers clearly reproduce Cameron's methodical methods for identifying and titling her work, just as her handwritten notations, captions, and marks to the letter or reverse side of the surviving prints also demonstrate her thoughtful care to provide clear textual references and literary interpretations for each photograph that she considered a complete work of art.

The *catalogue raisonné* also provides evidence that Cameron returned repeatedly to favourite subjects over time. Sometimes she reconceived a subject entirely or extended a thematic point of interest by portraying another character or scene from the same narrative source. Sometimes she gave a new title to an old photograph or chose to apply a title already used years before to a new and different image. Sometimes she would return to an earlier photograph and work in the darkroom to reverse its image, so that, for example, a profile that had originally faced in one direction would now face the opposite way in the newer photograph. By examining Cameron's working methods and by interpreting patterns that emerge from her choice of titles and narrative sources, we can determine that her photographs of 'fancy subjects' made use of, and relied upon, the inherently fluid and interconnected relationship that exists between texts and pictorial forms.[7] As she demonstrated in her earliest framed series of Madonna images, which she called *The Fruits of the Spirit* (1865), Cameron understood that texts and images bound one to the other in narrative photography, and that collectively, a group of allegorical photographs could tell a more persuasive story than any single image on its own. The nine photographs that comprise *The Fruits of the Spirit*, for example, include individual prints titled to correspond to the New Testament text from the Epistle of St Paul to the Galatians (5:22–3), which lists the cardinal virtues: 'love, joy, peace, long-suffering, gentleness, faith, meekness, temperance'.

Because Cameron embraced the narrative potential of the camera and gave special attention to religious imagery, young mothers and children, and portraits of the important cultural figures of her time, like Tennyson, Darwin, and Carlyle, historians have focused on how she used these particular subjects to elevate her art and 'ennoble Photography'. But Cameron's 'fancy subjects' *as a whole* have received relatively little attention compared to her portraits, particularly because when she indexed her albums and exhibitions, as we see in Figure 1, she grouped

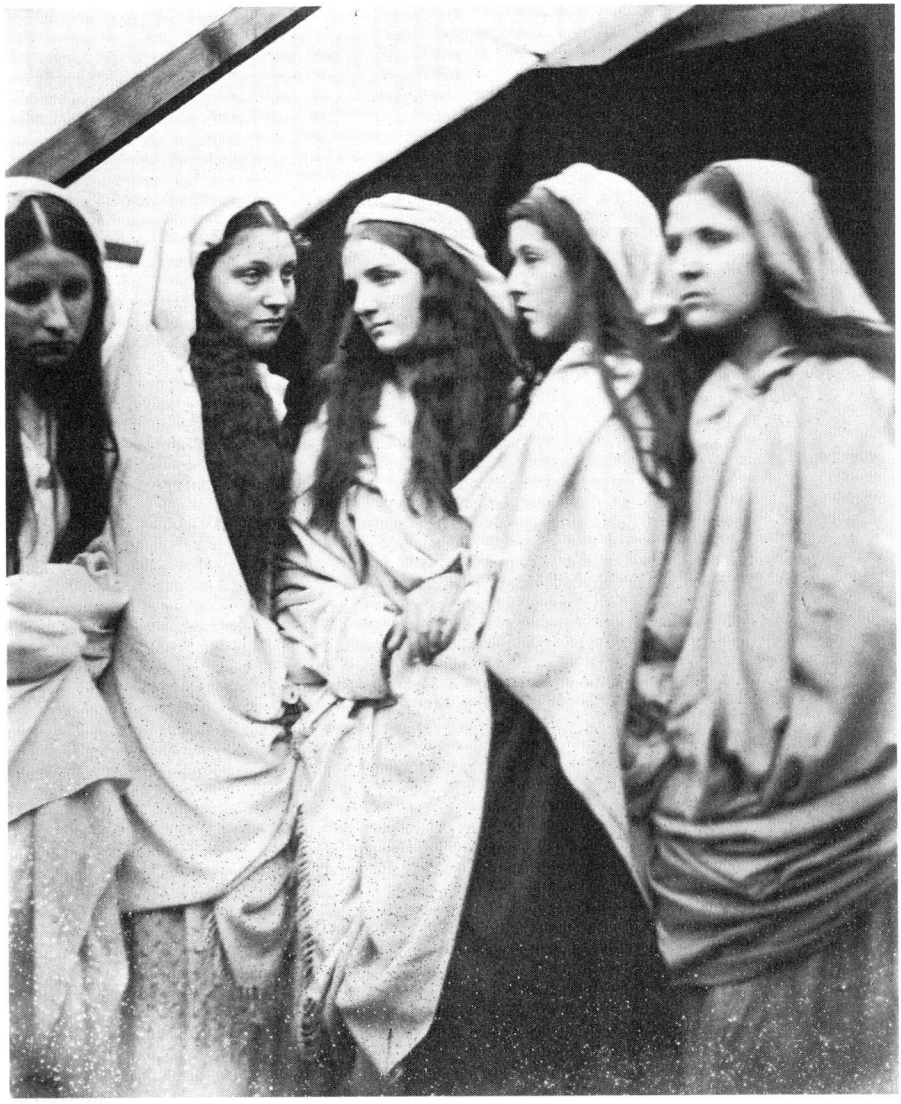

Julia Margaret Cameron, *The Five Foolish Virgins* (Cox 123), 1864.
Albumen silver print, 24.8 x 20 cm.

2

her allegorical works together and did not provide any particular context or perspective. In other words, despite her deep commitment to this pictorial work, she apparently gave little regard to its formal thematic coherence or to whether individual prints should be considered in relationship to others or to some greater purpose, leaving many questions unresolved to this day.

Like all allegories, where ideas and truths are represented indirectly, Cameron's 'fancy subjects' are inseparable from the act of storytelling, and like all narratives, dependent upon the multiple messages and meanings created by those literary sources. What did it mean in the mid-1860s to be engaged in 'making endless Madonnas and May Queens and Foolish Virgins and Wise Virgins' in photography? What was at stake in this activity, and what possible outcomes could Cameron have imagined would follow as a result of the wide distribution of these allegorical images? Many forms of debate among today's art historians and literary critics are embedded in these questions. Chief among them is the complexity of what we mean by the narrative image itself.[8] If we commonly refer to a 'story' as a succession of events, and to the 'text' as the spoken or written form that depicts those events in discourse, it is 'narration' that describes the process of delivering that story to a reader or listener. In visual art, where iconography defines the act of narration using abstract visual symbols, both popular and high art versions of different stories may coexist. Narration may be complicated further by the way that texts deliver stories in different expressive forms, like poetry, literature, music, and drama, for example, but also through expository means, like news accounts, satire, diaries, or essays, or in the visual arts, in paintings, book illustrations, popular prints, and photographs. Different individuals or communities might also interpret a story's many meanings according to their familiarity with, or political allegiance to, particular symbols, allegories, and textual references, further complicating otherwise simple interpretations of the narrative being represented or told.

As we shall see, Cameron's 'fancy subjects', like her image of *The Five Foolish Virgins* (Cox 123; Figure 2), consciously intertwine textual narratives and visual iconography, using signs and symbols in visual art to tell an allegorical story; for example, this photograph illustrates the New Testament Parable of the Ten Virgins from Matthew 25:1–13. This book provides evidence that Cameron understood and manipulated the narrative imagery she was creating. But because she joined together interdependent texts and images in her 'fancy pictures', we might also wonder if Cameron's narratives embodied fixed meanings and references that connected them to well-defined literary sources and historical events, or if her choices of pictorial and textual elements actually destabilized and undermined those connections. When narratives that seemed otherwise stable have become mutable, multiple associations may emerge and new meanings created. Because Cameron chose allegory as her primary artistic vehicle, it is helpful to appreciate that the earliest writings about her photography asked precisely these kinds of questions about her use of textual and pictorial narratives.

We begin Cameron's story with Virginia Woolf, who published one of the first biographies of the photographer in 1926. Ironically, it was Woolf's pen that first gave rise to 'Julia Margaret Cameron', casting her not as the decorated photographer, but instead as an idiosyncratic literary personality, a caricature starring in a work of dramatic fiction.

## Imagining Isumbras

In Virginia Woolf's three-act play, *Freshwater: A Comedy*, the author imagines the Victorian world of her great-aunt, portraying Julia Margaret Cameron as hopelessly idealistic and stodgy, even among her old-fashioned contemporaries. First written in 1923, and then later expanded and performed in 1935 for Woolf's Bloomsbury friends in her sister Vanessa Bell's London studio, the play's dramatic action was set in Cameron's own house in Freshwater, the small Isle of Wight village in which she lived.[9] There, Woolf portrayed the photographer with her neighbour, the poet Alfred Tennyson; her friend, the painter George Frederic Watts; and Watts's betrothed, the actress Ellen Terry – the four engaged in an imaginary dialogue about the exhausting process of creating great works of art. Toward the end of the first act, Woolf parodied Cameron by deriding her choice of subject matter and her efforts to turn the magic of ordinary, everyday life into remote and ancient stories, mocking her use of photography to look to the past rather than the future:

> **Mrs C.:** [*She goes to the window and calls out:*] Young man! Young man! I want you to come and sit to me for Sir Isumbras at the Ford. [*She exits. A donkey brays. She comes back into the room.*] That's not a man. That's a donkey. Still, to the true artist, one fact is much the same as another. A fact is a fact; art is art; a donkey's a donkey. [*She looks out of the window.*] Stand still, donkey; think, Ass, you are carrying St. Christopher upon your back. Look up, Ass. Cast your eyes to Heaven. Stand absolutely still. There![10]

Although Cameron never titled any of her photographs *Sir Isumbras at the Ford*, Woolf's ironic point is well made. Even if Woolf's literary group could not immediately place the reference, they would surely have understood 'Sir Isumbras' as cultural shorthand for a chivalric subject, one that had religious and medieval roots in the Crusades that placed it alongside other heroic tales like *King Arthur, Sir Gowther, Octavian*, and *Richard Coeur de Lion*.[11] Those in her audience with a deeper knowledge of English romantic poetry would also be able to recall Sir Isumbras's story as a familiar Orientalist tale. In brief, the fourteenth-century poem describes Sir Isumbras's noble origins and the knight's penance as he travels to free the Holy Land; it relates his wife's abduction and eventual recovery, his own personal sacrifice and despondency, and his loss of honour at the hands of a despotic Eastern sultan. Finally, it applauds his ultimate revenge in battle and in claiming foreign lands in the name of Christianity.

Because Woolf wrote her satire for a well-read and culturally astute group of literary friends, she could also have counted on those listening to 'Mrs C.' to have seen first hand, or to know through reproduction, John Everett Millais's painting of the same subject, called *A Dream of the Past; Sir Isumbras at the Ford*, which Millais had exhibited originally in 1857 at the Royal Academy. Woolf and her friends would have been able to place Millais as the artist for *Sir Isumbras* and recall his outmoded style as Pre-Raphaelite; to know, too, how Millais attempted to 'update' the Isumbras story in Victorian terms by joining it to sentimental themes like the vigilant father tending to his vulnerable children, and how this in turn inspired the art critic Tom Taylor to write additional romantic verses to accompany the painting.[12] But because Woolf knew that her audience expected parody, and that its members were well versed in the history of English art, she could also count on their knowing that both John Ruskin and William Michael Rossetti criticized Millais's painting for its stylistic faults and lampooned him for his efforts to use the high moralism of a tale like Isumbras to elevate mawkish and sentimental themes. In short, Isumbras was, in Woolf's eyes, a negative example of artistic overreaching and false pretensions. By extension, of course, Woolf was able to criticize Cameron.

But there is an important political dimension present in this subject as well. Shortly after it was exhibited, Frederick Sandys parodied Millais's painting in the *Cornhill Magazine* in a caricature that he called *The Nightmare*. In his caricature, Sandys substituted a braying donkey for Isumbras's knight's horse, replacing a noble steed with a vulgar ass, a substitution that Woolf emphasizes in her fictional scene involving Cameron. By replacing the knight's horse with a donkey, Sandys effectively devalued the supposed 'nobility' of the scene along with its symbolic idealization of nationalism, heroism, and paternalism. Sandys's send-up also ridicules the Pre-Raphaelite's painterly style, as he portrayed Millais in place of the knight, Dante Gabriel Rossetti in place of the girl, William Holman Hunt for the boy, and branded John Ruskin's initials into the rear flank of the donkey. In her analysis of the nineteenth-century reception of Millais's painting, Julie Codell wrote, 'Sandys's jibe was taken in good spirits as a gentle joke.'[13] But Codell also makes plain that embedded in Sandys's commentary was an overt criticism of the inflated nationalistic sentiments associated with romantic medieval poetry and the religious zealotry associated with the Crusades, and that this critique was even more effective because it censured the joining of 'legitimate' high art subjects with popular and vulgar forms.

For Virginia Woolf, *Sir Isumbras at the Ford* served a dual purpose in *Freshwater*: Isumbras was an archaic subject, an absurdist stereotype for an obsolete Victorian aesthetics as much as it was concise shorthand for the opposite impulses that described Woolf's own modern outlook, which focused on the complex interior spaces and dynamic interactions of contemporary social life. It proved a reliable token for mocking Pre-Raphaelite painting as an out-dated visual style. But Woolf's choice of the Isumbras tale also discloses her own thoughtful understanding about Cameron's process for choosing her narrative subjects. In particular, Woolf recognized that Cameron deliberately chose medieval subjects when those narratives embedded nationalistic sentiments. She also understood that the story itself could refer to, and be shaped by, a wide range of sources in medieval poetry, academic painting, and mass produced caricature, and that in this way, Isumbras was a perfect emblem to characterize Cameron's photography.

Woolf was in many ways correct: Cameron purposefully chose subjects like Sir Isumbras that relied upon the interplay of literary texts and historical images to influence and complicate the meaning of those narratives. She recognized that subjects like these resonated in literary, pictorial, and popular examples, that one expressive form influenced and affected the reception of another, and that the interpretation of these narrative subjects was deliberated culturally over time, taking shape in ever new and on-going forms.[14] Woolf also understood that Cameron took advantage of the vibrant interrelationship that mediates back and forth between literary texts and pictorial symbols, a dynamism that destabilizes the notion that fixed meanings must be attached decidedly to narrative photographs. In *Freshwater*, for example, she has Cameron exclaim, 'I have found him at last. Sir Galahad!' In doing so, Woolf references Watts's 1862 painting, *Sir Galahad*, which had become popularized through mass-reproduced prints into her own time, and she might have also intentionally referenced Cameron's characterization of her own son, Henry, whom she called 'Sir Galahad' because she admired his goodness and moral conduct.[15] As we examine the production and reception of Cameron's 'fancy subjects' in the chapters that follow, we will see that, like Woolf much later, Cameron thoughtfully considered how texts and pictorial forms influenced each other, how photographs could draw upon older graphic forms and make them new, and how she too could count on her audience to generate new meanings by challenging and reinterpreting the narrative stories she depicted.

## Image into allegory

Although *Freshwater* was not published in her lifetime, Woolf nevertheless reiterated the Victorian stereotypes embedded in the play when she composed Cameron's biographical sketch in 1926, which she wrote to accompany *Victorian Photographs of Famous Men and Fair Women*, the book of Cameron's photographs that she published with Roger Fry. As portrayed by Woolf, Cameron was a creative and inspired woman overflowing with unfocused and unpredictable energies, needing only to be surrounded by beauty; she was imperious and unstoppable in her efforts to shower her family and those she admired with the bounty of endless gifts. Only when she received a camera as a gift at the age of forty-eight was she able to realize

> an outlet for the energies which she had dissipated in poetry and fiction and doing up houses and concocting curries and entertaining her friends … The coal-house was turned into a dark room; the fowl-house was turned into a glass-house. Boatmen were turned into King Arthur; village girls into Queen Guinevere. Tennyson was wrapped in rugs; Sir Henry Taylor was crowned with tinsel. The parlour maid sat for her portrait and the guest had to answer the bell.[16]

Unique among her peers, Woolf wrote, Cameron was unfailingly generous, reliably unconventional, and above all, eccentric; she was 'like a tigress' around her children, uncaring about the brown stains that marked her hands from photographic chemicals or their harsh odour in her home, and 'uncompromising' about her art, which forced 'the carpenter and the Crown Princess of Prussia alike [to] sit still as stones in the attitudes she chose, in the draperies she arranged, for as long as she wished'.[17]

While it is not unusual for one generation to look down upon the aesthetic preferences of its predecessors, Woolf's assessments entered art history in 1926, and her book with Fry has cemented an unflattering depiction of the photographer as an eccentric woman who struggled to overcome her peculiarities and who created works of lasting cultural importance solely by virtue of the portraits she made of her famous male contemporaries. This unsympathetic portrait persists to the present day, as many of Cameron's biographers have felt compelled to retell an amusing anecdote that casts her in a dismissive light.[18] Woolf and Fry believed Cameron's portraits alone had lasting value and elevated them at the expense of Cameron's allegorical compositions, which they simply did not take seriously. In fact, all but two of the forty-four plates in *Victorian Photographs* reproduce portraits, minimizing and all but expunging from this early record the allegorical photographs that Cameron called her 'fancy subjects'. But we should not be surprised by their disapproval of Cameron's allegorical work, for several reasons.

For one, in writing her biography about Cameron (which became the model for all that have followed), Woolf relied upon the diaries, letters, and personal recollections of several of Cameron's child models (Agnes Weld, Laura Gurney, Lionel and Hallam Tennyson), who, as children, found her terrifying, along with those of extended family members who stayed with the Camerons in Freshwater as young adults (Anne and Hester 'Minnie' Thackeray), who found her both unpredictable and indomitable. Woolf's parents, Sir Leslie Stephen and Julia Prinsep Stephen (née Jackson), very likely enhanced these assessments by drawing upon their own published statements and personal memories.[19] Additionally, Woolf's knowledge of Cameron's photographs was limited; she did not have access to her great-aunt's entire photographic *oeuvre*, as Cameron's prints had been dispersed across the globe into many private collections.

Moreover, Cameron's photographs were situated within a set of well-established ideological attitudes that devalued the work of women artists; as Linda Nochlin reminds us, these attitudes assumed 'her defining domestic and nurturing function; her identity with the realm of nature; her existence as object rather than creator of art; [and] the patent ridiculousness of her attempts to insert herself actively into the realm of history by means of work or personal engagement in political struggle'.[20] As Griselda Pollock put it succinctly, 'High Culture systematically denies knowledge of women as producers of culture and meanings.'[21]

In Cameron's time, John Ruskin exemplified this arrogance when he criticized the painter Anna Mary Howitt, who in 1856 painted a work called *Boadicea Brooding over Her Wrongs*. Ruskin wrote to Howitt to dress her down for having the temerity to paint noble historical subjects, disqualifying her simply because she was a woman. Expressing his contempt, Ruskin declared: 'What do *you* know about Boadicea? Leave such subjects alone and paint me a pheasant's wing.'[22]

The visibility and potential impact of creative women were diminished when male critics preferred that gentle still lifes, rather than warrior queens, issued from the studios of its women artists. Similarly, their ability to give voice to what Nochlin calls 'the master discourse of the iconography or narrative' of their chosen subjects was impeded. Consequently, women artists faced an uphill climb in their efforts to contribute to a broad cultural dialogue, standing against those, like Ruskin, who would obstruct their way. The climb was steeper for artists like Cameron who used allegory in the relatively new graphic medium of photography. Yet when Cameron's 'fancy subjects' were criticized, the attacks seemed to strengthen her resolve. As this study makes clear, Cameron resisted any critique of her decision to represent allegorical and national subjects and chose instead to focus on these consistently, throughout her career. She even created her own pantheon of nationalistic warrior queens, producing photographs depicting *Boadicea* (Cox 521) in 1865; *Thalestris* (unknown or now lost) in 1867; and *Zenobia* (Cox 544) in 1870. We examine all three in Chapter 3.[23]

Cameron's chief interest in photography was in representing historical, literary, and allegorical subjects like these, subjects that held cultural significance and national historical importance: although she certainly cared about creating evocative portraits, her correspondence shows that she worked assiduously to master the iconography and narrative coherence of her allegorical compositions. A letter from George Frederic Watts to Cameron, dated 21 June 1865, provides evidence of their dialogue toward this end; its first lines are revealing:

> I have received with your letter two beautiful photos. More like old pictures than ever. I don't know that they are your very best but they are certainly amongst the most artistic. Some parts of the child with half a head are wonderful[.] More like Phidias & more anti pre-Raphaelite than anything I have seen.[24]

Cameron held on to Watts's letter for her own use at a later time and modified it by placing an asterisk after the phrase 'child with half a head'; then she wrote in the space above, 'called the Shunamite [*sic*] woman & her dead son', and 'G.F. Watts upon my photography'. Watts's letters to Cameron over the years refer consistently to her use of allegorical subjects, to the *Cupid*, to the *Alathea*, to the *Diana*.

Cameron's photograph of *The Shunamite* [*sic*] *Woman & her dead Son* (Cox 135; Figure 3) depicts a woman in a headscarf in front of a nearly naked recum-

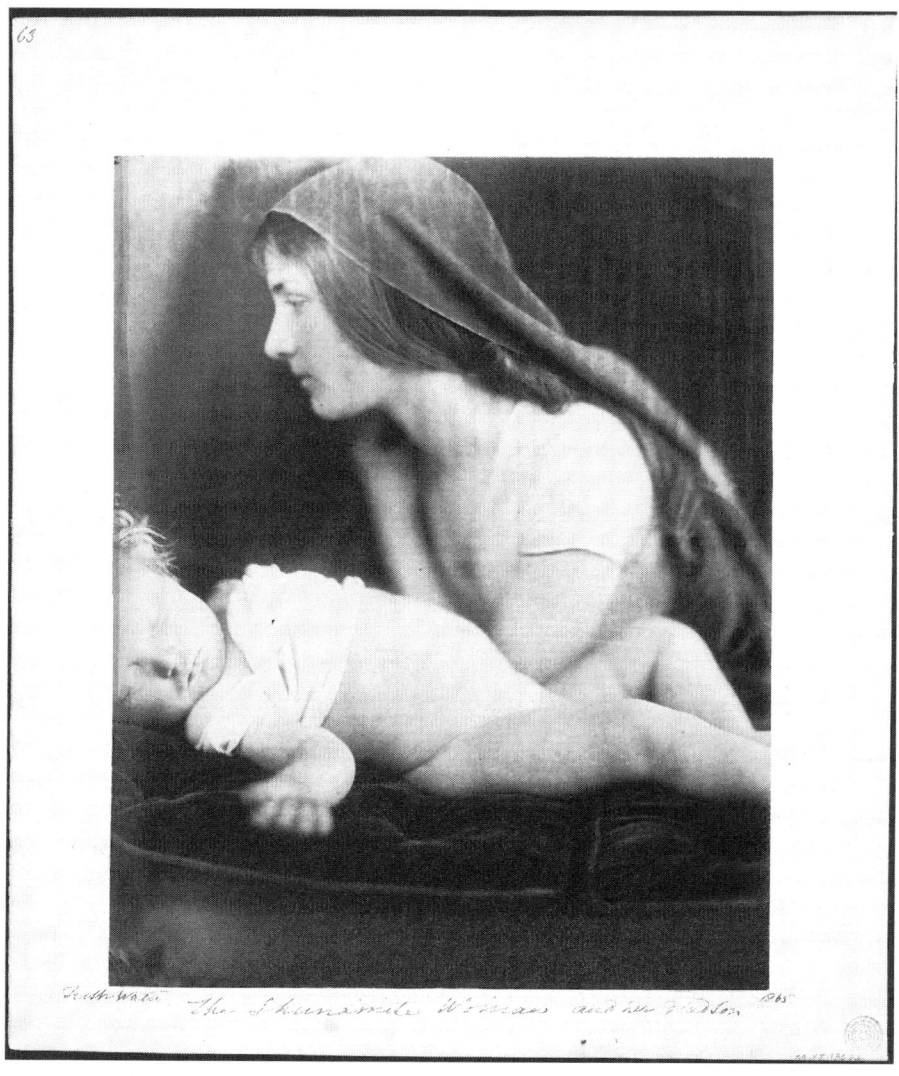

3     Julia Margaret Cameron, *The Shunamite Woman & her dead Son*
(Cox 135), 1865, albumen silver print, 27.1 x 21.3 cm.

bent child who appears asleep. As Watts wrote, the image indeed shows that
the camera's frame has seemingly cut off a portion of the child's head, just as it
has also cut off the child's feet, a fact left unmentioned by Watts. And as Watts
observed, the graphic modelling is rounded and full (like the sculpture of Phidias),
and the composition formal and symmetrical, 'like old pictures'. As recorded in
the copyright registers of 1865, over the course of several months, Cameron
clearly experimented with compositions using women and children, posing them
in arrangements that correspond to familiar subjects in religious art, including the

Mother and Child, Mary Madonna, and the infant *pietà*. To each of these photographs Cameron assigned a different narrative title, including: *Light and Love* (Cox 127), *Devotion* (Cox 128), *The Day-Spring* (Cox 129), *Prayer and Praise* (Cox 130), *Shepherds Keeping Watch By Night* (Cox 131), and *The First Born* (Cox 133).

The poses of the sitters in all of these photographs are similar to each other; their titles, in fact, are the only truly distinctive markers that allow us to tell them apart and to assign them different meanings and associations. Commenting on Cameron's repetitive Madonna studies, Watts cautioned her in this regard, urging her to introduce some compositional variety to the series: 'The expression is fine when Mary Madonna sits & you have had that view of head & identical expression over & over again. [F]or the purposes of sale[,] repetition will not do.'[25] Cameron's religious subjects are examined in detail in Chapter 2, but it is important to point out here how each of these titles bears multiple textual and pictorial references, making them as much specific subjects of the Old Testament (*The Shunamite Woman*, 2 Kings 4) and the New Testament (*Shepherds Keeping Watch*, Luke 2:8), as generalized emblems of family-centred Victorian domestic life and embodiments of motherly love and tenderness (*Prayer and Praise*; *Devotion*), or personifications of hopefulness, innocence, and joy associated with the dawn of a new day (*The Day-Spring*; *Light and Love*). Indeed, because allegory is a form of indirect representation, many of Cameron's admirers to this day have appreciated how these kinds of multiple associations are bound together in this related imagery.

What did Cameron hope to achieve by creating photographs like these, which contained multiple allegorical references, and by submitting them to competitions that were dominated by Photography Society jurists, whose commercial perspective generally disregarded such work? After all, photographic societies of the day encouraged photographers to use the medium for realistic purposes – to produce conventional portraits, landscapes, and still life arrangements that held commercial value. Their juries were predictably harsh toward Cameron, disparaging her choice of subject matter far beyond any superficial quibble they might have had with her technique or skill. By the end of 1864, she complained to her friend Sir John Herschel about this treatment: while she was happy to be included in their exhibitions, she was also pained by what she considered their unrefined preference for 'mere conventional topographic Photography – map making and skeleton rendering of feature & form'.[26]

Cameron allowed her increasing fluency in composing 'fancy subjects' to affect her stylistic approach to portraiture, not the other way around: whereas commercial photographers emphasized sharpness and overall diffused lighting in creating their portraits, Cameron chose strong raking light and soft focus instead, adopting this style from her Madonna series to suggest how a sitter's character emanated from within, using light to reflect an interior state of mind. Yet early in 1865, in response to an exhibition of her work at Colnaghi's, her print dealer, a reviewer claimed that her 'fancy subjects' were entirely ill-suited to photography. He particularly derided subjects that illustrated 'symbolic embodiments of the cardinal virtues', such as *Devotion* (Cox 128), a composition of a mother and child that the critic understood was related thematically to her nine-part series, *The Fruits of the Spirit*. 'This lady evidently possesses considerable artistic feeling', he declared, 'but we fear she is aiming to obtain from photography other results than those in which its strength lies.'[27]

In 1868, Cameron encountered similar resistance. At an exhibition of her photographs at London's German Gallery, for which she made the title list in Figure 1, she again exhibited 'fancy subjects' alongside portraits and figure studies. In response, the *Athenaeum* produced a critical review that disparaged her 'fancy subjects' outright, its reviewer apparently of the same mind-set as Ruskin, outraged that a woman would presume to represent national or historical subjects:

> Of these [photographs] we dismiss at once such as bear 'fancy' names, and pretend to subjects of the poetic and dramatic sorts. When such productions are [*sic*] due to the camera, or to any other scientific or mechanical instrument, aim at that which is properly brain-work, the less that is said about the results the better for all parties. In this case, when the poetic or dramatic titles have any aptitude, they are, to say the least, unpleasant, and often wreck that which, without an intend-edly [*sic*] suggestive name, would be grateful to the artistic eye.[28]

Although the focus of this attack was on photographs bearing 'fancy names' and 'poetic or dramatic titles', we might also ask: was it the particular allegor-ical subjects that displeased this critic, or was his chief objection that a woman produced them? Or, perhaps, did he object most to the pretensions of using photography allegorically, that is, to the idea of applying a 'mechanical art' for which thoughtful 'brain-work' was not typically required, to the fine arts?

In contrast to the narrow-mindedness of the photographic societies, Camer-on's social circle regarded her 'fancy subjects' as the intellectual focus and artistic inspiration, the driving force, of her photography. She found critical success in the *Illustrated London News*, which favourably reviewed her November 1865 exhibition at Colnaghi's. Paying special attention to her Madonna subjects, its critic praised her sitters for their 'rare and refined female loveliness', and paid special atten-tion to her *Prospero and Miranda* (Cox 1092, 1093), a theatrical subject drawn from Shakespeare's *The Tempest*.[29] Two months later, Coventry Patmore reviewed the same exhibition in *Macmillan's Magazine*. Although Patmore found difficulty in admiring Cameron's *tableaux vivants*, he praised her allegorical studies, which he referred to as 'heads in the grand style'.[30] Also in 1866, William Michael Rossetti, brother of the painter Dante Gabriel, published a full estimation of Cameron's subjects, finding her work 'magnificent': it was exceptional, he wrote, because of its ability to 'well-nigh re-create a subject; place it in novel, unanticipable [*sic*] lights; aggrandize the fine, suppress or ignore the petty; and transfigure both the subject-matter, and the reproducing process itself, into something almost higher than we knew them to be'.[31] By 1868, Cameron had won over the *Art-Journal*, too, which accepted her 'fancy subjects' as entirely appropriate for photography, its critic likening her compositions to the paintings of 'Caravaggio, Tintoretto, Giorgione, Velasquez, and others of the princes of their Art'.[32]

## Allegory and identity

Cameron exerted a strong will when it came to defining her subjects; she posed and lit her models with clear aims in mind, insisting they wear period costumes or drapery and hold certain props, and above all, that they maintain their poses and gestures long enough for their image to be recorded on the sensitized glass plate. A typical exposure could take several minutes. Because her sets had to be arranged and her models suitably attired, it would seem that Cameron's working method was deliberate and her intentions worked out in advance: her portrait sessions with Marie Spartali, daughter of a Greek consul-general, provide an instructive example. Marie Spartali was admired for her beauty; during the 1860s, she posed as a model for Rossetti and Burne-Jones. It is likely that they introduced her to Cameron, who made at least twenty-one photographs of Spartali in 1868 and 1870. Many of her prints of this sitter are not dated, and not all were registered for copyright protection.

On 15 September 1868, however, Cameron registered eleven photographs of Marie Spartali in dramatic or theatrical poses, all numbered sequentially. Here is how they were described in the copyright register for that date:

> 405. Miss Marie Spartali as Spanish Lady with black Veil, fan in one hand and Myrtle in the other, No. 1
>
> 406. Miss Marie Spartali as Spanish lady with cross in hand & beads round wrists, Eyes down, No. 2
>
> 407. Miss Marie Spartali, full face, head raised, right hand to broach, left hand to waist, No. 3
>
> 408. Miss Marie Spartali, White gown, dark bars, a bunch of grapes in hand close to cheek, grapes & leaves on lap, both hands seen, No. 4
>
> 409. Miss Marie Spartali in white gown, ¾ face bunch of grapes in right hand close to cheek, grapes on lap, No. 5
>
> 410. Miss Marie Spartali, full length with hat, beads round throat, Umbrella in hands, No. 6
>
> 411. Miss Marie Spartali, ¾ length, flowing hair with Ivy leaves, white robe & Ivy branch in hands, No. 7
>
> 412. Miss Marie Spartali, ¾ length, one hand raised, beads round wrist, ivy leaves between hands, hair flowing, No. 8

413. Miss Marie Spartali, full face, white robe, hands holding skirt – flowing hair, No. 9

414. Miss Marie Spartali, ¾ face, flowing hair, white dress with dark bars, one hand folded over other wrist, necklace round throat, No. 10

415. Miss Marie Spartali, as Spanish Lady, fan in right hand raised, & beads falling from left hand, No. 11.[33]

Cameron assigned allegorical titles to almost all of the individual prints from this series, titles that do not necessarily follow from the plainly factual and descriptive quality of the copyright registers. Matching the register to the prints in the *catalogue raisonné*, for example, we find that nos. 411 and 412 correspond to prints that she called *Memory* and *Mnemosyne* (Cox 467 and 468); 414 corresponds to *Hypatia* (Cox 469; Figure 4); 408 (or its slight variation, 409) correspond to *The Spirit of the Vine* (Cox 470); 407 corresponds to *Marie Spartali as The Imperial Eleänore* (Cox 471; Figure 5), and 415 corresponds to *La Donna at her Devotions* (Cox 473).

Spartali is costumed differently in the photographs; her props, hairstyle, and jewellery are altered in each image. Yet, since none of the registered prints include titles, it seems clear that Cameron gave these portraits allegorical titles after they were first produced. These images are curious hybrids: they insist on the camera's authority to ground the subject in real life, and they deny the realism of the camera and the specific identity of the sitter, now transformed into a 'fancy subject'. The photographs reflect Cameron's deliberate effort to create an artistic transformation, one that converted their graphic status as a 'sun recording from life' into narrative pictures that tell stories. *Mnemosyne*, for example, personifies Memory, and in Greek mythology is Mother of the nine Muses. *Hypatia*, a Platonic philosopher who lived in fifth-century Alexandria, is also the title character from a historical novel written in 1853 by Charles Kingsley. *The Imperial Eleänore* refers to a fictional figure from an 1864 poem by Tennyson. And while *The Spirit of the Vine* references the mythic story and wine-fuelled celebrations of the Dionysian ritual, *La Donna at her Devotions* is drawn from a dramatic scene in Byron's poem, *Don Juan*.

Each of these subjects is examined in greater detail below, but for the present purposes, it is important that each photograph insists upon its allegorical status as both narrative and pictorial. These shared attributes allow us to explore the particular cultural and historical contexts in which these photographs of Spartali acquired meaning for Cameron's audience. We might ask, for example, because they contained specific references to subjects drawn from history, mythology, and contemporary literature, what value and significance these subjects held in the mid-1860s? Was there any thematic coherence to this selection, or were they a random group of 'fancy pictures', chosen more for their pretensions to high art rather than to contribute to a unified narrative? These are important questions, because it is only through the process of encountering and confronting the

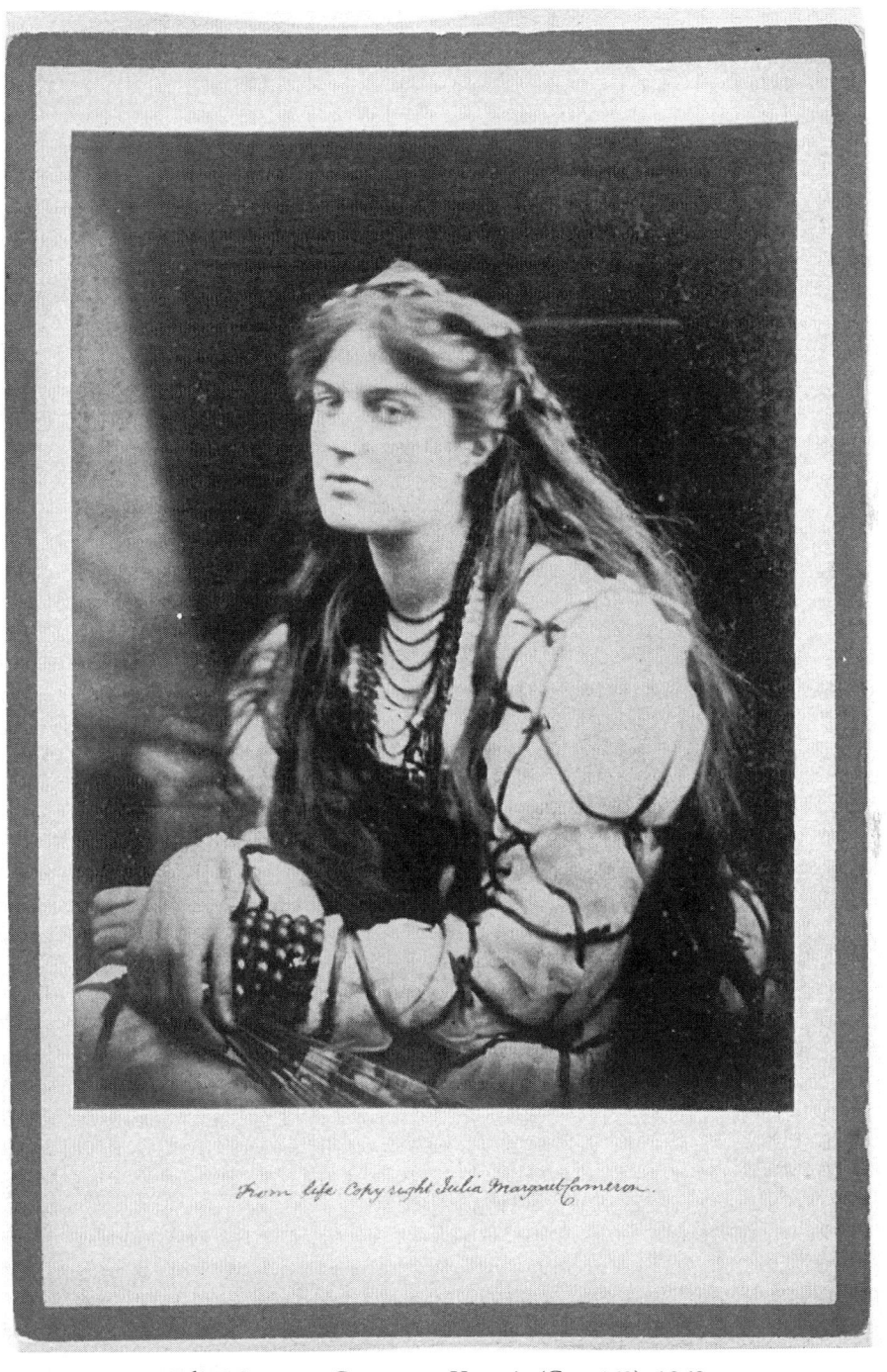

*From life Copyright Julia Margaret Cameron.*

Julia Margaret Cameron, *Hypatia* (Cox 469), 1868.
Albumen cabinet card, 12.2 x 8.9 cm.

**4**

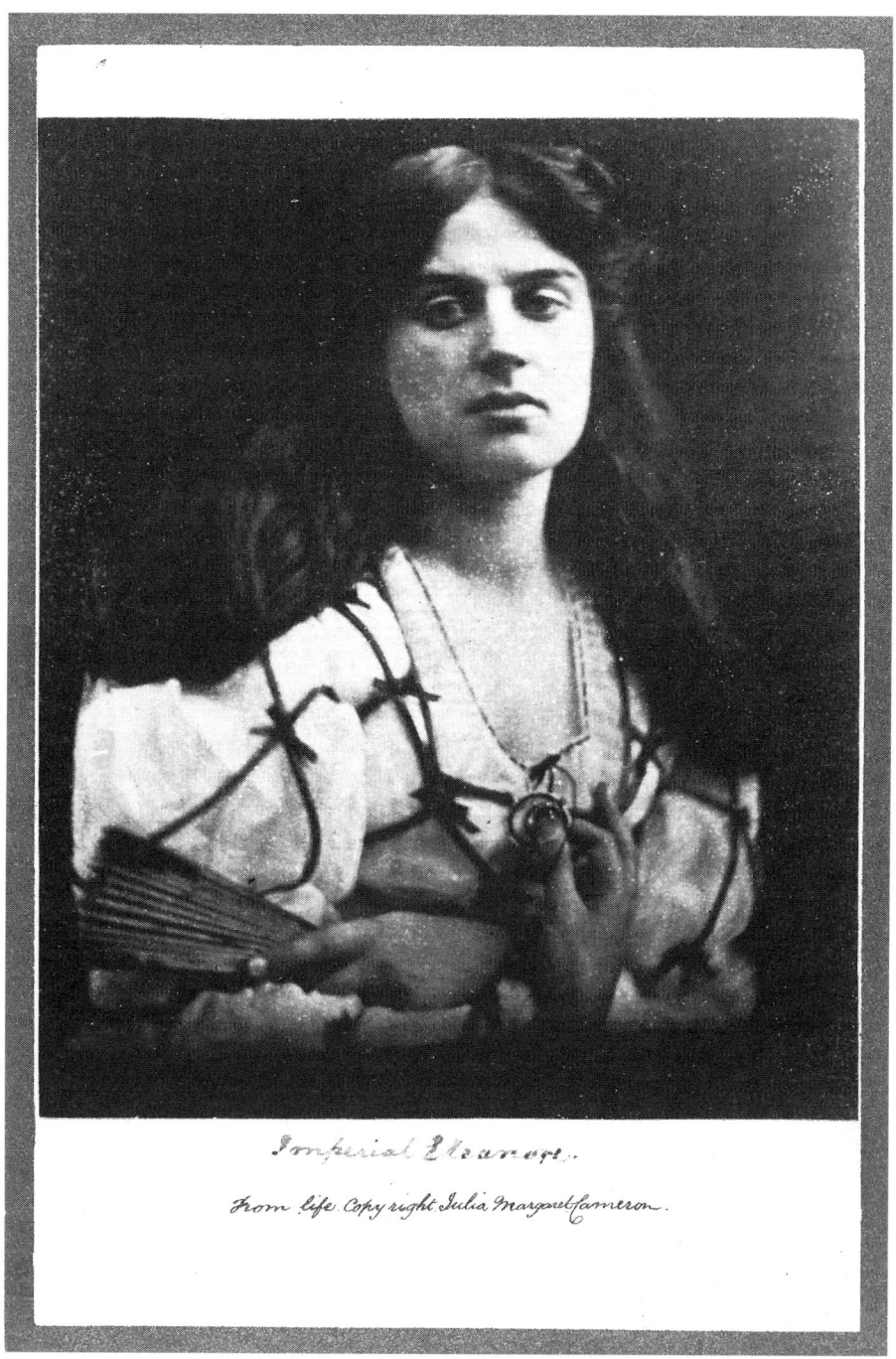

Julia Margaret Cameron, *Marie Spartali as The Imperial Eleänore*
(Cox 471), 1868. Albumen cabinet card, 12.2 x 9.8 cm.

narratives of history and by recognizing the way that representations like these produce new ways of knowing and being in the world that we are truly able to locate ourselves historically.[34]

During Marie Spartali's sitting with Cameron, for example, the sitter may indeed have collaborated with the photographer in striking poses that projected strength and self-possession and which denied the 'visual spectacle of women', as Deborah Cherry has suggested.[35] And as Sylvia Wolf has inferred, Cameron may well have chosen Spartali as her photographic model because of her 'exotic' looks, Greek heritage, and even her association with the Pre-Raphaelites.[36] But neither author has asked whether Cameron's photographs of Spartali functioned coherently as part of a substantial historical narrative. Indeed, among these images, Cameron's allegorical titles do not suggest any apparent connection, and although she numbered them from one to eleven, there seems to be no apparent 'progression' implied by the sequence. But by casting a wider historical perspective to this work, we can see that a theoretical and structural centre is present that makes the whole of the eleven images more than the sum of its constituent parts: Cameron relied upon the symbolic language of allegory, a strategy which functions in literature and art as an important means to connect the present to the past.

Allegory is the chief principle underlying the iconography of Cameron's 'fancy subject' pictures. In particular, the nostalgic, sentimental, and romantic works of the eighteenth century that preceded Cameron's imagery represented longing for a simpler, bygone era or an uncomplicated way of life. In such works, allegories give shape to social systems and values that are under siege or about to disappear, like the simple rural family menaced by the forces of industrialization or the innocent child of nature who appears unaware that events outside of her control will alter her life for the worse, ruining both nature and her innocence in the process. Allegory conveys these meanings because it engages the viewer in a dialogue between the seemingly intangible forces shaping the present and the ostensibly recoverable history of the past. As Craig Owens wrote, allegory functions 'in the gap between a present and a past which, without allegorical reinterpretation, might have remained foreclosed. A conviction of the remoteness of the past, and a desire to redeem it for the present – these are its two most fundamental impulses.'[37] In Cameron's work, allegory confiscates and appropriates imagery from the past and makes it new and culturally significant: we observe this process in action when Cameron gave allegorical titles to her prints of Marie Spartali.

But in depicting *Hypatia*, *Mnemosyne*, and the *Imperial Eleänore* in the new medium of photography, Cameron was not randomly choosing any historical narrative. Rather, she selected narratives that were important to the nation's cultural identity. Historians have shown that 'English national identity' emerged from many different sources around the turn of the eighteenth century, but that nationalistic pride was not expressed coherently across the land during that time as a vehicle of collective understanding. During the nineteenth century, however, when political culture began to centre on the nation's relationship to the world stage, national identity became connected broadly to 'the two "English empires," the empire of Great Britain and the British overseas empire'.[38] If the making of national identity also depended upon an intelligible 'imagined community' that could produce narratives that were broadly agreed upon by society, as Benedict Anderson has argued,[39] that infrastructure was built purposefully during this period. It was constructed historically much as a modern road is built physically, in overlapping strata, with cultural engineers excavating its past, storylines of heritage and tradition layering its foundations, narratives of unity and commemoration bonding its many layers, and tales of heroic bravery and personal sacrifice shaping and refining its surface.

Especially during the 1860s, new narratives emerged from the relationship between Britain and the colonial lands it occupied: in order to help sustain the country's political and economic power and win support for its policies, both at home and abroad, the nation's writers and artists created fresh approaches to tell old stories that would support its dominant role as a colonizer. Likewise, colonized peoples coped with the new authority imposed by the Empire either by absorbing or by opposing those points of view and cultural differences.[40] If colonialism disrupted the nation's myths of origin, like the supposed racial purity of England's Anglo-Saxon ancestors or its early adoption of Christianity as a national religion, it also provided an opportunity to debate the merits of those founding stories. And because colonialism also introduced disagreements about the social bonds that held the nation together, a space was opened up for new contributions to the dialogue that could help resolve those differences. These debates took many forms, but were characterized by a persistent conflict and lack of resolution during this period, in part because the relationship between London and its colonies was dynamic and in flux, and in part because of the latent political and cultural volatility between the two societies, where violence was suppressed or suspended, but never absent. This instability generated psychological states of anxiety and uncertainty in colonizers and colonized peoples alike, a feature that Cameron embedded in her most explicit photographs of the relationship between the two. Among her social circle, this instability up-ended the sure confidence of men like Lord Overstone and Tennyson that Britain's colonial activities were fair and honourable, as we explore below in Chapters 5 and 6.

Some of the architects of Britain's global political and cultural dominance, of course, were Cameron's close friends and neighbours, the same men of influence with whom she socialized at her sister's Holland Park salon after 1850, and later on, at her own home on the Isle of Wight.[41] This circle included Lord Macaulay of the Council of India, who, during the 1830s and 1840s, employed her husband

Charles as a Council member, and whose 'Minute on Indian Education' argued that it was Britain's mission to transform the people of India into 'a class of persons, Indians in blood and colour, but English in taste, in opinion, in morals, and in intellect'.[42] A frequent visitor was Thomas Carlyle, whose books, like *Past and Present* (1843), celebrated England's cultural ancestry in terms of its Anglo-Saxon roots, and whose political commentary of the 1860s argued for the nation's historical role in teaching the world how to live and how to act. Also included was Francis Turner Palgrave, whose poetry collection, *The Golden Treasury of English Verse*, celebrated the English lyrical voice. Palgrave frequently visited Tennyson and Cameron on the Isle of Wight, and in 1861 he dedicated his volume to the poet, expressing the hope of producing 'a true national anthology'.[43] Cameron's close friend, Sir Henry Taylor, an official in the Colonial Office, also regularly visited the photographer in Freshwater. Taylor, himself a poet, embodied Macaulay's 'civilizing mission' to spread English influence abroad by working to replicate the nation's governmental administration and political economy in the colonies.

The Holland Park circle also included well-established painters, poets, musicians, and literary critics; men of the University and of the Church; aristocrats who patronized the arts through their commissions and extensive collections; and reviewers of art and literature. Nationalism was a focal point of their many activities: Tennyson and Watts represented the heroic national past in poetry and in painting; Sir Henry Cole collected national historical artefacts for his Museum to represent the nation's shared and collective identity; Austen Henry Layard and William Gifford Palgrave literally excavated foreign lands in their effort to recapture remnants of the nation's cultural past; and George Grote and Benjamin Jowett, who translated and reinterpreted ancient Greek and biblical texts, did so as a way to re-evaluate the foundational role of those texts for the nation's current needs. By actually reconceiving the 'original meaning' of St Paul's *Epistles* or Plato's *Dialogues*, for example, Grote and Jowett independently engaged their intellectual peers in debate about whether these ancient documents were being used legitimately by their present exponents to justify the contemporary religious practices or political actions that were the supposed foundation of their beliefs. Cameron was not only familiar with the published works of each of these men, she often engaged them personally in debate or wrote about their works in letters to others, clearly articulating her own point of view, which was not always in agreement.

Like these influential men, Cameron also wanted to contribute to the on-going narrative of British national identity, and she chose allegorical photographs as her primary instrument. By arranging her sitters to represent 'fancy subjects', she could personify these intellectual and political ideas figuratively. Consequently, she chose familiar narratives and well-known parables and legends to engage with these men, but also with the larger intellectual audience that made Grote, Jowett, Carlyle, and Tennyson famous authors. This was the same public that bought Christmas editions of Tennyson's *Idylls of the King* and Palgrave's *The Golden Treasury*; the same art lovers that attended Watts's exhibitions at the Royal Academy; the same audience that viewed the Elgin Marbles in the British Museum and visited Cole's South Kensington Museum to appreciate the best in historical design and applied art. This public's enthusiasm for Thackeray influenced his publisher to produce numerous illustrated editions and made journals like *Punch* and the *Illustrated London News* household names. Its appetite for visual imagery supported the Arundel Society's production of fine art prints as well as the livelihood of celebrity-chasing photographers who made *cartes-de-visite* and cabinet photographs of famous men to be pasted into albums. In such a context, where artists and authors influenced each other, where popular and high art forms crossed multiple boundaries, and where cultural ideas were as much the subject of debate as the expressive forms they took, it makes less sense to think about the uniqueness of these different artistic forms and more about the shared spaces they occupied and the interdisciplinary effect of their imagery.[44]

Because of these overlapping and multiple influences, Cameron began producing hybrid works of art when she took up photography. The term 'hybrid' neatly describes this imagery because these photographs contained converging and intersecting references, fused together multiple sources of imagery and expressed opposing forces that coexisted simultaneously, or created new narrative structures that generated multiple ways to interpret a story. Three examples illustrate this aspect of Cameron's hybrid approach: in Chapter 1, we will see how Cameron engaged her audience with a sentimental story of primitive simplicity and childhood innocence common to the 'fancy subject' model of the eighteenth century. In representing the story of *Paul and Virginia*, the title characters of a French book of the same name that was widely popular in English translation, Cameron drew upon illustrated books, fashionable wallpaper, and contemporary photographs as source material. She also relied on the way this popular imagery took on new meanings in different contexts, from Thomas Carlyle, who used the novel as a means to idealize colonial emigration, to Prince Albert, who romanticized the tale in terms of his own Anglo-Saxon heritage. In Chapter 5, we will examine how Cameron drew upon caricatures in *Punch* and graphic art in the *Illustrated London News* when she photographed Prince Alamayou, the orphaned child of the vanquished king of Abyssinia, which had been overrun by a British military expedition in 1868. And in Chapter 6, we will see how Cameron studied earlier graphic illustrations of Tennyson's *Idylls of the King* prior to producing her own photographic interpretations of scenes from that epic poem, replacing, where she could, Tennyson's voice with her own, both in textual and in pictorial form.

Hybridity is also a valuable way to describe how two or more interpretations of the same narrative could be joined together to create a new reality, one that manifested psychological anxiety and social instability because it held together at least two contradictory points of view. As we shall see, in Cameron's hands, hybrid works of art embody ambivalence as much as they do conflict, especially when they stand in opposition to a prevailing interpretation about a historical event or stake out an ambiguous position in order to avoid expressing explicit disagreement with a dominant viewpoint. Several chapters illustrate how Cameron produced photographs that held simultaneously contradictory positions: in Chapter 2, we will see that Cameron chose religious subjects that could support both orthodox and radical 'free-thinking' positions, especially with regard to important moral questions. In Chapter 3, we will examine how Cameron embraced historical and mythological stories from fifth-century BC Athens as contemporary civic models, using photography to comment on the classical past and interpret Hellenism for the Victorian present. And in Chapter 4, we will investigate how Cameron chose Byronic subjects to offer her own take on contemporary historical and political events, fusing together Oriental and Western ideas of beauty, honour, duty, and nationalism in her allegorical imagery.

Narrative instability; submerged narratives; hybrid imagery; narrative 'gaps': during the 1860s and 1870s, Cameron constructed 'British national identity' as a tentative, even contentious undertaking, but she embraced this narrative project as one that required vigilant attention and constant revision.

## Cameron's project

Until now, the full range of Cameron's photographic 'fancy subjects' have been regarded as frivolous; following Emily Tennyson and Virginia Woolf, critics have called them idiosyncratic, unconcerned with serious purpose or intent. Modern scholars rejecting this view have focused narrowly on Cameron's religious subjects or her pictures of children and motherhood, extracting a small number of images from the much larger whole.[45] By contrast, my objective is to offer a new and broader historical framework to help contextualize Cameron's 'fancy subjects' as important contributions to the on-going dialogue of her time about British national life and to explain how these contending forces and social conflicts shaped her thematic selection. It is important, too, that Cameron's personal biography as a British landowner in the colonies also shaped her worldview. Consequently, this study also clarifies her own idealization of colonialism, both as a Freshwater resident and Ceylonese plantation owner, helping to explain why she embedded photographs with complex narratives about British colonial history, especially as these were expressed in terms of reclaiming a lost heritage or reconnecting with a distant and remote element of the national inheritance.

I have grouped together Cameron's 'fancy subjects' in the context of several larger themes that she used to address these controversial cultural and political debates. Importantly, because she consciously wove together her allegories and her portraits in albums and exhibitions, and because the men she portrayed were also writing and helping to shape the nation's cultural identity, I have examined her allegories and portraits together in each chapter, taking particular note when certain portraits and 'fancy subjects' were hung in the same exhibition. In addition, each chapter is arranged chronologically to capture the ways that Cameron constructed her historical narratives in response to timely political and cultural events. In particular, we shall examine her engagement with religious arguments that pitted High Church doctrines against those of the Low Church; her confrontation with contemporary political interpretations about the Greek classical past as they were used to support or undermine governmental reforms; and her nostalgic critique of material conditions in the Empire, especially in relation to her idealization of colonial lands as unspoiled. Cameron's worldview was romantic: her 'fancy subjects' romanticize the simple and uncomplicated life of the past and venerate old traditions; they celebrate inspirational stories of atonement, redemption, and deliverance; they elevate patriotism, nationalism, and nobility.

Chapter 1 examines the photographs Cameron made of two children to represent the central protagonists of the sentimental novel, *Paul and Virginia*. Written originally in French in 1788 by Jacques-Henri Bernardin de Saint-Pierre and translated shortly thereafter into English, Saint-Pierre's tale became one of the most widely published novels of the century. *Paul and Virginia* takes place on a remote island colony, and in order to help contextualize the story's importance, this chapter also explores how Julia Margaret and her husband Charles regarded their own island homes on the Isle of Wight and the island of Ceylon, especially in relation to their ownership of the land, the impact of the colonial condition, and their romantic attitudes about art. In *Paul and Virginia*, one of the first allegorical photographs that she produced in 1864, Cameron demonstrated her interest in taking a sentimental story about exiled children and connecting it to conflict-filled narratives about colonialism then facing Britain, including the intersection of race and slavery, the origins of English ancestry, the birth of Christianity as a national religion, and the spread of national economic and labour policies in the colonies.

Cameron's religious images of Madonnas and children, especially the nine photographs that she grouped together and called *The Fruits of the Spirit*, are the focus of Chapter 2. Inspired by the unorthodox approach to biblical criticism of her friend Benjamin Jowett, Cameron created *The Fruits of the Spirit* to put forward what she called a 'theological work in photography'. A frequent visitor to the Tennysons and the Camerons on the Isle of Wight, Jowett published his most controversial essay on biblical interpretation in 1860 in a volume called *Essays and Reviews*. Chapter 2 contends that Jowett's volume inspired Cameron to create religious photographs that conveyed both High Church and Broad Church inter-pretations and that stood in opposition to both the rigid orthodoxy advocated by

Jowett's opponents and the one-dimensional typological approach to visual art promoted by Anna Jameson.

A similar responsiveness to mid-Victorian thinking about classical antiquity informs Cameron's photographs devoted to classical Greek subjects, which are the subject of Chapter 3. George Grote's historical essays about ancient Greece inspired both Charles and Julia Margaret Cameron. Grote was a political radical who was associated with Jeremy Bentham, and a close friend of Charles. In his numerous essays and books, Grote advocated that Britain adopt a participatory brand of democracy that was modelled on ancient Athens. Julia Margaret, through her husband, and very probably through her own reading, was exposed to Grote's histories in 1866, but his intellectual contribution to her artistic work has been overlooked until now. Chapter 3 addresses this oversight by examining how Cameron created a coherent body of classical imagery, and how, like Grote, she used stories from Greek myths as a way to engage with the debate over the practice of British civic life.

Cameron's photographs containing Byronic subjects are the focus of Chapter 4. The extent to which she drew subjects and meaning from Byron, both in terms of his Romantic subject matter and the political context of his poetry, has not been recognized and fully appreciated. Cameron stayed away from maudlin or carnal themes that many of her contemporaries used to disparage the poet. Henry Taylor, for example, famously disliked Byron's works and disapproved of his continuing fame. Cameron apparently disagreed with Taylor. As we shall see, she chose the poet's heroic and selfless subjects that served patriotic, noble, and nationalistic ends as suitable subjects for her photographs. In fact, in Cameron's Byronic subjects, she represented narratives of personal sacrifice and loss in which the grand ambitions of country and nation take priority over narrow familial bonds. As a result, she produced allegorical photographs that invited multiple and often contradictory interpretations, as her national heroines and defenders of liberty both celebrated and undermined the British imperial cause.

Chapter 5 examines Cameron's photographs of colonial conflict, responding to hostile encounters in Jamaica and Abyssinia and examining the whirlwind of controversy that swept up her social circle, particularly Lord Overstone, but also Carlyle, Taylor, and Tennyson: in 1868, at London's German Gallery, she exhibited recently made portraits of Edward John Eyre, the colonial governor of Jamaica who had brutally suppressed an insurrection in 1865, along with portraits of Carlyle, who publicly supported Eyre as his most ardent defender. Shortly thereafter, she rushed last-minute prints into circulation that depicted refugees from the 1868 war in Abyssinia; these studio-produced images deliberately re-enact scenes of violence and aggression. Cameron's Abyssinian photographs are analysed in relation to these historical events, and in relation to other works, particularly her portraits of disguised British Orientalists (some of which she included in the exhibition) who had achieved fame by infiltrating colonial lands on behalf of the Empire.

On the Isle of Wight, Alfred Tennyson was not only a close friend and neighbour, but also an inspiring figure whose poetry provided a rich source of literary material for Cameron to represent photographically. Her illustrations for Tennyson's *Idylls of the King*, which she undertook in 1874 with the poet's encouragement and advice, are the focus of Chapter 6. This chapter examines how Cameron interpreted Tennyson's epic narrative and selectively counterbalanced the poet's repeated cries for war and national rejuvenation with her own emphasis on the moral guidance and 'temperate qualities' that she found in the voices of his female characters. By pairing together her photographs with lines of Tennyson's verse that she selected, Cameron emphasized these female voices in her illustrated volumes, expressing anxiety about the legitimacy of the nation's imperial cause and questioning its effects on British domestic life. In her photographs, she tempered Tennyson's strident call to strike out against 'the heathen' by focusing on how his female characters positively expressed the lyrical, tolerant, and altruistic qualities of English civic life. In doing so, she implied that a generous and compassionate hand could secure the nation's future more effectively than could hostile manoeuvring or outright war.

In 1875, Charles and Julia Margaret Cameron decided to move permanently to Ceylon for the remaining years of their lives. Chapter 7 concentrates on the photographs she made during this time and explains the commercial decisions she made prior to leaving England to publicize her volumes illustrating Tennyson's *Idylls*. While residing there in 1877, she was visited by the botanical painter Marianne North, which allowed both Cameron and North to create works of art in each other's presence. In their imagery, both women expressed a profound cultural displacement and commented on the exoticism, primitivism, cultural inferiority, and dependence they found in the colony. Cameron's Ceylonese photographs contain a complex dual reality: on the one hand, she experienced Ceylon as an extension of Britain, where it felt 'natural' to live off the land as a coffee grower and exporter; on the other hand, living in Ceylon made it possible for her to experience a 'return to origins', a position that allowed her to repudiate the repressive influences of colonialism that might one day threaten her island paradise.

This chapter also examines Cameron's 1877 portrait photograph of Marianne North looking up from reading George Eliot's novel, *Daniel Deronda*. Eliot's novel had been published in instalments the previous year. By connecting the portrait to the central themes of the novel, which involve the return of the protagonist to his Jewish roots in the ancient land of Palestine, Cameron embodies the British colonialist's conflict in the image. The presence of *Daniel Deronda* in Cameron's portrait of Marianne North not only grounds the two artists in place and time, it also metaphorically marks this photograph as a sign of the colonialist's unresolved conflicts. Cameron's final work in portraiture is thus revealed to be yet another expression of the ambivalence that is also present in her allegorical 'fancy subjects': for Cameron, celebrating the cultural extension of Britain's national borders across the globe, as measured by the long reach of George Eliot's novel from its publication in London to its reception in Ceylon, is countered by the photographer's heartfelt desire to interpret her own return to the island colony as an act of moral redemption.

## Notes

1  Letter from Emily Tennyson to Edward Lear, quoted in Colin Ford, *The Cameron Collection: An Album of Photographs by Julia Margaret Cameron Presented to Sir John Herschel* (London: Von Nostrand Reinhold and the National Portrait Gallery, 1975), p. 127, plate 44.

2  See Rosemary Mitchell, *Picturing the Past: English History in Text and Image, 1830–1870* (New York: Oxford University Press, 2000).

3  *The Discourses of Sir Joshua Reynolds, with Explanatory Notes by John Burnett* (London: James Carpenter, 1842), esp. Discourse Fourteen. See also: Martin Postle, *Angels and Urchins: The Fancy Picture in 18th-century British Art* (Nottingham: Djanogly Art Gallery and Lund Humphries, 1998).

4  Letter from Julia Margaret Cameron to Sir John Herschel, dated 31 December 1864, quoted in Ford, *The Cameron Collection*, p. 141.

5  R. Derek Wood, ed., *Julia Margaret Cameron's Copyrighted Photographs* (London: privately published, May 1996), copy archived at the Royal Photographic Society, Bath, and online at: www.midley.co.uk/cameron/cameron.pdf

6  Julian Cox and Colin Ford, eds., *Julia Margaret Cameron: The Complete Photographs* (Los Angeles: J. Paul Getty Trust, 2003).

7  Michael Baxandall, *Patterns of Intention: On the Historical Explanation of Pictures*, (New Haven: Yale University Press, 1985); W. J. T. Mitchell, *Iconology: Image, Text, Ideology* (Chicago: University of Chicago Press, 1986), chapter 2.

8  There is a vast literature on narrative and narration. Of particular importance to this study, see: Shlomith Rimmon-Kenan, *Narrative Fiction: Contemporary Poetics* (London: Methuen, 1983); Marie Maclean, *Narrative as Performance: The Baudelairean Experiment* (London: Routledge, 1988); Wallace Martin, *Recent Theories of Narrative* (Ithaca, NY: Cornell University Press, 1986); Frederic Jameson, *The Political Unconscious: Narrative as a Socially Symbolic Act* (Ithaca, NY: Cornell University Press, 1981); M. M. Bakhtin, *The Dialogic Imagination: Four Essays*, ed. Michael Holquist (Austin: University of Texas Press, 1981); Homi K. Bhabha, ed., *Nation and Narration* (London and New York: Routledge, 1990); Robert Scholes, James Phelan, and Robert Kellogg, *The Nature of Narrative*, rev. (New York: Oxford University Press, 2006).

9  Virginia Woolf, *Freshwater: A Comedy* [1935], ed. Lucio P. Ruotolo (San Diego: Harcourt Brace Jovanovich, 1976), p. v.

10  *Ibid.*, p. 16.

11  See Lee Manion, 'The Loss of the Holy Land and *Sir Isumbras*: Literary Contributions to Fourteenth-Century Crusade Discourse', *Speculum*, 85 (2012), 65–90. On the Isumbras story, see also: Samara P. Landers, 'And Loved He Was With All: Identity in *Sir Isumbras*', *Orbis Litterarum*, 64: 5 (2009), 351–72; Raluca Radulescu, 'Pious Middle English Romances turned Political: Reading *Sir Isumbras, Sir Gowther,* and *Robert of Sicily* in Fifteenth-Century

England', *Viator*, 41:2 (2010), 333–60.On the persistence of these themes in Victorian and in modern times, see Debra N. Mancoff, *The Arthurian Revival in Victorian Art* (New York: Garland, 1990) and Mark Girouard, *The Return to Camelot: Chivalry and the English Gentleman* (New Haven: Yale University Press, 1981).

12  Julie Codell, 'Sir Isumbras, M.P.: Millais's Painting and Political Cartoons', *Journal of Popular Culture*, 22:3 (1988), 29–45.

13  *Ibid.*, 33.

14  Julia Thomas, *Pictorial Victorians: The Inscription of Values in Word and Image* (Athens, OH: Ohio University Press, 2004), Alison Byerly, *Realism, Representation, and the Arts in Nineteenth-Century Literature* (Cambridge: Cambridge University Press, 1997), and Martin Meisel, *Realizations: Narrative, Pictorial, and Theatrical Arts in Nineteenth-Century England* (Princeton: Princeton University Press, 1983).

15  Victoria C. Olsen, *From Life: Julia Margaret Cameron and Victorian Photography* (New York: Palgrave Macmillan, 2003), p. 236.

16  Virginia Woolf, 'Julia Margaret Cameron', in Virginia Woolf and Roger Fry, *Victorian Photographs of Famous Men and Fair Women* [orig. London: Hogarth Press, 1926] repr. (London: Chatto and Windus, 1992), p. 18.

17  *Ibid.*

18  Janet Malcolm is emblematic: 'The trouble is that Cameron *was* the heroine of a screwball comedy. There is too much evidence of the picturesque behaviour for it [earlier criticism] to be summarily dismissed as a calumny [...] If Cameron's Madonna and Child pictures and her illustrations of scenes from Tennyson seem less silly to us than they did to the puritanical modernists, even the most catholic of postmodernists will have to acknowledge that these photographs bear unmistakable traces of the conditions under which they were taken, and that these conditions were often comical.' Original emphasis; from 'The Genius of the Glass House' [1999], in *Forty-One False Starts: Essays on Artists and Writers* (New York: Farrar, Straus, and Giroux, 2013), p. 154.

19  Agnes Grace Weld, *Glimpses of Tennyson and Some of His Relations and Friends* (London: Williams and Norgate, 1903); Lady Laura Troubridge (née Laura Gurney), *Memories and Reflections* (London: Heinemann, 1925); Anne Thackeray Ritchie, *From Friend to Friend*, ed. Emilie Ritchie (London: John Murray, 1919); Hester Thackeray Ritchie, ed., *Thackeray and His Daughter: The Letters and Journals of Anne Thackeray Ritchie* (New York and London: Harper and Brothers, 1924); Lord Hallam Tennyson, ed., *Tennyson and His Friends* (London: Macmillan, 1911); Julia Prinsep Stephen, 'Julia Margaret Cameron', in Sir Leslie Stephen and Sir Sidney Lee, eds., *Dictionary of National Biography*, vol. 3 (London: Oxford University Press, 1921).

20  Linda Nochlin, 'Women, Art, and Power', in *Women, Art, and Power and Other Essays* (New York: Harper and Row, 1988), p. 2.

21  Griselda Pollock, *Vision and Difference: Femininity, Feminism and the Histories of Art* (London: Routledge, 1988), p. 17.

22  Quoted by Deborah Cherry, *Painting Women: Victorian Women Artists* (London: Routledge, 1993), p. 187.

23  Cox identifies the work (Cox 521) from its inscription in Cameron's hand, *Boadicea*, but dates it 1864–66, with attribution in the copyright records. However, the image corresponds well to '#190 – Miss Mackensie, both arms extended, holding dagger, full length, white dress dark drapery', which was recorded in the registers on 15 September 1865. Cox and Ford, *Julia Margaret Cameron*, p. 274.

24  Letter from G.F. Watts to Julia Margaret Cameron, 21 June 1865, National Portrait Gallery, London, NPG-P125.

25  Letter from G.F. Watts to Julia Margaret Cameron (undated, but probably 1865), National Portrait Gallery, London, NPG-P215, pp. 2–3.

26  Julia Margaret Cameron to Sir John Herschel, 31 December 1864, reprinted in Colin Ford, *The Cameron Collection*, pp. 140–1.

27  *Photographic News*, 9 (6 January 1865), 4.

28  'Fine Arts Gossip', *Athenaeum*, 15 February 1868, p. 258.

29  *Illustrated London News*, 11 November 1865, p. 463; and 18 November 1865, p. 486.

30  'Mrs Cameron's Photographs', *Macmillan's Magazine*, 13 (January 1866), 230–1.

31  Quoted by Joanne Lukitsh, *Cameron: Her Work and Career* (Rochester, NY: International Museum of Photography at the George Eastman House, 1986), p. 47.

32  'Minor Topics of the Month', *Art-Journal*, 1 March 1868, p. 58.

33  Wood, *Julia Margaret Cameron's Copyrighted Photographs*, 15 September 1868.

34  Jameson, *Political Unconscious*, pp. 34–5.

35  Cherry, *Painting Women*, p. 198.

36  Sylvia Wolf, *Julia Margaret Cameron's Women* (Chicago: Art Institute of Chicago, 1998), pp. 54, 64, 226.

37  Craig Owens, *Beyond Recognition: Representation, Power, and Culture* (Berkeley: University of California Press, 1992), p. 53.

38  Krishan Kumar, *The Making of English National Identity* (London: Cambridge University Press, 2003), p. 179; Stefan Collini, Donald Winch, and John Burrow, *That Noble Science of Politics: A Study in Nineteenth-Century Intellectual History* (Cambridge: Cambridge University Press, 1983); Bernard S. Cohn, 'Representing Authority in Victorian India', in Eric Hobsbawm and Terence Ranger, eds., *The Invention of Tradition* (Cambridge: Cambridge University Press, 1983); and Catherine Hall, *Civilizing Subjects: Metropole and Colony in the English Imagination, 1830–1867* (London: Polity Press, 2002).

39  Benedict Anderson, *Imagined Communities* (London: Verso, 1983).

40  Edward W. Said, *Orientalism* (New York: Vintage, 1978); Edward W. Said, *Culture and Imperialism* (New York: Vintage, 1993); Homi K. Bhabha, *The Location of Culture* (London: Routledge, 1994), and Bhabha, *Nation and Narration*.

41  Caroline Dakers, *The Holland Park Circle: Artists and Victorian Society* (New Haven: Yale University Press, 1999).

42  Thomas Babington, Lord Macaulay, 'Minute on Education', in W. Theodore de Bary, ed., *Sources of Indian Tradition*, vol. 2 (New York: Columbia University Press, 1958), p. 49.

43  Francis Turner Palgrave, 'To Alfred Tennyson, Poet Laureate' (May 1861), preface to *The Golden Treasury of the Best Songs and Lyrical Poems in the English Language*, ed. F. T. Palgrave (London: Penguin, 1991), p. 3.

44  Carlo Ginzburg, James D. Herbert, W. J. T. Mitchell, Thomas F. Reese, and Ellen Handler Spitz, 'Inter/disciplinarity', *Art Bulletin*, 77:4 (1995), 534–52. Thomas, *Pictorial Victorians*; on the periodical press, Peter Sinnema, *Dynamics of the Printed Page: Representing the Nation in the 'Illustrated London News'* (Aldershot: Ashgate, 1998).

45  For religion, see Mike Weaver, *Whisper of the Muse: The Overstone Album and Other Photographs by Julia Margaret Cameron* (Malibu: J. Paul Getty Museum, 1986); for motherhood, see Carol Mavor, *Pleasures Taken: Performances of Sexuality and Loss in Victorian Photographs* (Durham, NC: Duke University Press, 1995) and Carol Armstrong, 'Cupid's Pencil of Light: Julia Margaret Cameron and the Maternalization of Photography', *October*, 76 (Spring 1996), 114–41; for Cameron's 'self-reflexive' identification with her subjects, see Carol Armstrong, *Scenes in a Library: Reading the Photograph in the Book, 1843–1875* (Cambridge, MA: MIT Press, 1998).

# 1

# Saint-Pierre's exiles:
# myths of origins and national identity

## Sites of romantic inspiration: the Cameron's island homes

In 1860, shortly after the Camerons had settled close to the Tennysons in Fresh-water, Julia Margaret wrote to her husband Charles, who was then in Ceylon, the island colony located just off the south-eastern tip of India: 'This island might equal your island now for richness of effects.'[1] These might seem like incongruous sentiments, since at the time Charles was not travelling abroad for leisure or recreation, like a tourist; but rather, as he had done intermittently throughout the 1850s, to assess the health of his coffee plantations and measure their projected yield. Nevertheless, the letters written between Charles and Julia Margaret show the joining of one island to the other was common in their thinking and that their deep connection to their two island homes was part of an extended dialogue over many years. To the Camerons, possessing land in Ceylon and on the Isle of Wight was more than having a simple place to reside. As we shall see, their two island homes offered them ideal spaces upon which they could project their Romantic descriptions of the land and landscape, plan and strategize where they should put down roots and raise their children, and express a kind of longing, a yearning that was born of their displacement and ambivalence as British colonists. Their correspondence expresses this longing and displacement, often in fervent tones.

It is useful to begin here with a brief overview of the Camerons' attachment to their island homes, their attitude about these locations, and their thoughts about the uniqueness of island colonies, where we might locate the origins of Julia Margaret's project to photograph subjects of national importance. Islands, especially remote, tropical, and even deserted islands located far from England's shores have long claimed a special importance in the literature of colonialism.[2] Daniel Defoe's *Robinson Crusoe* (1719) established an early model. Crusoe's island captured the eighteenth-century popular imagination because of its isolation and detachment from the world. As remote sites surrounded by water, islands reminded colonists of the dangers of sea travel and the perils of being far from civilization. Islands were also imagined in romantic terms, as if they existed in a perfect state of balance and harmony, self-contained, ruled by nature and not by man. But in fiction as in life, islands had to be inhabited to be of interest: when populated, they could then be described as a kind of crossroads, a zone of commerce and cultural exchange where colonialists could confront what they imagined to be their 'savage' or 'primitive' others, where they could hear different languages, see different races.

These attitudes persisted in British fiction of the nineteenth century and are present as well in the Camerons' correspondence to each other. They also inform Julia Margaret's first allegorical photograph, very likely made when Charles was in Ceylon in 1864. This photograph portrays two Western children exiled on the island colony of Mauritius, an island located in the middle of the Indian Ocean; she titled her image *Paul and Virginia* (Figure 6). Taken from the French novel written in 1788 by Jacques-Henri Bernardin de Saint-Pierre, *Paul et Virginie*, Cameron's photograph helps to establish that the colonial condition was at the forefront of her ambitious project. But Cameron's colonial island consciousness was not simply a product of her imagination or of responding to an influential and popular novel. Before we consider the making and reception of *Paul and Virginia*, we return to the Cameron's two islands, the better to understand their romantic attachment to their island homes.

Charles's regular voyages to Ceylon were reminders that the Camerons were not quite settled in England, in large part because their economic foundations were not stable or secure. Even in 1860, economic uncertainty was a constant presence. Although Charles Cameron had retired from governmental service in India and returned to England in 1848, twelve years had passed and his Ceylonese plantations still did not provide the family a sufficient income. Charles's trip that year was to provide direction to his foreman and overseers and to test new methods for drying coffee and shipping it to Europe. Tropical island crops like tea, coffee, and rubber faced a high degree of risk because of the seasonally violent weather, and in 1860, the Ceylonese coffee crop experienced an unusually low yield. Julia Margaret's attentions were elsewhere; her focus was social and cultural. Following the Camerons' return to England in 1848 and shortly after joining the social circle surrounding her sister Sara Prinsep at Little Holland House, Julia Margaret set up her own literary and artistic salon in 1859, embracing Alfred, Lord Tennyson as a central figure. The two became neighbours in Freshwater on the Isle of Wight. According to one of her contemporaries, Cameron established herself as a kind of Madame Recamier to Tennyson's Chateaubriand.[3]

To draw the island parallels ever closer in 1860, Julia Margaret named one of her recently acquired Freshwater cottages 'Dimbola', after the Camerons' largest plantation in Ceylon. It is useful to compare this act of naming to her calling Ceylon 'your island' in her letter to Charles. The act of naming here is more than a shorthand reference between intimates; it is integral to both the formation of

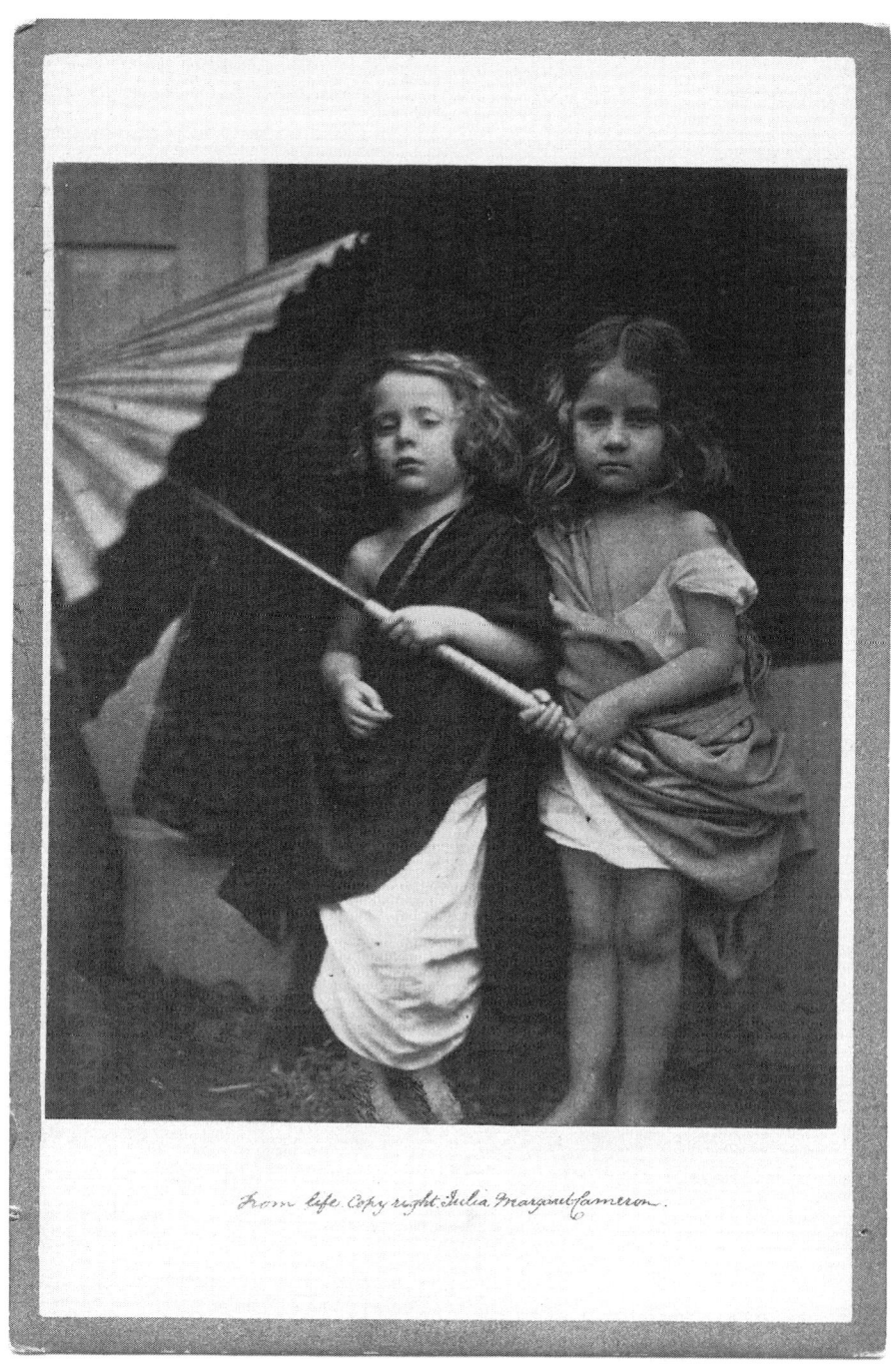

*From life Copyright Julia Margaret Cameron.*

6    Julia Margaret Cameron, *Paul and Virginia (William Frederick Gould;*
*Elizabeth Keown) (Cox 23),* 1864. Albumen cabinet card, 117 x 96 mm.

identity and the claiming of ownership. To the Camerons, and, importantly, to the literary and artistic circle surrounding Julia Margaret, Dimbola in Freshwater became both an extension of, and a metaphorical substitute for, the island colony of Ceylon, combining the key associations of both territories, drawing these places together as possessions that shared an unusual identity as idyllic island homes. Similarly, when Julia Margaret calls Ceylon 'your island' in her correspondence with Charles, she uses the possessive reference to disclose Charles's figurative attachment to the land and his literal ownership as a landowner. By means of this parallel line of association, Julia Margaret's use of the possessive 'your' also allows her to unite the fragment of their plantation estate with the entire island colony, and in so doing, she symbolically unites the British nation and its remote island colony across the globe.

During her lifetime, Julia Margaret Cameron was written into the history of Freshwater as if she and her husband were committed, lifetime residents, or as if they longed to be.[4] But this view of the Camerons as happily landed retirees is false; the two did not rest easily in England after flourishing as a Society couple in Calcutta. As early as January 1851, in fact, they even made plans to return to the East and live in Ceylon, at least until Charles was offered a much-anticipated position as governor of Malta or the Ionian islands.[5] Charles had every reason to be optimistic about his chances for being named to such an appointment: years earlier, from 1829 to 1833, Charles briefly left his post in the Council of India and joined Sir William Colebrooke as part of a Commission to make recommendations to the Colonial Office regarding the laws and colonial administration of Mauritius and Ceylon. Their report, the *Royal Commission to Examine and Report upon the Present State of the Laws, Regulations and Usages in the Settlements of the Cape of Good Hope and the Island of Mauritius and Ceylon*, recommended establishing new laws and a formal penal code on the islands, as well as the formation of a constitutional government based upon the British example.[6] After Charles was ultimately passed over for both of these governing posts, it appears the family settled in England by default, for clearly, had he been appointed to govern either of these island colonies, Julia Margaret and the family had already decided to follow.

The Camerons' Freshwater years were also spent in regular correspondence with several of their grown sons in Ceylon and with the land overseers managing their estates.[7] The two were also tied, at least sympathetically, to another island colony across the globe: from 1862 to 1867, their eldest son Eugene, a colonel in the Royal Artillery, was stationed as an aide to the governor of Barbados. Although Eugene visited the Isle of Wight in 1867, when he sat for his portrait (Cox 605, 606), he served during a period of great turmoil and economic unrest in the West Indies, capped by the Gordon Riots of 1865 in Jamaica, unrest that was forcibly put down by its Governor-General, Edward John Eyre. And not long afterward, in 1869, the Camerons' second son, Ewen, married Annie Chinery from nearby Lymington, and subsequently used his legacy to purchase his own Ceylonese coffee estate adjoining his parents' plantation in Rathoongodde.[8]

The correspondence between Julia Margaret and Charles after they settled in England affirms that the couple believed their two island homes shared both physical characteristics and economic similarities. For example, in a letter to Julia Margaret from Ceylon, dated 11 December 1850, Charles wrote:

> Juley love – Think of me sitting after dinner in the old Rathoongodde Bungalow (the new one is not yet finished) drinking port wine sent to Clerihew [one of the land overseers that the Camerons' employed] in former days by your father – It seems like a dream. I left Kandy about 9 am this morning and came … as far as Haragam. There we mounted our ponies and rode hither. The journey did not fatigue me at all. The sun was very hot but an umbrella gave me protection against that … I saw some beautiful mountain views in the course of that ride and Rathoongodde truly surpassed my expectations in regard to romantic beauty. The idea I had formed of it from Clerihew's drawings and descriptions was surprisingly correct. We arrived a little before 4 o'clock and after washing my hands and face I walked out with Clerihew. We first visited his newly invented apparatus for drying coffee which seems excellent. Then we went to the new Bungalow. It promises to be very comfortable and very pretty. This old one is much worse than I expected … after going over the new bungalow, we went to look at a waterfall which Clerihew had brought to view by clearing away forest. It is enchanting – in no gentleman's grounds either in England or Scotland have I seen a more lovely spot – you must come and see it. I shall describe it more at length in a future letter.[9]

In this letter, Charles expresses the temporal nature of his immediate trip (leaving at 9 a.m., arriving at 4 p.m.) but he also invokes the nostalgic passage of time (the reference to Julia's father and the contrast implied between the old bungalow and the new and as yet unfinished modern dwelling) and the dream-like state that such meditations can create; these have the powerful effect of collapsing time (sipping port wine after dinner, as in former days). Writing from tropical Ceylon, Charles insists that his gentlemanly identity and class status is secure and that his plantation's views compare favourably to known 'gentleman's grounds' back home. And importantly, Charles's account also privileges the visual as the cornerstone of his experience: 'I saw some beautiful mountain views in the course of that ride'; 'we went to look at a waterfall'; 'you must come and see it. I shall describe it more.'

For Charles, as for his intimate reader Julia Margaret, Time, Identity, and the Visual were the three inseparable conditions of his experience. The three were intertwined symbolically, helping Charles bridge the actual physical distance between Freshwater and Ceylon but also stabilize the narrative disjunctions that might otherwise have weakened his sense of order. These three elements were also present for Julia Margaret in 1874, when the Camerons decided to leave

England for Ceylon; the priorities and impressions she expressed then, as she sailed through the Suez Canal on her final voyage abroad and which are discussed later, in Chapter 7, were identical to Charles's sentiments as he expressed them in 1850. Moreover, Charles's discourse, in which he collapses time, asserts his English gentleman's identity, and expresses preference for the visual over other senses, provides compelling evidence for his fixation on those rhetorical and perceptual frameworks that are known to him; they provide comfort and assurance, as if they are permanent. Yet these same rhetorical devices are simultaneously called into question by other aspects of his letter that suggest he is 'uncertain of the boundaries of society, and the margins of the text'.[10] For although someone in the household prepared his dinner, brought the ponies, provided soap and fresh water, and remembered the umbrella, those individuals remain unknown and invisible. And in Charles's letter to Julia Margaret, romance and industry clashed: in his reference to the new apparatus to dry coffee, Charles alludes unmistakably to the exchange value of the crop in marketplace terms, and to his ownership of the land, which guaranteed him the legal right to farm coffee for profit. Yet to Charles the landscape was steeped in an idealized, that is, timeless and pictur-esque, 'romantic beauty'.

The romantic beauty of the island is the subject of another letter sent to England before the close of the week. It includes a pen-and-ink drawing by Charles depicting three buildings on the Rathoongodde estate, along with the evocative verbal depiction of a waterfall (Figure 7). In this letter, Charles privileges the visual by combining descriptive elements that both map the land that describe an idealized view of an island paradise. The act of mapping the land is useful to the landowner in many ways. Whether officially created by governments and the professional geographers or cartographers they employ or produced by transient travellers, maps draw upon a set of rhetorical codes and representational devices that are inherently unstable because they almost always require an explanatory table or a narrative in order to decode the symbols and visual shorthand they contain. Maps were among the first documents, of course, that were produced to depict newly colonized lands. Mapping the colonial lands, with designated codes used to mark the principal (or planned) transportation routes, such as roads and railways, served practical purposes, and even the earliest British maps of Ceylon were careful to inscribe plantation boundaries and often included the names of plantation owners.[11] But Charles's rough sketch marking the location of buildings and terrain does more than represent an interesting or notable topographic feature of Dimbola. By moving from an aerial perspective to a figure-ground representa-tion with a perceptible horizon and perspective, Charles introduces distinctive romantic references: the bungalow placed at the centre of two outbuildings, with its thatched roof; the harmonious array of the architecture, which is laid out on a symmetrical plan; the suggestion of a pathway on the hill above the cabins; the foam and spray created by the waterfall, possibly at the lower right of the drawing. These are not areas awaiting European improvement; rather, they are elements of the familiar travel-writer's trope of the romantic and untouched 'natural' island.[12]

At the same time, Charles engages in the practice of his own renaming of the landscape, a picturesque expression of repossessing the land:

> O Juley! Juley! How I wish you could see all that I have been seeing for the last few days ... If you follow the path which winds round the grassy hill on the right you come in about 200 yards to a deep ravine down which flows a lovely mountain

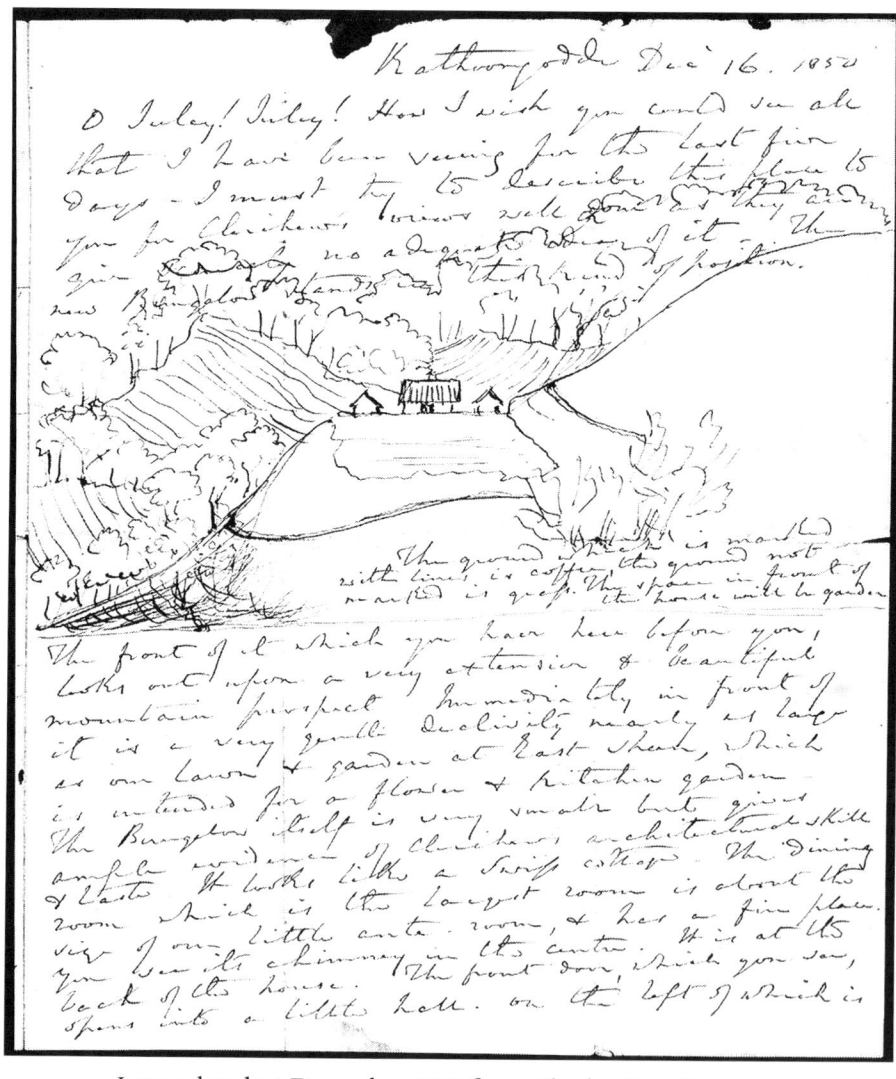

7    Letter dated 16 December 1850 from Charles Hay Cameron
to Julia Margaret Cameron.

stream which I have christened the Julia oya (I believe it is the very same stream that I used to call by that name when looking at the plan of the estate at Calcutta). When it crosses the path it forms a beautiful cascade falling in two white and foaming sheets of water, over the smooth face of a huge and solid mass of granite rock ... It would be nothing less than an eternal shame to you to be the owner of such a place and not to come and see it.[13]

As in his previous letter comparing 'the idea' he had formed of the land, 'from Clerihew's drawings and descriptions' or from poring over official government-sanctioned maps, to his actual experience before the sites he owned, Charles insists that the visual beauty of the mountain stream, the pathway leading to the cascade, and the foaming sheets of water, can only be truly experienced *in person*. Nevertheless, these experiences are captured and possessed rhetorically, just as they are simultaneously rebranded, passing from pagan, profane, and Ceylonese, to spiritual, sacred, and British. As a British waterfall, it can then be christened in the name of Julia herself.

Back in Freshwater, around 1860, Charles composed a poem that again reflects upon his relationship to island life, revealing his complex thoughts about possessing the land, especially a land steeped in a rich cultural past. In the manner of an English gentleman, Charles surveys the view from his own home, as well as the topography surrounding the town of Freshwater, from which the River Yar issues and flows north toward the town of Yarmouth, there emptying into the Solent, the channel that separates the Isle of Wight from England.

> The English Channel famed in war,
> The Solent sea and winding Yar
> Have cut an islet, yet not quite
> An islet from the Isle of Wight,
> For 'twixt the Channel famed in war
> And silent sources of the Yar,
> Dry land the twentieth of a mile
> Unites it to the parent isle.
>
> There dwell I, fronting Afton Down,
> With Yarmouth for my nearest town,
> The little Yarmouth where the Yar
> Though hindered by its gathering bar
> After four miles of winding reach
> At length divides the yellow beach,
> And meets in Solent's brine the rills
> That southward flow from Hampshire's hills.
>
> There dwell I, nowise unreproved,
> By those who, loving and beloved,
> Think that to them I ought to give
> The remnant that I have to live.

> Nor can they cease to wonder why
> I let the gusty Solent lie
> 'Twixt me and them, 'twixt me and all
> That men 'The World and Life' do call.[14]

In these lines, Charles evokes the Isle of Wight's distinct topography, but also underscores its connection to historical wars endured by England, on England's southern coast, and therefore, to the legacy of preserving and defending the (home)land, that is, the British nation itself. Curiously, Charles places himself on Afton Down, facing the southern periphery of the Isle of Wight and therefore looking *outward* toward the Channel. Yet he uses this vantage point to reflect upon the world *north* of where he stands, including the River Yar, the block of land he calls the islet 'not quite' cut into the Isle of Wight by the river, the Solent, and the mainland, which Charles refers to by its county name, Hampshire. Charles seems to say that he remains connected to the nation's home, mindful of its historical origins, and connected to its deepest traditions and memory. His poem expresses his awareness of how topography and culture work together to mark both the land and the sea, uniting the two in the process.

Charles also places himself and his family at the nexus of land and sea, a liminal place of superiority rather than disadvantage because from Charles's vantage point he can occupy both positions simultaneously. From this place of privilege – literally, high ground – he can project his connection to the imperial centre and affirm his ties to it, comparing the 'islet' on 'the parent isle', formed by the Yar, to the relationship of the Isle of Wight and Hampshire. From Charles's site, therefore, he could survey the geography and assess the contour of the land as if a map surveyor, using this perspective to appreciate how the island is cut from, yet is also united to, a larger landmass, and symbolically, how the smallest part of a nation is connected to its centre. It is compelling to think of this poem's island imagery as a sentimental reflection on the British Empire itself, where the romantic rills of Hampshire winding down to meet the Solent represent the imperial centre, while the coffee plantations in Ceylon represent its colonial 'other'.[15]

Julia Margaret also cherished the same privileged vantage point on the Isle of Wight that was described by Charles. In a letter written to Charles in 1865, she described her view from Freshwater's 'Dimbola' and the picturesque landscape she encountered. Julia Margaret and Charles both defined their place in the world from the perspective of being 'at home', tied literally and figuratively to the land: like Charles, Julia Margaret also defined Freshwater in relationship to England. As much a landowner as Charles, she described the picturesque scenery she experienced from that home: 'The elms make a golden girdle around us now. The dark purple hills of England behind are a glorious picture in the morning when the sun shines on them and the elm trees ... there is something so wholesome in beauty, and it is not for me to try to tell of all we have here in those delicate tints of a distant bay and the still more distant headlands. These I see every day with my own eyes.'[16]

In this letter, Julia Margaret asserts her stability, her contentedness, and her optimism as expressed by her trust in nature. This is also a trust that is guaranteed by her familiarity with place, her ownership of the land, but also, importantly, cultural belonging; the elms create a warm embrace, the hills are soft and picturesque, the landscape is wholesome because it is natural and sustaining. But the land also has a cultural, and therefore political, identity as well, because culture imbues otherwise simple topography with complex meanings, investing it with cultural associations, personal memories, political and economic expectations, and a historical legacy: 'It is in culture that we can seek out the range of meanings and ideas conveyed by the phrases *belonging to* or *in a* place, being *at home in a place*', wrote Edward Said.[17] Whether in Calcutta, where Charles and Julia Margaret Cameron wed and raised their children; in Kent, where they initially settled upon their return to England and reclaimed their connection to British society; in Ceylon, where they imagined themselves occupying the land; or in Freshwater, where they relocated in order to be close to the Tennysons, Charles and Julia Margaret Cameron were 'at home', because culturally, the two had never abandoned their British identity.

## Saint-Pierre's island exiles

In 1864, when Julia Margaret photographed two local children as the title characters of Saint-Pierre's popular novel *Paul et Virginie*, she was continuing a long tradition of illustrating scenes from this popular and much-loved book. Saint-Pierre's story takes place on an island colony, the Île de France, which had earlier been called Mauritius under the Dutch, and later returned to that name under the British. Sitting in multinational waters in the Indian Ocean, the place appealed to the European powers for years as a strategic naval site because it could be used as a staging ground to launch conflicts with India, advance the slave trade in Madagascar, and promote international commerce. Although Saint-Pierre's novel was about French subjects rather than British, its story appealed to a broad European audience and had transnational appeal, and for that reason, *Paul and Virginia* became one of the most widely translated and widely published works of literature during the nineteenth century, one that achieved far-reaching influence across the globe.[18]

Helen Maria Williams's translation of 1795 was the first to help popularize the novel in England. She abridged the text for English readers, omitting long philosophical sections and inserting her own sonnets to punctuate the novel with a self-consciously romantic sentimentality. By 1789, Saint-Pierre himself noted the success of the novel in England, and especially its popularity among women readers.[19] This broad appeal led James Cobb to adapt the story in 1800 for the London stage, where once again, he shifted its setting for a British audience by transposing Mauritius into an unnamed British-occupied colony in the West Indies, where its land is worked by 'English planters'. Cobb, an official of the East India Company, also transformed the story politically, re-imagining the island in idealized terms of British national identity: 'it is the boast of Britons', one of his characters declares, 'that from the moment a slave imprints his footstep on our shore, the moment he breathes the air of our land, he becomes free'.[20]

*Paul and Virginia* tells the story of two French women who are exiled on Mauritius, each of whom is pregnant, one deserted after the death of her husband and cast out by her aristocratic family; the other abandoned in poverty by the unmarried father of her child. On Mauritius, the two outcast mothers give birth to their children and resolve to live communally and raise them as siblings. Their island home is a precious and fragile utopia, but also a clear alternative to – and rejection of – the modern-day world, especially its commercial values and social conventions. Living close to the land and surrounded by nature, with few wants and no external influences, the women raise their children aided by two black slaves. When Paul and Virginia grow to adolescence, however, and experience strong feelings for each other that cannot be acted upon, the harmony of the group begins to disintegrate, and Virginia is sent to France to rejoin her mother's aristocratic family. The idyllic harmony of the island dissolves irreversibly when Virginia drowns in a shipwreck upon her return from France.

Photography was still brand new for Cameron in 1864 when she chose her subject and composed her models; in fact, *Paul and Virginia* was her first 'fancy subject'. After receiving a camera from her daughter, she experimented with various portraits and figure studies while she learned the mechanics of the new craft. But in the act of composing *Paul and Virginia*, she crystallized an artistic working method that provided room for her to experiment and then to choose among provisional results for the most successful outcome. Four images of *Paul and Virginia* document the earliest of her efforts to devise such a working method (Cox 20–3). The last of the four she evidently considered her 'final image' (Cox 23), as she copyrighted this photograph on 27 March 1865 with the intention of mass-reproducing it for sale. By the end of the year, she had included the photograph in her exhibitions at Colnaghi and Company (July) and at the French Gallery (November). To allow for even greater public awareness, she produced the work in reduced size as an albumen print on a gold-edged cabinet card (4⅝ in. x 3¾ in. / 117 mm x 96 mm) (Figure 6), and over the next few years, she included a large print of *Paul and Virginia* in virtually every photographic album that she created for her family and friends.[21] Although we have no idea of the edition size or how many reduced-format prints were in circulation, Cameron certainly did not produce the cabinet cards herself, and very likely did so only to promote the sale of her full-size works.[22]

Cameron's photograph draws much of its power from the romantic trope of the remote island home that was present in Saint-Pierre's story and its connection to the allegories of homelessness, exile, and primitive innocence that are personified by the two children. But in 1865, when Cameron made plans to publish her photograph widely, *Paul and Virginia* directly intersected with two contemporary controversies that gave new meaning to the story of exiled European children on a remote island colony: these were a crisis in the Colonial Office over how to stabilize the economic conditions that sustained colonialism, which was accompanied by a larger public examination about emigration both as a solution for overcrowding at home and as a way to extend British influence abroad. These two debates were connected by a resurgent interest in the popular legends and the visual iconography that united Victorian Britain to its early and primitive past. This interest was expressed formally in governmental competitions for fine arts prizes and informally in numerous essays that appeared on the subject of colonial expansion to remote areas of the world by authors like Edward Gibbon Wakefield and Thomas Carlyle.

At the same time, from the 1840s to the 1860s, the Colonial Office, and in particular, its colonial land and emigration commission, vigorously debated the merits versus the costs of introducing itinerant labourers in island colonies like Jamaica, Mauritius, and Ceylon to help advance their economic prosperity. These policy decisions were accompanied by related efforts to try to stimulate British emigration to those colonies. Within the Colonial Office, the debates circled around Lord Stanley (14th earl of Derby), Lord Grey (colonial secretary 1846–52), and the permanent under-secretaries for the colonies Sir James Stephen (until 1847), Herman Merivale (1854–59), and Sir Frederick Rogers (1859–71), as well as members of the land and emigration commission like Thomas Frederick Elliot and Sir Henry Taylor. Under Stephen and Merivale, the Colonial Office defended British law prohibiting slavery and in its place sought to import coolie labourers from India into island colonies to promote their economic development, while others in Britain called their efforts little more than a new kind of forced labour.[23] These included members of the Anti-Slavery Society like Lord Brougham and religious humanitarians like Bishop Samuel Wilberforce of Oxford.

While Saint-Pierre downplayed slavery in *Paul and Virginia*, he also embedded an important subplot of emancipation versus indentured labour in the novel to create dramatic tension. In order to describe an idyllic world in his novel, Saint-Pierre marginalized the plantation economy that sustained slavery and focused instead on the romantic myth of an unspoiled natural world that could lead to prosperity only if selfless individuals, like Paul and Virginia, were free to cultivate it properly. To Cameron, the setting of this sentimental story against the harsh economic realities of colonialism and political debates about indentured labour and emigration made the subject of *Paul and Virginia* resonate with multiple meanings and conflicting interests.

In her photographs of the two children, Cameron followed Saint-Pierre's narrative and portrayed them as diminutive and passive. As innocent children, both Paul and Virginia embody multiple social and allegorical references: the children represent mythical and idealized children of nature, raised largely in the company of their own society, built around their mothers–and the slaves who tend to their needs. This unconventional family group forges a new social bond and lives in virtual isolation, cut off not only from the outside world, but also from the island's other communities. In this sheltered society, the two unrelated children are raised as brother and sister, yet they also fall in love, as if it were preordained, and express eternal devotion to each other. In addition, the two children also lead uncorrupted lives characterized by the spiritual harmony they have found in nature, thereby embodying moral goodness and virtue. When they enact dramatic stories from the Bible in theatrical performances for their mothers, they do so naively, expressing enduring moral lessons rather than any particular religious beliefs. Consequently, in Saint-Pierre's world, these 'native mimes'[24] may be considered 'pre-religious', largely because their moral actions stand apart from the lessons of formal institutional Christianity, to which Paul and Virginia's mothers have expressed their firm opposition. Among this small group, piety is not expressed as a function of organized religion; rather, religion is presented as an institutional practice of civilized society which, within the context of the novel, must not be trusted. Finally, as island children reared in isolation from the civilized ways of the colony and Europe, Paul and Virginia are written as inexperienced and guileless, easily deceived by a treacherous aunt, a dishonest priest, and a scheming governor. Their simple world eventually becomes undermined by an economic system of wage-labour that is based on exploitation. Once these forces have conspired to invade their arcadia, the pure and natural society is easily destroyed.

Virginia's demise is often taken as an additional example of the intrusion of corrupt Western morals upon the untouched moral universe of the island. Death enters where it had not been known before, and symbolically destroys the small society, when, toward the end of the novel, Virginia, now a young woman, acts upon the conventions of modesty that she learned while visiting France. Rather than protecting her life and virtue, these actually work against her own natural sense of self-preservation, but it is a lesson learned too late. The shipwreck where this occurs – the climactic scene in the novel – takes place when Virginia refuses to remove her heavy layered dresses in the presence of a sailor who is trying to save her before the boat submerges. Refusing to disrobe, Virginia goes down with the ship.[25] Although this scene embodies the high-minded sense of female virtue and pathos associated with Victorian social conventions, Cameron did not choose to represent it, focusing instead on pre-adolescent children who are clothed in rags but free from harm.

The colonial condition is ever-present in the novel. Virginia's death exemplifies the triumph of nature over the corrupting influences of Western civilization, but it also has the effect of stimulating feelings of melancholy in the reader and nascent political awakening on the island: Anna Neill has written that *Paul and Virginia* 'secures a society of tears, whose collective imaginary can restore the strong narrative of moral order to the weaker one of political confusion'.[26] To Neill, the sensation of melancholy opens up a new emotional space in the novel, an expressive moment she calls 'colonial' because it focuses the reader to recall what happened to indigenous peoples before colonialism took root in such remote places. In the novel, Saint-Pierre's narrator reminds readers that the story of Paul and Virginia survives only in legend and myth; it is not preserved in stone, like the monuments erected by kings of grand civilizations. As the narrator (*le vieillard*) insists: 'No marble was raised over their humble mounds, no inscription was cut to their virtues, but their memory has remained indelible in the hearts of those who experienced their kindness.' Memory alone preserves the story of Paul and Virginia. Nature has finally erased the physical bodies of the two, and the tomb in which they were buried stands overgrown and unmarked as if it were a just and heroic reclamation of their simple lives. Readers are also told that their memories continue to live on, preserved by the names that islanders subsequently gave to different sections of the island. Yet while these warm and compassionate memories are preserved, the 'other lives' of the island, represented by the two adult slaves who helped to look after the children as they grew up, are overlooked as if they are insignificant, just as they have been nearly erased by history itself.

## Children of the colonies

*Paul and Virginia* is not a 'children's story', nor was the novel written to be read by or to young children.[27] Rather, the novel appeared in the Romantic tradition of Rousseau as a sentimental romance and bitter morality tale that, for emphasis, was situated in the idyllic setting of a distant island colony. Carlyle was much closer to Saint-Pierre's ideal reader: in his history of the French Revolution, Carlyle called *Paul et Virginie* a 'Noteworthy Book',

> which may be considered as the last speech of old Feudal France … Everywhere wholesome Nature in unequal conflict with diseased perfidious Art; cannot escape from it in the lowest hut, in the remotest island of the sea. Ruin and death must strike down the loved one; and, what is most significant of all, death even here not by necessity, but by etiquette. What a world of prurient corruption lies visible in that super-sublime of modesty![28]

Scholars who have studied the literary reception of *Paul et Virginie* have noted that its popularity during the nineteenth century was connected to the illustrations that frequently accompanied the text: of all the editions of the novel that were produced throughout its publication history (more than 269 distinct editions appeared until 1962), almost half were illustrated by engravings.[29] Moreover, the graphic art that illustrated the novel generated an additional popular secondary market, giving rise to a wide array of vignettes and scenes from the novel that appeared on fabrics and tapestries, plates and cups, porcelain and fans, and wallpaper produced in England, France, and Germany for an international buying public.[30] Among the reading public in nineteenth-century France, the book's visual illustrations were often more vivid and well known than the text itself.[31] And for British readers, more than sixty English editions were published throughout the nineteenth century.[32]

The Didot edition of 1789 established the iconographical model for almost all subsequent editions by featuring an engraving by the celebrated artist Jean-Michel Moreau (le jeune); Figure 8 shows a reproductive engraving of Moreau's design. This image portrayed Paul and Virginia huddled together beneath the billowing fabric of Virginia's petticoats under the watchful gaze of *le vieillard*. Moreau le jeune's illustration soon became the novel's signature arrangement of the two central characters, and a version of this composition appears in virtually every subsequent popular illustrated edition of the novel.[33] The seminal illustration depicts a memorable scene that occurs early in the novel: at this early point in the story, Paul and Virginia are about five years old. Reflecting upon an encounter with the children who were taking cover from a sudden rain-shower under Virginia's upturned petticoat, *le vieillard* recalls, 'Both were laughing heartily at being sheltered together under an umbrella of their own invention. The sight of these two pretty heads encircled by the billowing petticoat brought to my mind the children of Leda, enclosed in the same shell.' The graphic images that represent Paul and Virginia under their fabric canopy often situate them in a forested setting, depicting them in modest, but not 'proper' European clothes, and barefoot, as they have no need for shoes. At the same time that these visual devices situate Paul and Virginia in their tropical home, the visual iconography also looks back to earlier visual art in order to borrow well-known symbols. As Moreau le jeune undoubtedly knew from ancient Roman art, the billowing drapery over the head of an idealized figure (known as *velificatio*), as in the Ara Pacis, could personify an abstract idea, depict a timeless moment, or visualize a privileged and isolated world. Artists well versed in this ancient iconography were reinforced by the novel's classical references that related the children to the mythological story of Leda, who gave birth to twin infants conceived by Zeus.

Cameron probably chose to represent this particular scene from the novel because of its broad familiarity in popular literature and visual culture. It is also

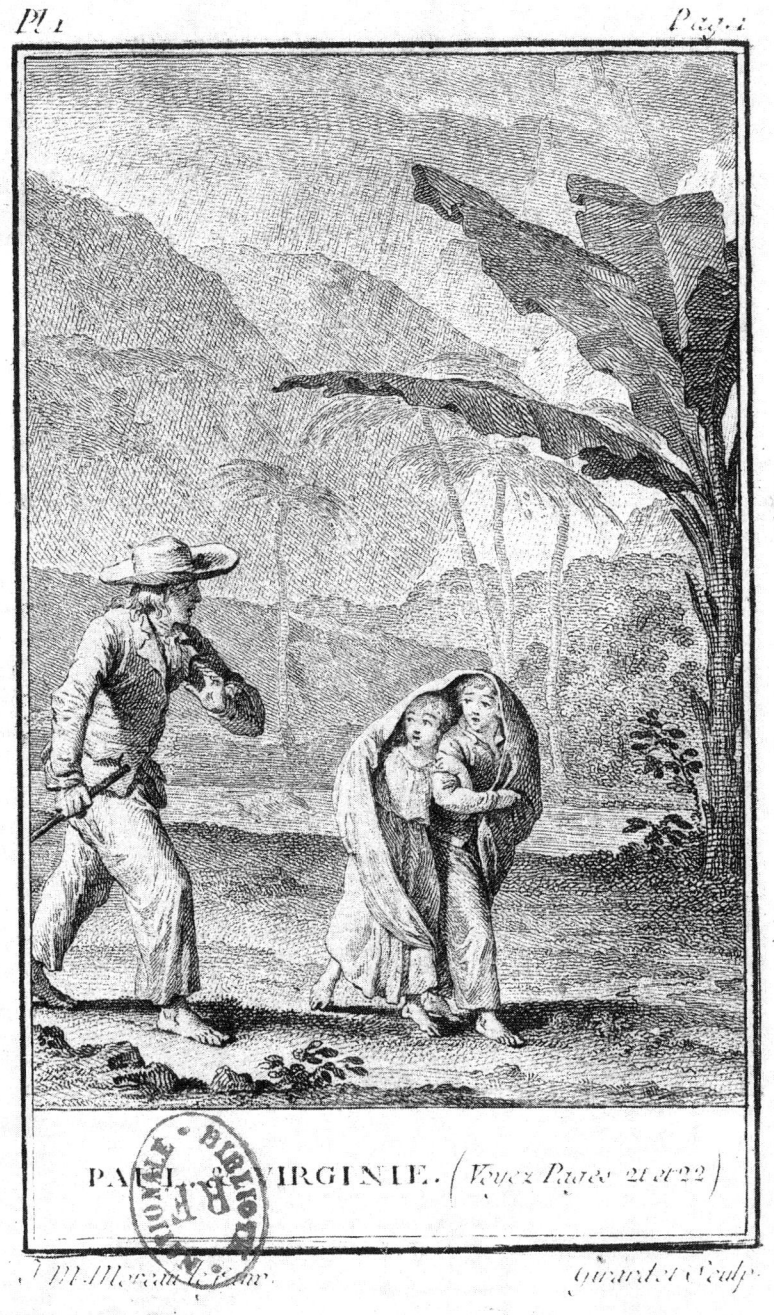

Jean-Michel Moreau (le jeune), *Paul et Virginie se protégeant de la pluie et rencontrant le narrateur*, frontispiece, engraving by Abraham Girardet, in Jacques-Henri Bernardin de Saint-Pierre, *Paul et Virginie* (Paris: Didot, 1789).

possible that she remembered the novel or even saw the French wallpaper during her childhood in France.[34] In her photographic sitting, she posed the two young children close together toward the front of the picture plane and within a shallow spatial field, using Moreau le jeune and his followers as a compositional guide. She clothed her models in costumes that resemble unstructured cotton or oversized flimsy gowns, as opposed to tailored outer garments, with Paul in dark fabric and Virginia in light. While the drapery appears oversized, because it is bunched up in multiple folds on the children's bodies, Cameron arranged the children's arms and legs to be bare in three of the four photographs, and in each image the children stand barefoot. Cameron placed an open umbrella in their hands as a substitute for the fabric petticoats that the novel says billowed up to protect the children; this was a creative solution to a difficult formal problem, since long exposure times logistically prohibited photographers from trying to depict the ephemeral, like weightless, airborne fabric. But attentive viewers would also have recognized the umbrella as Indian in origin, and might even have connected it to commercial photographs of island peasants in exotic lands; for example, Skeen and Company, a firm that operated in Ceylon, produced such imagery for the British market.[35] The umbrella itself could have dated from the Camerons' return from Calcutta in 1848 or been a more recent gift from one of Charles's visits to Ceylon. In order to help define the three-dimensionality of the pictorial space and suggest volume, Cameron tilted the umbrella at a 45-degree angle. In two of the images produced during this sitting, a female assistant's forearm and hand can be seen adjusting Paul's costume, and in the 'final image', that is, the one selected for mass production, Cameron manipulated the glass plate negative itself, scratching away bits of the photographic emulsion in an effort to provide greater visual definition to the feet of the boy, whose pose appears awkward and his feet oddly indistinct.[36]

In representational art, children carry a special narrative burden, and Cameron's *Paul and Virginia* is no exception. In the tradition of Western visual art that Cameron inherited, images of children were used to embody themes like purity and innocence, sentimentality, and nostalgia; to symbolize the idealized past and as-yet-unknown future; to represent peacefulness and harmony; to give visual form to unquestioning faith, or to the ideal of domestic tranquillity; or to portray an image of unconditional honesty and goodness, especially if that was threatened by corruption or evil.[37] These ideas were at the heart of the eighteenth-century 'fancy picture', and drew upon the philosophy of Jean-Jacques Rousseau (1712–78), as much as Saint-Pierre himself. This tradition continued in painting of the Victorian era, but during a time when the prevailing Enlightenment understanding of childhood as an innocent and blissful stage of life was being re-evaluated, pictures of children grew more complicated. Cameron's contemporaries increasingly considered childhood a period of instability and irresponsibility, easy corruption and weakness, immaturity and ignorance, and inferiority, especially as compared with adulthood. Under the influence of British colonialism during the nineteenth century, the developmental model of childhood – in which gradual learning, increased understanding, and steady maturity would accompany children's increased participation in adult society – was replaced by a new understanding of childhood itself. According to the new model, 'childhood' was an expression of primitivism and uncivilized behaviour; as a result, a new and wide gulf separated 'inferior children' from the superiority of adults.

It is evident that representations of children, and of childhood itself, cannot be separated from the historical moment that created them. This is especially true under British colonialism, which imposed its own conditions and expectations: Ashis Nandy has written that colonialism 'drew a new parallel between primitivism and childhood … What was childlikeness of the child and childishness of immature adults now also became the lovable and unlovable savagery of primitives and the primitivism of subject societies.'[38] During the nineteenth century, childhood was a useful construct under British colonialism because it could be used to reinforce a theory of progress, one that fit efficiently into a before-and-after narrative of moral, social, and economic development. For example, missionaries and educators made use of this concept to help them visualize how social and economic progress could be achieved. Children's natural physical development could also provide an evidentiary model for social uplift and improvement. As a result, according to Nandy, the ignorance and innocence associated with childhood could be shown to give way to enlightened states of knowledge, civilization, and modern attitudes, and consequently, these themes emerged as popular representational tropes under British colonialism. White children, especially when represented in a colonial context and as juxtaposed against non-white colonial 'others', also acquired a new visibility and importance as a subject for the camera, because in the colonial context, white children were often inflected with layers of meaning that invoked questions of inclusion and exclusion, emigration and citizenship, identity and nationality.[39]

## Emigration, emancipation, indentured labour

Because *Paul and Virginia*, following Moreau le jeune's graphic model, extracts the children from the larger historical context where the land had been carved into plantations and where slavery was present, Cameron disengages the colonial narrative from the historical memory of the novel. This extraction allowed Saint-Pierre (who marginalized these elements in his novel) and Cameron to acknowledge, and yet also to remove, the condition of slavery that defined the island's economic system. In one instance of *Paul and Virginia* wallpaper, slaves dance nearby the child couple, replacing *le vieillard* (Figure 9); in this case, slavery is present but strategically turned into a picturesque vignette, and the personal

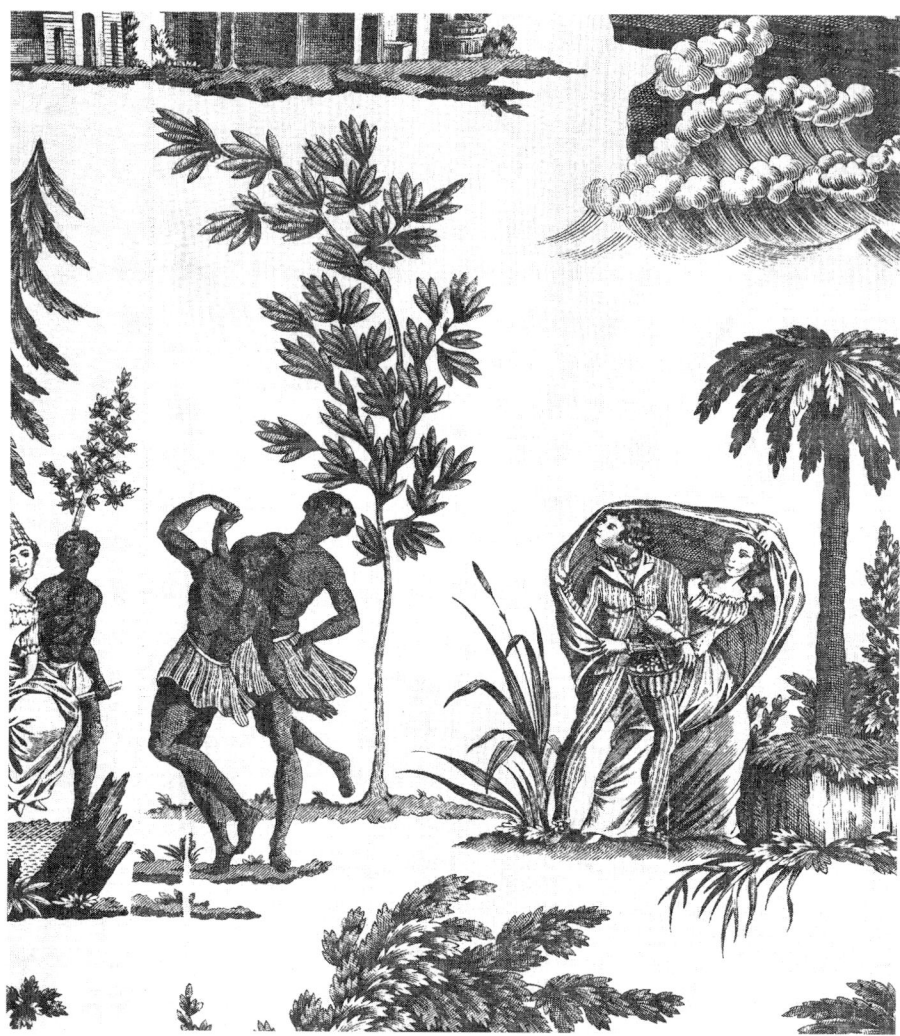

9     Textile, *Paul et Virginie*, c. 1795. Detail. Produced by Petitpierre et Cie.,
France, Nantes. Cotton, printed by engraved copper plate on plain weave.
Warp x Weft, 170 x 126 cm.

hardship and exploitation of slavery is omitted. In *Blind Memory*, Marcus Wood's
survey of visual representations of slavery, he contends that 'It may not be possible
to find solutions to the questions of how to read, or how to see, visual representations developed out of the Western myths devoted to the memory of slavery.'[40]
This difficulty is compounded further when references to slavery are not overt,
but contained in subtext or indirect association. Because of slavery's historical
role in colonization, and its subordinate, though enabling role in Saint-Pierre's
novel, Wood's observation is useful to emphasize how slavery is present in visual

representations developed out of the Western myths devoted to colonization, immigration, and nationalism, even when slavery itself is not explicitly visible; as he notes, it is impossible for us to make direct contact with the historical experience of slavery. Similarly, for Cameron, slavery was not available for her to represent directly. Instead, she chose other visual strategies, which we will explore below, that allowed her to substitute Paul and Virginia's Anglo-Saxon ancestors as effective stand-ins to represent the condition of slavery.

In Mauritius, slavery was a fact of the island's economic life, and in Europe, inseparably connected to debates about colonial expansion, emigration, and indentured labour. As represented by Saint-Pierre, slavery was 'benevolent' under the French. Throughout the novel, the author portrays Marie, the slave attached to Virginia's mother, Madame de la Tour, and Dominigue, who belonged to Marguerite, Paul's mother, as if they were intimate extensions of the women and their children. This close-knit society is solidified further when Marie and Dominigue marry each other, a familial act that was very likely impossible for slaves attached to the colony's plantations. This difference is explicitly emphasized in the novel when Paul and Virginia 'rescue' a runaway female slave. In this scene, the two white children return her to the plantation from which she fled, and Virginia naively and ineffectively advocates on behalf of the woman for mercy and forgiveness. Immediately after this scene, Paul and Virginia get lost in the forest on their return home, but it is Dominigue who rescues the children. Later, when Dominigue ages and grows too feeble to work outside, Paul gladly relieves Dominigue of his burdens. Madame de la Tour, who has left behind the aristocratic social conventions of France, expresses further solidarity with the slave and Creole populations of the island by casting off her Western dresses for plain Indian cotton, clothing herself in the same simple garments worn by the island's slaves. Finally, toward the close of the novel, when Dominigue and Marie have joined their mistresses in following Virginia and Paul to their graves, Saint-Pierre replaces the term 'esclaves' for 'fidèles serviteurs', a semantic change that he employs to signify common bonds and unity, in stark contrast to the economic and social realities that defined the slaves from those who own them.[41]

From the time that it was acquired in 1810 from the French during the Napoleonic Wars, Mauritius also retained the name Île de France. Consequently, for most of the nineteenth century, the island took on a double identity as both British and French, its Dutch identity long having been abandoned. This double identity was also experienced by the colony's European population, which was largely francophone, although a British governor ruled the island. In order to pacify the plantation owners and keep the fragile economy intact, Britain initially maintained laissez-faire economic policies and did very little to curtail the slave trade, in spite of having outlawed slavery in 1807. Under the general terms that described the island's transfer to Britain, all of the existing rights and institutions of the French were to be preserved under British law, including schools, the Roman Catholic Church (which continued to receive state support), and the ownership of French plantations, which produced sugar as their exclusive export crop.[42] The British established Mauritius as a crown colony (with an autocratic governor and a Crown-appointed council), while older sugar-producing colonies of the West Indies like Jamaica and Barbados were governed by two-house legislatures (one Crown-appointed; one elected by colonists).[43] Colonists understood their role was to maintain a steady flow of sugar to London, while keeping the island port a British oasis in the vast sea, and consequently out of the hands of Britain's economic and political rivals. Nevertheless, a clandestine slave trade flourished in Mauritius until 1818, when the British imposed a series of regulations to curtail the practice, which had little practical effect. Only after October 1826, following the visit of the Commission of Eastern Enquiry, did the large-scale illicit trade start to decrease.[44] By 1830, when the population in the entire island numbered approximately 100,000, some 76,000 were slaves imported from Africa.[45] But it was not until 1835 that slavery was finally abolished on the island, in large part owing to the importation of more than 25,000 'coolies' from India and Africa, the brainchild of Cameron's close friend, Sir Henry Taylor, and his associates in the Colonial Office.[46]

In spite of its small size, Mauritius was a major focal point for the Colonial Office, becoming an open playing field upon which colonial administrators experimented with theories on how to govern an antagonistic population of colonists and indentured servants on a remote island. Using Mauritius as a model, they tested theories that were designed to ameliorate social tensions, like tinkering with the island's educational system, but their social engineering efforts largely failed.[47] Around 1840, Merivale, together with his associate Henry Taylor, supported a new idea to make Mauritius economically sound by proposing to import coolies from India, theorizing that these labourers would be grateful to work on British plantations and that once trained, would be suitably conditioned to work for the Empire in other colonial situations. Merivale regarded this a kind of 'grand experiment', one that could provide a model for solving similar problems in Jamaica and the West Indies. According to Merivale, Mauritius was superior to West Indian islands like Trinidad or Jamaica because of its close proximity to

> the great reservoir of free labour, British India. The cost of conveying a Coolie from India to Mauritius is believed to be not a third of that of carrying him to Trinidad, and no source has hitherto been found, except British India and China, from which any regular supply of laborious immigrants for hopeful cultivation can be derived … In ten years, nearly 150,000 Coolies have been imported into Mauritius: they constitute much more than half the inhabitants of the colony: they are not voluntary immigrants in the ordinary sense, led by the spontaneous desire of bettering their condition: they are not slaves, seized by violence, brought

over in fetters, and working under the lash. They have been raised, not without effort, like recruits for the military service, imported under government care, assigned by the local authorities to masters, but with their freedom and rights carefully watched over, and their option to return to the mother country after a limited period of industrial service, carefully secured to them.[48]

With the demise of slavery in Mauritius this new system of indentured labour rose to take its place, and from the late 1830s to the 1860s, Henry Taylor played an instrumental role in overseeing its policies and administration, creating a system of government-subsidized indentured labour as the 'best hope' to ensure the colony's financial solvency.[49]

The activity in Mauritius coincided with an important imperial policy shift that was associated with the politician and pro-emigration propagandist Edward Gibbon Wakefield, an early advocate for colonizing Australia and New Zealand. As early as 1831, Wakefield distinguished between colonies that he deemed fit or unfit for settlement, regarding Mauritius and Ceylon as 'unsuitable' because they were small, one- or two-crop islands, and Canada or Australia, by contrast, as better able to receive large numbers of emigrants.[50] Even into the 1870s, Britain's social and economic policies in Mauritius and Ceylon largely failed, proving Wakefield correct in his assessment of the complicated factors that were necessary to sustain land ownership. In reality, then, Mauritius had become a significant problem for the Colonial Office by 1860 as it experienced lingering social troubles stemming from its transfer from French to English rule, the resistance of its plantation owners to the emancipation of their slaves, and a colonial government hampered by administering an indentured labour system. By contrast, Cameron's photograph of *Paul and Virginia* represented a safe haven where peace and harmony prevailed, rather than the failed proving ground of colonial economic policies. At the same time, however, the photograph could represent the hardy persistence of the island's white settlers who took shelter against economic adversity, much as Saint-Pierre's children took cover against the storm. As a modern allegory, such an image could help to construct and support a new mythology, one that could support advocates for expanding colonial emigration and colonial rule, like Wakefield and Carlyle.

## Cameron's Anglo-Saxon doubles

In London, those who supported the nation's emigration policies, like Carlyle, eagerly seized upon Saint-Pierre's novel as a propagandistic tool, embracing it as a symbol of the imagined peace and prosperity that could be found in the colonies. Carlyle knew of Saint-Pierre's *Paul et Virginie* at least as early as 1823, when he convinced his publisher George Boyd to allow his half-brother, John A. Carlyle, to translate *Paul et Virginie* from French into English for contemporary readers. Carlyle supported this venture despite the fact that there were already several English translations of the novel still in print. As he advised his brother, the new translation would be useful for helping him earn 'respectability' as he made his way in society. Were he to encounter any difficulties during the course of his translation, Carlyle himself agreed to correct the manuscript and even review proof sheets prior to its publication. Perhaps he even wrote, or rewrote, entire sections of the novel. Carlyle even suggested to his half-brother that he rely strongly on earlier English translations, urging him to come close to, but only just avoid, committing outright plagiarism: 'You will get the French copies and the existing translations, by [the courier] Farries; and then I read [advise] you, betake yourself to the duty with might and main. I have no doubt you will do it in a sufficient manner. You have only to consult the old copy at any dubious point, and never to be squeamish in imitating it. All that Boyd wants is a reasonable translation, which no one can prosecute him for printing. Those already before the public are very good.'[51]

When reviewing his brother's proof sheets, Carlyle commended the translation, but at the same time he disparaged Boyd's plan to include prefatory remarks by John M'Diarmid, editor of the *Dumfries Courier*. Carlyle complained: 'There cannot be a greater difference between M'Diarmid and St. Pierre. I hate M'Diarmid's flirting would-be-sentimental style of writing as sincerely as I admire the simple unaffected narrative of Pierre.'[52] Over Carlyle's protests, M'Diarmid reinforced the romantic qualities of the novel, just as Carlyle had foretold. However, M'Diarmid unexpectedly shifted attention from the scene of Virginia's tragic demise on to the fate of Paul, characterizing *Paul et Virginie* 'as the story of "the sorrows of Paul, like *The Sorrows of Werther*"'. As Ian Henderson noted recently, 'it is a modern tendency to be so distracted by Virginie's fate as to subordinate the story of Paul, which is of equal importance'.[53] And while much of the critical analysis of *Paul et Virginie* has focused largely on readers' interpretations in the late eighteenth century, less attention has been devoted to the novel's importance during the nineteenth, when more than 200 translated editions were produced in a wide array of formats and languages.[54]

Nineteenth-century readers apparently enjoyed both the sentimental and the stoic elements of the novel. In France, Flaubert and Balzac knew they could reliably draw upon *Paul et Virginie* as shorthand for over-the-top sentimentality and lugubrious fiction. In *Madame Bovary*, for example, Flaubert comically used *Paul et Virginie* as a foil to describe his heroine's dreamy and inwardly focused state of mind. Emma fantasizes of romantic love in a far-off primitive land, and the act of reading such an engrossing novel is sufficient to transport her from her own dismal reality.[55] Readers were also able to find stoic expressions in the novel itself, as Saint-Pierre sprinkled various classical inscriptions throughout the novel. Although these had no logical place in a primitive tropical colony, especially one populated by social outcasts, Saint-Pierre nevertheless inserted elevated moral attitudes as expressions of his characters' classical goodness and in spite of their low social status. In Saint-Pierre's story, *le vieillard* recites Latin from Horace, whose verses are etched into the bases of steles and flagpoles, and regularly compares the two children to the gods of ancient Greek mythology. When they attain age twelve, he writes, 'Their silence, the simple grace of their posture and the beauty of their bare feet would have made you think of a classical sculpture in white marble representing two of Niobe's children.' In the novel, during the scene of the climactic shipwreck, the sailor who tries to save Virginia 'is as muscular as Hercules', and Virginia's whole demeanour throughout her final ordeal is unwaveringly 'noble and assured'. As David Menhennet has written, 'Patience and courage in adversity; virtue in the face of temptation and injustice; modesty and death rather than immodesty and rescue; solitude as preferred to the society of cultivated but loose-living people – all these qualities are elevated in *Paul and Virginia* to the status of an ideal way of life.'[56]

After assisting his brother in translating *Paul et Virginie*, Thomas Carlyle referred periodically to the novel as one of inspiration and hope, and ironically, as a kind of antidote to excessive sentimentalism. For example, in a letter of 1837 to David Lester Richardson, a recent émigré to the East and editor of the *Bengal Annual* and the *Calcutta Literary Gazette*, Carlyle gamely attempted to support Richardson's decision to emigrate to India, in spite of the editor's expressed dismay at feeling 'in exile' in the East. Carlyle wrote:

> But as for you, my dear Sir, you have other work to do in the East than grieve. Are there not beautiful things there, glorious things; wanting only an eye to note them, a hand to record them? If I had the command over you, I would say, Read *Paul et Virginie* then, read the *Chaumière Indienne* [both novels were written by Saint-Pierre, and many published volumes bound the two stories together]; gird yourself together for a right effort, and go and do likewise or better! I mean what I say. The East has its own phases; there are things there which the West yet knows not of; and one Heaven covers both.[57]

For Carlyle, Saint-Pierre's stories set in island colonies were uplifting Eastern tales that promised emigrants the rewards of peaceful colonial settlement, especially if one believed the policies of Merivale, Wakefield, or Taylor would succeed.

Whether 'the East' was located in Mauritius or India, Carlyle believed it was a knowable and expansive territory, its natural and simple state evidence of its fertility and economic promise. The Camerons knew the Carlyles well after Charles and Julia Margaret returned to England in 1848; they met often at Little Holland House and, in the company of men like Thackeray, Watts, and Henry Taylor, debated such matters as how England might expand its colonial reach. Reginald Horsman has written that, in Carlyle's view, England had been assigned two essential undertakings in world history: 'the industrial task of conquering "half or more" of the planet, "for the use of man," and the constitutional task of sharing the fruits of conquest, and showing other peoples how this might be done'. Carlyle advanced domineering racial theories to support this view, privileging the Teutonic peoples, which included the Germans, the Norsemen, and the Anglo-Saxons as colonizers of the world. As Horsman noted, Carlyle even claimed that the 'Normans were Saxons who had learned how to speak French'. Carlyle's Anglo-Saxons emerged from 'the shores of the Black Sea' and 'out of Hartzgebirge rock'. Because of their dominant global status, he wrote, they had the right to claim any 'vacant Earth' that could be rendered useful as their own: 'No property is eternal but God the Maker's', Carlyle insisted; 'whom Heaven permits to take possession, his is the right; Heaven's sanction is such permission.'[58]

In 1843, Carlyle wrote that England should not be deterred from spreading its material goods and its population of white Anglo-Saxons across the globe by means of settlement or trade. He made this argument in *Past and Present* in the context of promoting emigration:

> Our little Isle is grown too narrow for us; but the world is wide enough yet for another Six Thousand Years. England's sure markets will be among new Colonies of Englishmen in all quarters of the Globe. All men trade with all men, when mutually convenient; and are even bound to do it by the Maker of men. Our friends of China, who guiltily refused to trade, in these circumstances, – had we not to argue with them, in cannon-shot at last, and convince them that they ought to trade! 'Hostile Tariffs' will arise, to shut us out; and then again will fall, to let us in: but the Sons of England, speakers of the English language were it nothing more, will in all times have the ineradicable predisposition to trade with England. Mycale was the *Pan-Ionian*, rendezvous of all the Tribes of Ion, for old Greece; why should not London long continue the *All-Saxon-home*, rendezvous of all the 'Children of the Harz-Rock', arriving, in select samples, from the Antipodes and elsewhere, by steam and otherwise, to the 'season' here! – What a Future; wide as the world, if we have the heart and heroism for it, – which, by Heaven's blessing, we shall:
>
> > 'Keep not standing fixed and rooted,
> > Briskly venture, briskly roam;
> > Head and hand, where'er thou foot it,
> > And stout heart are still at home.
> >
> > In what land the sun does visit,
> > Brisk are we, whate'er betide:
> > To give space for wandering is it
> > That the world was made so wide.'
>
> Fourteen hundred years ago, it was by a considerable 'Emigration Service', never doubt it, by much enlistment, discussion and apparatus, that we ourselves arrived in this remarkable Island, – and got into our present difficulties among others![59]

Carlyle promoted emigration and colonial expansion in *Past and Present* as if these forces operated independently of global economic forces, oblivious to the emerging global financial crisis of 1847. His commentary also helps to explain his particular interest in Mauritius, upon which he seems to have projected his desires for the island to be settled with 'Children of the Harz-Rock'. And his evident interest in contributing to the publication of a new English edition of *Paul and Virginia* several years earlier seems less an act of appreciation for the novel or the career of his half-brother and more an effort to celebrate the island colony as if it were a suitable home for English emigration. Carlyle referred to England's own historical origins, 'fourteen hundred years ago', when 'we ourselves arrived in this remarkable Island', drawing a connection from ancient Anglo-Saxon settlement to present-day colonial emigration as a way to legitimatize British overseas expansion.

By 1848, however, Britain's colonial experiments were failing internationally and its colonial governments experiencing armed resistance. Former slaves in the island colony of Jamaica were among the first to defy London, as they resisted imperial laws and fought against efforts to import Indian coolies. The confrontation provided new source material for Carlyle, which resulted in his virulent, racist essay of 1849, 'Occasional Discourse on the Negro Question'. Carlyle's concerns to uncover the root causes of the 1848 revolutions across Europe stoked his invective against those who laboured in the plantations of Jamaica, leading to his condemnation of what he called a black inferior race.[60] As we shall see in Chapter 5, in 1865 Carlyle supported Jamaica's colonial governor, Edward John Eyre, who crushed an uprising of indentured labourers, just as earlier, in *Past and Present*, he argued that it was legitimate for Britain to intimidate the Chinese in the first Opium War to 'convince them that they ought to trade'.[61] At the same time, Carlyle adopted utopian imagery in his essay, promising readers a return to a golden age of prosperity, however misplaced it might be within his assault on reason and law:

> The West Indies grow pineapples, and sweet fruits, and spices; we hope they will, one day, grow beautiful, heroic human lives too, which is surely the ultimate object they were made for; beautiful souls and brave; sages, poets, what not – making the earth nobler round them, as their kindred from of old have been doing; true 'splinters of the old Hartz Rock;' heroic white men, worthy to be called old Saxons, browned with a mahogany tint in those new climates and conditions.[62]

Earlier, in *Past and Present*, Carlyle introduced the notion 'Children of the Harz-Rock' as if it was a parable of origins, and he used that emblem again here as a basis of imagined national identity. To Carlyle, this founding myth depended upon a theory of ancient, unbroken bloodlines and a heroic calling for Britons to take over distant lands, one that allowed 'old Saxons' to make the earth 'nobler' through their actions. As a legend of origins, the myth became new again in

Carlyle's hands: he reinvigorated the Saxon myth by promoting emigration and finding ancient justification for Britain's policies of colonial expansion. And in 1849, Carlyle became specific about the role of race in his prescriptions for settling the globe: the 'splinters of the old Hartz Rock' were indeed the children of 'heroic white men', that is, like Paul and Virginia, white Anglo-Saxon children.

## Ancestral archetypes

By mid-century, popular writers like Anna Jameson had helped to establish the essential historical role of two young fair children in shaping England as a Christian nation and in promoting a wide understanding of that iconography in visual art. As Mike Weaver has shown, Cameron drew liberally upon Jameson's popular books and the graphic reproductions of the Arundel Society as explicit references for her artistic compositions.[63] In her book, *Legends of the Monastic Orders* (1850), Jameson described a foundational story of England's past that was embedded in the traditional iconography of Pope St Gregory, who discovered two young English slaves in the Roman Forum, and being touched by their innocence and fair complexions, brought them freedom and religious deliverance. According to Jameson: 'We have all learned in our childhood of the famous legend which makes Gregory the Great the father of Christianity in England.' This story 'tells how he became interested for the poor benighted islanders, our fair-headed ancestors, (*non Angli sed Angeli!*) and represents St. Augustine of Canterbury as the first *Christian* missionary in this nation'.[64] The story powerfully unites the virtues of the Pope's kindness toward the fair young children, and how he granted them freedom, returned them from exile, and led them to spiritual redemption. At the same time, this traditional narrative venerates Anglo-Saxon racial identity as a marker of ancient heritage and Christianity as a fundamental pillar of English culture.

In Jameson's telling, the phrase '*Non Angli sed Angeli*' are the words Pope Gregory spoke in the year 573 when he visited the slave market in the Roman Forum and came across the two blond (and by some accounts, blue-eyed) children. In recognizing their light-coloured features as unusual signs of racial difference he asked where the children originally came from and was told the two were English (*Angli*). In reply, the Pope remarked, '*Non Angli sed Angeli*' ('[They are] not English, but Angels'). For Jameson, this brief phrase condensed the story into a tale of recognition and redemption. But these words were apparently only the first part of the Pope's longer phrase, '*Non Angli sed Angeli, si forent Christiani*', the second part of which translates as: 'if they were but Christians'. Importantly, the second part completes the Pope's expression both conceptually and politically, as it contextualizes the phrase's religious, cultural, and imperialistic implications. In addition, the second part of the sentence deepens the meaning of 'angels' to register the word as a symbol of Christianity and the origins of Christian national identity in England. In mid-Victorian England, these two senses were united in the iconography of the story. In addition, the phrase '*Non Angli sed Angeli*' also introduces Gregory's central role in shaping England as a Christian nation, effectively establishing the Pope as a founder of the modern state: following his encounter in the slave market, Gregory sent Augustine to England to 'Christianize' the pagan land. In essence, the story deftly summarizes one of the core myths of English national identity, as the story collapses England's imagined ancestry in Saxon racial terms, shows how it overcame its pre-Christian ignorance, and commemorates its ultimate religious deliverance. National identity and spiritual redemption were made possible by the foresight and kindness of the Pope.

As a result, this rich and symbolic imagery was among the most well-known examples of British art during the nineteenth century, a common iconographic theme used to decorate public works, including governmental and religious buildings. In 1840, for example, shortly after the Houses of Parliament were destroyed six years earlier, Members created a Royal Fine Arts Commission to oversee the redecoration of the Palace of Westminster. Early plans for paintings and wall coverings prominently included the representation of 'Anglo-Saxon captives exposed for sale in the market-place of Rome'. As imagined in the rebuilding scheme, this painted composition was to form one of the chief iconographic focal points in the building itself, and would provide visual and didactic lessons about the historical formation of the nation. Once the scheme was announced by the Commission, the public was invited to comment on the submissions through journals like the *Illustrated London News*.[65] Representing the general popular acclaim for the project as a whole, the *Art Union* helped to cement the view that history painting of the kind proposed by this subject was best suited to represent the country's ancestral heritage; the entire decorative scheme proposed was described in the following terms: 'Six subjects have been selected: in three Britain appears sunk in ignorance, heathen superstition, and slavery; in the other three she appears instructing the savage, abolishing barbarous rites, and liberating the slave.'[66] If the first three represented the uncivilized past, the second three represented the civilizing mission of the modern nation.

The overall effect was intended to be instructive and inspirational: ignorance would be portrayed giving way to education, pagan rites yielding to religious observance, slavery giving way to emancipation: the effect would summarize the aims of Britain's Colonial Office in visual terms. The historical panel featuring *St Gregory in the Roman Forum* was to be painted in the building's central corridor, representing Britain's inglorious and humble past in ignorance but also the seeds of its enlightened Anglo-Saxon and Christian Victorian present. The Fine Arts Commission purchased four oil paintings representing such historical moments because they were deemed important to British national identity, including George Frederick Watts's *Alfred inciting the Saxons to prevent the Landing of the Danes*.[67] This

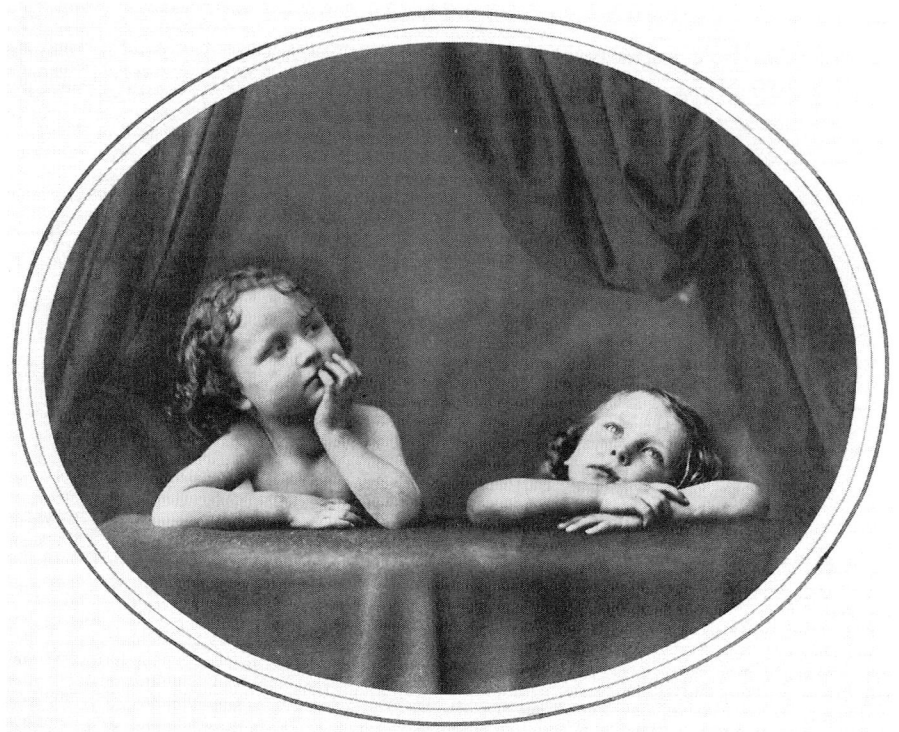

**10**          Oscar Gustave Rejlander, *Non Angeli sed Angli*, 1857.
                    Albumen print, oval, 16.1 x 20 cm.

panel was destined to hang in the Houses of Parliament in Westminster; nearby, the Painted Chamber 'was to refer to the "acquisition of the countries, colonies and important places constituting the British Empire"'.[68]

Because of the Commission's prominence, other artists of the period also experimented with compositions depicting the Pope in the Roman Forum; for example, the title *Non Angli sed Angeli* was used by John Everett Millais and by George Scharf in several drawings, paintings, and engravings. In mass produced graphic art, the image of the two fair English boys gained currency as the mast-head of the *Anglo-Saxon*, a short-lived magazine of 1850 that promoted the racial theories of Robert Knox and the social theories of Thomas Carlyle; *Non Angli sed Angeli* was printed on the mast-head under the image of the two children.[69] And Oscar Gustave Rejlander, one of Julia Margaret-Cameron's earliest photographic mentors whose photography was therefore well known to her, also titled his photograph of two children, posed as angels in the manner of Raphael's *Sistine Madonna*, *Non Angeli sed Angli* (Figure 10). Note that Rejlander inverted the phrase, transposing the words *Angli* and *Angeli*. In 1857, Rejlander had exhibited this photograph in the Manchester Fine Arts Exhibition to much public acclaim.

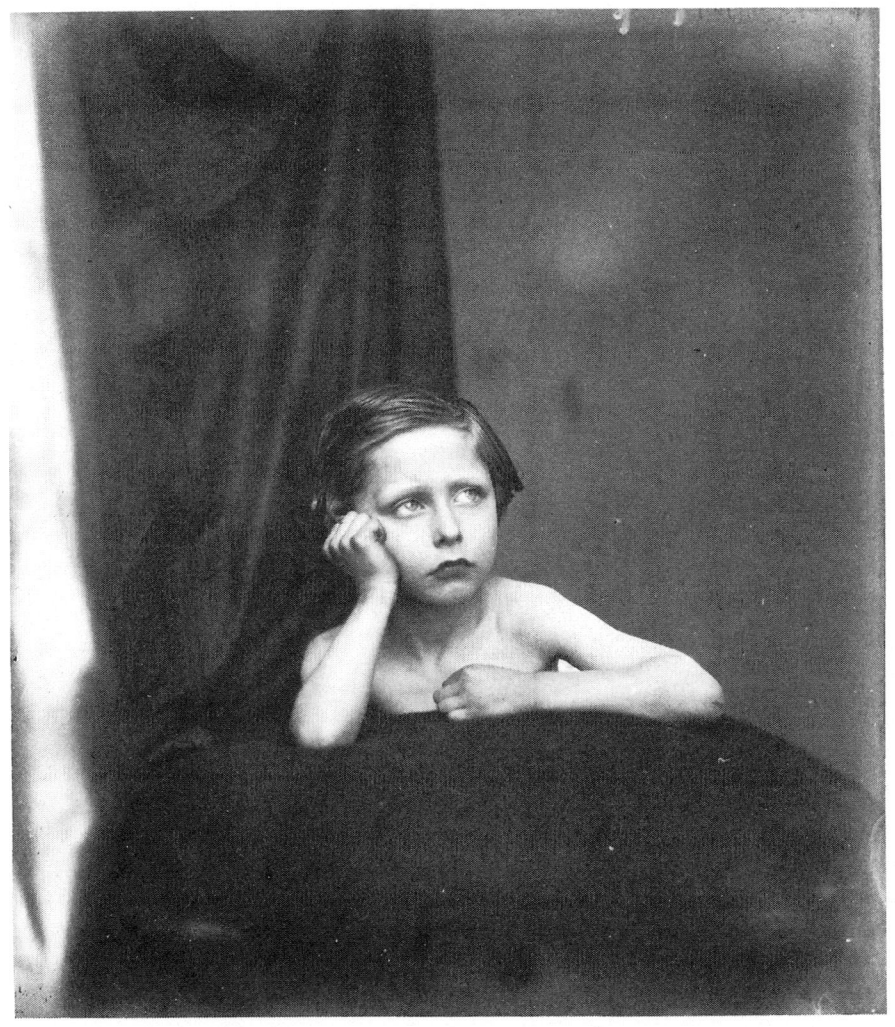

Leonida Caldesi, *Prince Arthur*, 1857. Albumen print,17.8 x 15.1 cm.      **11**
Acquired by Prince Albert, Royal Collection Trust/
© Her Majesty Queen Elizabeth II 2014, # RCIN 2900255.

Whether he inverted *Angli* and *Angeli* on purpose, or by accident, is less important
to this story than the fact that Prince Albert purchased Rejlander's photograph
and mounted it in the photographic album of the royal family, both as a sincere
marker of the Anglo-Saxon heritage he shared as much as a statement supporting
European unification.[70]

The phrase clearly resonated with the Prince: that same year, Albert commissioned the Caldesi firm to photograph his own son, Prince Arthur, in the same

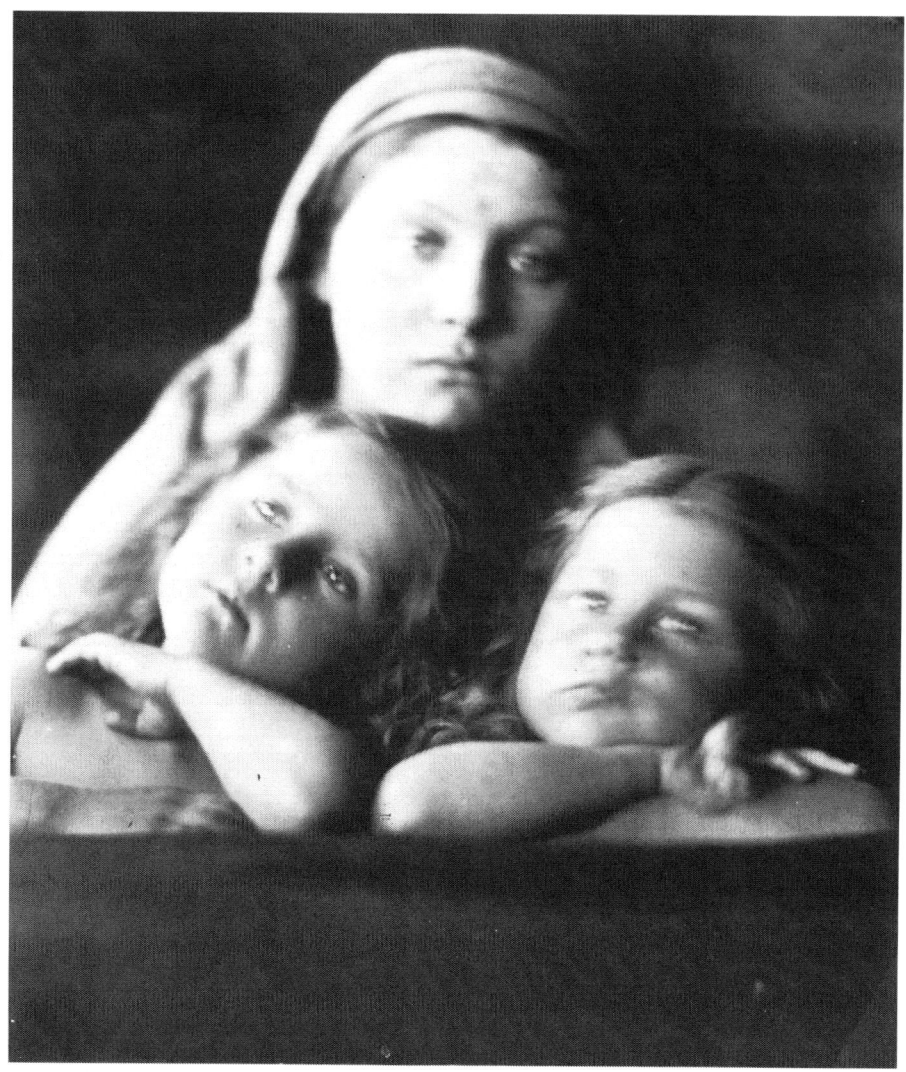

**12**     Julia Margaret Cameron, *Madonna with Two Children* (Cox 66), c. 1864.
Albumen print, 25.3 x 21.4 cm.

'angelic' pose used by Rejlander. He inserted this image, too, in the royal album
(Figure 11).[71] Several years later, around 1863, Prince Albert and Queen Victoria
together commissioned William Theed to sculpt a marble portrait of the royal
couple dressed in heroic Anglo-Saxon costume. The twin portrait allowed the pair
to reclaim their own heritage both personally and politically, symbolically uniting
the British and the German people from ancient times to the present day, realized
in the marriage of Victoria and Albert.[72] Following Rejlander's photographic
example, Cameron herself experimented with the idea of posing two children

in the manner of Raphael's *Sistine Madonna*. In 1864, in several photographs of the *Madonna with Two Children* that she produced that year (Figure 12), Cameron modelled the Keown sisters almost exactly like the two winged angels portrayed originally by Raphael and appropriated later by Rejlander (Cox 65, 66). She made these images at precisely the same period in 1864 that she was representing the story of *Paul and Virginia*.

Cameron's *Paul and Virginia* therefore allowed her audience to explore the multiple identities of the two children: as naive siblings, as potential lovers, in the context of their shifting national identities, in relation to their family connection to their mothers, in relation to the volatile colonial space which defined them and marked them as outcasts. The photograph's multiple associations also encouraged Cameron's audience to contend with competing perspectives; for example, the children are self-contained but also isolated by and diminished within the frame; in the shallow picture plane they appear submissive in their expressions and pose; their white ethnicity is latent rather than overtly striking as a marker of their identity.[73] As Richard Dyer has claimed, the children's identity as colonists is dependent upon 'the specificity of [their] whiteness, even when the text itself is not trying to show it to you, doesn't even know that it is there to be shown'.[74] Half-clothed and barefoot, the two children do not proclaim any particular nationality, but lay claim instead to a kind of universal subjectivity as children-in-and-of-nature, pure and innocent, and as a result, even stateless and transnational, rather than possessing any fixed nationality alone. In literary theory, the 'transnational subject' is one that is able to cross boundaries to another side, transgressing borders and creating new alliances.[75]

As transnational subjects, the two children in Cameron's photograph become no longer identified as French or British, but instead assume re-imagined identities as a new kind of childhood archetype: Anglo-Saxon children possessing an ancient lineage, associated with the race (white) and religious identity (Christian) of multiple European nations. Carlyle made this transformation explicit in *Past and Present* when he linked England's racial ancestors to what he called 'the Emigration Service' started by Pope Gregory and Augustine, using this legend as if it were an acceptable historical claim for modern-day London to become the rendezvous point for the 'Children of the Harz-Rock'. By assigning these legendary ancestors a transnational identity, Carlyle was able to carve out a new cultural space for the children. In this new space, fair and blue-eyed ancestors could represent a pure link to a reimagined British heritage where Anglo-Saxon children were both innocent and chosen by God. We have seen this narrative promoted by Anna Jameson and in the Houses of Parliament, as well as by the National Church. But in Carlyle's hands, this story of purity and innocence also created its opposite: Because he was threatened by Jamaica's mixed racial past and needed a compelling narrative of pure historical origins to legitimize his views on emigration and Anglo-Saxon racial superiority, Carlyle urged his brother to publish a new translation of *Paul et Virginie* at precisely the same time that he was gathering material for his essay on the 'Negro Question'.

The convergence of Cameron's formal interest in and narrative exploration of this rich iconography suggests that it held several important and interrelated meanings for her and her contemporaries: by selecting this particular narrative, she was able to represent a founding moment in the story of the nation's origins when it was primitive and crude, even ungovernable, and therefore unrecognizably English. In representing pre-Christian Britain and colonial Mauritius as pagan lands, she was able to elevate organized religion as an important feature that defined the nation's character. And in describing ancient Britain and the island colony as untamed territories that were fragmented and in need of being united as a people and liberated through faith, she emphasized their common archaic origins, much as the Royal Fine Arts Commission recognized this ancient and dark period in the nation's history as representing its 'inglorious' past. Consequently, Cameron's photograph of *Paul and Virginia* embodied elements that celebrated Britain's civilizing and colonial mission as much as it lamented the demise of paradise and innocence that was brought about by colonial expansion.

## Notes

1 Letter from Julia Margaret Cameron to Charles Hay Cameron, 25 May 1860, quoted in Julian Cox and Colin Ford, eds., *Julia Margaret Cameron: The Complete Photographs* (Los Angeles: J. Paul Getty Trust, 2003), p. 22.

2 See Diana Loxley, *Problematic Shores: The Literature of Islands* (London: Macmillan, 1990) and Chris Bongie, *Islands and Exiles: The Creole Identities of Post/Colonial Literature* (Stanford: Stanford University Press, 1998).

3 Wilfred Ward, 'Tennyson at Freshwater', *Dublin Review*, 150 (1912), 68; quoted in Cox and Ford, *Julia Margaret Cameron*, p. 23.

4 Anne Isabella Thackeray Ritchie, *From Friend to Friend* (London: John Murray, 1919), esp. pp. 2–37; Virginia Woolf and Roger Fry, *Victorian Photographs of Famous Men and Fair Women* (London: Chatto and Windus, 1992).

5 As Charles wrote to Julia Margaret in a letter dated 28 January 1851:'If Malta or the Ionian islands is given to me then my plan must be postponed, but of that there is very little chance. Lord Grey thinks that the E.I. Directors [Directors of the East Indian Company] ought to give me one, and so I think we may be pretty sure that I shall go without.' Cameron papers, Getty Research Institute, Los Angeles, Box 11.

6 G. C. Mendis, ed., *The Colebrooke-Cameron Papers: Documents on British Colonial Policy in Ceylon, 1796–1833*, 2 vols. (London: Oxford University Press, 1956).

7 These included the management and shipping firms of Clerihew; Pitts and Gavin; Wilson Ritchie and Co.; and Keir Dundas & Co. Cameron Papers, Getty Research Institute, Los Angeles, Boxes 1 and 11.

8 Cox and Ford, *Julia Margaret Cameron*, p. 512.

9 Letter from Charles Hay Cameron to Julia Margaret Cameron, 11 December 1850, Cameron Papers, Getty Research Institute, Los Angeles, Box 1.

10 Homi K. Bhabha, 'DissemiNation': Time, Narrative, and the Margins of the Modern

Nation', in Homi K. Bhabha, ed., *Nation and Narration* (London and New York: Routledge, 1990), p. 296.

11  Mary Louise Pratt, *Imperial Eyes: Travel Writing and Transculturation* (New York: Routledge, 1992); Jeremy Black, *Maps and Politics* (London: Reaktion Books, 1997).

12  Malcolm Cook, 'Bougainville and One Noble Savage: Two Manuscript Texts of Bernardin de Saint-Pierre', *Modern Language Review*, 89:4 (1994), 842–55; Nelson F. Adkins, 'Wordsworth's Margaret; or the Ruined Cottage', *Modern Language Notes*, 38:8 (1923), 460–6.

13  Letter from Charles Hay Cameron to Julia Margaret Cameron, December 16, 1850, Cameron Papers, Getty Research Institute, Los Angeles, Box 1.

14  Quoted in full in Brian Hinton, *Immortal Faces: Julia Margaret Cameron on the Isle of Wight* (Newport, Isle of Wight: Isle of Wight County Council, 1992), p. 6.

15  Bhabha, 'DissemiNation', p. 319.

16  Quoted (without full attribution or date) in Hinton, *Immortal Faces*, pp. 2–3.

17  Edward Said, *The World, the Text, and the Critic* (Cambridge, MA: Harvard University Press, 1983), p. 8, original emphasis.

18  Paul Toinet, *Paul et Virginie: repertoire bibliographique et iconographique* (Paris: G.-P. Maisonneuve et Larose, 1963); Peter Mortensen, 'On Seeing Miss Helen Maria Williams Weep at a Tale of Distress' [1787], *British Romanticism and Continental Influences* (Basingstoke: Palgrave Macmillan, 2004), pp. 122–3; David Menhennet, 'International Bestseller: *Paul and Virginia*', *Book Collector*, 38 (1989), 483–502.

19  Malcolm Cook, *Bernardin de Saint-Pierre: A Life of Culture* (Oxford: Legenda, 2006), pp. 115, 123.

20  James Cobb, *Paul and Virginia … in two acts* (New York: Longworth, 1806), p. 14.

21  The photograph appears in the Mia Album, the Watts Album, the Herschel Album, the Overstone Album, the Lindsay Album, the Thackeray Album, the Henry Taylor Album, the Norman Album, and the A. A. Taylor Album; Cox and Ford, *Julia Margaret Cameron*, Appendix C, Albums.

22  Philippa Wright, 'Little Pictures: Julia Margaret Cameron and Small-Format Photography', in Cox and Ford, *Julia Margaret Cameron*, p. 84.

23  Russell Smandych, '"To Soften the Extreme Rigor of Their Bondage": James Stephen's Attempt to Reform the Criminal Slave Laws of the West Indies, 1813–1833', *Law and History Review*, 23:3 (2005), 537–88; David McNab, 'Herman Merivale and the Native Question, 1837–1861', *Albion*, 9:4 (1977), 359–84.

24  Anna Neill, 'The Sentimental Novel and the Republican Imaginary: Slavery in Paul and Virginia', *Diacritics*, 23:3 (1993), 43.

25  Pratima Prasad, 'Intimate Strangers: Interracial Encounters in Romantic Narratives of Slavery', *L'Espirit Createur*, 47:4 (2007), 1–15; Clifton Cherpack, '*Paul et Virginie* and the Myths of Death', *PMLA*, 90:2 (1975), 251.

26  Neill, 'The Sentimental Novel', 38.

27  This is evident from its publishing history, despite the fact that in France, several 'children's editions' were produced during the nineteenth century. Ruth Carver Capasso, '"La Bibliothèque rose": Children, and Imperialism in Nineteenth-Century France', *French Review*, 77:2 (2003), 283.

28  Thomas Carlyle, *The French Revolution, A History*, [1837], repr. (University of Adelaide, 2014, ebooks.adelaide.edu.au/c/carlyle/thomas/french_revolution/index.html), vol. 1, Book 2, chapter 8.

29  Simon Davies, 'Paul et Virginie 1953–1991: The Present State of Studies', *Studies on Voltaire and the Eighteenth Century*, 317 (1994), 258.

30  Toinet, *Paul et Virginie: repertoire bibliographique*, pp. 187–90.

31  Valérie David, 'Sur l'iconographie de *Paul et Virginie*', in Jean-Paul Racault, ed., *Etudes sur Paul et Virginie* (Paris: Publications de l'Université de la Réunion, 1986), p. 248.

32  See J. H. Bernardin de St-Pierre, *Paul and Virginia*, trans. Helen Maria Williams [1796], repr. (Oxford: Woodstock Books, 1989), p. 1.

33  For example: 1796 edition, London: Yernor and Hood; 1806 edition, Paris: Didot; 1820 edition, London: John Sharpe; 1834 edition, Boston: Lilly, Wait and Col; 1838 edition, Paris: L. Curmer; 1868 edition, Paris: Alphonse Lemierre.

34  Hugh Orange and John Beaumont, 'The Chevalier de L'Etang (1757–1840) and His Descendants, the Pattles', *Virginia Woolf Bulletin*, 7 (2001), 51–62; 8 (2001), 31–48; 9 (2002), 70–2.

35  *Allegory and Illusion: Early Portrait Photography from South Asia*, 16 October 2013 – 10 February 2014, exhibition checklist, Rubin Museum of Art, www.rubinmuseum.org/uploads/documents/Allegory%20and%20Illusion%20Approved%20Image%20Checklist.pdf, see item no. 94.14.0071.

36  Cox and Ford, *Julia Margaret Cameron*, p. 52.

37  Anne Higonnet, *Pictures of Innocence: The History and Crisis of Ideal Childhood* (London: Thames and Hudson, 1998).

38  Ashis Nandy, *The Intimate Enemy: Loss and Recovery of Self Under Colonialism* (Delhi: Oxford University Press, 1983), pp. 15–16.

39  Nicholas Thomas, *Colonialism's Culture: Anthropology, Travel, and Government* (Princeton: Princeton University Press, 1994), esp. chapter 4.

40  Marcus Wood, *Blind Memory: Visual Representations of Slavery in England and America, 1780–1865* (New York: Routledge, 2000), p. 6.

41  Suzanne R. Pucci, 'Snapshots of Family Intimacy in the French Eighteenth Century: The Case of *Paul et Virginie*', *Studies in Eighteenth Century Culture*, 37 (2008), 115, n. 25.

42  Hugh Tinker, 'Between Africa, Asia and Europe. Mauritius: Cultural Marginalism and Political Control', *African Affairs*, 76:304 (1977), 323.

43  James Patterson Smith, 'Empire and Social Reform: British Liberals and the "Civilizing Mission" in the Sugar Colonies, 1868–1874', *Albion*, 27:2 (1995), 255.

44  Richard B. Allen, 'Licentious and Unbridled Proceedings: The Illegal Slave Trade to Mauritius and the Seychelles during the Early Nineteenth Century', *Journal of African History*, 42:1 (2001), 91–116.

45  Tinker, 'Between Africa, Asia and Europe', 324.

46  Hugh Tinker, *A New System of Slavery: The Export of Indian Labour Overseas, 1830–1920* (London: Oxford University Press, 1974); Marina Carter, *Voices of Indenture: Experiences of Indian Migrants in the British Empire* (London: Leicester University Press, 1996).

47  According to Merivale, 'Children of most native races are fully or more than a match for those of Europeans in aptitude for intellectual acquirement. Indeed it appears to be a singular law of nature, that there is less precocity in the European race than in any other. In those races in which we seem to have reason for believing that the intellectual organization is lower, perception is quicker, and maturity earlier.' Quoted in McNab, 'Herman Merivale and the Native Question', 370.

48  Herman Merivale, 'Appendix to Lecture XI. Employment of Slave Labour', in *Lectures on Colonization and Colonies, Delivered before the University of Oxford in 1839, 1840, & 1841, and Reprinted in 1861* (London: Oxford University Press, 1928), p. 345.

49  Patterson Smith, 'Empire and Social Reform', 267; Vijaya Samaraweera, 'Governor Sir Robert Wilmot Horton and the Reforms of 1833 in Ceylon', *Historical Journal*, 15:2 (1972), 214; Bruce Knox, 'The Queen's Letter of 1865 and British Policy Towards Emancipation and Indentured Labor in the West Indies, 1830–1865', *Historical Journal*, 29:2 (1986), 345–67.

50  K. M. de Silva, 'The Third Earl Grey and the Maintenance of an Imperial Policy on the Sale of Crown Lands in Ceylon, c. 1832–1852', *Journal of Asian Studies*, 27:1 (1967), 7.

51  Letter, Thomas Carlyle to John A. Carlyle, 9 May 1823, *Carlyle Letters Online* (www.carlyleletters.dukejournals.org) DOI: 10.1215/lt-18230509-TC-JAC-01; CL 2: 347–9.

52　Quoted in Edwin W. Morris, Jr., 'Carlyle, Bernardin de Saint-Pierre, and Madame Cottin', *Victorian Newsletter* (1968), 45.

53　Ian Henderson, 'Reading Lessons: A New Appreciation of Bernardin de Saint-Pierre's *Paul et Virginie*', *Studies on Voltaire and the Eighteenth Century*, 2 (2003), 314. Unfortunately, Henderson mis-attributes the volume's actual translation by John A. Carlyle to 'McDiarmid.'

54　Toinet, *Paul et Virginie: repertoire bibliographique*, pp. 63–98.

55　Lisa Lowe, *Critical Terrains: French and British Orientalisms* (Ithaca: Cornell University Press, 1991), p. 95.

56　David Menhennet, 'International Bestseller: *Paul and Virginia*', 495.

57　Letter, Thomas Carlyle to David Lester Richardson, 19 December 1837, *Carlyle Letters Online* (www.carlyleletters.dukejournals.org) DOI: 10.1215/lt-18371219-TC-DLR-01; CL 9: 372–5.

58　Reginald Horsman, 'Origins of Racial Anglo-Saxonism in Great Britain before 1850', *Journal of the History of Ideas*, 37:3 (1976), 400.

59　Thomas Carlyle, *Past and Present* [1843] (London: Chapman and Hall, 1872), pp. 229–30.

60　Aileen Christianson, 'On the Writing of the "Occasional Discourse on the Negro Question"', *Carlyle Newsletter*, 2 (1980), 290.

61　Simon Gikandi asserts that Carlyle showed his readers 'that although the colonies are important to the power of England, they are not part of the culture of Englishness', in *Maps of Englishness: Writing Identity in the Culture of Colonialism* (New York: Columbia University Press, 1996), p. 64.

62　Thomas Carlyle, 'Occasional Discourse on the Negro Question', *Fraser's Magazine for Town and Country*, 40 (1849), 534.

63　Mike Weaver, *Julia Margaret Cameron, 1815–1879* (Southampton: John Hansard Gallery, 1984).

64　Mrs [Anna] Jameson, *Legends of the Monastic Orders as Represented in the Fine Arts* (London: Longman, Brown, Green, and Longmans, 1850), p. 49, original emphasis.

65　*Illustrated London News*, 8 July 1843, contains illustrations of the intended interior decorations.

66　T. S. R. Boase, 'The Decoration of the New Palace of Westminster, 1841–1863', *Journal of the Warburg and Courtauld Institutes*, 17:3/4 (1954), 341.

67　*Ibid.*, p. 343; see also, Billie Melman, 'Claiming the Nation's Past: The Invention of an Anglo-Saxon Tradition', *Journal of Contemporary History*, 26:3/4 (1991), 575–95.

68　Boase, 'The Decoration of the New Palace of Westminster', 342.

69　Horsman, 'Origins of Racial Anglo-Saxonism', 407.

70　The portrait of Prince Arthur of the same year, is doubly fitting for the child, who was the offspring of the duke of Saxe-Coburg-Saalfeld, and eventual first monarch of the House of Saxe-Coburg and Gotha, named after the ducal house to which Prince Albert belonged, and the young Queen Victoria, daughter of Prince Edward, duke of Kent and Strathearn and Princess Victoria of Saxe-Coburg-Saalfeld, who united Great Britain to the House of Hanover.

71　Higonnet, *Pictures of Innocence*, pp. 44, 127–29.

72　The marble is installed in the Frogmore Mausoleum; a plaster cast is in the National Portrait Gallery in London. See also, Melman, 'Claiming the Nation's Past', 575–95 and Margaret Homans, *Royal Representations: Queen Victoria and British Culture, 1837–67* (Chicago: University of Chicago Press, 1998).

73　On whiteness, see: Ann Louise Keating, '"Whiteness", (De)Constructing "Race"', *College English*, 57:8 (1995), 901–18; J. P. Bowles, 'Forum: Blinded by the White. Art and History at the Limits of Whiteness', *Art Journal*, 60:4 (2001), 39–67; Nell Irvin Painter, *The History of White People* (New York: W.W. Norton, 2010), pp. 154–83.

74　Richard Dyer, 'The Matter of Whiteness', in *Privilege: A Reader*, ed. Michael S. Kimmel and Abby L. Ferber (Boulder, CO: Westview Press, 2003), p. 28.

75　Margaret Cohen and Carolyn Dever, eds., *The Literary Channel: The Inter-National Invention of the Novel* (Princeton: Princeton University Press, 2002).

# 2

# Jowett's scriptures:
# the moral life and the state

## Theological questions on the Isle of Wight

On 31 December 1864, Julia Margaret Cameron sent her friend Sir John Herschel a gift of photographs and a letter informing him about a turning point in her creative life. After a year spent experimenting with different subjects, she seized upon the goal of pursuing a religious iconography in photography. The following declaration accompanied her post: 'Yesterday I dispatched for you & dear Lady Herschel one series of my Photographs which form I think now a theological work of some Interest.'[1] In her bold and assertive way, Cameron claimed the specific and determined aims of an artist who sought to influence her friends as well as a larger public: she produced a *series* of photographic works; this series possessed both *coherence and meaning*; and above all, the imagery expressed a particular *theology*, a formal interpretation or point of view about the relationship of God and mankind, a public statement made for serious consideration and discussion. Cameron was the first person to articulate such an ambitious goal in the new art form; not one of her photographic contemporaries could make a similar claim.

She called her series the *Fruits of the Spirit*. It contained nine photographs, each titled for one of the nine Christian virtues described by St Paul in his *Epistle to the Galatians* from the New Testament. According to Paul, 'The fruit of the spirit is love, joy, peace, patience, kindness, goodness, faithfulness, gentleness and self-control. Against such things there is no law' (Galatians 5:22–23). Each photograph in the series depicted Mary Hillier, Cameron's parlour maid, posed to represent the Madonna, accompanied by one or two local children (Figure 12, 13, and 14). Herschel's letter had no sooner been delivered, when on 12 January 1865, Cameron presented a large framed work containing this series to the British Museum, 'Being the *Fruits of the Spirit*, Illustrated from Life'.[2] Throughout the year, she exhibited these nine photographs together, as a unit, and alone, as separate photographs, at Colnaghi's and in other venues. At the same time, she created additional imagery expressing these and similar Christian virtues by

exploring the religious iconography of the Virgin Mary, including The Annunciation, The Three Marys, The Holy Family, and The Salutation.

What compelled Cameron to produce a body of religious imagery representing the Christian Madonna, to draw upon the Bible for inspiration, and to use
photography to illustrate her new theology 'from Life'? Were her photographs
of the Madonna and Child emblematic of her own personal, deeply felt maternal
sensibilities, evidence of her faith and religious devotion, expressions of her political views, or all three, and how did she reconcile her personal thoughts and expressions with the public theological argument that she said she wanted to make?
How, too, did she regard the relationship between the specific biblical text and
her imagery? For example, in drawing upon St Paul's Epistles, did she wish to
emphasize the 'mystical Paul', who wrote that Christ's divine intercession was
required for the soul's redemption, or the 'practical Paul', who offered practical
lessons about how to lead a just and moral life?[3] As a group of photographs, we
might also ask how the *Fruits of the Spirit* series made its theological point, and
whether it did so successfully, by focusing on the principal issues that were at
stake for clergy and laity alike in Cameron's interpretation and in relation to the
accepted doctrines of the Church of England. For example, did Cameron and her
contemporaries regard her photographs as sacred and devotional, to be revered
like holy icons or objects that possessed mystical power, or did they embrace a
more secular function, using ancient morality tales containing 'essential truths' as
a way to communicate worldly lessons for the present day? In other words: did
her photographs have the power to convince, persuade, and influence others in
theological terms?

These and related questions were topical matters in Cameron's circle. In
fact, on the Isle of Wight, religion was a matter for public discussion and debate
among its famous residents. In June 1860, for example, the celebrated lecturer
Dr Joseph Wolff visited the island to raise funds for the building of a new church
in Somerset. Wolff was a converted Jew who had become a zealous Christian
missionary. Following his travels in the East to convert 'the heathen', especially
Jews, he wrote the *Mission to Bokhara* (1845), and by 1847 had become well known
as a regular speaker for the London Society for Promoting Christianity amongst
the Jews. He was known popularly for his spirited, inspiring, and entertaining
lectures; his contemporaries often celebrated Wolff as full of 'rich orientalisms'
owing to his penchant to drop the names of Eastern monarchs and speak in their
foreign tongues.[4] In her journal entry of 13 June 1860, Emily Tennyson wrote
how Wolff spoke that day in the Freshwater schoolroom, attended by Alfred,
Mrs Cameron, and the Freshwater curate and his wife, Mr and Mrs Isaacson. She
recalled how Alfred and Mrs Cameron caused a small delay in the proceedings by
walking to the meeting, while everyone else in the party drove, and that Wolff
delayed speaking to the congregation until the two arrived. At the event, Wolff's

tales of religious conversion apparently inspired the Tennyson boys, Hallam and Lionel, to donate all of their pocket-money to his church-building campaign.[5]

While Wolff's visit to the Isle of Wight was extraordinary, Benjamin Jowett, Regius Professor of Greek at Oxford, visited Freshwater regularly. From the 1850s, Jowett visited the Tennysons nearly every summer and almost every Christmas, and during the 1860s, he stayed often with the Camerons nearby, becoming the Isle of Wight's most famous (and soon thereafter, infamous) regular theological visitor. In 1860, in fact, he became an accidental national figure, the result of writing a scholarly essay in an otherwise unexceptional religious book called *Essays and Reviews*. Almost immediately following its publication, Jowett was elevated to the centre of a national dispute about the nature of biblical interpretation, the application of Church law in education and political life, and the expression of faith, especially among the clergy and university professors. These disputes were not confined to learned men in smoke-filled clubs; they were discussed publicly among Cameron's social circle in Freshwater and London and were the subject of correspondence with her dear friends, like the Herschels. They even followed her when she went to church in Freshwater: in 1861, for example, in the midst of the initial hostile public reaction to *Essays and Reviews*, Jowett sought relief from the pressure in Oxford by visiting the Tennysons on the Isle of Wight; after having attended the local church together, Jowett himself noted, 'the clergyman of this parish does call me and others "Judas Iscariot" in his sermons'.[6]

Jowett's controversial essay, 'On the interpretation of scripture', became a lightning rod for the theological and academic 'culture war' that began with his essay and lasted throughout the decade. For a scholarly book concerned with highly nuanced religious interpretations, the volume itself became an unusual publishing phenomenon: by 1862, at the height of the controversy it helped incite, more than 20,000 copies of *Essays and Reviews* had been sold in England alone.[7] Thirteen editions were published by 1869, as well as an 'authorized edition' published by Bernhard Tauchnitz in 1862 for the continent, which provided for its 'authors and publishers a handsome profit and [made] the book a notable best-seller'.[8] According to Ieuan Ellis, 'The essays were exported to France and Germany, a French translation was prepared, and a Parsee was dispatched from Bombay to render them in his own language. Circulating libraries loaned out the volume and its answers at 2d per day; it was displayed on railway bookstalls and hawked by newsboys along with *Punch* and *The Times*.'[9] Significantly, criticism of *Essays and Reviews* created its own publishing event: by 1865, for example, some 400 books, pamphlets, and articles had been written about the essays and the essayists, both favourable and in opposition to the positions taken, which in turn provoked additional demand for the original volume.[10]

Cameron's theological interests coincided with a particular rift in the Church of England, one that emphasized opposing theological perspectives of the High

Church (a branch sometimes called Anglo Catholic) and the Low Church (often referred to as Evangelical). In many respects, the schism of the 1860s was reminiscent of sixteenth-century debates following King Henry VIII's establishment of the Church of England, which separated the National Church from Rome and placed it under state control. From the early years of the nineteenth century, the High and Low Church rivalry placed different emphases on such matters as liturgy and the sacraments and on the interpretation of scripture, with the High Church tending to more traditional, ceremonial, and ritual approaches and the Low to more evangelical practices. In spite of these differences, generally speaking, the Church of England made it possible for individuals to approach the question of spiritual truth in many different ways; importantly, as a *National Church*, it guaranteed Protestant independence from Rome.

By mid-century, the Broad Church movement emerged, drawing inspiration from Coleridge's writings, along with a partisan approach to politics and to teaching that favoured liberal thinkers and many who did not conform at all to established Church doctrines. They were opposed, both spiritually and politically, by members of the Oxford Movement, whose orthodox religious positions had been published since the 1830s in pamphlets, called 'tracts', which led to their loosely defined label, Tractarians. The Tractarians were led by Edward Pusey, John Keble, and John Henry Newman, who believed the Church of England had lost its traditional obedience in Catholic traditions; they argued, moreover, that the liberal elements within the Church posed a grave threat to its central role in civic life. This erosion of tradition and orthodoxy, they feared, reflected weakness in the Church among its leaders, and more ominously, could lead to disestablishment across a broad political spectrum. As a consequence, as Frank Turner and Jeffrey Von Arx have written, by the 1860s, when the Church of England increasingly defined itself as a 'distinct corporate body clearly defined by devotion, doctrine, and ministry', these actions 'had the effect of exacerbating and hardening the differences between churchmen and doubters'.[11]

Rather than a narrow-minded theological clash over the finer points of Church doctrine, then, the debate between Broad Church members and the Tractarians during the 1860s was central to narrating the nation's religious identity because it implicated the future of the Anglican Church as a state institution. Rigorous political debate was an essential feature of this public conversation: as an example, William Ewart Gladstone, who was later to serve as Prime Minister, wrote a book in 1838 called *The State in its Relations with the Church*, in which he argued for a kind of nationalist orthodoxy to the country's affairs that would join together national interests with the doctrines of the Church of England. His proposal was hardly inclusive; rather, he proposed that both Nonconformists and Roman Catholics alike should be *excluded* from participating in state affairs. But before Gladstone's argument was able to gain momentum, Thomas Babington

Macaulay countered his proposal by forcefully defending political and religious heterodoxy, effectively saving Gladstone's political future.[12]

Indeed, questions of religious identity and faith as they were expressed through the Church were among the chief forces defining the nature of social interactions in mid-nineteenth century England; in this context, ideas about religious devotion and Christian morality took centre stage. As John Wolffe and others have noted, 'religion was taking a central role in the development and articulation of national consciousness in the British Isles. This applies equally whether we are concerned with the assertion of overarching "British" identity; with the awareness of the Scots, Welsh and Irish of their own distinctiveness; or with the attitude of the whole towards continental Europe and the rest of the world.'[13] Moreover, by mid-century, Anglican evangelicals and Nonconformists, as well as Anglo Catholics, staked equal claims to Christian heritage in England and therefore a purchase on British national identity. Two parallel directions emerged which directly linked politics and religion: on the one hand, national identity was complicated by questions of allegiance that lingered from the Reformation to the present and by the uncertain political connection of the four English Kingdoms to a national centre that was increasingly preoccupied with managing its colonial possessions. On the other hand, the debate over national religious identity was expressed in theological terms within the Anglican Church itself. Opposing sides disputed scriptural doctrine, the application of Church laws, and the expression of Christian morality in everyday life.[14] During this era, membership in the Church of England was a condition of employment at Oxford and Cambridge. Consequently, the Broad Church drive to 'reform the university', which took root as a movement to modernize higher education, threatened conservatives as if it were a secular drive to undermine Church influence and encourage liberals to embrace modern science. In short, the larger conversation into which Cameron hoped to insert her 'theological photographs' was one that captivated the intellectual, political, and religious elite in England; the risks were high, as the character and future of these bedrock state institutions were on the line.

## Photographing 'the Madonna'

When Cameron chose to represent the *Fruits of the Spirit* in nine photographs, she was faced with a number of pictorial challenges, including how to use the realism of the camera to depict an abstract idea or moral concept, and how to choose a suitable and familiar religious iconography as an appropriate vehicle for this subject in photography. She expressed this dual problem by joining together abstraction and realism, by framing her subject as 'Being the *Fruits of the Spirit*, Illustrated from Life', and by drawing upon familiar Madonna and Child iconography. Michaela Giebelhausen has described this impulse as a kind of 'Protestant biblical naturalism' in the paintings of the Pre-Raphaelites, but as we shall see, Cameron's photographs depart significantly from the Pre-Raphaelite aesthetic and from the religious impulses that gave rise to that movement.[15] Yet because she chose to mine the established iconography of Christian art, she was faced with the problem of how to re-imagine this subject in photography. The Madonna and Child had been popular during the Renaissance and ever since by means of reproduction in books, woodcuts and engravings, and other popular reproductions. How could she vary the Madonna and Child with sufficient distinctiveness so that her nine-part photographic series could convey the unique attributes of the particular virtues being represented, while at the same time provide enough consistency to maintain evident connections between the nine images?

Cameron used the same group of models in the series as a way to approach this difficulty, and in each print, she altered their poses in slight variations. At the same time, throughout 1864, she studied the familiar iconographic grouping of the Madonna and Child by arranging her maid, Mary Hillier, accompanied by one or two children, in variations inspired by Raphael, Guido Reni, and other masters of the Italian Renaissance. She called these works after their common titles: *La Madonna Adolorata* (Cox 48); *La Madonna della Ricordanza* (Cox 49); *La Madonna Aspettante* (Cox 50). Cameron gave her photographs of the Madonna specific meanings and connected them to the abstract virtues in St Paul's *Epistle* by means of her careful use of titles for each work. As a result, the actual title bears a substantial narrative responsibility to signify precisely which abstract religious idea or value is being represented in the photograph. As Mike Weaver recognized, one might easily confuse the sacred and the secular in these works: for example, when comparing *Fervent in Prayer* (Cox 54) to *Goodness* (Cox 42), he interpreted the first as a sacred picture 'of a Madonna and child' but the second as a profane work that could not break free of the realism of the model, or in Weaver's words, 'very much Mary Hillier, doubtless bearing the *persona* of the Madonna but in charge of a half-draped child'.[16] Carol Mavor, by contrast, regarded this ambiguity an asset, calling Cameron's genius the purposeful blurring of such distinctions: 'Cameron's "Madonna pictures," she wrote, 'become undecidable [*sic*] in their representation: they are a tribute to both the Virgin and Mary Hillier. They are just as much indebted to portraiture as to religion.'[17] And Carol Armstrong interpreted Cameron's Madonna photographs as a kind of self-referential substitution, in which Mary Hillier and 'the Madonna' both stand in as proxies for the photographer's creative activity.[18]

Each interpretation has advanced our understanding of Cameron. The question, however, is not how convincingly one thinks Cameron managed to represent her living models as idealized forms in art or whether a particular photograph of the Madonna is more or less sacred than another, since subjective assessments might reasonably change over time and differ in relation to one's taste, education, culture, religion, or gender. Rather, by asking instead how Cameron's contemporaries interpreted the *Fruits of the Spirit* series, we may investigate how successfully the imagery realized her efforts to express a 'theology' of art that was photographic in nature, which is to say, portable and reproducible and which merged realistic and abstract elements together in the same image. By examining different interpretive approaches, we are able to connect these photographs to larger cultural and political forces that shaped the debate about the Anglican Church in relation to British national identity. We gain some initial insight by examining each image in the *Fruits of the Spirit* series and the apparent difficulty that Cameron experienced in assigning titles to each photograph.

At least four of the nine photographs in the series contain multiple inscriptions. Unfortunately, the copyright registers are of little help to explain how Cameron assigned a specific title to each image, as she did not explicitly title every photograph in the register, and several entries marked *Holy Family* actually correspond to titles she subsequently reconceived and retitled as parts of the *Fruits of the Spirit* series. For example, on the back of one image, which depicts Mary Hillier alone, clasping her hands together in front of her breast, Cameron wrote, as if in the act of deliberating, 'Shall this be *Joy*?' and then added, but then apparently reconsidered and struck out, the following two words: 'or *Goodness*' (Cox 36). In the end, she decided upon *Joy*, which she then wrote in ink on the mount under the print, allowing her to title another print (Cox 42) *Goodness* and include that image in the *Fruits of the Spirit* series. But this evidence of her uncertainty and deliberation suggests that she found the two virtues, or perhaps her representation of those virtues, compatible or possibly even equivalent. As another example, Cameron portrayed the Madonna and Child using Mary Hillier and Freddy Gould as models (Cox 38); she first called this work *Repose*, but at the same time she also considered another title for the same composition: in the Lindsay Album, the same image bears the title *Peace*. And in a third example, under a photograph of Mary Hillier accompanied by the two Keown sisters, who portray Christ and St John (Cox 43), Cameron wrote *Faith*. Yet another print of the same image, which she placed in the Norman Album, she called the photograph *Holy Family*. Cameron's habit of appending numerous re-inscriptions to her works emerged with this series; established here, she employed the practice throughout her career.

Cameron also experimented with producing more than one picture from the same negative, which is to say, she reversed the image in at least one instance to create different positive prints under a new title. *Love* (Cox 35), for example, portraying Hillier and the Keown sisters, is also known as *The Madonna Pensosa* (*sic*) when she printed the same negative in reverse. Two versions of *Temperance* also exist; each a mirror image of the other (Cox 46 and 47) (Figure 13 and 14). In a like manner, Cameron gave other photographs new titles when she produced

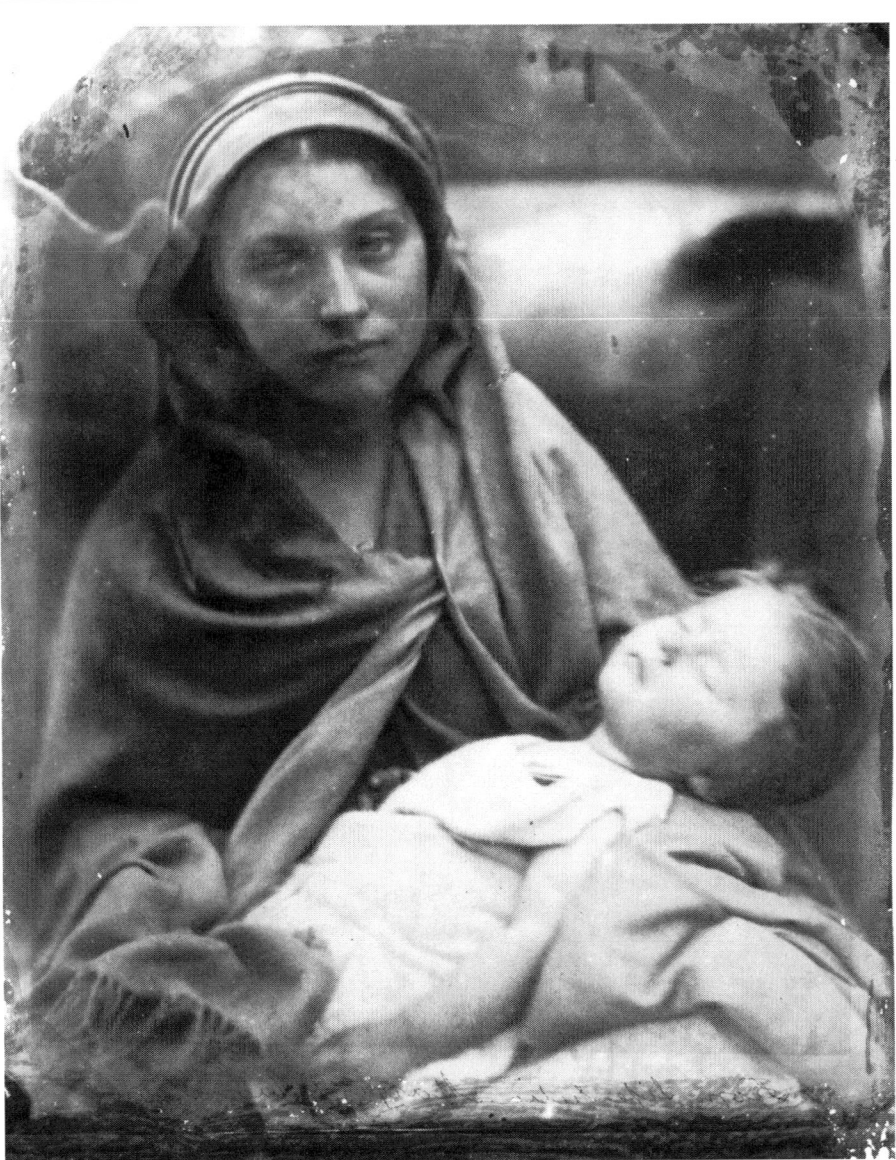

Julia Margaret Cameron, *Temperance* (Cox 46), c. 1864.
Albumen print, 28.6 x 22.3 cm.

**13**

numerous prints that she trimmed in different styles: for example, *Blessing and Blessed* (Cox 56) was trimmed with an arched frame, but when printed in a rectangular frame, Cameron gave two different titles to these prints, calling them *La Beata* and *Divine Love*. And Cameron also experimented with other models besides Mary Hillier for her Madonna imagery: Kate Dore also posed for *Joy* (Cox 211); Mary Kellaway posed for *A Spanish Picture* (Cox 73) and *The Mother Wing* (Cox 74);

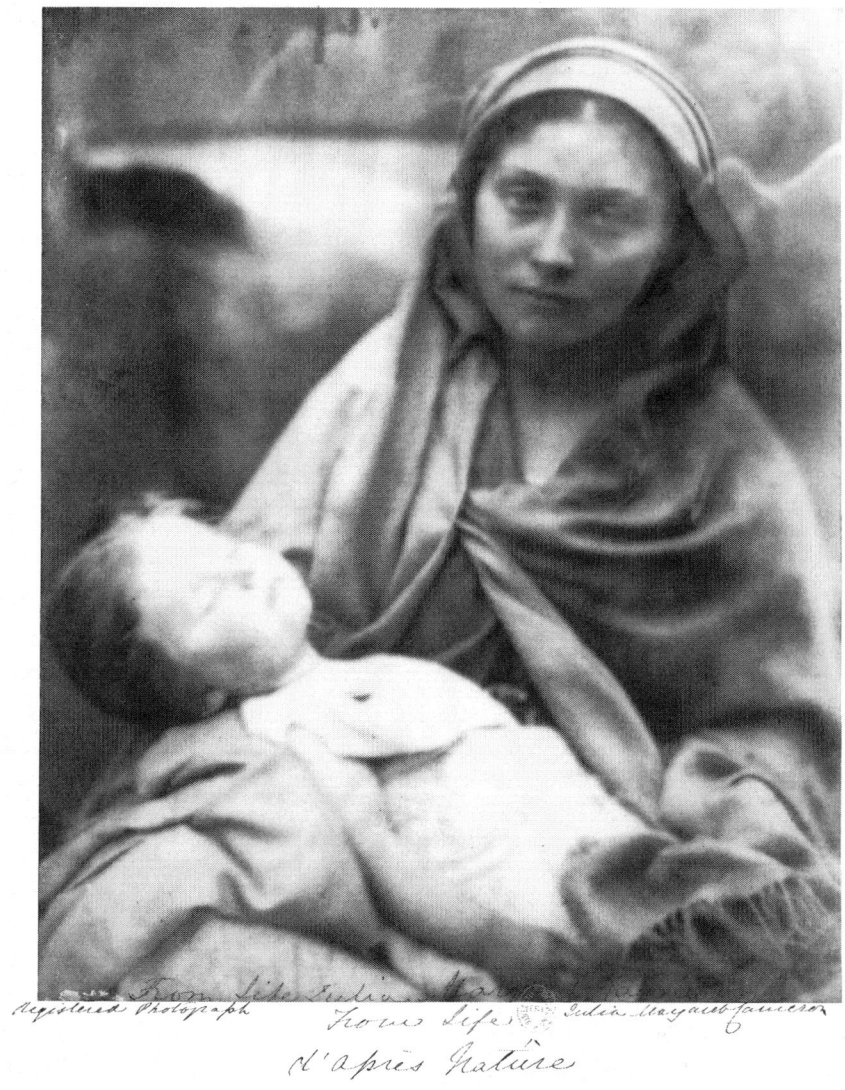

**14**                Julia Margaret Cameron, *Temperance* (Cox 47), 1864.
Albumen print, 26.3 x 20.9 cm (reverse printing of Figure 13).

and Mary Ryan posed as the Virgin Mary of the Annunciation in *A study – after the manner of Francia* (Cox 110) and in *After Perugino* (Cox 113).

These examples demonstrate that the physical and material qualities that describe photography as a representational art form enabled Cameron to explore, both conceptually and concretely, how the same image could take on different meanings. We might identify four areas in which she actively experimented with photography's expressive possibilities as part of her creative process; throughout 1865, she experimented with all four in the religious studies she made through the Madonna images. These are: a) photography's pictorial qualities, which represent the world graphically in both positive and negative values; b) photography's reproductive character, which enables a single negative to produce multiple positive prints and in a variety of dimensions or formats for different purposes; c) the uncanny nature of the photographic print, in which space is flattened, transforming the world into a recognizable two-dimensional picture which at the same time possesses 'lifelike' qualities of naturalism – which Cameron's experimentation involved, in her words, 'rounding' or 'modelling', which enlivens an otherwise two-dimensional form; and, d) photography's ability to depict narrative elements and abstract conceptual ideas that she described as, respectively, 'real' and 'ideal'. Put another way, she used the camera to represent people and objects naturally, and used those realistic qualities as a way to tell narrative stories and allegories.

Cameron wove these four elements together in her practice; if she did not actually articulate the terms used here, she certainly practised the art with these principles in mind. We have already seen how Cameron produced *Love* (Cox 35) and *Temperance* (Cox 46 and 47) as straightforward positive prints from their respective negatives, but that she also reversed the negative to produce another, different, photographic positive. She made multiple prints of these religious images, trimming them accordingly in frames or for placement in a wide variety of photographic albums, and she allowed others to print her work in different formats, including miniature editions. *Mary Mother* (Cox 101), for example, was produced in a rectangular and an oval mount, in reduced format as a *carte-de-visite* and cabinet card, and as an albumen print and a carbon print (Figure 15). Cameron understood that her images were portable, and that cabinet- and *carte*-sized photographs were as collectible as works sold in larger formats.[19]

When Cameron's critics in the photographic press opposed her preference for soft focus, which she believed produced a suitable dramatic effect, she dismissed their assessments as narrow and uninformed. In 1864, for example, she exhibited twenty-three photographs at the ninth annual exhibition of the Photographic Society in Edinburgh and included three additions to the nine photographs in the *Fruits of the Spirit* series, along with a number of portraits. Critics ridiculed her photographs for their 'complete absence of definition' and their 'sketchiness', terms of derision that the *Photographic Journal* reiterated again in 1865.[20] Complaining to Herschel, Cameron wrote that these critics were unable or unwilling to value her photographs in the soft focus style she favoured, in her words, using 'that roundness & fullness of form & feature[,] that modelling of flesh & limb which the focus I use only can give tho' called & condemned as "out of focus"'.[21] Years later, writing her autobiography, she praised her own 'Raphae-

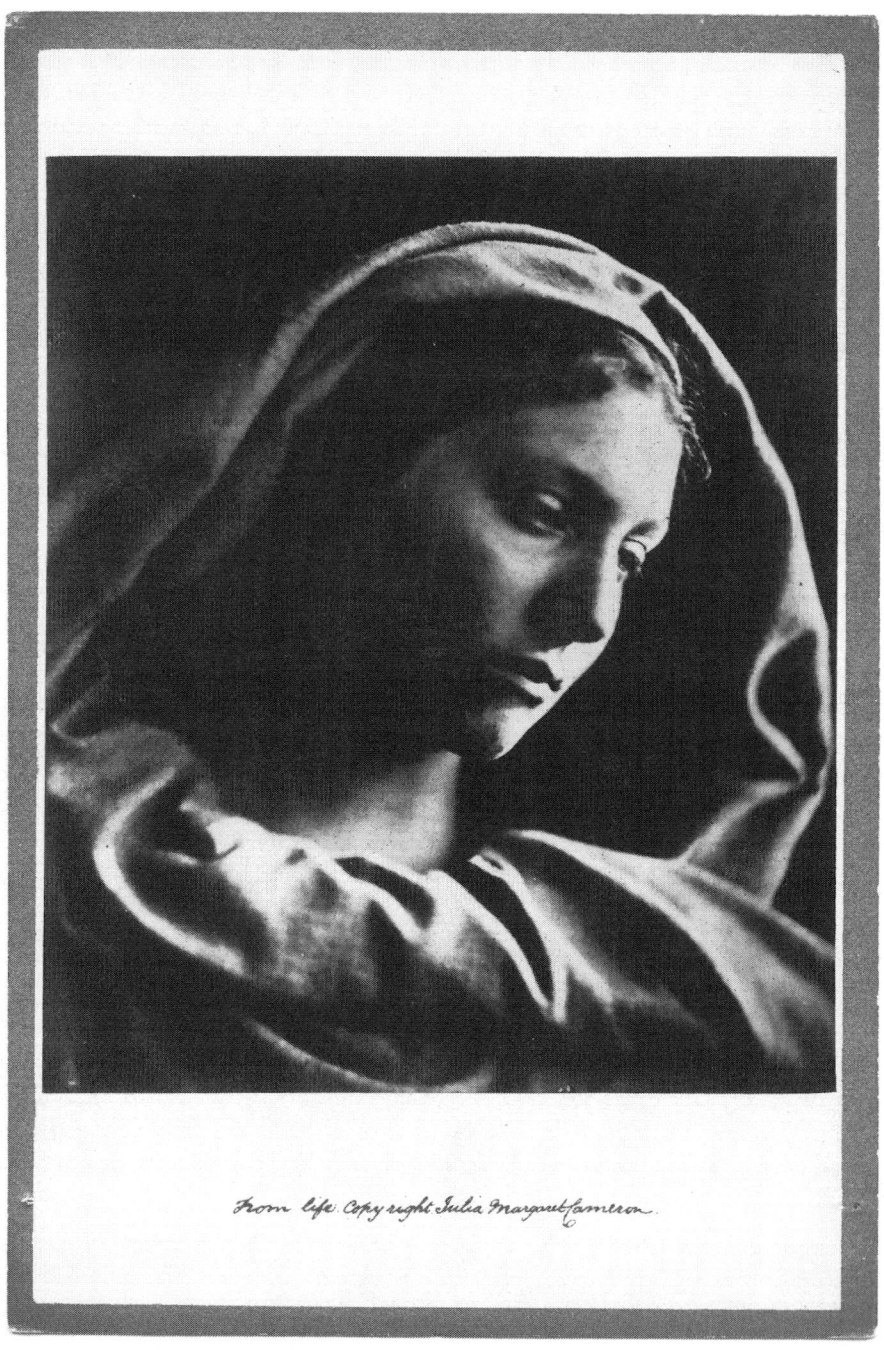

*From life. Copyright Julia Margaret Cameron.*

**15**     Julia Margaret Cameron, *Mary Mother* (Cox 101), c. 1867.
Albumen cabinet card, 116 x 97 mm.

lesque Madonna, called "La Madonna Aspettante,"' as a work that 'cannot be surpassed'.[22]

Cameron's 'illustrations from life' also represented a narrow and exclusive slice of real life, a fact recognized by Coventry Patmore, who in writing about her photographs deflected attention away from her 'fancy subjects'– her Madonnas – and focused instead on Cameron's real-life models, women like Mary Hillier. According to Patmore, 'She knows a beautiful head when she sees it – a very rare faculty; and her position in literary and aristocratic society gives her the pick of the most beautiful and intellectual heads in the world.'[23] Even sympathetic critics like Patmore grew weary of seeing the same model over and over again. Another critic writing in the *Illustrated London News* agreed: 'Mrs Cameron is very felicitous in her choice of female models for her fancy subjects. However, one particular model – invaluable in many subjects, and especially where an expression is required of gentle pathos or piteousness – is reproduced so often as to greatly detract from the variety one expects in so large a collection.'[24] To these critics, Cameron's 'illustrations from life' stripped away what a much later critic would call the 'aura' from the work of art, since in these photographs, the depiction of Mary Hillier was a real and persistent presence, an unwelcome intrusion to the suspension of belief that was necessary in appreciating allegorical photographs.

During the 1930s, Walter Benjamin described how traditional works of art, especially religious paintings that were situated uniquely in cathedrals and churches and therefore surrounded by ritual and ceremony, also embodied the authority of their uniqueness as singular objects, a status he called their 'cult value'.[25] Photography, he argued, destroyed the aura of traditional works of art by introducing reproducibility and by separating the work of art from its original place as a centrepiece of ritual. By severing such works from the 'fabric of tradition' that gave them meaning as inspirational or devotional objects, photography liberated art. Benjamin also recognized that when Cameron's critics identified Mary Hillier as a 'beautiful head' or a 'particular model – invaluable in many subjects', those critics also took on a new and unprecedented role, one that made it possible for them to imagine themselves as if *they* were the creative agents behind the camera, substituting themselves for Cameron in her role as photographer. Imagining such an analytical role-reversal is hardly possible prior to photography. Rather, it is only made possible by the camera's naturalism and by photography's ability to strip away cult value from the subject. Consequently, Cameron's critics and her admirers alike were able to identify with the photographic subject in new ways, introducing new critical judgements about her models, their use in different allegorical compositions, and their ability to convey multiple meanings in each image.[26]

If photography liberated the idealized image of the Madonna from its dependence on ritual, it also introduced a new concept of art production in which reproducibility itself, rather than the uniqueness of the image, became a defining feature of the work of art, according to Benjamin. Cameron recognized this fact intuitively when she produced two almost-identical images of Mary Hillier and the young Percy Keown, titling both images *La Madonna Riposata* (Cox 51 and 52). She included both prints in the album she gave to Lord Overstone in August 1865, but did not mount them next to each other. Rather, under one of these prints, she marked, without a trace of irony, 'from another negative than the one seen page 19'. Tellingly, the two images are *almost the same*, but not quite identical, as are the two reversed images of *Temperance* (Figure 13 and 14): they duplicate the subject matter in virtually the same pose and do not re-present it in a different manner. Neither one nor the other is able to stake a claim as *the* original idea or *the* authoritative print. Instead, both photographs appear curiously as if they are a partial representation of a much larger idea, one that may not be fully realized. Despite their evident independence from each other, the two images are also clearly connected, a fact explicitly noted by Cameron herself. And yet paradoxically, in the face of some uncertainty about which print most fully realized her vision, she inscribed her unconventional notation to insist on the independence and singular value of each print. Cameron repeated this practice once again in 1865 when she constructed a photographic album for Sir Coutts Lindsay: she produced two almost-identical images of the sitters but, in this particular album, she maintained their difference and uniqueness as separate images by applying two different titles. One is known as *La Madonna della Pace / Perfect in Peace* (Cox 53; no. 14 in the Lindsay Album); the other is titled *La Madonna Esaltata / Fervent in Prayer* (Cox 54; no. 28 in the Lindsay Album).

In making numerous photographs of the Madonna, posed in a variety of styles and formats, trimmed in a wide array of mounts, and presented in multiple, closely aligned prints, Cameron used photography to emancipate the subject from its singular value in painting, where it could only be seen as a unique image that was fixed into an architectural niche or altarpiece. Hilary Fraser has described how, during this time in England, imagery of the Madonna was increasingly secularized and humanized and her feminine qualities assigned to abstract moral values, while at the same time, traditional and religious responsibilities of women were increasingly blended together with their maternal role as keepers of the home and hearth.[27] By creating multiple photographs of Mary Hillier as the Madonna, Cameron also humanized her subject by stripping away the aura from the photograph, allowing her viewers to see the Madonna as a flesh-and-blood woman. She therefore humanized 'the Madonna' in two important ways, first by embodying the moral lessons of Paul, secondly by emancipating the image from one fixed reference point.

Confronted with numerous photographic prints of the same subject, Benjamin claimed it made little sense to elevate any one print as more or less 'authentic' than any other: because of photography's realism and ability to produce multiple prints of the same subject, everyday subjects take on greater meaning and value. Therefore, according to Benjamin, 'the instant the criterion of authenticity ceases to be applicable to artistic production, the total function of art is reversed. Instead of being based on ritual, it begins to be based on another practice – politics.'[28] The remainder of this chapter asks, then, to what extent did Cameron's religious photographs enter the realm of everyday politics by offering new interpretations of biblical narratives? Stripped of their aura as unique objects, did Cameron's multiple prints of the Madonna reinforce the devotional role of art or challenge its place in national culture?

## Visual art and the politics of biblical interpretation

For many years, the assertion that Cameron held Tractarian religious beliefs and expressed these values in her photographs has remained unchallenged. Mike Weaver's scholarship advanced this interpretation in several important essays, books, and exhibitions. He concluded that the photographs in the *Fruits of the Spirit* series and similar iconography do more than simply demonstrate Cameron's personal devotion. Drawing largely upon extant letters she wrote to family members expressing her own deeply felt religious feelings, Weaver made the case that Cameron's beliefs were also expressions of personal politics, and that her choice of allegorical subjects emerged from this wellspring. For Weaver, there was no middle ground: Cameron absorbed the fears and concerns of the High Church, he insisted, because she 'was probably a Tractarian but not a Catholic':

> The historical and the devotional were one to Mrs Cameron. Thus in her work we find the embodiment of the ideas of Keble and Newman [ …] So it was that Mrs Cameron's treatment of her friends, her servants, her acquaintances, her heroes, and those whom she snatched off the streets like any scout for a model agency had but one aim – to show their divine and superhuman aspect […] She clearly regarded her photographs as theophanies, manifestations of God in terms of living persons – both indexes and icons of the true, the good, and the beautiful.[29]

Using Cameron's photographs alone to make his case (there is no evidence that Cameron exchanged letters with Keble, Newman, or Pusey; no collection of 'tracts' to which she ever referred in her correspondence; no particular expression of devotion to Tractarian theology), Weaver nevertheless characterized her as a religious extremist, calling her a 'theological feminist' or type of female Christian warrior for whom 'the subjects of the Women at the Sepulchre, the Angel at the Tomb, Mary Magdalene in the Garden, and the Three Marys put women in the position of witnesses charged with the task of bringing men to the faith'.[30]

Rather than considering the *Fruits of the Spirit* a work whose central purpose was to question or examine the role of ritualism, dogma, and orthodoxy in the Church as part of an extended dialogue in the public sphere about that very subject, Weaver argued Cameron's private devotions were sufficient to explain the impetus for her religious imagery. In a circular fashion, Weaver used her religious photographs to confirm that very devotion. Because Cameron called photography a 'divine art' and urged her husband and children to believe in God, Weaver presumed that Cameron obediently and reflexively also complied with what he called 'the accepted role for women Anglo-Catholics' by articulating a one-dimensional and 'archaic ritualism'.[31] This adherence to ritual, explained Weaver, helps us understand why Cameron chose the religious subject matter she did and why she adopted typology as her preferred interpretive approach to the Bible.

Typology is a method of biblical analysis that is founded on two shared belief systems: first, that the New Testament is the ultimate realization of the Old Testament, and second, that there are elements in the Old Testament that anticipate and predict the New. Typology is also a form of allegory. As understood by Weaver, typology seeks figurative parallels and correspondences in the two texts, examining the way that biblical characters behave, the form by which symbols are revealed, and the structure in which narrative episodes are written, all from the perspective of prophecy, revelation, and divine foretelling. Fundamental to this idea is the conviction that the older text of the Hebrews prefigures the Christian revelation and, according to the idea of progressive revelations, leads to a 'new dispensation'. To the Tractarians, as much as to the evangelicals in the London Society for Promoting Christianity amongst the Jews, Christianity was founded historically upon the beliefs and laws of Judaism; both groups believed that, once all remaining Jews had been converted, Christians of all denominations would unite and usher in a new era of religious harmony.[32]

The importance of a common religious identity cementing the nation informed Carlyle's belief in its Anglo-Saxon origins as much as it did Gladstone's early expressions of Christian orthodoxy. In visual art, it also informed the activities of the Pre-Raphaelite Brotherhood. William Holman Hunt, for example, travelled to the Holy Land in 1854 to paint present-day individuals who he believed retained the physical characteristics of those born in biblical times. In Jerusalem, he read the Old Testament, Talmud, and Josephus and studied rabbinical law; he visited the ancient synagogues and personally surveyed the landscape and terrain for areas he thought remained untouched by modern hands.[33] His sponsors were the evangelical London Society's missions to convert the Jews, who put him in touch with Jewish models in Jerusalem, and he was encouraged by the Tractarian tendencies of his fellow Pre-Raphaelites. He wrote to Millais, for example, of his interest in painting a dying goat in a barren landscape to represent 'the scapegoat' as a sign from God, 'sent a way into the wilderness bearing all the sins of the children of Israel which of course was instituted as a kind of Christ'.[34] Cameron had known Hunt and Millais since the 1850s; they had met at her sister's salon in Holland Park. In 1864, she pursued Hunt in London in order to photograph him in the same costume he wore while in Jerusalem (Cox 685, 686, 687).

Extrapolating from Cameron's interaction with Hunt, on the one hand, and her apparent familiarity with Anna Jameson's popular books on the art of the Renaissance, on the other, Weaver held that Cameron interpreted the world principally through typology, and that she used typology to advance Tractarian politics: 'Hitherto, Cameron's photographs have been seen as vaguely allegorical, but they are more properly described as typological or typical – illustrative in a profound, biblical sense.'[35] Yet despite his insistence, neither Anglo Catholics nor Broad Church Protestants exclusively practised typology as a form of biblical interpretation; rather, both religious groups used typology as a way to reinvigorate Christianity; by animating the Christian narrative they made it seem familiar and preordained.[36] Moreover, Tractarianism was an extreme rather than mainstream religious practice, one that placed emphasis on the ritual of divine worship. Tractarians expressed this commitment in daily prayer, confession, feasts and fasts; in the personal expression of faith, particularly conveyed by private devotion, piety, and discipline; and by actively partaking in 'the doctrine of reserve' in the course of practising one's faith. This doctrine held that only by means of a slow and guided awakening to the mysteries of Christianity could the faithful come to find Christ in Scripture and in daily life.

Significantly, Keble and his colleagues in the Tractarian movement did *not* encourage believers to express their private devotions in the visual arts, either through the act of creating or consuming the arts. Rather, they advised *against* believers' reading daily papers and gazing upon the graphic imagery one might find there, calling such exposure particularly inappropriate to the contemplative and internal processes of sacred devotion. In his *Lectures on Poetry* (1832–41), for example, Keble sought to establish poetry as superior to all other expressive forms: he considered poetry 'the best, most oblique and sacred manner of expression available to the [Tractarian] believer' because it was able to stress 'the supernatural, sacramental element within poetry as a spontaneous overflow of spiritual feeling'.[37] For Tractarians, the 'doctrine of reserve' addressed the question of how to properly express religious feeling and how to 'regulate' and exert self-control over those very feelings.[38] This doctrine was called 'On Reserve in Communicating Religious Knowledge'. It was published in two instalments in 1837 (tract 80) and 1840 (tract 87). As Joshua King has written, these two tracts counselled believers to resist 'the perceived excesses of nineteenth-century print culture'; readers were cautioned against 'discuss[ing] the most sacred subjects in the daily periodical' (Part 2: 47) and warned about the influence of 'the bad instruments of the world (such as the daily periodical)' (Part 2: 125).[39] Above all, the doctrine asserted that only a confirmed believer could fully grasp the deep meaning of the scriptural laws; that all expressions of faith should be contained inwardly and expressed indirectly, if at all; and that in every instance, all elements of originality, novelty, and innovation were to be avoided. 'Reserve' was exemplified by reverential distance and awe in the presence of the mysterious and unknowable divine. It was a movement that sought to reclaim purity, and therefore celebrated virginity, celibacy, self-containment, and lack of touch.[40] There is no evidence that Cameron held such extreme views; in fact, others have celebrated Cameron's haptic enthusiasm as 'evidence' of her maternal expressions in photography.[41]

Mid-Victorian book illustration, particularly in the works of poetry illustrated by the Pre-Raphaelites and others in Moxon's 1857 editions of Tennyson's poems, did much to satisfy the public's desire to visualize the intense emotions and psychological drama of religious devotion, Keble's apparent disapproval notwithstanding. As Susan Casteras has described, the graphic interpretations of many Pre-Raphaelite paintings emphasized these elements because of their reduced scale and economical expression in line drawings and wood engravings. According to Casteras, illustrations 'of Hunt's "Lady of Shalott," Millais' "Mariana," and Rossetti's "Palace of Art" and "Mariana of the South" all emphasize highly keyed emotions, centring these on melodramatic moments of crisis both psychologically and pictorially'.[42] For example, as a black-and-white print, Rossetti's *Mariana of the South* draws upon Dürer's *Birth of the Virgin* series and packs into the frame devotional symbols of penitence, supplication, and prayer as the central figure kisses the feet of a hanging crucifix.[43] Similarly, in Eleanor Vere Boyle's illustration of Tennyson's *The May Queen* (1861), the heroine submits to her death by embracing the feet of the crucified Christ, which is rendered as a vision made substantial in an open field, surrounded by a tangle of lilies and vines.[44] Both Rossetti and Boyle stress the supernatural and use Christian iconography to emphasize the embodiment of faith.

Vocal members of the Broad Church dismissed the supernatural as a retreat from the real world and embraced instead the importance of engaging actively with it: Charles Kingsley and Thomas Hughes, for example, promoted an oppositional counter-movement to the Tractarians they called 'muscular Christianity'. Founded in physicality and exemplified by the rough-and-tumble world of Hughes's *Tom Brown's School Days*, muscular Christianity was based upon a participant-based morality having its roots in the Old Testament. As headmaster of Rugby School, Thomas Arnold taught that moral struggles were ever-present in daily life and that a person must fight for fundamental truths daily by taking part in worldly affairs.[45] In contrast to the withdrawal preached by Tractarians, Kingsley insisted that muscular Christians engage with biblical stories for their historical significance, cultural meanings, and contemporary applications, argue with those who held other faiths, and promote religious dialogue in everyday events. Frederick Denison Maurice's book, *The Kingdom of Christ* (1838), epitomized this approach by arguing that the shared belief system of the National Church was sufficient to express the sacredness of daily life, able to overcome differences in race or family lineage.[46]

In this context, where religious disagreement fed the public appetite for social and political controversy, and where a print market had long existed to produce reproductions of religious and devotional paintings, English printmakers and a new breed of photographers responded by promoting their stock of religious subjects. For example, firms like S. B. Beal offered a *Catalogue of Photographs* from which sacred and secular selections could be purchased by mail or through the firm's 'Fine-Art Gallery', located at St Paul's Churchyard, London. In Oxford, one could purchase 'religious prints and photographs' directly from Mowbray's Photographic Studio on Cornmarket Street. Mowbray also sold other explicitly Christian images, including 'Carte Photographs of Bishops, Priests, and Deacons, in the proper Vestments', at one shilling each. Both Beal and Mowbray advertised in the annual publication of the Anglican Church, *A Kalendar of the English Church and Ecclesiastical Almanack*, as well as in other pamphlets and broadsides, but their names are largely forgotten today as producers of commercial religious photographs, perhaps because they served a broad public, as opposed to offering limited edition portfolios to print connoisseurs.[47] These English firms shared the commercial photographic market and demand for religious imagery with international businesses like Goupil in Paris and Alinari in Florence; both firms operated large graphic arts workshops that produced and widely distributed fine art reproductions of religious subjects.[48]

During the 1860s, the English market was saturated by the availability and affordability of cabinet photographs and *cartes-de-visite* produced by Leonida Caldesi, who gained access to all of the public art collections in London and who sold his reproductive photographs through the Colnaghi firm, which marketed his goods to a mass audience. The rise of this market was accompanied by newly accessible books, like those written by Anna Jameson, which helped a middle-class public understand these graphic reproductions as their own, and which encouraged the acquisition, display, and discussion of religious art.[49] At the high end of the market, fine arts enthusiasts like members of the Arundel Society and the art unions commissioned expensive reproductions of Renaissance works in luxuriously bound print portfolios.[50] But whether prints were high-end or cheaply acquired, a robust market fed popular interest in religious imagery, a market that was fuelled by the debates between the High and Low Church movements.

## Church and state, types and anti-types

Cameron knew Benjamin Jowett personally from his visits to the Tennysons, which he made during regular breaks from Oxford, and in 1864, she managed to take his portrait during Jowett's Christmas holiday that year. Cameron enjoyed his stays and the young students who often accompanied him.[51] In order to entice him to return to her company each time he visited Freshwater, Cameron hired

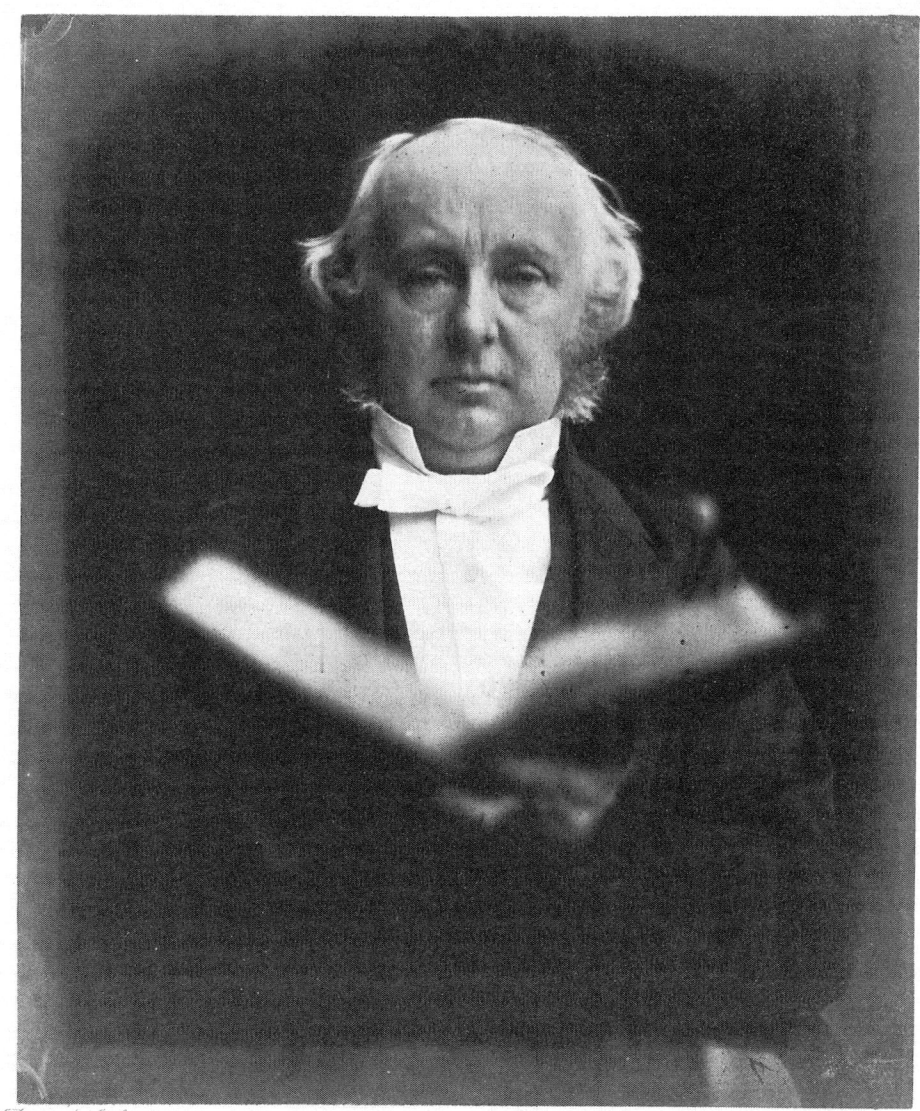

**16**        Julia Margaret Cameron, *Benjamin Jowett* (Cox 698), c. 1865.
Albumen print, 26.5 x 21.6 cm.

carpenters to join one of the neighbouring cottages on to Dimbola; she named the new structure 'The Porch', a reference to Jowett's translations of Plato, to honour the scholar and encourage his future visits.[52] In early 1865, Cameron travelled to London on a mission: she registered her portrait of Jowett (Cox 699) for copyright protection on 11 January; the following day, she delivered the *Fruits of the Spirit* to the British Museum.[53] At each destination, she staked out new ground to advance her new theology of photography.

Cameron depicted Jowett as the scholar he was, serious, intent, alert, and inquiring (Figure 16). He casts his gaze directly at the viewer, looking up from a large open book, an image of dignity, nobility, and learning, returning the viewer's gaze as if in the midst of lecturing, preaching, or reading aloud. Too large to be an actual volume of *Essays and Reviews*, which had been issued *in-octavo*, he holds a folio-sized volume, which becomes as much a commanding presence as the sitter himself; its prominence suggests a ceremonial Bible or other significant work.[54] Following her copyright registration at the Public Record Office, Cameron sent Jowett's portrait to Colnaghi's for sale, and over the course of the next several years, she included the portrait in no fewer than five of her photographic albums, often placing it alongside prints depicting the *Fruits of the Spirit* and other religious subjects.

As we have seen, religious discussion during the 1860s was animated by popular debates over the Old and New Testament, and in particular, the controversy separating High and Low Church practice centred on how to interpret the gospel of Paul. In his book of 1859 on St Paul's Epistles, Jowett devoted a considerable section to an academic question that from an orthodox point of view was potentially heretical: 'Is it possible for the Same Word to have Two Meanings in the Same Passage?'[55] During this period, Jowett pioneered an innovative approach to interpreting the Bible that combined learned translation from the Greek, philology and linguistic analysis, and a historical interest in reconstructing the historical audience for whom the Epistles were originally written. However, Jowett's volume on St Paul drew little attention from the public as it contained long passages in Greek and an esoteric philosophical argument. Awareness of his writings, however, changed dramatically the following year with the publication of *Essays and Reviews*.

In large part owing to its scholarly approach, somewhat arcane language, and complex intellectual arguments, *Essays and Reviews* might seem an unlikely text to cause such controversy. In its foreword, the writers acknowledged that the book departed from accepted convention, imploring readers to receive the essays 'as an attempt to illustrate the advantage derivable to the cause of religious and moral truth, from a free handling, in a becoming spirit, of subjects peculiarly liable to suffer by the repetition of conventional language, and from traditional methods of treatment'.[56] Using coded words and phrases, they advocated for the so-called 'free handling' of interpretation, where all forms of knowledge, including religious subjects, could be approached by means of discovery, intellectual investigation, and open debate. These methods, common enough today in academia as the process of intellectual discovery that is a cornerstone of logical and critical thinking, were not embraced at the time in theology because they opened the door to questioning accepted doctrine. In particular, Church members were expected to receive Scripture as undeniably truthful, and therefore would not imagine subjecting it to scrutiny for coherence or correctness, nor would they interrogate its logic. At stake were the traditional authority of the Church and the influence of its foundational texts. *Essays and Reviews* threatened to destabilize received meanings, and in the process, introduce the potential for doubt or disbelief. There was also the risk of competing moral codes, where the act of discovery and the role of scepticism faced off against traditional belief systems founded largely on faith and received truths.[57]

Because national identity was tied to religious expression, this conflict was not confined to the Anglican Church's convocation or ecclesiastical courts. Nor was the conflict defined as an esoteric academic debate limited to committees of Oxford dons. Rather, this was a highly visible national conflict, in part because Prime Ministers appointed Church officials as bishops and to their university positions at Oxford and Cambridge. At stake too was the role of the Church in the University, which taught England's ruling elite and shaped its future colonial administrators. *Essays and Reviews* therefore put biblical interpretation before the public eye and into a new space that was not confined to the exclusive power of bishops. Rather, by widening the discursive field to encompass the sciences, arts, and letters, *Essays and Reviews* might be said to have expanded public dialogue about religion in daily life.[58] For example, one of the essayists, Henry Bristow Wilson, contributed to the volume by directly questioning the traditional role of the National Church – both in terms of its everyday role for individuals and its far-reaching aspirations. According to Wilson, its national status guaranteed all citizens the freedom to expand their spiritual life in harmony with the nation's moral centre. Wilson wrote that such growth could occur only when the National Church was free and just:

> We all know how the inward moral life – or spiritual life on its moral side, if that term be preferred – is nourished into greater or less vigour by means of the conditions in which the moral subject is placed. Hence, *if a nation is really worthy of the name*, conscious of its own corporate life, it will develop itself on one side into a Church, wherein its citizens may grow up and be perfected in their spiritual nature […] If the national Church is to be true to the multitudinist principle, and to correspond ultimately to the national character, the freedom of opinion which belongs to the English citizen should be conceded to the English Churchman; and the freedom which is already practically enjoyed by the members of the congregation, cannot without injustice be denied to its ministers.[59]

For Wilson, the Church's chief role was to preserve and elevate an individual's moral life; religious insistence that individuals adhere to supernatural beliefs or miracles stood in opposition to that spirit. To the Essayists, the integrity of Protestant beliefs and the importance of free opinions were fundamental to national identity. As Wilson wrote, the supernatural had no role in the activities of a modern nation:

> It cannot concern a State to develop as part of its own organization a machinery or system of relations founded on the possession of speculative truth. Speculative doctrines should be left to philosophical schools. A national Church must be concerned with the ethical development of its members. And the wrong of supposing it to be otherwise, is participated by those of the clericalty who consider the Church of Christ to be founded, as a society, on the possession of an abstractedly true and supernaturally communicated speculation concerning God, rather than upon the manifestation of a divine life in man.[60]

Wilson and Jowett both believed rational thought would unlock the literal interpretation of the Bible and liberate the interpreter; both Essayists considered the freedom to pursue such enquiry an inalienable right of citizenship. As Wilson wrote: 'Under the terms of the sixth Article [of the Thirty-Nine Articles of the Church] one may accept literally, or allegorically, or as parable, or poetry, or legend, the story of a serpent tempter, of an ass speaking with man's voice, of an arresting of the earth's motion, of a reversal of its motion, of waters standing in a solid heap, of witches, and a variety of apparitions.'[61]

For his contribution to *Essays and Reviews*, Jowett was attacked for claiming the Bible should be read like 'any other book', with its parables, allegories, and narratives informed by history and language, and its influence subjected to methodical enquiries informed by science. To Jowett, the aim of interpretation was to restore a work's original meaning as much as possible, to what it was trying to convey when first conceived, and he believed biblical interpretation should be no different. According to Jowett, the Bible 'is to be interpreted like other books, with attention to the character of its authors, and the prevailing state of civilization and knowledge, with allowances for peculiarities of style and language, and modes of thought and figures of speech'.[62] His essay also contended that religion could be relevant in people's lives only when it was acknowledged to have 'progressed' over time. Arguing against a rigid and unchanging canon-based law, Jowett asked: 'In what relation does [Scripture] stand to actual life? Is it a law, or only a spirit? for nations, or for individuals? to be enforced generally, or in details also?'; in short, he asked, is everything 'done or said by our Saviour and His Apostles, to be regarded as a precept or example which is to be followed on all occasions and to last for all time?'[63]

In opposition to many key elements expressed by the Articles of Faith, Jowett even declared that the power of religion was more human and temporal than it was mystical and eternal. In fact, he rejected the immutability of Christian doctrine, calling it contrary to the ever-present experience of change that affected every person every day:

That can hardly be, consistently with the changes of human things. It would be a rigid skeleton of Christianity (not the image of Christ), to which society and politics, as well as the lives of individuals, would be conformed. It would be the oldness of the letter, on which the world would be stretched; not 'the law of the spirit of life' which St. Paul teaches.[64]

Consequently, Jowett argued that it was necessary to separate politics and law from the framework of spiritual life, because otherwise, 'the great principles of truth and justice have no longer room to make themselves felt'. A more responsible political position, he argued, was to emphasize the principles of liberty and freedom learned from Christian teachings and elevate those as 'a counsel of perfection'; all else, wrote Jowett, must be of 'this world'.[65]

Members of the High Church responded vehemently to Jowett, vilifying him as the chief radical dissenter at Oxford. Jowett's opponents even argued for his outright dismissal for contradicting the Articles of Faith. All of the Essayists were accused of rejecting the authority of the Bible as the Word of God, denying the fact of miracles, including Christ's, and questioning the infallibility of God. For Broad Church members, on the other hand, *Essays and Reviews* created a new opportunity for them to engage in rational dialogue about Church doctrines, especially on the role of interpreting biblical stories, Christian morals, and Church laws. The dispute also broke down along partisan political lines that reflected the fissures in English religious and political belief: for example, Arthur Penrhyn Stanley, Jowett's friend since their undergraduate days and a Professor of Ecclesiastical History at Oxford prior to his appointment as Dean of Westminster in 1864, who was long identified with the Broad Church movement, organized a defence fund to support the Essayists.[66] On the other side, Edward Pusey and John Keble, two prominent Tractarians, published lengthy treatises of their own condemning the Essayists.[67]

The case generated a great deal of public opinion following the episcopal censure of the book in February 1861. Yet the bishops' persecution of the Essayists did not play well outside Oxford. In 1861, for example, the editors of *Punch* took the side of the Essayists, addressing the following lines to the Church bishops:

> Those *Essays and Reviews*
> How idle to abuse
> In terms of vague unmeaning condemnation:
> Do you think the people look
> For your censure of the book?
> No, ye Bishops, but expect your refutation.[68]

Nevertheless, the bishops kept the matter open for three years, threatening the Essayists with multiple suspensions and fines. But on 8 February 1864, the Privy Council finally acquitted the group. This action was widely interpreted as a victory for liberal reformers and a defeat for the orthodox Church.[69] *The Times* reported the event:

The broad fact remains that a book which aroused the greatest public dissatis-
faction and which was almost judicially condemned by the Bench of Bishops
has been found practically unassailable in point of law ... Right or wrong; the
question is definitively settled, the members of the Church are released from
all legal obligation to maintain a higher authority for the Scriptures than that
claimed for *Essays and Reviews*.[70]

Although the court case was settled, the public debate was not. Cameron and her
circle on the Isle of Wight were invested deeply in the outcome. Emily Tennyson,
for example, faithfully recorded each moment of hope and despair as Jowett's
fortunes rose and fell during those years. Julia Margaret Cameron was also
affected by Jowett's experience. She confessed her engagement with 'theological
questions' in her letter to Herschel, but it is also clear from her photographic
activity during this time that she was engaged in developing a novel approach to
interpreting religious imagery that had meaning for both sides of the debate over
the role of interpretation in the National Church. In her photographs, she created
a new space of ideological common ground because it was focused on moral
teachings. This foundation was at the heart of Cameron's 'theological work' in
photography.

## Jowett's opposition to typology

How did Cameron draw lessons from Jowett's approach to interpreting Scripture?
In particular, Jowett's essay struck an important blow to typology, undermining
its legitimacy as an interpretive approach to the Bible by dismissing its mystical
elements and reliance on dogma. In her *Fruits of the Spirit* series, Cameron also
rejected typology in favour of drawing upon Paul's advice on how to lead a moral
life.

Jowett called the search for types and anti-types in biblical interpretation
misleading and false. In his view, many of the clerical interpretations that were
based upon typology produced conflicting accounts, and all were speculative.
Many symbols cancelled each other out, for example, and legitimate narrative
explanations for supernatural prophecies could hardly be authenticated. We have
seen that Jowett tended toward a literal over a mystical approach in his analysis
of biblical language, and thought that one only had to strip away the layers of
history, mythology, and linguistic idiosyncrasies from the text in order to recover
original meanings. He also considered interpretation a discursive process, arguing
that the 'free handling' of religious texts meant that one had to apply metaphor,
figures of speech, and allegory to understanding the Bible in conversational
terms.[71] Above all, this approach had to apply its lessons to everyday life, where
there was no place for supernatural beliefs. Jowett argued against the Church's
narrow adherence to dogma, believing it actually obscured what interpreter's

aims should truly be, which is to say, to bring light by restoring a text's original meanings. For example, Jowett wrote,

> He who reflects on the multitude of explanations which already exist of the 'number of the beast,' 'the two witnesses,' 'the little horn,' 'the man of sin,' who observes the manner in which these explanations have varied with the political movements of our own time, will be unwilling to devote himself to a method of inquiry in which there is so little appearance of certainty or progress. These interpretations would destroy one another if they were all placed side by side in a tabular analysis ... Or to take an example of another kind, the Protestant divine who perceives that the types and figures of the Old Testament are employed by Roman Catholics in support of the tenets of their church, will be careful not to use weapons which it is impossible to guide, and which may with equal force be turned against himself. Those who have handled them on the Protestant side have before now fallen victims to them, not observing as they fell that it was by their own hand.[72]

Jowett's rejection of typology was consistent with his interest in recovering original meanings; like language, he understood that the meanings of symbols and types could also be altered historically: 'what the authors of the New Testament books had written ought simply to be taken at face value and that one would be "guided" into an understanding of it'.[73]

In order to arrive there, however, the symbols, allegories, and parables that had gained authority from the typological methods of the past needed to be disassembled, because, according to Jowett, they were historical aberrations. References to the New Testament, for example, were not *already present* in the Old Testament, as typology taught. Rather, writers who imagined such foretelling frankly misunderstood their interpretive task and had *read into* these texts during the course of time:

> The office of the interpreter is not to add another [interpretation], but to recover the original one; the meaning, that is, of the words as they first struck on the ears or flashed before the eyes of those who heard or read them. He has to transfer himself to another age; to imagine that he is a disciple of Christ or Paul; to disengage himself from all that follows ... All the after-thoughts of theology are nothing to him; they are not the true lights which light him in difficult places. His concern is with a book in which as in other ancient writings are some things of which we are ignorant; which defect of our knowledge cannot however be supplied by the conjectures of fathers or divines. The simple words of that book he tries to preserve absolutely pure from the refinements or distinctions of later times.[74]

Importantly, Jowett argued for the integrity of the text: 'One could not understand Paul by cross-reference to verses taken out of context from some other part of the Bible, as though the scriptures had sprung – whole and entire – from a single mind.'[75]

Jowett's essay empowered Cameron to articulate her own interpretation of biblical scenes. Significantly, she first chose subjects illustrating St Paul's moral code, creating photographs that combined the real and ideal, taking moral examples from everyday life. Although she drew upon the established iconography of the Madonna, she complicated her photographic imagery by intentionally introducing repetitions, indeterminate spaces, ambiguous symbolism, and multiple inscriptions, and embodied these ideas pictorially in repeated poses and multiple versions or interpretations of her negatives, and she inscribed these ideas textually in the multiple titles she gave her works. Rather than subscribing to fixed biblical doctrines, she engaged in the on-going dialogue about those interpretations with those who agreed with Jowett's views *and* opponents who stood against him, making portraits of both groups.

Cameron also extended the formal boundaries of photography when she thought this made sense. Just as she scratched into the emulsion of *Paul and Virginia*, she manipulated the medium in her religious subjects if she thought it could enhance an image. In one depiction of the *Madonna* (Cox 18), for example, she added a halo to her model, and in another, represented disembodied rays of light to suggest otherworldly mysticism, in a work she called *The Nativity* (Cox 90). Similarly, Cameron removed unwanted objects or an unsightly background from an image altogether: she did this in *La Madonna Vigilante* (Cox 55) and in *A Spanish Picture* (Cox 73). Cameron's approach to traditional religious framing is also apparent in several *Madonna and Child* images from 1864 and 1865 (Cox 75, 76, 82), where she erased photographic emulsion or created an original framing template in order to remove unwanted areas of the picture while creating a soft arch to the top of her image at the same time, or used an oval frame, as she did with *Mary Mother*.[76] These examples show Cameron enjoyed experimentation, dispensed with pre-conceived ideas about display or framing, and was eager to adopt untested techniques to realize her vision.

There is no reason to believe Cameron thought that any metaphysical transformation took place when she manipulated photographic emulsion. Rather, it is apparent that she let the compositional needs of each subject guide her hand. For example, in several images illustrating Percy Keown, a sleeping baby, several prints are made from two negatives joined at the mid-point and printed as composite images. These create an unsettling horizontal black line that divides the top half from the bottom (Cox 139, 143, 145) (see Figure 17). In spite of this 'technical imperfection', Cameron registered each of these prints at the Public Record Office, all seemingly having equal importance to her. Yet it is also true that four additional prints of similar subject matter (in which Cameron's model Mary Hillier is posed bending over a different sleeping baby) bear at least four different registered titles (Cox 149–53 and 155–61). These include the following: a) *My Grandchild, Archie Cameron, aged 2 years & 3 months*, b) *My grandchild my chef*

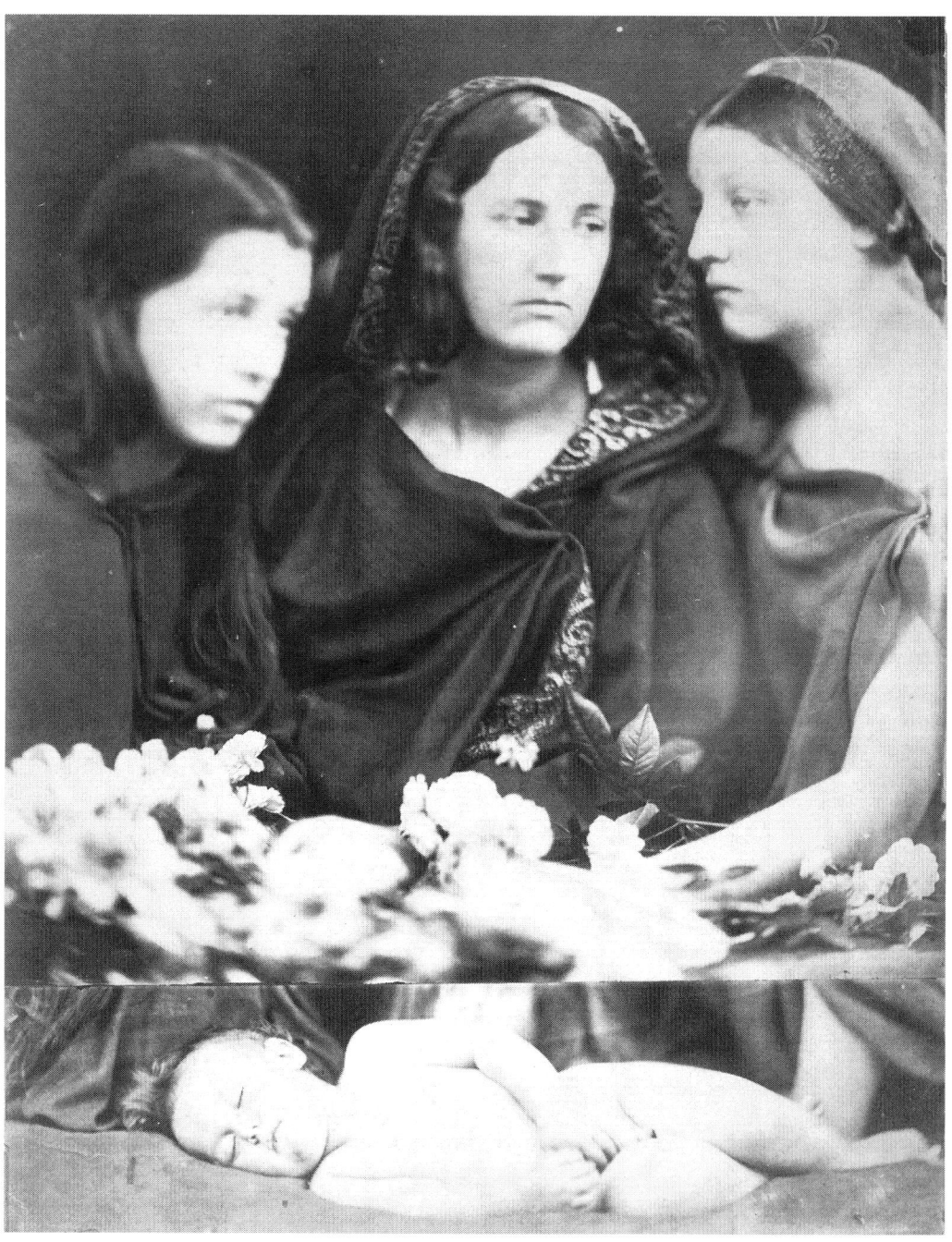

17          Julia Margaret Cameron, *[Daughters of Jerusalem and child]*
(Cox 143), c. 1865. Albumen print, 34.5 x 26.2 cm.

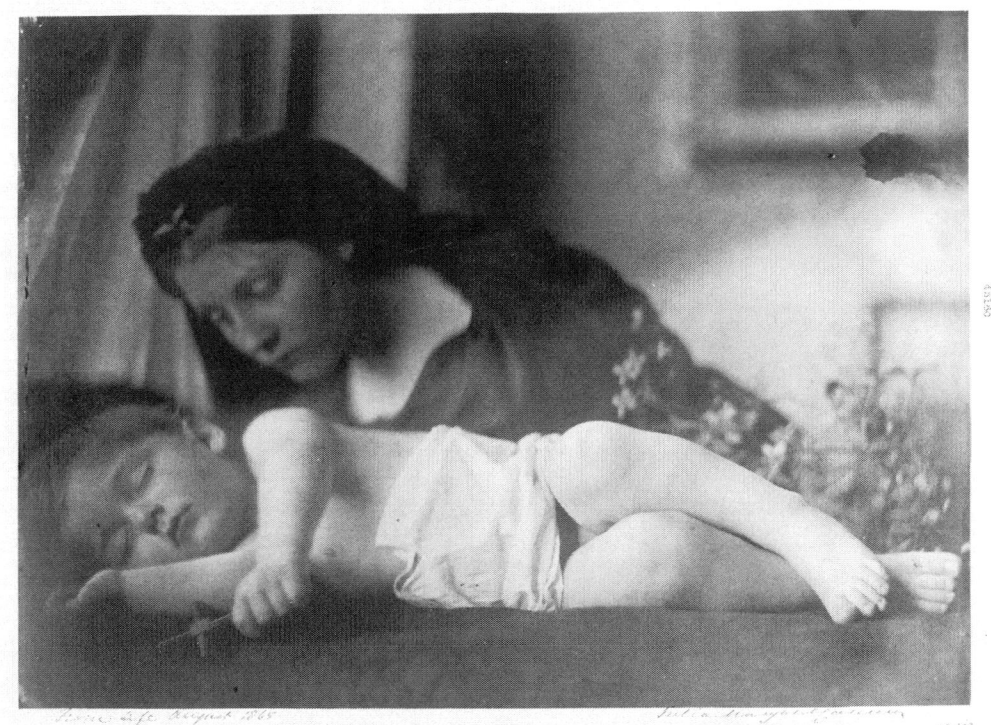

Julia Margaret Cameron, *The Shadow of the Cross* (Cox 157), 1865.          **18**
Albumen print, 27.1 x 36.5 cm.

*d'oeuvre*, c) *For Signor my chef d'oeuvre, My grand child age 2 years & 3 months, Born at Barbados, May 1863*, and d) *Light and Love (June 1865)*.[77] Two months later, Cameron posed models in the composition once again and produced *The Shadow of the Cross* (August 1865), the most fully realized of the series from a photographic point of view, the small cross clutched in the child's hand no longer blurred, as in the earlier composite image, and the image no longer a composite of two negatives (Cox 157) (Figure 18).[78] Cameron was nothing if not persistent: in one image, Mary's head might be in greater shadow, and therefore less sharply defined, but in a second image details like the small cross become perfectly distinct and clear. Later, as evident in the layout design in the album she created for Lord Overstone, she paired the two sitters, Hillier and Keown, again in new compositions called *La Madonna Esaltata / Fervent in Prayer* (Cox 54), *La Madonna della Pace / Perfect in Peace* (Cox 53), and *La Madonna Riposata / Resting In Hope* (Cox 51).

When Cameron depicted the bodies of her child models as insistently 'real bodies' and less evidently idealized as painterly subjects, the flip side of this traditional iconography emerges. This occurred when Cameron's photographs revealed the nude model's human form in such a way that it broke with established convention by exposing the child's sexuality. For example, when the gender of Cameron's models for Christ and St John is revealed as female, her allegorical illusion effectively disappears, as in *Spring* (Cox 1085), *Gentleness* (Cox 41), and *Goodness* (Cox 42). In these photographs, the model's gender destabilizes the compositions from within.[79] In other photographs, when she switched the gender of her angels from male to female, such as *The Angel at the Tomb* (Cox 264) and *The Angel at the Sepulchre* (Cox 268), which represent the biblical account of a male angel and a female follower of Christ, or in *The Return after Three Days* (Cox 148), where the angel is depicted in the company of witnesses (and/or other angels) that are not present in the biblical narrative, Cameron embarked upon her own novel 'free interpretation' of Scripture. This 'free handling' also permitted her to replace the male Paul with a female model when she reinterpreted Raphael's *St Cecilia Altarpiece*, which she titled *St Cecilia / after the manner of Raphael* (Cox 125). In all of these images, Cameron was clearly content to occupy an indeterminate space rather than to insist on a fixed iconography or orthodox interpretation of her subject.

In these photographs, Cameron charted new territory in her interpretation of biblical narratives: on the one hand, she drew upon Scripture to provide lessons on how to lead a moral life, as in the *Fruits of the Spirit* series, and on the other hand, following an approach advocated in *Essays and Reviews*, she brought those lessons into contact with a modern, personalized interpretation informed by new insight, much like Jowett's theology was informed by new archaeological expeditions across the globe which uncovered evidence that sometimes contradicted accepted biblical narratives.[80] Thrust into this modern world, Cameron's photographs embody signs of instability, her interpretations of Scripture more personal and unique than programmatic or dogmatic. In forging her way, Cameron challenged the authority of the established iconography by replacing religious and cultural doctrines with a dynamic process of interpretation that denied any single claim to truth, or correctness, or established and fixed knowledge.

## Defenders and dissenters: reconciling the National Church

In her biblical imagery, Cameron expressed a kind of ambivalence that corresponds to the unresolved question about the interpretation of scripture in the National Church and the continuing debate over secular reforms to biblical scholarship then taking place in Oxford. She occupied a middle ground in these debates that revealed itself in the two exhibitions she organized in July and November 1865. In these one-person exhibitions, Cameron brought together her allegorical works of 'theological interest' with her portraits of individuals who were closely associated with both sides of the public debate surrounding *Essays and*

*Reviews*. On 30 June 1864, for example, Cameron registered for copyright protection two photographs of men who represented opposing politics and religious beliefs; both were frequent visitors to the Isle of Wight. These were Aubrey De Vere, a Catholic convert who was a close friend of Henry Taylor and Tennyson, and Henry Halford Vaughan, a 'free-thinking reformer' who was married to her niece, Adeline Maria Jackson. Vaughan was also Regius Professor of Modern History at Oxford and a colleague of Jowett's. Described by one contemporary as 'a High Churchman turned radical', Vaughan helped to lead the reform movement at the University.[81] She photographed De Vere in several variations (Cox 650, 651, 652) and printed his image in an arched frame similar to Jowett's (Cox 699). In her portraits of the two men, Cameron represented each person sympathetically, posing them against type as if to counter expectations. De Vere appears absorbed, for example, holding himself together while glancing down, metaphorically looking within, as if seeking inspiration or enlightenment. In the portrait of Vaughan, by contrast, the sitter casts his eyes out of the frame and heavenward in a representational gesture for seeking divine guidance (Cox 824, 825). Both sitters appear absorbed, reinforced by Cameron's framing in a roundel (Cox 824) or topped by an arch (Cox 825).

Although Jowett had been acquitted, his enemies froze his annual salary as a kind of punishment, limiting him to £50 per year, strapping him financially. Throughout 1864, in fact, Jowett's antagonists and his supporters alike effectively kept the controversy alive in the public sphere:[82] in February, for example, the published debates between Charles Kingsley and John Newman emerged over the question of orthodoxy in the Anglican Church. Newman issued his autobiography, *Apologia Pro Vita Sua*, in regular bi-monthly instalments, which culminated in June. During that same period, Jowett endured debates in Oxford's Upper House of Convocation on the arguments he presented in *Essays and Reviews*. In March, a proposal to endow Jowett's chair failed by a large margin, and then in April 1864, Bishop Samuel Wilberforce, who had been an ardent critic, submitted yet another petition to condemn the Essayists. By September, the public tide had turned somewhat, and Jowett and his colleagues received new support. Finally, 14 February 1865 brought an end to Jowett's immediate financial crisis when his annual compensation was raised to £500. These trials kept the public controversy popular and current: in the same month, a twelfth edition of *Essays and Reviews* was published in a print run of another 1,000 copies, priced to sell at the nominal cost of five shillings.

By July 1865, then, when Cameron exhibited her religious images of the *Fruits of the Spirit* and various Madonna studies in the French Gallery, the ideas debated in *Essays and Reviews* and the controversy surrounding Jowett were very much alive. In fact, they might be said to have influenced her selection of photographs to display in the exhibition. In the gallery, in addition to the *Fruits of the*

*Spirit* series, Cameron displayed *Light and Love* (Cox 127); *Contemplation* (Cox 62); *La Madonna Aspettante* (Cox 50); *La Madonna Adolorata* (Cox 48); *La Madonna Riposata* (Cox 51); *La Madonna della Ricordanza* (Cox 49); *Grace thro' Love* (Cox 57); and *Blessing and Blessed* (Cox 56).She also included another image called *Charity*, which at this point remains unidentified; though not explicitly one of the *Fruits of the Spirit*, this work could have been a re-titled version of *Goodness* (Cox 42) or another image of the Madonna.

Also in 1865, Cameron exhibited portraits of well-known intellectual figures who were prominent on both sides of the debate surrounding *Essays and Reviews*; she copyrighted these works, made them available for sale at Colnaghi's, and included them prominently in the second of her two exhibitions that year along-side her religious subjects. These included Jowett's supporters, like Henry Liddell, Dean of Christ Church; Henry Hart Milman, the Dean of St Paul's; and Thomas Hughes. Hughes still enjoyed notoriety for *Tom Brown's School Days* (1857), but by 1865, Hughes emerged an ardent supporter of the Essayists and became known for his volume, *Tracts for Priests and People*. This book erased much of the goodwill following *Tom Brown*, however, as critics either vilified or commended Hughes for trying to stake a 'middle position' between those attacking the Essayists and those defending them.[83] Hughes responded by insisting the Bible was not an object to be worshipped, but rather contained 'the highest of all truths', that is, instructions on how to lead a moral life.[84]

Arthur Penrhyn Stanley, Dean of Westminster, whom Cameron later photo-graphed around 1868 (Cox 852; previously unidentified), and Henry Liddell were two of the most influential liberal voices in the Broad Church movement. The two circulated petitions, provided moral support, and used their influence to increase Jowett's annual income during his years of persecution.[85] Both were also close to Jowett's fellow Essayist, Frederick Temple, whose essay, 'The Education of the World' also first appeared in *Essays and Reviews*, and who was assumed to be one of the group's organizers. Cameron took Temple's photograph sometime after 1866 (Cox 791) as part of her participation in, or exploitation of, the larger contro-versy. During Temple's sitting, Cameron took at least two exposures, reversing one in printing, making its identification unknown until now; she also produced a reduced-size cabinet print (Cox 839) for collectors. Like other images of public intellectuals connected to this debate, those who filled albums with portraits of celebrities collected Cameron's portraits of Temple, Stanley, Hughes, and Liddell.

Many of these men were among the 393 signatories to a protest against the prosecution of Jowett published in *The Times* on 4 March 1863. Other prominent 'free thinkers' who signed this petition included John Morley, then editor of the *Fortnightly Review*, Frances Turner Palgrave, author of *The Golden Treasury*, and Henry Taylor's associate from the Colonial Office, Herman Merivale, who had recently been appointed Professor of Political Economy at Oxford.[86] During this time, Cameron photographed several of Jowett's students from Oxford, notably Albert Edmund Parker, Lord Morley (Cox 716), and William Creedly (Cox 642, 643); two years later, in 1867, Cameron photographed Frank Charteris (Cox 631, 632) and Adolphus Liddell (Cox 704) when they accompanied Jowett to the Isle of Wight on break from the University.

Jowett and Temple became public figures following the publication of *Essays and Reviews*, and while public attention had died down in 1866, in October 1869 new pressure grew for Temple to repudiate his earlier free-thinking positions and disown his fellow Essayists if he wanted to accept appointment as Bishop of Exeter. Temple refused to comment publicly and did not republish his offending essay from the 1860 volume.[87] But once installed as bishop, Temple confirmed the Essayists' positions upholding freedom of interpretation:

> It seems to me that, whether we like it or not, we are of necessity involved in what Dr Arnold spoke of some years ago, – namely, the general discussion, all over the Christian world, of the degree and limits of the inspiration of the Bible. It is a question of absolutely enormous importance. The progress of discovery and historical research has made it quite impossible for us to leave it alone; it is forced upon us on every side. It is quite impossible that this great discussion should really come to a worthy end unless it is conducted with real freedom on the part of those who take any real share in it.[88]

Temple managed to maintain both sides, affirming his devotion to Christian religious principles without adhering strictly to the Articles of Faith; professing his faith in the Bible without following its restrictive laws; laying claim to the universality of Christian moral truths without denying that new historical research and scientific discoveries could undermine those foundations.

Like Temple, Cameron maintained an important equilibrium in representing both sides of the religious controversy, at least photographically. In 1872, for example, she photographed Leslie Stephen (Cox 758, 759) and Samuel Wilberforce (Cox 830, 831), who occupied celebrated, if opposing sides in the Jowett affair, and expressed independent public positions with respect to the role of the Church in the functioning of the state. Stephen, for example, had been ordained in 1862 at Trinity Hall, Cambridge, but left the Church when he began to doubt the literal truth of Noah's flood. Working as a journalist after leaving Cambridge, he argued unsuccessfully for university reform during the debates over *Essays and Reviews*. When he left the Church he no longer possessed internal influence, but in 1866 began to write articles on theological controversies, arguing on behalf of free thinking and discovery, the scientific method, and the value of a secular system of higher education.[89] Wilberforce, by contrast, who in the early 1860s was Bishop of Oxford and in 1869 named Bishop of Winchester, wanted the Essayists removed immediately from their posts, insisting that such men 'cannot, consistently with moral honesty, maintain their posts as clergymen of the Established

Church'.[90] Assuming leadership against the Essayists in the House of Bishops, he joined Pusey to censure Jowett and condemn the publication. Tellingly, Cameron did not favour any one side, at least photographically: she included portraits of both men in her pantheon. As Temple had avowed, the learned discussion about English national identity could take place only with the participation of all those who held a stake in the outcome. To some, however, it appeared the National Church had split; to others, the same Church was now 'doubly inscribed', a complex zone in which two contradictory attitudes inhabit the same space.

In early 1866, following her two exhibitions the previous year, Cameron wrote once again to her friend Herschel, continuing the intellectual conversation that she had begun in her correspondence two years earlier about creating a theological statement in photography. The two friends apparently had read a recently published controversial book by the Cambridge historian John Robert Seeley. Seeley's work, *Ecce Homo*, was introduced anonymously to the English reading public as a new contribution to understanding the life of Jesus. The book appeared in 1865, just as the controversy surrounding *Essays and Reviews* was beginning to wane. It came on the heels of Ernest Renan's *Vie de Jésus* and David Friedrich Strauss's *Life of Jesus*, which had both appeared in English late in 1864. By September of its first year, sales of *Ecce Homo* reached 12,000 volumes, a degree of popularity for a religious book unmatched since *Essays and Reviews*.[91] Unlike Renan and Strauss, however, Seeley avoided theological questions about atonement, inspiration, miracles, or deity. Instead, he continued the arguments about 'free interpretation' that Jowett and his colleagues had begun in *Essays and Reviews*.

Seeley wrote that Jesus was significant because he 'set the first and greatest example of a life wholly governed and guided by the passion of humanity'.[92] Although his stated aim was to reconcile the question of Jesus's dual role as divine and human, Seeley dealt principally with his humanity. In *Ecco Homo*, Seeley promoted Christianity as a belief in universal morality, devoting the second half of his book to the 'laws' that Jesus handed down to his followers:

> The *law of philanthropy* required that they provide generously for the 'physical needs and distresses of their fellow creatures.' The *law of edification* required that they both seek new members and guard the purity of one another. It thus divided into the *law of mercy* by which the faithful offered help to 'the neglected, outcast, and depraved part of society,' and into the *law of resentment*, which required criticism of the proud and the wilfully immoral. Finally, there was the *law of forgiveness*, which defined the way in which a Christian was to receive the treatment of others. He must, like his master, be prepared always to forgive and recognize that 'there is no injury so deadly but that it comes under this general rule.'[93]

To Seeley, religion provided access to a unique internal moral code, much like Jowett had argued many years earlier in his own book on St Paul. Above all, he wrote, Jesus intended his moral laws to be internalized, and Paul put them into popular discourse so that they could be 'written on the heart'. Following these teachings, each individual was expected guide his own internal moral life.

Once again, a controversy erupted over *Ecce Homo*. High Church critics, on the one hand, regarded the book with suspicion and hostility because Seeley deliberately avoided the question of Christ's miracles and divinity, skirting concepts like resurrection, atonement, and a second coming. One critic castigated Seeley as a Broad Churchman 'muddling his brains with the works of Renan and other blasphemers, … descending upon a sliding scale to the very depths of atheism'.[94] Others, especially Broad Churchmen, found his book a reasoned and non-dogmatic approach to understanding Jesus's moral teachings. Jowett's friend Stanley wrote approvingly, 'Let the "enthusiasm of humanity" have its perfect work … and the English nation would undergo a regeneration such as no critical discoveries could undermine, and no theological controversy could embitter.'[95]

But Seeley's work also drew criticism *from* both sides because it seemed like an apology *for* both sides: one reviewer claimed that it was difficult to tell whether Seeley 'was an orthodox believer on his road to liberalism, or a liberal on his road to orthodoxy'.[96] Herschel seemed mystified as to how to respond to Seeley, confessing this confusion in his correspondence with Cameron: 'There is a great deal … that I certainly would not have written', he wrote to his friend in September 1866; 'These chapters about the Law of [Resent]ment and about a man being a law unto himself – taken together, admit of being pushed to very ugly conclusions.'[97] But Herschel had been cautious, too, with respect to disavowing his support for or rejection of the ideas contained in *Essays and Reviews*: in April 1864, at the height of the warring petitions for and against Jowett, a group of London chemists tried to recruit him to sign a petition condemning the Essayists.[98] Herschel refused, calling the declaration 'an infringement of that social forbearance which guards the freedom of religious opinion in this country with special sanctity'.[99] Like Seeley, Thomas Hughes, and Frederick Temple, Herschel took what we might call a double position, staking a claim in two spheres, denying neither. These were Cameron's intellectual models when she created her own theological work in photography: by liberally interpreting religious iconography, by emphasizing the human over the mystical and supernatural, and by taking morality as her chief subject, Cameron infused her religious photographs with the 'freedom of religious opinion'.

## Notes

1  Letter from Julia Margaret Cameron to Sir John Herschel, 31 December 1864, National Portrait Gallery, London, NPG-P201.
2  Julian Cox and Colin Ford, eds., *Julia Margaret Cameron: The Complete Photographs* (Los Angeles: J. Paul Getty Trust, 2003), p. 76, n. 102.

3   The term 'practical' is used by Benjamin Jowett, *The Epistles of St. Paul to the Thessalonians, Galatians, Romans* (London: John Murray, 1859), Book 1, p. 239.

4   Joseph Leech, *The Church-Goer: Rural Rides; Calls at Country Churches* (Bristol: John Ridler, 1847), pp. 233–41.

5   *The Letters of Emily Lady Tennyson*, ed. James O. Hoge (University Park, PA: Pennsylvania State University Press, 1974), p. 149.

6   See Evelyn Abbott and Lewis Campbell, eds., *The Life and Letters of Benjamin Jowett*, vol. 1 (New York: E. P. Dutton, 1897), p. 323.

7   Richard D. Altick, *The English Common Reader: A Social History of the Mass Reading Public, 1800–1900*, 2nd edn (Columbus: Ohio State University Press, 1998), p. 390.

8   *Essays and Reviews: The 1860 Text and Its Reading*, ed. Victor Shea and William Whitla (Charlottesville: University Press of Virginia, 2000),p. 14.

9   Ieuan Ellis, *Seven Against Christ: A Study of 'Essays and Reviews'* (Leiden: Brill, 1980), pp. 183–4.

10  *Ibid.*, p. 117.

11  Frank Turner and Jeffrey Von Arx, 'Victorian Ethics of Belief: A Reconsideration', in W. Warren Wagar, ed., *The Secular Mind: Transformations of Faith in Modern Europe* (New York: Holmes and Meier, 1982), p. 87.

12  Thomas Babington Macaulay, 'Gladstone on Church and State', in *Critical and Historical Essays Contributed to the Edinburgh Review*, 5th edn in 3 vols. (London: Longman, Brown, Green, and Longmans, 1848), vol. 2, pp. 430–503.

13  See John Wolffe, *God and Greater Britain: Religion and National Life in Britain and Ireland, 1843–1945* (London: Routledge, 1994), pp. 31, 121; Olive Anderson, 'The Growth of Christian Militarism in Mid-Victorian Britain', *English Historical Review*, 86:338 (1971), 46–72; Richard Brent, *Liberal Anglican Politics: Whiggery, Religion, and Reform, 1830–1841* (Oxford: Clarendon Press, 1987); Jonathan Parry, *The Politics of Patriotism: English Liberalism, National Identity and Europe, 1830–1886* (Cambridge: Cambridge University Press, 2006), esp. chapter 2; Adele M. Ernstrom, '"Why should we be always looking back?" "Christian art" in Nineteenth-century Historiography in Britain', *Art History*, 22:3 (1999), 421–35.

14  Linda Colley, *Britons: Forging the Nation, 1707–1837* (New Haven: Yale University Press, 1992).

15  Michaela Giebelhausen, *Painting the Bible: Representation and Belief in Mid-Victorian Britain* (Aldershot: Ashgate, 2006), p. 33.

16  Mike Weaver, *Julia Margaret Cameron, 1815–1879* (Southampton: John Hansard Gallery, 1984), p. 23, original emphasis.

17  Carol Mavor, *Pleasures Taken: Performances of Sexuality and Loss in Victorian Photographs* (Durham, NC: Duke University Press, 1995), p. 47.

18  Carol Armstrong, 'Cupid's Pencil of Light: Julia Margaret Cameron and the Maternalization of Photography', *October*, 76 (Spring 1996), 114–41.

19  Philippa Wright, 'Little Pictures: Julia Margaret Cameron and Small Format Photography', in Cox and Ford, *Julia Margaret Cameron*, pp. 81–94.

20  'The Photographic Exhibition: Portraiture',, *Photographic News*, 8 (15 July 1864), 339–40. The Edinburgh exhibition was reviewed in the *Photographic Journal*, 15 February 1865, pp. 195–6.

21  Letter from Cameron to Herschel, 31 December 1864, National Portrait Gallery, NPG-P201.

22  Julia Margaret Cameron, 'Annals of My Glass House' [1874], in Violet Hamilton, *Annals of My Glass House: Photographs by Julia Margaret Cameron* (Claremont, CA: Scripps College, 1996), p. 13.

23  Coventry Patmore, 'Mrs Cameron's Photographs', *Macmillan's Magazine*, 13 (January 1866), 230–1.

24 'Fine Arts', *Illustrated London News*, 18 November 1865, p. 486.Cameron's repetitive use of Hillier was discouraged by Watts: letter from G. F. Watts to J. M. Cameron, undated, National Portrait Gallery, NPG-P215.

25 Walter Benjamin, 'The Work of Art in the Age of Mechanical Reproduction', in *Illuminations*, trans. Harry Zohn (New York: Schocken Books, 1969), p. 225.

26 Benjamin wrote, 'The audience's identification with the actor is really an identification with the camera. Consequently the audience takes the position of the camera; its approach is that of testing. This is not the approach to which cult values may be exposed.' *Ibid.*, pp. 228–9.

27 Hilary Fraser, *The Victorians and Renaissance Italy* (Oxford: Blackwell, 1992), esp. pp. 83–4.

28 *Ibid.*, p. 224.

29 Mike Weaver, *Whisper of the Muse: The Overstone Album and Other Photographs by Julia Margaret Cameron* (Malibu: J. Paul Getty Museum, 1986), pp. 24, 26.

30 Weaver, *Julia Margaret Cameron, 1815–1879*, p. 23.

31 As Weaver writes, 'bringing men to the faith' was an explicit role for Anglo-Catholic women; *ibid.*, p. 15. See also, 'Women and Anglo-Catholicism', in John Shelton Reed, *Glorious Battle: The Cultural Politics of Victorian Anglo-Catholicism* (Nashville: Vanderbilt University Press, 1996), chapter 10. Stephen Cheeke also urges against reading unintended meanings for references to 'the divine' in his 'Browning, Renaissance Painting, and the Problem of Raphael', *Victorian Poetry*, 49:4 (2011), 450.

32 William Thomas Gidney, *The History of the London Society for Promoting Christianity amongst the Jews from 1809 to 1908* (London: London Society for Promoting Christianity amongst the Jews, 1908), and V. D. Lipman, 'The Age of Emancipation', in *Three Centuries of Anglo-Jewish History* (Cambridge: Cambridge University Press, 1961), pp. 69–106.

33 On Hunt's religious pilgrimage, see Albert Boime, 'William Holman Hunt's "The Scapegoat": Rite of Forgiveness/Transference of Blame', *Art Bulletin*, 84:1 (2002), 94–114.

34 Quoted *ibid.*, p. 107.On Hunt's frame, see Judith Bronkhurst, 'Holman Hunt's Picture Frames, Sculpture and Applied Art', in Ellen Harding, ed., *Re-Framing the Pre-Raphaelites: Historical and Theoretical Essays* (Aldershot: Scolar Press, 1996). On Hunt's symbolism, see Linda Freedman, '*The Scapegoat* and the Story of Grace', *Word and Image*, 26:2, 142–9.

35 Weaver, *Julia Margaret Cameron, 1815–1879*, p. 15.

36 George P. Landow, *Victorian Types, Victorian Shadows: Biblical Typology in Victorian Literature, Art, and Thought* (Boston: Routledge and Kegan Paul, 1980), pp. 15–22, and Herbert Sussman, *Fact into Fiction: Typology in Carlyle, Ruskin, and the Pre-Raphaelite Brotherhood* (Columbus: Ohio State University Press, 1979), pp. 10–30.

37 Emma Mason, 'Tractarian Poetry: Introduction', *Victorian Poetry*, 44:1 (2006), 1–2.This entire issue is devoted to Tractarian poetry.

38 *Tracts for the Times by members of the University of Oxford*, 6 vols. (London and Oxford, 1833–41), vols. 4 and 5.

39 Joshua King, 'John Keble's *The Christian Year*: Private Reading and Imagined National Religious Community', *Victorian Literature and Culture*, 40:2 (2012), 400.

40 According to F. Elizabeth Gray, 'Keble's famous dictum, "Don't be original!" … implicitly linked originality – stylistic as well as doctrinal – with heresy'. See her '"Syren Strains": Victorian Women's Devotional Poetry and John Keble's *The Christian Year*', *Victorian Poetry*, 44:1 (2006), 62, and Duc Dau, 'Perfect Chastity: Celibacy and Virgin Marriage in Tractarian Poetry', *Victorian Poetry*, 44:1 (2006), 78.

41 Mavor, *Pleasures Taken*, chapter 2; Armstrong, 'Cupid's Pencil'.

42 Susan P. Casteras, *Pocket Cathedrals: Pre-Raphaelite Book Illustration* (New Haven: Yale Center for British Art, 1991), p. 11.

43 *Ibid.*, figure 47, p. 81.

44  Julia Thomas, *Pictorial Victorians: The Inscription of Values in Word and Image* (Athens, OH: Ohio University Press, 2004), p. 73.

45  William E. Winn, '*Tom Brown's Schooldays* and the Development of "Muscular Christianity"', *Church History*, 29:1 (1960), 64–73.

46  Frederick Denison Maurice, *The Kingdom of Christ, or Hints to a Quaker respecting the principles, constitution and ordinances of the Catholic Church*, ed. Alec R. Vidler [1842 edn], 2 vols. (London: SCM Press, 1958).

47  *A Kalendar of the English Church and Ecclesiastical Almanack for the Year of Grace, 1866* (London: Church Press Co., 1866). Beal's advertisement is on p. 39; Mowbray's on p. 27.

48  See Hélène Lafont-Couturier, Pierre-Lin Renié, DeCourcy E. McIntosh, and Gerald M. Ackerman, *Gérôme and Goupil, Art and Enterprise* (Paris: Réunion des musées nationaux, 2000), and *Fratelli Alinari: Photographs in Florence, 150 years of Picturing the World, 1852–2002*, ed. Arturo Carlo Quintavalle and Monica Maffioli (Florence: Palazzo Strozzi, 2003).

49  Laurie Kane Lew, 'Cultural Anxiety in Anna Jameson's Art Criticism', *Studies in English Literature, 1500–1900*, 36:4 (1996), 829–56.

50  Anthony Hamber, '*A Higher Branch of the Art*': *Photographing the Fine Arts in England, 1839–1880* (London: Gordon and Breach, 1996), esp. chapters 3 and 5. On the art unions, see Lyndel Saunders King, *The Industrialization of Taste: Victorian England and the Art Union of London* (Ann Arbor: University of Michigan Press, 1985).

51  Letter from Anne Thackeray Ritchie to Walter Senior, quoted in Helmut Gernsheim, *Julia Margaret Cameron: Her Life and Photographic Work* (New York: Aperture, 1975), p. 29.

52  See Victoria C. Olsen, *From Life: Julia Margaret Cameron and Victorian Photography* (New York: Palgrave Macmillan, 2003), p. 123; Brian Hill, *Julia Margaret Cameron: A Victorian Family Portrait* (New York: St. Martin's Press, 1973), pp. 135–6; Gernsheim, *Julia Margaret Cameron*, p. 38.

53  Jowett is recorded in the registry of the Public Record Office, Kew, COPY 1/8, 11 January 1865; in the British Museum, Cameron's gift was recorded on 12 January 1865. See Cox and Ford, *Julia Margaret Cameron*, p. 76, n. 102.

54  *Essays and Reviews*, ed. Shea and Whitla, p. 14.

55  Jowett, *The Epistles of St. Paul*, pp. 125–35.

56  *Essays and Reviews*, ed. Shea and Whitla, p. 135.

57  See Van Harvey, *The Historian and the Believer: The Morality of Historical Knowledge and Christian Belief* (Urbana: University of Illinois Press, 1996), pp. 102–26.

58  Homi K. Bhabha, 'DissemiNation: Time, Narrative, and the Margins of the Modern Nation', in Homi K. Bhaba, ed., *Nation and Narration* (London and New York: Routledge, 1990), p. 293. See also Edward W. Said, *The World, the Text, and the Critic* (Cambridge, MA: Harvard University Press, 1983), p. 273.

59  Henry Bristow Wilson, 'Séances historiques de Genève: The National Church', in *Essays and Reviews*, ed. Shea and Whitla, pp. 302, 294, my emphasis.

60  *Ibid.*, pp. 302–3.

61  *Ibid.*, p. 292.

62  Benjamin Jowett, 'On the Interpretation of Scripture', in *Essays and Reviews*, ed. Shea and Whitla, p. 519.

63  *Ibid.*, pp. 492–3.

64  *Ibid.*, p. 493.

65  *Ibid.*

66  Ellis, *Seven Against Christ*, p. 178.

67  *Ibid.*, p. 181.

68  'Abuse for Argument', *Punch, or the London Charivari*, 9 March 1861, p. 105.

69  Ellis, *Seven Against Christ*, pp. 184–90.

70  *The Times of London*, 10 February 1864, p. 9.

71 Jowett, 'On the Interpretation of Scripture', p. 478.

72 *Ibid.*, p. 483.

73 Peter Hinchliff, *Benjamin Jowett and the Christian Religion* (Oxford: Clarendon Press, 1987), p. 75.

74 Jowett, 'On the Interpretation of Scripture', p. 481.

75 Hinchliff, *Benjamin Jowett*, p. 76.

76 Karl M. Birkmeyer, 'The Arch Motif in Netherlandish Painting of the Fifteenth Century: A Study in Changing Religious Imagery', *Art Bulletin*, 43:2 (1961), 99–112.

77 Joanne Lukitsch, *Cameron: Her Work and Career* (Rochester, NY: International Museum of Photography at the George Eastman House, 1986), pp. 14–15; Weaver, *Whisper of the Muse*, p. 33; Weaver, *Julia Margaret Cameron, 1815–1879*, p. 31; Gernsheim, *Julia Margaret Cameron*, plate 138.

78 Weaver, *Julia Margaret Cameron, 1815–1879*, p. 32.

79 According to Weaver, 'A certain theological androgyny offered the possibility to photograph nude children, something that might otherwise have been taboo in the Victorian period' (*Whisper of the Muse*, p. 34). But if Ruskin denounced even the High Renaissance of Michaelangelo for debasing the piety of earlier Italian art, along with, closer to his own day, Edward Burne-Jones's eroticized figures, there would seem to be little room for such elasticity to relax criticism against Cameron's contrived biblical scenes. *John Ruskin and the Victorian Eye*, ed. Harriet Whelchel (Phoenix: Phoenix Art Museum and Harry Abrams, 1993). Carol Mavor has interpreted the photographs containing nude child models as evidence for Cameron's interest in sexuality and desire (*Pleasures Taken*) and Carol Armstrong as expressions of maternal identity and self-reflexivity ('Cupid's Pencil').

80 For example, the excavations at Nineveh caused numerous artistic and religious reinterpretations of biblical fact about the 'holy land'. Andrew M. Stauffer, 'Dante Gabriel Rossetti and the Burdens of Nineveh', *Victorian Literature and Culture*, 33:2 (2005), 369–94.

81 Ellis, *Seven Against Christ*, p. 40.

82 Shea and Whitla provide a chronology, *Essays and Reviews*, pp. 624–5.

83 Ellis, *Seven Against Christ*, pp. 131, 133.

84 Thomas Hughes, 'Religio Laici', in *Tracts for Priests and People*, 2nd edn (Boston, MA: Walker, Wise, and Co., 1862), p. 27.

85 'Jowett's Trial in the Chancellor's Court at Oxford: An "Obscure and Obsolete Process"', in *Essays and Reviews,* ed. Shea and Whitla, pp. 778–802.

86 See 'The Oxford "Protest Against the Prosecution of Professor Jowett"', in *Essays and Reviews*, ed. Shea and Whitla, p. 659.

87 Frederick Temple, 'Address to the Upper House of Convocation, 11 February 1870', in *Essays and Reviews*, ed. Shea and Whitla, pp. 684–6.

88 *Ibid.*, p. 686.

89 On Stephen, see Turner and Von Arx, 'Victorian Ethics of Belief', pp. 88–97.

90 Quoted *ibid.*, p. 89.

91 See Daniel Pals, 'The Reception of *Ecce Homo*', *Historical Magazine of the Protestant Episcopal Church*, 46:1 (1977), 67, n. 17.

92 John Robert Seeley, *Ecce Homo: A Survey of the Life and Work of Jesus Christ*, [1865] (London: J.M. Dent and Co., c. 1907), 150. See also James R. Thrane, 'Ecce Homo: The "Passion of Humanity"', *Encounter: Creative Theological Scholarship*, 34:2 (1973), 139–46.

93 See Pals, 'The Reception of *Ecce Homo*', 71, my emphasis.

94 *Ibid.*, 78.

95 *Ibid.*

96 [J. H. Newman], 'Ecce Homo', *Month*, 4 (1866), 564, quoted in Pals, 'The Reception of *Ecce Homo*', 78.

97  Quoted in Colin Ford, *The Cameron Collection: An Album of Photographs by Julia Margaret Cameron Presented to Sir John Herschel* (London: Van Nostrand Reinhold and the National Portrait Gallery, 1975), p. 142.

98  'The Declaration of Students of the Natural and Physical Sciences' (16 April 1864 to May 1865), in *Essays and Reviews*, ed. Shea and Whitla, pp. 665–6.

99  W. H. Brock and R. M. Macleod, 'The Scientist's Declaration: Reflexions on Science and Belief in the Wake of *Essays and Reviews*', *British Journal for the History of Science*, 9, pt 1, no. 31 (1976), 47.

# 3

# Grote's Hellenism:
# Victorian Parnassus on the Isle of Wight

It is to the Greeks that we turn when we are sick of the vagueness, of the confusion, of the Christianity and its consolations, of our own age. (Virginia Woolf, 'On Not Knowing Greek', 1925)

## Knowing Greek

Virginia Woolf and her sister, Vanessa Bell, owned most of the photographs that Woolf and Fry published in their 1926 book about Cameron. Although their volume reinforced the view that acclaims Cameron's portraits at the expense of her 'fancy subjects', Woolf and Bell preserved in their families' collections a number of allegorical photographs that were inspired from classical Greek literature. Cameron gave these works classical titles to signify their meaning and connect them to ancient Greek history or to the legendary figures described by Homer and Ovid. These works include *Sappho* (Cox 253), *Aurora* (Cox 380), *The Echo* (Cox 181), *Memory (Mnemosyne)* (Cox 467), *Cassiopeia* (Cox 339), and *Venus Chiding Cupid and Removing His Wings* (Cox 903). In tracing the provenance of these photographs, it is likely that they were handed down to Woolf and Bell through the matrilineal Jackson–Duckworth–Stephen family. But it is highly unlikely that Cameron's titles based upon classical Greek myths would have been overlooked by Virginia Woolf, who just prior to publishing the first illustrated book about her great-aunt Julia had also authored a provocative essay about the persistence of ancient Greek culture in English arts and letters. This essay, 'On Not Knowing Greek', is still powerful today as a meditation on the limits of understanding ancient literature, especially one written in a foreign tongue.

In her essay, Woolf wrote of experiencing a remarkable contradiction, a paradox expressed by her desire to comprehend ancient Greek culture, literature, and history, a yearning to grasp the subtle meanings of Greek beyond 'incongruous odds and ends'. In spite of this longing, she found her ambitions stalemated against the extreme difficulty of mastering the ancient language. In frustration, Woolf concluded, 'it is vain and foolish to talk of Knowing Greek, since in our ignorance we should be at the bottom of any class of schoolboys, since we do not know how the words sounded, or where precisely we ought to laugh, or how the actors acted, and between this foreign people and ourselves there is not only difference of race and tongue but a tremendous breach of tradition'.[1] Ancient Greek cannot be understood in the present day, she argued: it is unknowable because the space of time and difference separates the Hellenistic world from today and these distinctions cannot be easily re-contextualized without losing meaning and doing harm. One cannot look back into the ancient world transparently through an unmediated lens, as if that world were somehow left intact, and try to resolve ambiguities in usage or meaning, and come to learn, therefore, just when to laugh or cry when reading a text. 'The meaning', Woolf writes, 'is just on the far side of language.'

Importantly, Cameron's friends and contemporaries thought quite differently, a fact that Woolf understood well and satirized in her drama, *Freshwater*. In Woolf's send-up, Watts, Tennyson, and the entire retinue surrounding Cameron venerate the aesthetic influence of ancient Greece, and the photographer, too, finds its power irresistible:

> **Tennyson**: There is something highly pleasing about the death of a young woman in the pride of life. Rolled round in earth's diurnal course with stocks and stones and trees. That's Wordsworth. I've said it too. 'Tis better to have loved and lost then never to have loved at all. Wearing the white flower of a blameless life. Hm, ha, yes let me see. Give me a pencil. Alexandrines? Iambics? Sapphics? Which shall it be?
>
> [*He begins to write.* **Watts** *goes to his canvas and begins painting out the picture.*][2]

In her stage directions, Woolf might well have also written: **Cameron** *sets up the photograph.* Woolf knew that during the 1860s, ancient Greece was promoted as a model for British public life, influencing the production of literature and visual art, the development of school curricula, even parliamentary debates about the role of democratic government.

To the Victorians, the Hellenistic world – particularly that of the fifth century BC – provided important historical lessons about rational thought, ethical behaviour, humanism, and artistic perfection. Consequently, one could not begin teaching these lessons too early to children to provide inspiration and guidance, and in Victorian England, ancient Greek influenced the course of elementary school curriculums, where it was taught as an important foundation of civil society, literature, and politics. At Rugby School, for example, Thomas Arnold wrote of training young English minds to follow the logical patterns established by the ancient Greeks.[3] And in 1856, Charles Kingsley wrote a children's book to describe the debt England owed to the ancient Greeks:

As you grow up ... you will find that we owe to these old Greeks the beginnings of all our mathematics and geometry – that is, the science and knowledge of numbers, and of the shapes of things, and of the forces which make things move and stand at rest; and the beginnings of our geometry and astronomy; and of our laws, and freedom, and politics – that is, the science of how to rule a country, and make it peaceful and strong. And we owe them, too, the beginning of our logic – that is, the study of words and reasoning; and of our metaphysics – that is, the study of our own thoughts and souls.[4]

Kingsley's book, *The Heroes*, gained such favour in the Tennyson household that in January 1859, Emily read it to her children.[5] In 1860, in Freshwater, Cameron sent her fourteen-year-old son Hardinge across the green to Farringford so that Tennyson could tutor him in Greek. She regularly received Tennyson's friend, the Greek scholar Benjamin Jowett, during his Oxford vacations, often accompanied by several students who were also studying the language.[6] No evidence suggests that Cameron herself knew Greek, but as Isobel Hurst and Yopie Prins have argued, the extent to which Victorian women studied the classics and made use of them in their work has been largely underestimated.[7] In addition, a growing body of Greek works in English translation, especially after mid-century, opened up this literature to those unfamiliar with the original language. Lorna Hardwick, for example, has argued that 'there were more opportunities for those outside the traditional aristocratic or scholarly fields to publish' their translations, and Shanyn Fiske has expanded our understanding of how women attained classical knowledge outside formal systems of education.[8]

In fact, numerous English translations and adaptations of classical texts proliferated during this time. In 1861, for example, Matthew Arnold wrote that English translators should use the poetic style of hexameters, because he thought this style best approximated the original Homeric verse. Sir John Herschel, who preferred a less restrictive style, disputed those guidelines in 1862. The following year, Tennyson published his own Homeric translation into classical hexameters.[9] Around Tennyson's hearth in Farringford, statesmen like Gladstone, critics like Palgrave and Arnold, scholars like Jowett, and poets like William Allingham and the young John Addington Symonds, all gathered to debate these matters seriously.[10] As related by Symonds, their debates focused on matters that were both literary and technical, involved questions of meaning and interpretation, and covered such topics as the use of 'correct' poetic metre in translations of the *Iliad* and *Odyssey*, 'the proper means of getting a certain pause', how to 'give equivalent suggestive sounds', and whether certain lines should be translated 'Jove and Greeks', or 'Zeus and Achaeans'.[11] But these debates were not academic: rather, by studying the Greek language, especially as found the *Iliad* and the *Odyssey*, by reclaiming Sappho's fragments and learning from her lyric voice, and by studying Greek iconography and rediscovering ancient design principles as much as the foundation of Platonic thought, Victorians believed they could revive the ethos of humanism they associated with the Hellenistic world. Consequently, they were eager to draw favourable parallels between the values and wisdom of the ancient Greeks and the modern ideals that shaped contemporary England.[12]

Cameron produced photographs inspired by classical Greek mythology as a part of this process of rediscovery. Her photographs portraying Greek gods and goddesses, muses, nymphs, and heroines were made to portray modern incarnations that personified ancient Greek values rather than provide literal illustrations of specific scenes from classical literature. Drawing upon material from numerous literary sources, she also found visual inspiration in public exhibitions at the Royal Academy, the British Museum, and the South Kensington Museum. At South Kensington, for example, her friend, the Museum Director Sir Henry Cole had collected photographic albums and plaster casts of ancient and Renaissance sculptures since the 1850s, making them a staple of his acquisition policy. In 1864, when Cole accepted the first of Cameron's photographs into the Museum's collection, he had also secured exchange agreements with other European countries to help expand its collections of plaster casts, an increasingly popular attraction for museum visitors.[13] Cameron had access to numerous classical sources and did not need to reach back to the original texts of Homer or Ovid for inspiration. Rather, she chose many of the same ancient subjects that her contemporaries found inspirational: she portrayed Boadicea, the Iceni warrior queen, whom Tennyson fashioned an ancient prototype for Britannia; she re-imagined the fifth-century philosopher Hypatia, the protagonist of Charles Kingsley's novel of 1853 of the same name; and she gave human form to Robert Browning's poem *Balaustion's Adventure*, itself a retelling of Euripides' play, *Alcestis*. Among her contemporaries in photography, Cameron alone explored these allegorical subjects as a way to represent the presence of classical ideals in contemporary English life. Over a ten-year period, she produced more than fifty such photographs, using children and women as her principal models, returning regularly to this classical theme as a fertile creative space (Table 1).

Despite broad evidence attesting to Cameron's persistent interest in and reference to the mythological stories of ancient Greece, she never described this imagery as if it were interconnected, or intended to stand alone as a coherent body of work. Critics of the time generally thought these photographs represented only some vague and undefined notion of 'classical beauty', and, consistent with their preference for Cameron's portraits over her allegories, they viewed these photographs as if they were sentimental or romanticized genre studies, paying more attention to the erotic femininity of her models and less to the classical subjects or their sources. Cameron's own comments about idealized beauty also helped to dissociate this imagery from its classical roots, although Emily Tennyson's *journal* makes clear that the Camerons were often present at Farringford

Table 1 *Cameron's classical imagery*, organized by title and date of copyright

(Brackets indicate approximate dates for titles, or unidentified or unknown works; PRO indicates record in the Public Record Office)

| | Cox catalogue raisonné number(s) | 1864 | 1865 | 1866 | 1867 | 1868 | 1869 | 1870 | 1871 | 1872 | 1873 | 1874 |
|---|---|---|---|---|---|---|---|---|---|---|---|---|
| Alethea | 348, 349 | | | | | | | | | x | | |
| [Astarte]: French Gallery 1865 | ? | | [x] | | | | | | | | | |
| Aurora | 85, 380 | | x | x | | | | | | | | |
| A Bacchante | 512 | | | | x | | | | | | | |
| Balaustion | 202, 203 | | | | | | | | x | | | |
| Boadicea | 521 | [x] | | | | | | | | | | |
| Cassiopeia | 339 | | | x | | | | | | | | |
| Ceres | 350 | | | | | | | | | x | | |
| Circe | 983 | | x | | | | | | | | | |
| Clio | 255 | | x | | | | | | | | | |
| Cupid | 898, 899, 900, 901, 902, 956 | | | | | | | | | | | |
| Cupid and Psyche | 1070, 1071 | x | | | | | | | | x | x | |
| Daphne | 389 | | | x | | | | | | | | |
| [Diana]:Watts Letter 1865 | [522] | | [x] | | | | | | | | | |
| The Double Star | 860 | x | | | | | | | | | | |
| The Echo | 181, 182, 183 | | | | | x | | | | | | |
| Egeria | 379, 402 | | | x | | | | | | | | x |

| | Cox catalogue raisonné number(s) | 1864 | 1865 | 1866 | 1867 | 1868 | 1869 | 1870 | 1871 | 1872 | 1873 | 1874 |
|---|---|---|---|---|---|---|---|---|---|---|---|---|
| [Ganymede]: 1873 Exhibition | ? | | | | | | | | | | [x] | |
| God of Love | 879 | | | x | | | | | | | | |
| Hypatia | 469 | | | | | x | | | | | | |
| Marie Spartali as The Imperial Eleanore | 471 | | | | | x | | | | | | |
| Infant Jupiter | 892, 893, 894 | | | | | | | | | x | | |
| Infant Undine | 976 | x | | | | | | | | | | |
| Lady Elcho as a Cumean Sibyl | 216, 217 | | x | | | | | | | | | |
| Love in Idleness | 957 | | | x | | | | | | | | |
| Melpomene | 401 | | | x | | | | | | | | |
| Memory (Mnemosyne) | 467, 468 | | | | | x | | | | | | |
| The Morning Star | 511 | | | | x | | | | | | | |
| Mountain Nymph | 335, 336 | | | x | | | | | | | | |
| Oenone | 541 | | | | | | | x | | | | |
| [Persephone]: Herschel Letter 1866 | [528] | | | | | | | | | | | |
| Pomona | 346, 347 | | | | | | | | | x | | |
| Psyche | 249, [256] | x | | | | | | | | | | |
| Sappho | 252, 253, 254, [340] | | x | | | | | | | | | |
| Sister Spirits | 146, 558 | | x | | | | | | x | | | |
| Spirit of the Vine | 470 | | | | | x | | | | | | |

| | Cox catalogue raisonné number(s) | 1864 | 1865 | 1866 | 1867 | 1868 | 1869 | 1870 | 1871 | 1872 | 1873 | 1874 |
|---|---|---|---|---|---|---|---|---|---|---|---|---|
| A Sibyl (three versions) | 538, 539, 540 | | | | | | | x | | | | |
| Teachings from the Elgin Marbles | 1110 | | | | x | | | | | | | |
| 2nd Version of Study after the Elgin Marbles | 1111 | | | | x | | | | | | | |
| [Thalestres]:PRO 7/4/67 | ? | | | | [x] | | | | | | | |
| [Ulysses]; untitled portrait of Charles Cameron | 595 | x | | | | | | | | | | |
| [Urania]: French Gallery 1865 | ? | | [x] | | | | | | | | | |
| Venus Chiding Cupid | 903 | | | | | | | | | | x | |
| A Vestal | 182, 245, 246 | x | | | | x | | | | | | |
| Whisper of the Muse (two versions) | 1086, 1087 | | x | | | | | | | | | |
| Young Astyanax | 955 | | | | | | | x | | | | |
| Young Endymion | 896 | | | | | | | | | | x | |
| Zenobia | 544 | | | | | | | x | | | | |

when the assembled company discussed ancient Greek art and culture. Cameron probably knew of the sculptural casts acquired by the Tennysons in 1860, including the *Nike fastening her Sandal*, which was thought at the time to be a genuine work by Phidias, like the sculptures of the Parthenon and the Venus of Milo.[14] And she probably knew the original texts – even if in translation – from which she drew her subjects, especially the *Metamorphoses* of Ovid and of Apuleius, Homer's *Iliad*, and Virgil's *Aeneid*. In 1873, Cameron presented a volume of Apollonius that was produced in 1780 as a Christmas gift to Tennyson.[15]

Virginia Woolf recognized that Cameron's Greek subjects were made as a way to transmit the enlightened, democratic, moral, and ethical image of ancient Greece into Victorian England. But Woolf also wrote that efforts to capture Hellenism as if it were a 'lost original' could not be truly accomplished in nineteenth-century England. Rather, she argued that modern knowledge of ancient Greece was based only on pieces and fragments ('these few words cut on a tombstone, a stanza in a chorus, the end or the opening of a dialogue of Plato's, a fragment of Sappho'),[16] meaning that knowledge about the past was incomplete and unfinished, and could only be so. 'Truth', wrote Woolf, is always partial and imperfect. When reconstructing a nation's cultural history, she wrote, it is a fallacy to study only the parts in isolation, as if they were unconnected to the whole, as one might study Phidias in solitude in the British Museum, for example, or ponder the plaster cast of an ancient subject in modern London. Rather, for Woolf, reading and interpreting the past with a modern sensibility could lead only to an arrogant and false over-confidence, one that disregards the incompleteness of the original text.

Cameron's photographs of ancient Greek subjects embody the partial truths and multiple sources that Woolf found present in modern interpretations of the ancient past. Each of the photographs listed in Table 1 portrays an ancient subject that has been reinterpreted for a modern audience. As we shall see, each also embeds a complex literary and political dialogue borne of a partial text or fragmentary origins. In creating these photographs, Cameron was advised by three close contemporaries who helped her select her subjects, developing her Parnassus of ancient Greek subjects. These men also provided practical and intellectual guidance as she pursued this imagery: the painter George Frederick Watts generously offered Cameron practical advice on how to pose her sitters and compose her pictures. Her friend and neighbour Tennyson provided a flowing storehouse of literary and symbolic engagement with the ancient Greek themes. And her connection to George Grote, through his historical volumes that reinterpreted Greek history and myth, contributed an intellectual, moral, and political framework that supported her interest in re-examining the ways ancient history informed contemporary civic life in Britain. Together, these three helped sustain Cameron's commitment to represent classical subjects in photography, and consequently, these influential voices are the principal centres of focus for the following three sections.

## Watts and his 'teachings'

Cameron first exhibited her classical photographs in 1865 at the French Gallery, where she displayed *Circe* (Cox 983); *Astarte, Queen of Heaven* (presently unknown); *Urania* (presently unknown); *A Vestal* (Cox 182, 245, 246); *The Morning Star* (Cox 511); and two versions of *Sappho* (Cox 252, 253). Prior to this exhibition, Cameron corresponded extensively with Watts, to whom she periodically sent examples of her photographs asking for advice and support. Watts responded to Cameron with suggestions to improve her compositions, poses, and expressions, and also commented on her prints' tonality, shading, and framing. Many of these photographs were actually works-in-progress, but Watts clearly appreciated the unfinished style and sometimes-incomplete rendering or tonal fixing of the prints. Cameron had met Watts years earlier at Little Holland House and admired his paintings exhibited at the Royal Academy, many of which were based upon the study of classical Greek compositions.

When Lord Elgin brought the Parthenon Marbles to Britain in 1816, artists like William Hazlitt were overwhelmed by their natural depiction of 'veins, wrinkles in the skin, indications of the muscles under the skin'.[17] Without exaggeration, the Marbles influenced every aspiring artist in England during the time of Ruskin, becoming shorthand for human perfection and artistic excellence; prints, photographs, and plaster casts reproduced them in numerous ways. As a young man, Watts admired the Marbles too, but he did not wholly discard the academic approach to art favoured by Sir Joshua Reynolds.[18] In a painting of 1850, Charles Couzens depicted Watts contemplating an artistic problem while metaphorically drawing inspiration from a plaster Greek frieze representing a section of the Parthenon.[19] The ancient sculptures attained great popularity: in 1857, for example, Roger Fenton sold stereoscopic photographs of the Marbles on display in the British Museum, and published these photographs in the December 1859 issue of *Stereoscopic Magazine*.[20] In art criticism they were often used as examples of ancient naturalism, deemed superior to anything that could be produced by modern industrial means. Or they were used colloquially to represent an ideal of classical beauty, as when Ruskin visited Watts at Little Holland House in 1859 and came upon two of Cameron's sisters, calling them 'Elgin Marbles with dark eyes'.[21] It is not known precisely when Julia Margaret first saw the Marbles in the British Museum, but on 1 March1860, Emily Tennyson recorded in her journal that their neighbour presented the Tennysons with a gift of wallpaper 'with a border from the Elgin Marbles'.[22]

Watts developed an idealized signature style in painting and sculpture that was much admired by his contemporaries, one that drew upon the *Discourses* of Reynolds by combining the idealism associated with Homer's epic style with Phidias' practice of drawing upon nature; but over time, Watts's aesthetic priorities placed a premium on idealized form over naturalism.[23] Recently, Elizabeth Prette-john offered a revision of Watts's aesthetic choices, turning these apparent deficits into artistic assets. According to Prettejohn, 'Watts was among the first and most perceptive artists to revere the anti-neoclassical aesthetic of the Parthenon marbles in what might be called their translation into English – broken, frayed, detached from context – the state of ruination, perhaps, but also that of modernity'.[24] In this reappraisal of the artist, Prettejohn interestingly employed the same terms Virginia Woolf used to describe the difficulty of forming a coherent framework from fragmented bits of a remote culture and foreign language.

According to Prettejohn, Watts learned from the Marbles' fragments how ancient sculpture could come alive into a living presence through the practice of making art. In Watts's sculpture *Clytie*, for example, he could create a kind of modern metamorphosis, breathe life into inert stone, and in his painting, *The Wife of Pygmalion: A Translation from the Greek*, he could animate the living woman hidden in Pygmalion's statue. Both works, she contends, provide evidence that Watts regarded Phidias as if he were a living artist whose work was relevant and accessible to the present day. According to Prettejohn, 'Watts is willing to find the spiritual quality of the sculptures in their actual physical appearance in modern reality, rather than trying to imagine them as they might have appeared when they were first made; for Watts the Parthenon sculptures are both ideal and material at once'.[25]

Watts admired the symbolic solemnity and dignity of ancient Greek sculpture; classical titles provided his nudes with a mythological narrative and lent gravity to his genre studies. Watts also understood how he could borrow arcane subjects from the Hellenistic world, appropriating allegories to flatter his contemporaries as a way to secure portrait commissions. For example, in 1846, he used the language of classicism to appeal to Alexander Ionides, an early patron and member of the Holland Park circle, to commission a painting from him. To help seal the deal, Watts claimed that ancient Greek motifs would project upon Ionides's portrait noble attributes like heroism and patriotism:

> Some patriotic subject! Something that shall carry a moral lesson, such as Aristides relinquishing his right to command to Miltiades. Thus those who look upon it may recollect that the true Hero & patriot thinks not of his own honour or advantage & is ever ready to sacrifice his personal feelings & his individual advancement for his country's good, such subjects grandly painted & in a striking manner would not be without their effect upon generous minds.[26]

Watts offered similar kinds of classical 'lessons' to Cameron, emphasizing the gravitas of ancient nationalistic values, the human potential locked away in ageless stone, and the modernity of the old and broken fragment, re-envisioned in a modern and contemporary light. In gratitude, she commemorated his influence and encouragement in 1865 in two photographs of classical artistic inspiration that she called *Whisper of the Muse* (Cox 1086, 1087). Both photographs depicted

Watts as the central artistic figure in the composition; in one, the two children who represent Muses both rest on his arms, in the other, one Muse literally whispers in his ear. In a letter of 21 June that year, Watts praised Cameron for her study of *The Shunamite [sic] Woman & her dead Son* (Cox 135) (Figure 3), using classical references the two apparently shared, calling the composition 'wonderful[;] more like Phidias & more anti pre-Raphaelite than anything I have seen'.[27]

Two years later, in 1867, Cameron honoured Watts again in photographs she titled *Teachings from the Elgin Marbles* and *2nd Version of Study after the Elgin Marbles* (Cox 1110, 1111). In these two photographs, she posed her models in the manner of the Fates from the Parthenon's west pediment, as if animating the sculptures by substituting modern women (Figure 19). Soon thereafter, she presented both works in an album of her imagery to her friend Herschel. In 1864, in fact, she had written to Herschel using classical terms to summarize her artistic ambitions.[28] Cameron could have been emulating Watts's efforts to transform the ancient sculptures into contemporary women, using photography to unite the ideal and the real in one. Herschel later confirmed this impression when he wrote to Cameron about another classical subject that she called *Mountain Nymph Sweet Liberty* (Cox 335). This image, he wrote 'is really a most astonishing piece of high relief – She is absolutely alive and thrusting out her head from the paper into the air.'[29] Herschel's extraordinary comment is comparable to another made by Algernon Charles Swinburne after he reviewed Watts's entries in the Royal Academy exhibition of 1868, using similar terms. Swinburne claimed that in Watts's hands, 'a picture may share the gracious grandeur of a statue, a statue may catch something of the subtle bloom of beauty proper to a picture'.[30]

Cameron relied upon Watts to tutor her in the fine art of composition. In a letter of 1865, for example, Watts offered Cameron advice concerning a photograph she had called *Diana*, a work that has been unknown previously (Cox 522), but which we may now identify from Watts's verbal description and accompanying sketch (Figure 20).Watts wrote: 'The photographs come to hand to day[;] though fine in texture; seem to me to be less good than any you have done for a long time. I can't think you have taken a favourable view of the face of the young lady who poses for Diana, [but] avoid such arrangements of lines as these.'[31] To make his criticisms clear, Watts included a line drawing in the letter itself, reproducing from the photograph Cameron's sitter and her general pose, and added, for emphasis, '*I mean these*', followed by another sketch that specifically abstracted what Watts considered the disagreeable elements in Cameron's composition, drawing a kind of parallelogram as a guide. Watts intended these sketches to help Cameron improve compositionally in making later photographs.

In his *catalogue raisonné* of 2003, Julian Cox remarked that more than a third of Cameron's total photographic output consisted of portraits of women, and about an eighth of those remained unidentified, by which he meant the sitters'

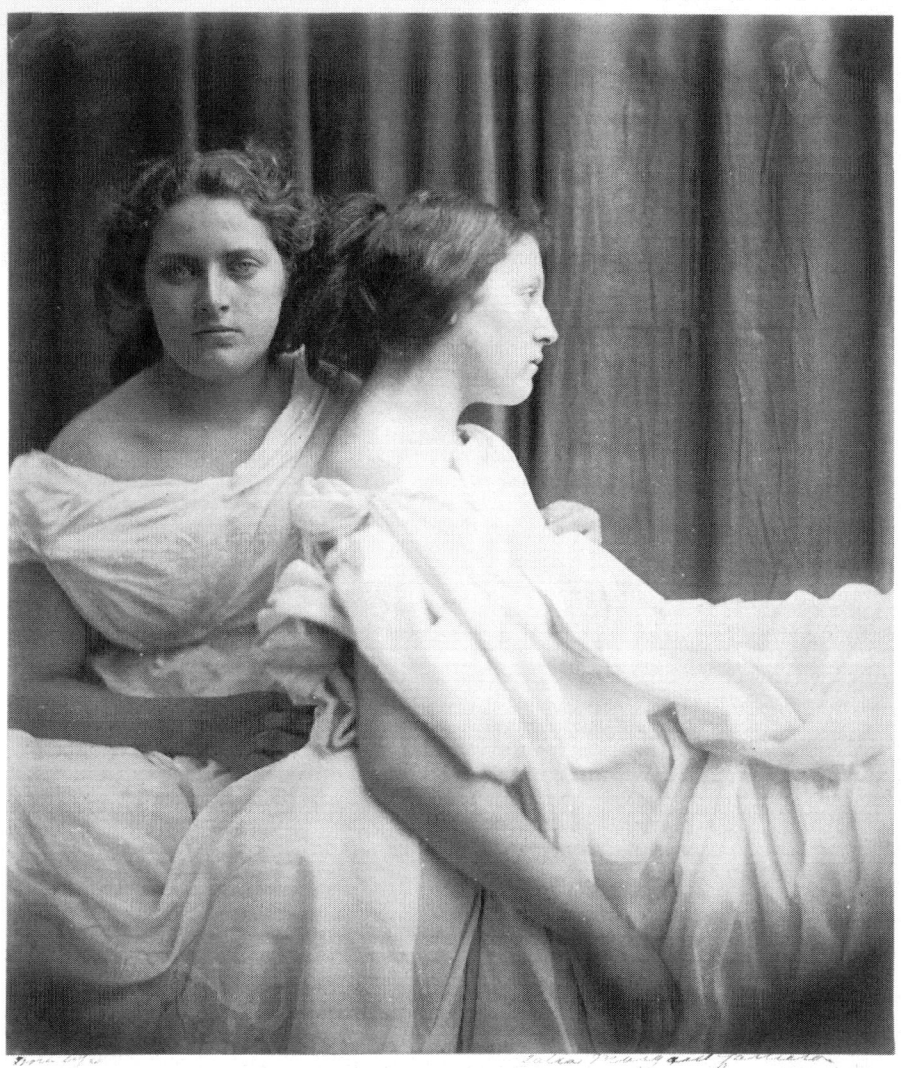

19          Julia Margaret Cameron, *2nd Version of Study After the Elgin Marbles*
(Cox 1111), 1867. Albumen print, 58.2 x 46.5 cm.

identities remained unknown, rather than the actual titles Cameron gave them,
although these facts, too, remain unclear for a large number of works containing
both male and female models.[32] *Diana* provides an example of one of these previously unknown works. While we might not know the sitter's identity, Watts's
diagram helps us identify the allegorical subject from his description and the

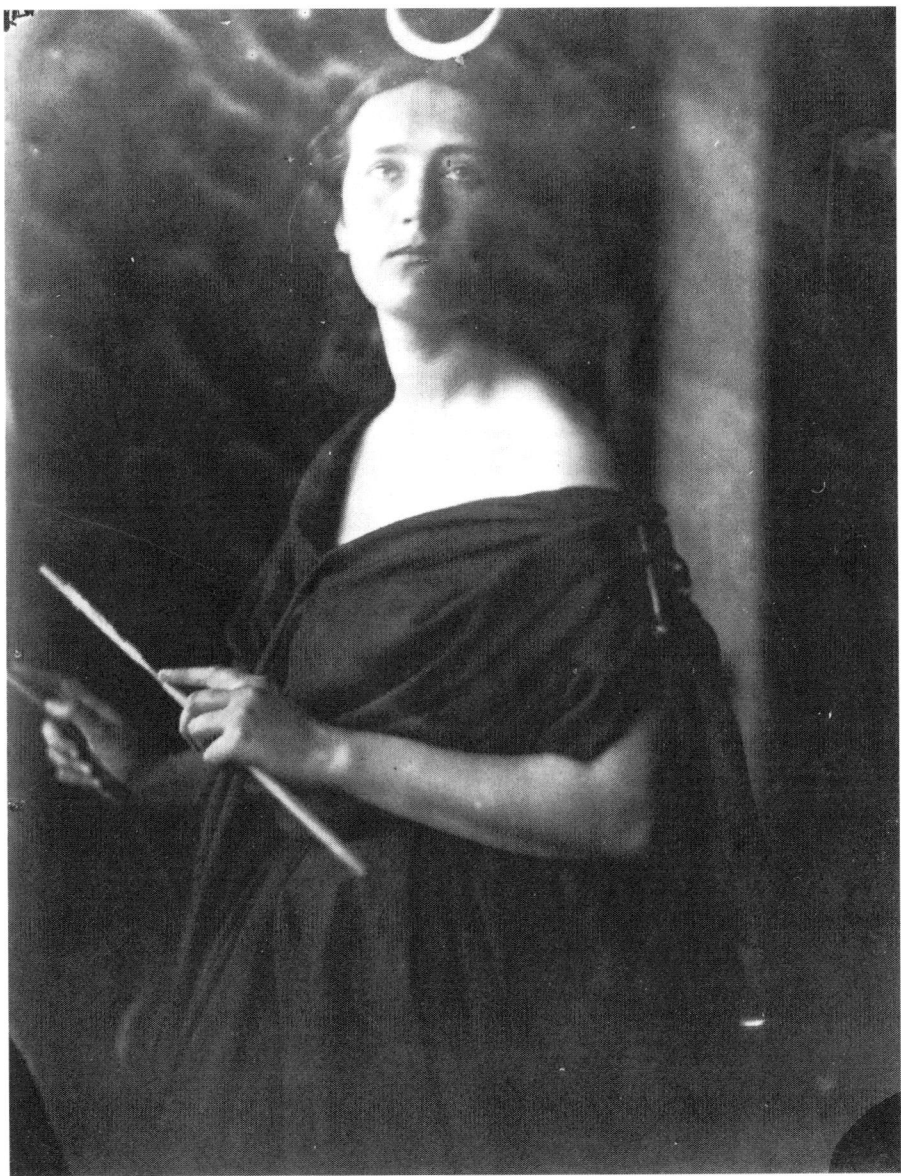

Julia Margaret Cameron, *Diana* (Cox 522), c. 1864. Albumen print, 26 x 20 cm.        **20**

traditional iconography associated with Diana since ancient times. The photograph portrays a woman posed in the manner depicted by Watts's line drawing, with her forearm positioned frontally across her torso, and her drapery arranged similarly to that in Watts's illustration. Additionally, as the goddess of the hunt, Cameron's model holds an arrow in her left hand and a bow in the other, and as goddess of the moon, Cameron's model wears a moon crown on her forehead; both elements are present in the photograph to confirm her identity.

A year following Watts's critique of *Diana*, Cameron created another allegory she called *Proserpina (Persephone)*, taking her subject from Ovid; she offered a print to Herschel for his evaluation. Herschel responded: 'Proserpina is awful – if ever she was "herself the fairest flower" her "cropping" by "Gloomy Dis" has thrown the deep shadows of Hades into not only the colour but the whole cast & expression of her features.'[33] *Proserpina* remains unidentified, and Cox's *catalogue raisonné* does not identify a particular sitter for the image. While several of Cameron's compositions might seem appropriate as a possible image for *Proserpina*, the date of Herschel's critique and its particular objections narrow down the possibilities to several extant works, all of which are rendered dark and in shadow. One, in particular, matches the deep shadow and 'whole cast & expression of her features' (Cox 528); it, too, is cropped severely, in the manner of a classical roundel. Herschel's allusion to lines from Milton's *Paradise Lost* (IV, ll. 269–70), in which Proserpina is described as much more fair than the flowers she picks, and to Hades himself as 'Dis', provides another example of the shared discourse of classical subject matter and literature shared by Herschel and Cameron.

Given the wide range of classical subjects available to her, it is apparent that Cameron decided to portray women and children almost exclusively. One cannot find any works depicting adult males as classical gods or heroes, either separately or together with mortals. Cameron's Parnassus was female and juvenile: her classical heroines included solitary figures like *Sappho*, *Daphne*, and *Oenone*; historical queens like *Boadicea*, *Zenobia*, and *Cassiopeia*; and children representing innocence, like *Young Endymion*, *Cupid*, and *Young Astyanax*. Cameron learned from Watts how to compose her models in a classical space and help them appear to come alive like the Parthenon statues; to turn a two-dimensional photographic rendering into sculptural high relief. She also learned to value the partial and the fragmentary, as when Watts praised her image of the Shunammite Woman 'with half a head'; in other photographs, like the *Whisper of the Muse*, Cameron accepted cut-off or partial bodies to help convey movement and dynamism. Finally, from Watts Cameron learned to portray the artistic effect of a naturalistic model, though detached and isolated in space: in Cameron's hands, Daphne, Echo, and the Mountain Nymph all appear to have just caught their breath, or, as in a painting by Watts, appear suspended in time, ready to leap out of the picture or endure some unforeseen physical change. Cameron's photographs of Daphne, Sappho, Oenone, Psyche, and Cassiopeia might all be called 'arrested images', much as Herschel uncannily described the *Mountain Nymph*; they are visual analogues to the physical metamorphoses their characters had endured in the original classical texts, caught in-between two transitional states, representing a moment of extreme emotion or physical and psychological transformation.[34]

## Tennyson and Sapphic desire

If Cameron learned from Watts how to animate the ancient Greek sculptures in the British Museum, her friend and neighbour Tennyson, who drew inspiration from ancient Greek poetry but refused to be limited by what he considered artificial rules for how to translate those poems into English, reinforced this important 'lesson'. Emily Tennyson recorded in her journal how Alfred devoted much of November 1863 to writing Greek translations, working on translations of the *Iliad* in blank verse and his poem, *Milton. Alcaics*.[35] In December of that year, William Allingham described dinner conversations continued over three evenings on the same subject of 'Classic Metres'.[36] Together with his poem *Boadicea*, which he had worked on since at least 1859, Tennyson published his classical 'Experiments' in poetry in the volume *Enoch Arden* (1864). To this day, Tennyson scholars are still engrossed in defending or challenging the poet for his decision to forego hexameters in favour of blank verse, or for what they deem the critical success or failure of his 'Hendecasyllabics' and his incorporation of Sapphic verse. But what is apparently lost in these debates and the disclaimers of the time was Tennyson's insistence that every translation after the antique must also stand on its own as a modern interpretation: as he wrote in 1865, 'I know my Alcaics were not exactly after the Horatian model but was Horace exact to his Greek model? Was I not at liberty to modify them to suit the genius of the English language?'[37] Later, in the 'Eversley edition' of his collected works (1907–08), he stated these opinions overtly: 'My Alcaics are not intended for Horatian Alcaics, nor are Horace's Alcaics the Greek Alcaics, nor are his Sapphics which are vastly inferior to Sappho's, the Greek Sapphics ... I have no doubt that an old Greek if he knew our language would admit my Alcaics as legitimate.'[38]

Tennyson's debt to Sappho has been traced to his early friendship with Arthur Hallam, and scholars agree Sappho's influence is clearest in his early works, especially his poems *Mariana in the South*, *Eleänore*, and *Fatima*. Scholars today also agree how, especially during the Victorian era, 'Sappho' as both author and subject became shorthand for unrequited heterosexual, not homosexual, love. In Ovid's 'Sappho to Phaon' parable from the *Heroides*, for example, Sappho's desire is expressed as heterosexual longing, as Sappho throws herself from a cliff in despair after having been rejected by Phaon, a ferryman who does not return her love. Following Ovid, Roman authors also transposed Sappho's desire for a woman into heterosexual longing and passion.[39] Yet Sappho's love for another woman is clear from her poetic fragments, and Tennyson understood her intent in this way. Sappho's verse, now called '*fragment 31*', provides an important example:

> Just like a god he seems to me
> That man who sits
> Across from you so closely
> Attentive to your sweet words.[40]

In Tennyson's time, these few lines were known by three titles: *Ode to Anactoria*; *To a Beloved Woman*; and, *To a Maiden*. The original Greek was known to contain several words with 'feminine signatures', which is to say, the ancient words convey gender specificity that indicates that the speaker and the object of her affection are both women.[41] Many translators reinterpreted this verse before it made its mark on Victorians; it passed through Longinus' discourse on the sublime in AD 250 and Plutarch's on the passions in AD 60. But Tennyson re-imagined the poem, starting with Sappho's fragment, which describes the desire of a woman who gazes upon her female beloved, but who feels excluded because that woman is preoccupied with a man. Tennyson then transposes the gender of the lovers. Instead of same-sex longing, especially in *Eleänore*, for example, Tennyson inverts the action into a male speaker's longing for a woman who is involved with another man.[42]

Sappho's survival into the nineteenth century and beyond came at the cost of suffering numerous re-translations and reinterpretations. As Yopie Prins has written, 'it is within the context of many versions by many translators that we can understand the fragment [31] to be "not one passion, but a congress of passions," carrying Sappho beyond the treatise on the sublime and into the long tradition of decomposing and recomposing the Sapphic corpus'.[43] Like the Parthenon Marbles that Cameron used to honour Watts's influence, ancient Greek fragments became sites of similar, numerous projections, representing 'not one passion, but a congress of passions'. For example, the pediment sculptures themselves were reinterpreted by the Victorians as the Three Fates; later, they were called the goddesses Hestia, Dione, and Aphrodite, and even later, the unnamed 'Figures K, L, and M'.

In 1855, Tennyson published his poem *Maud; A Monodrama*. The following year he enlarged that work in a second edition, noting that he meant by 'monodrama' a a modern type of poem that 'has been made into a drama where successive phases of passion in one person take the place of successive persons'.[44] In framing his poem using these terms, Tennyson put aside the questions of classical metre that occupied him earlier and shifted his attention to voice and expression. As a result, he updated Sappho's 'poetry of sensation' and her interest in revealing inner states of mind. Inspired in this way to make antique forms modern, Tennyson put into modern English verse what Hallam called 'sensuous perception'.[45] As Prettejohn writes, Sappho's second ode, *fragment 31*, was the ancient source that inspired Tennyson's highly emotional narrator in *Maud*. In this poem, Sappho describes the powerful physical and psychological effect of being in her lover's presence:

> Nothing see mine eyes, and a noise of roaring
> Waves in my ear sounds;
> Sweat runs down in rivers, a tremor seizes
> All my limbs, and paler than grass in autumn,
> Caught by pains of menacing death, I falter,
> Lost in the love-trance.[46]

Tennyson's subjects were Victorian, but his dramatic expressions were drawn from this model. As Dwight Culler has established, the idea of the monodrama and the poetry of sensation captivated the Victorians. Culler wrote that Tennyson created a new model that depended upon 'a solitary figure, most frequently a woman, who expressed through speech, music, costume, and gesture the shifting movements of her soul. That the figure was solitary and that virtually the entire text consisted of her utterance was evidence of an attempt to focus on her subjectivity; that she was feminine was a further indication that the drama was one of passion.'[47]

Like Tennyson, Cameron also chose classical subjects that allowed her to pose solitary female models to express an arrested emotional moment, one that simultaneously revealed 'the shifting movements of her soul'. An important consequence of this approach is that Cameron portrayed her heroines without the male protagonists that commonly accompany their stories: Echo appears without Narcissus; Oenone without Paris; Daphne without Apollo; Psyche without Eros; a Bacchante without Dionysus. The passionate individual, experiencing both discord and isolation, demanded solitary representation in order to express her subjective voice. Cameron's classical photographs also demonstrate sympathy with Sapphic verse; a 'congress of passions' is expressed in each image. In *The Echo* (Cox 181), for example, Cameron depicts her model turning within the picture plane as if to express her heroine's unsuccessful attempt to communicate with her inattentive lover, who gazes only at his own reflected image. In *Daphne* (Cox 389), Cameron narrowly confined her plane of focus so that her model's left shoulder would be blurred, allowing the figure's twisted movement in space to represent her flight from Apollo or the startling beginning of her metamorphosis from flesh-and-blood female into bay laurel tree. In *Psyche* (Cox 249), she portrayed her model in a melancholy half-slumber, as if awakening unsteadily as she did each morning from her nightly rendezvous with Eros, a more composed image than the provocative and untitled similar image (Cox 256) that portrays the same model as *Psyche* in a groggy state of *déshabillé* with unkempt hair and half-open eyes. In *Oenone* (Cox 541), Cameron imagined her character's pain, desolation, and hopelessness as she witnesses her husband Paris's cruel betrayal. Photographically, Cameron isolates each individual, the visual analogue of arresting form that ties her to Tennyson's lyric voice. As in Tennyson's poems, a solitary female figure expresses a moment of desire, longing, or extreme despair, an intense and dramatic moment frozen in time.

Cameron also created a number of classical studies that used the ancient Greek Muses to represent a succession of passionate emotions similar to those found in Sapphic monodrama. For example, she portrayed *Mnemosyne*, the personification of memory (Cox 467, 468) and mother (with Zeus) to the other Muses, along with *Urania*, the Muse of astronomy, which she exhibited in 1865, but which is now lost or unknown, *Clio*, the Muse of history (Cox 255), which she copyrighted on 16 September 1865, and *Melpomene*, the Muse of tragedy (Cox 401), which she registered for copyright protection in June 1866. Cameron also pursued this theme by portraying the female object of affection that haunts the unstable protagonist in Tennyson's poem *Maud*; Tennyson's unpredictable male narrator is by turns despondent, jealous, war-like, and melancholy. Cameron likewise represented *Maud* in a moment of melancholy (*Maud by Moonlight*, Cox 240), in a passionate daydream of her own (*The Passion Flower at the Gate / Maud*, Cox 386), even in a rare moment of self-possession and self-control (*Maud*, one of three discrete titles used for positive images from the same negative, Cox 255). In these photographs, Cameron used Tennyson's poem to represent the 'successive phases of passion' that describe his character's moods. Scholars have long recognized how Tennyson's interest in Sapphic passion aligns well with this poem, because Maud is both the object of the narrator's extreme emotions and the instigator for those unstable thoughts.

Cameron represented Sappho photographically in three compositions (Cox 252, 253, 254) that suggest the importance the ancient poet had for the photographer. For the most part, these photographs portray the *opposite* of unsteady emotion; they are dignified portraits that suggest composure, solidity, and self-possession. Although Cameron did not include a lyre as a signifying prop, she nevertheless portrayed Sappho holding a musical instrument in two of the versions in order to convey the lyric qualities of her poetry. In one photograph (Cox 252), her model, Mary Hillier, holds a pan flute; in the other (Cox 254), perhaps a violin. In the third image (Cox 253; Figure 21), she portrayed *Sappho* standing in profile without a prop, quietly composed, stately, even noble. Cameron gave a print of this photograph to Watts, with the appreciative inscription '*A gem for the Signor from JMC*'. To Tennyson, she sent a different image altogether (Cox 340), one that portrays Sappho equally well by depicting her model crowned with a band of laurel leaves, the traditional iconography of poetry and ancient symbol for Sappho. Tennyson's gift was not titled. It depicted one Mrs Keene, the same model who sat for the *Mountain Nymph* (Cox 335) and *Cassiopeia*, 1866 (Cox 339), but the allusion to Sappho is embedded in the iconography. Simeon Solomon, in his watercolour painting of 1864, *Sappho and Erinna in a Garden at Mytilene*, also used the laurel crown to identify Sappho.

These personifications were clearly important to Cameron, who, like Tennyson, cultivated a creative debt to Sappho; these portraits seem to elevate the ancient poet to a dignified place of honour. In addition, evidence suggests that Sappho also inspired Cameron to use the art of allegory to experiment with unconventional depictions of sensation and expression in photography. On the Isle of Wight, the ancient Greek poet was very much admired, and not exclusively for her metre or lyric voice. Cameron's neighbour Tennyson, of course, acknowledged his debt to Sappho in his 1832 poems *Fatima* and *Eleänore*, and

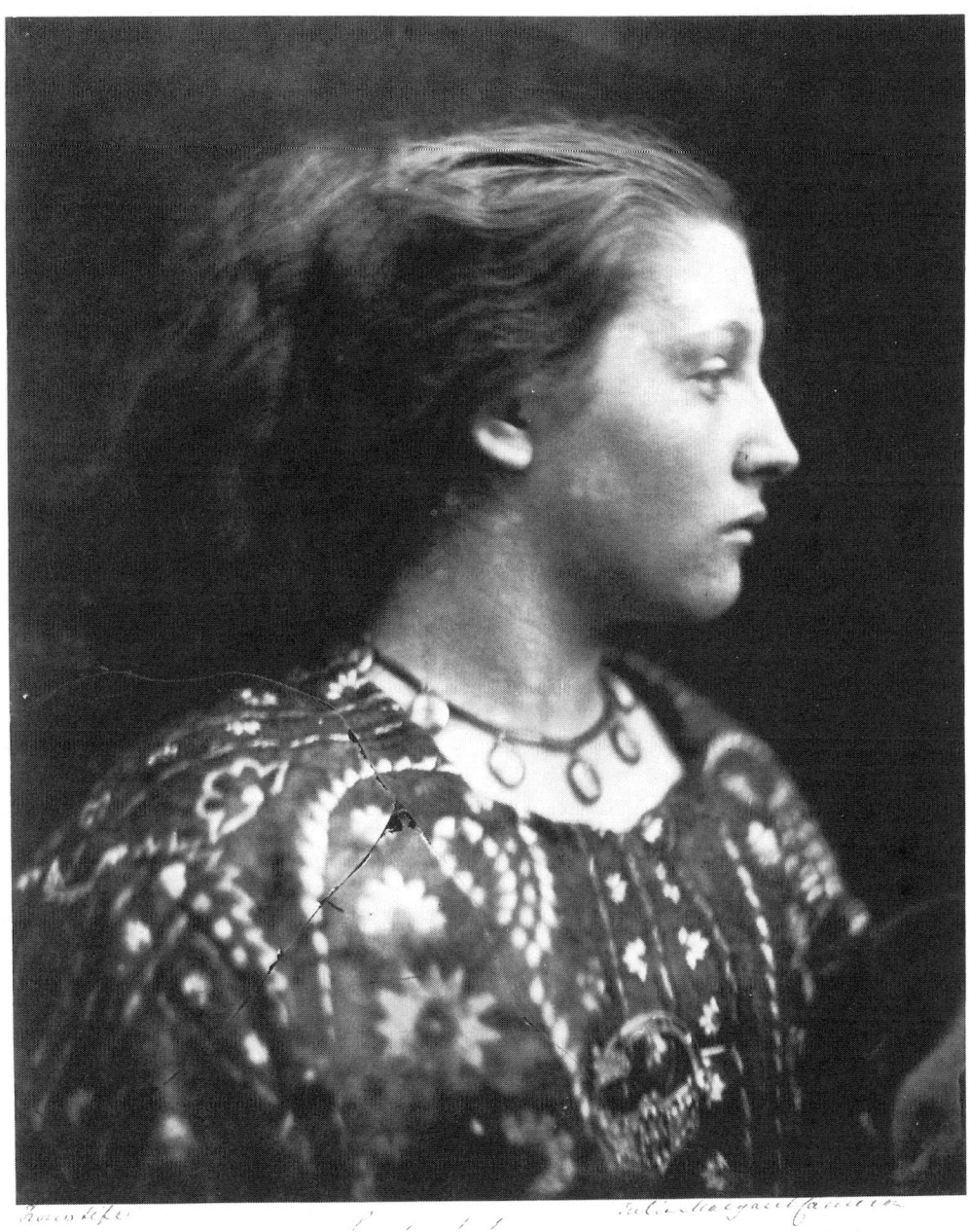

Julia Margaret Cameron, *Sappho* (Cox 253), 1865. Albumen print, 35.5 x 28.2 cm.    **21**

reiterated that inspiration again in 1842, when he reprinted *Eleänore*. But as we have seen, in these poems, Tennyson consciously turned Sappho's lyrics of female passion for another woman into expressions of male heterosexual desire.[48] In 1866, however, Cameron's other poetic neighbour, Algernon Charles Swinburne, bravely redirected the expression of 'Sapphic desire' back to its original female-centred object. In *Poems and Ballads*, Swinburne corrected Sappho's yearning as same-sex desire, and this precedent enabled Cameron to re-imagine Sapphic desire photographically.

Swinburne's 1866 poem, *Anactoria*, marks a turning point in the Victorians' understanding of the ancient Greek poet. In his poem, Swinburne imagined Sappho and her beloved Anactoria as passionate lovers, intertwined by desire and emotional need, consumed by the emotional fire of their mutual love:

> My life is bitter with thy love; thine eyes
> Blind me, thy tresses burn me, thy sharp sighs
> Divide my flesh and spirit with soft sound,
> And my blood strengthens, and my veins abound.
> I pray thee sigh not, speak not, draw not breath;
> Let life burn down, and dream it is not death.
> I would the sea had hidden us, the fire
> (Wilt thou fear that, and fear not my desire?)
> Severed the bones that bleach, the flesh that cleaves
> And let our sifted ashes drop like leaves.
> I feel thy blood against my blood: my pain
> Pains thee, and lips bruise lips, and vein stings vein.
>
> (ll. 1–12)

To Yopie Prins, *Anactoria* expresses an 'allegory of sublime rhythm', one that scandalized Swinburne's readers. She writes that Swinburne shocks because he 'doubles the pain and directs it both ways, like the verbal doubling in "lips bruise lips" and "vein stings vein," leaving us unable to distinguish any longer between "thy blood" and "my blood." Divided into many parts, separate but also together, different but also the same, Sappho and Anactoria embody the paradox of "flesh that cleaves".'[49] In Swinburne's verse, according to Prins, 'to cleave' means to join as much as to separate. Used metaphorically, the verb defines Sappho's rhetoric as much as her body, but also describes the generative and creative activities of the poet, the sculptor, and the photographer.

Swinburne's poem caused a sensation in Freshwater, which it would have been impossible for Cameron to ignore. Indeed, Swinburne laid the groundwork for Cameron to create a new homage to Sappho by depicting intimacy between two women. This is contained in her Elgin Marbles photographs, both of 1867, introduced earlier. Because of their unambiguous titles, *Teachings from the Elgin Marbles* and *2nd Version of Study after the Elgin Marbles*, the two photographs have understandably been directly connected to their artistic 'source' in the British Museum. But like the story of Pygmalion, whose emotional response to the sculpture he created helped to animate the lifeless form before him, Cameron started with the sculptural group but then nestled the two women into each other in her imagery. In both photographs, she costumed her models in drapery meant to suggest Grecian gowns and posed them in direct physical contact with each other; one model, Mary Hillier, rests into the shoulder and torso of the other, Cyllena Wilson. In the first image, the two women seem to communicate with each other as one whispers into the other's ear, while the other listens attentively. In the second image (2$^{nd}$ Version; Figure 19), one stares out of the picture plane to the right while the other engages directly with the viewer's gaze, as if unflinchingly acknowledging their embrace and intimacy. In both photographs, Wilson seems to embrace Hillier, as her left arm supports Hillier from behind and her right hand holds her arm in front. And in both works, their gowns fall away from their necklines to reveal their bare shoulders.

In these two photographs, Cameron depicted scenes of human tenderness and affection, frank sexuality, and arrested animation. By using the Marbles as a narrative setting, she made 'presentable' the image of two interconnected women for her Victorian audience because it was modelled on the familiar ancient Phidian sculptures. Solomon's watercolour painting and Swinburne's contemporary poem may provide a broader context for this Sapphic imagery, but in 1867, Cameron's photograph of two ancient Greek women embracing moved the image from documentary re-enactment to allegory. Under the cloak of allegory, she could portray the reciprocal touch of two modern women, their shared physical and emotional confidence, even their sexual familiarity. By framing this scene as 'inspired by the Elgin Marbles', she effectively distanced her subject as if it were a remote ancient portrayal, creating an idealized abstraction. Most contemporary scholars have largely ignored the physical intimacy between the two women, preferring instead abstract references to Cameron's 'search for beauty' or her commitment to 'high art', or have searched the personal biographies of the two models, one a housemaid, the other an adopted daughter, for clues to the deeper meaning of the photographs. Others have complained that the photographs were 'failures' because they tried to impose unrealistic ideas of classical perfection on real flesh-and-blood women.[50] But in using Phidias as her ancient model and her contemporary shield, Cameron successfully deflected any possible complaint about sexual transgression or erotic temptation, creating instead a sensual photograph inspired by classical form that was both humanized and idealized.[51]

Cameron's debt to Sappho, Tennyson, and Swinburne is also present in her photograph called *Marie Spartali as The Imperial Eleänore* (Cox 471) (Figure 5). Cameron titled this photograph after Tennyson's poem *Eleänore* at the conclusion of an extensive portrait session with her model, Marie Spartali, in September 1868. Why did Cameron portray *The Imperial Eleänore* in 1868? The poem itself was not much admired by Tennyson's critics or his friends. When first published along with other 'love-poems' bearing women's names, like *Adeline, Lilian, Madeline, Rosalind, Margaret,* and *Kate,* for example, Tennyson's friend Edward FitzGerald derided them as 'ladies' poems'. FitzGerald remained unsupportive when Tennyson reprinted *Eleänore* in 1842: he called *Eleänore* 'a bore' and derided it as appealing only to women who imagined themselves as similarly adored by love-struck men, mocking the idea that any of the poem's admirers would 'think herself the original of one of that stupid Gallery of Beauties'.[52]

But Cameron understood that Tennyson's *Eleänore* was also associated with Sappho because the poet infused *Eleänore* with Sapphic fragments that he used in earlier publications as epigraphs. In the final stanza of *Eleänore,* Tennyson transposes his understanding of Sapphic love into heterosexual longing:

> I watch thy grace, and in its place
> My heart a charmed slumber keeps,
>     While I muse upon thy face;
> And a languid fire creeps
>     Thro' my veins to all my frame,
> Dissolvingly and slowly. Soon
>     From thy rose-red lips MY name
> Floweth; and then, as in a swoon,
> With dinning sound my ears are rife,
>     My tremulous tongue faltereth,
>     I lose my colour, I lose my breath,
>     I drink the cup of a costly death,
> Brimm'd with delirious draughts of warmest life.
> I die with delight before
>     I hear what I would hear from thee;
>     Yet tell my name again to me,
> I would be dying evermore,
> So dying ever, Eleänore.

(ll. 126–44)

In Sappho's ancient poetry, the presence of the beloved alters the narrator's senses: sounds become muffled and eyesight grows dim; the skin burns and breath is caught short; the whole body trembles and shakes. Tennyson's narrator in *Eleänore* is similarly transfixed. But Tennyson also structured the poem to convey that its narrator can only observe Eleänore from afar, whereas Cameron's photograph portrays the direct confrontation between Eleänore and the viewer. In fact, in the poem, Tennyson's narrator is a wholly passive observer, emotionally removed but visually entranced, and becomes engaged only when Eleänore utters his name. But because Cameron's model engages the viewer directly, the photographer seems to have re-imagined the poem as a kind of Sapphic provocation, in spite of Tennyson's portrayal of heterosexual longing. As Elizabeth Prettejohn argued for *Anactoria*, Swinburne's Sappho 'betrays not the slightest awareness of the modern moral censure that would condemn her same-sex desire; she is tormented by love, but not by … remorse'.[53] The same might be claimed for Cameron's photograph of *Eleänore*: she confronts the viewer directly, unconcerned that she is the object of desire of an unseen admirer.

Two distinct groups of photographs emerge from the more than fifty discrete classical titles identified in Table 1. One depicts solitary and emotionally expressive heroines; many of these personifications correspond to Greek heroines that are also the subject of Tennyson's poems. The other group portrays a different kind of protagonist, one associated with action and resistance rather than quiet reserve and diffidence; these titles focus on ancient imperial queens celebrated in legend and history. This imagery includes *Persephone (Proserpina)*, queen of the underworld and *Cassiopeia*, queen of Ethiopia (Cox 339). On 4 July 1867, Cameron deposited for copyright protection an image she called *Thalestres* (Thalestris), the Amazonian queen of legend who was said to have wanted to breed a superior race with Alexander. Cameron's warrior queens include *Boadicea* (Cox 521), queen of the Iceni tribe, and the subject of Tennyson's poem of the same name, and *Zenobia* (Cox 544), queen of Palmyra, who, like Boadicea, fought off the invading Romans in her effort to defend her country's independence and preserve its national honour.

It would seem an oversimplification to describe Cameron's warrior queens as heroic, assertive, and bold and her woodland nymphs as passive, dutiful, and obedient, but this stark dichotomy effectively represents the double bind of women portrayed in the classical myths as much as it describes Cameron's approach to retelling those narratives. While all of these female subjects might be said to possess idealized feminine 'beauty' in some way, the warrior queens possess courage, learning, independence, and the virtues of heroic leadership admired by Cameron and her circle, including humility, selflessness, and patriotism. Above all, if Cameron's nymphs are mute, her warrior queens are boisterous and cannot be silenced. As Tennyson wrote in *Boadicea*:

> 'Up, my Britons! on, my chariot! on, my chargers, trample them under us!'
> So the Queen Boadicea, standing loftily charioted,
> Brandishing in her hand a dart and rolling glances lioness-like,
> Yell'd and shriek'd between her daughters in her fierce volubility.
>
> (ll. 69–72)

Boadicea is lioness-like, but in contrast, Echo and Oenone stand invisible in the shadows, demure, retiring, silent. In fact, in Cameron's photographs the mute nymphs come close to the impotent and emasculated boys: compare Cameron's

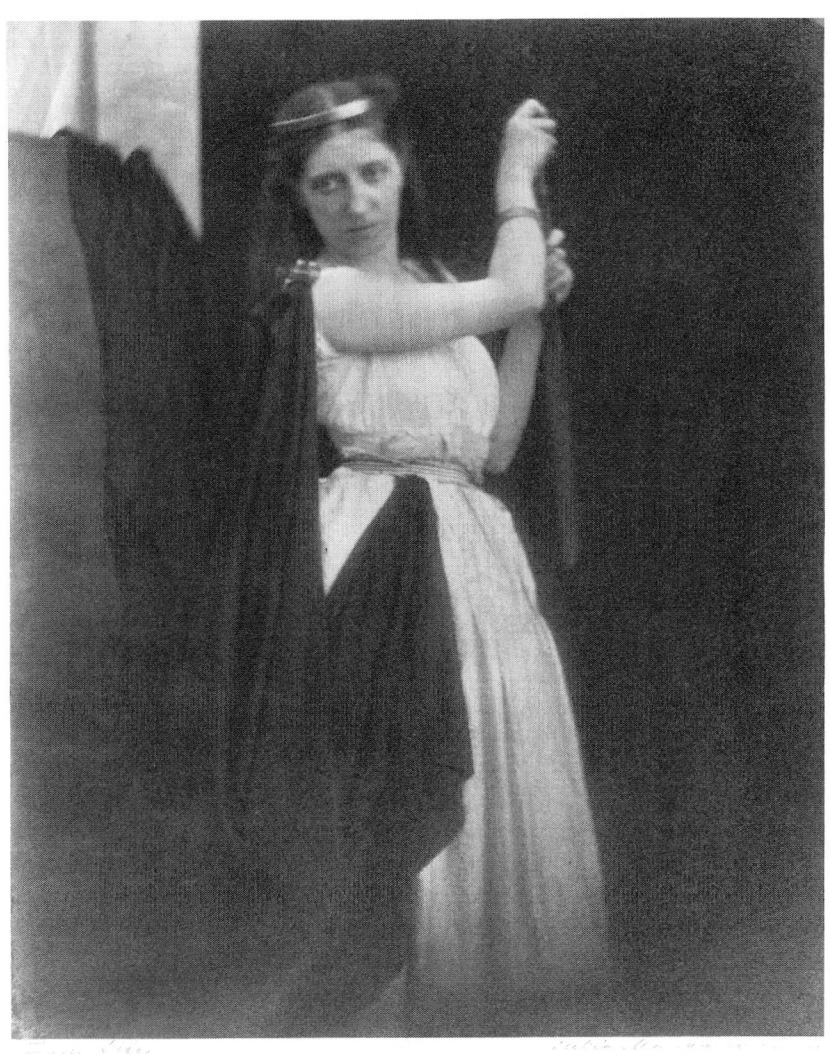

22    Julia Margaret Cameron, *Boadicea* (Cox 521), c. 1864–66.
Albumen print, 26.7 x 21 cm.

sleeping *Endymion* (Cox 896), portrayed at the moment he gets scooped up by the light of the moon goddess Selene; the chastened and humiliated *Cupid*, pouting at having his wings removed by Venus (Cox 903); the *Infant Jupiter* (Cox 892, 893, 894), imagined as a vulnerable child, incapable of expressing wrath, powerless to rain down thunderbolts from the heavens. These subjects fit a pattern of myths that were retold by Sappho in her poetry in which a pre-adolescent youth becomes incapacitated sexually or rendered powerless, or, as in the case of Endymion, is secreted away, never able to reclaim his independence or be reunited to human society.[54]

By contrast, Cameron's warrior queens are animated in their depiction of national pride. *Boadicea*, for example, is vigorous, forceful, and powerful (Figure 22): she stands tall and leans with authority upon a sceptre; she twists in motion in the frame, shifting to her side as if to address someone's presence; she wears a sober look of seriousness or concern; she stands poised, ready to roar. The legends of Boadicea and Zenobia were noteworthy examples of national pride, as these two heroines resisted invasions from outsiders: in AD 61, Boadicea defended the land of ancient Celtic Britain, and in AD 267, Zenobia defied Rome's central authority by establishing her own kingdom in the lands of the eastern Empire, including present-day Palestine, Lebanon, Syria, and Asia Minor. In London during the 1860s, the two warrior queens were symbols of female power and national honour fused together, and became allegories of patriotism that took shape in several forms. In 1859, for example, the American artist Harriet Hosmer depicted *Zenobia* in marble and exhibited her full-size sculpture in 1862 in London at the International Exhibition, which took place on the grounds of the South Kensington Museum. If Cameron did not see the work in the exhibition herself or hear about it from her circle, it is possible that she knew of the legend of Zenobia from other sources, like Anna Jameson's *Memoirs of Celebrated Female Sovereigns* (1831). Following Jameson's description of the typical iconography, Cameron portrayed Zenobia in her prime as 'Queen of the East', boldly displaying the elaborate jewellery associated with her pride, ancestry, and regal bearing, and free of the chains that would confine her at the end of her life (Cox 544).[55]

Boadicea also defended Eastern lands, an important symbol for an expanding empire that was rapidly moving east, even though Boadicea's Celtic tribes histori-cally occupied territories on the same English island. In 1843, the subject of *Boadicea* was submitted as one of the formal proposals for a historical panel in the competition to redecorate the Palace of Westminster, the same exhibition for which Watts had won a prize for his *Caractacus led in triumph through the streets of Rome*. Although the entry, proposed by H. C. Selous, was not successful, his depiction of *Boadicea* had a popular afterlife as a mass-reproduced lithographic print.[56] The subject was also popular in drama: in 1857, Sir Coutts Lindsay (Cox 707) re-imagined the story of *Boadicea* as a theatrical performance.[57] Lindsay's

*Boadicea* dramatized the queen as victorious by portraying her as brave and noble, especially in defeat, as she died honourably by defending her family and people.[58] In 1864, Tennyson recast *Boadicea* as a triumphant and victorious warrior who shrieks and roars, unabashed in her vocal, cathartic violence: 'Burst the gates, and burn the palaces, break / the works of the statuary, / Take the hoary Roman head and shatter it / hold it abominable, / Cut the Roman boy to pieces' (ll. 64–6).

Tennyson and Cameron both used Boadicea and Zenobia for their allegorical role in representing the defence of patriotic honour and national independence. Boadicea symbolically represents the presence of earlier empires on British soil and, Zenobia, the fragile détente that existed between Britain and its Eastern colonies. Both images, whether depicted in poetry or photography, provided inspiration to Britain as it faced an increasing number of economic and political challenges to its undisputed rule. For Cameron and her circle, these political metaphors were particularly vivid, the subject of parliamentary debate as much as continuing discussions in Holland Park and on the Isle of Wight.[59]

## Grote, Plato, and English politics

On the day before Christmas 1865, Benjamin Jowett arrived in Freshwater from Oxford to stay with the Tennysons, and on Monday, 1 January 1866, he read from the tenth book of Plato's *Republic*, the final story sometimes called the 'Visions of Er'.[60] Cameron was probably present for Jowett's reading and for the ensuing discussion about the fate of human souls after death. Cameron's familiarity with the works of Plato has never been discussed as germane to her photography, nor has her connection to the chief intellectual and political controversies surrounding the way Plato's texts were interpreted by her contemporaries. However, by revisiting a handwritten letter that was unfortunately transcribed incorrectly in 1975, we may restore to Cameron an important intellectual link to Platonic philosophy. By examining this connection, we may also contextualize her interest in classical iconography more broadly and explain how that imagery was interpreted politically. In a letter from Sir John Herschel to his friend Julia Margaret, dated 25 September 1866, the scientist wrote: 'I rejoice to hear that Mr Cameron is so much recovered and can relish his Grote on Plato.'[61] When this letter was first transcribed from Herschel's hand, *Grove* was misread for what was really *Grote*, which unfortunately deflected attention away from the influence of this important writer. Read correctly, this letter actually restores Grote and Plato to an active intellectual place in the Cameron household.

While George *Grove* was a historian of music, it was George *Grote*, the radical philosopher and utilitarian follower of Jeremy Bentham, former Member of Parliament, and celebrated historian of ancient Greece and Platonic philosophy, who was a long-time friend of Julia Margaret's husband, Charles. In the Victorian era, George

Grote gained notoriety as one of the most prolific writers on the Hellenistic world, interpreting its literature, moral life, philosophic outlook, and forms of government for contemporary British men and women. During the 1820s and 1830s, George Warde Norman (Cox 726), George Grote, and Charles Cameron formed close bonds as members of London's Political Economy Club. Grote's first significant books examining Greek mythology were published in 1846, and additional volumes followed these on Greek history and on Plato in 1865. In particular, his twelve-volume *History of Greece* (1846–56) gained the author widespread fame for his authoritative analysis of Greek history and literature. Scholars today have demonstrated that Grote's works were read widely among British readers and displaced earlier histories of Greece written by Connop Thirwall and William Mitford.[62]

In his analysis of the Homeric myths as well as in his interpretation of Plato, Grote drew attention to those aspects of ancient Greece that he believed were favourable antecedents to utilitarian political philosophy. He used Athenian democracy to inform contemporary ideas about the civic role of English government, particularly in relation to public debates about democracy, parliamentary representation, and the act of voting; these issues were deeply controversial on the eve of the Second Reform Act. Frank M. Turner described his influence: 'Grote championed the civic skills of the sophists, the logic and science of Socrates, and the searching examinations of received ideas presented by Plato's dialogues. Grote's narrative and analysis constituted a far ranging polemic in defence of free expression, intellectual individualism, science, and critical philosophy.'[63] If earlier historians had blamed democratic institutions for misleading or corrupting the Athenians, Grote blamed the insidious influence of ancient myths and superstitions. Much like Jowett before him, Grote believed that rational thought and dissent went hand in hand with good government.

Grote's historical research also argued that ancient Athenians were the first to establish the secret ballot. As a Member of Parliament, Grote tried to establish the secret ballot in England, a cause he championed throughout his life, along with James Mill and the Benthamites.[64] However, the secret ballot stood in opposition to the long-standing English practice of public voting, where individuals gathered at local meeting points called 'the hustings' and voted collectively by a show of hands. Grote believed that such public displays made it impossible for working men to vote against the interests of their employer while it simultaneously exposed them to bribes, corruption, and intimidation. But the secret ballot also had negative connotations in England and was not accepted until 1872, when the Ballot Act was passed. As Nadia Urbinati explained, attitudes of religious morality and national identity were intertwined in explaining this resistance:

> The secret ballot was associated with immorality (hypocrisy, cunningness, deceitfulness) and wicked habits ('servility, secretiveness, mental slavery, and effeminacy') – the same vices Protestant rhetoric usually attributed to Catholics. Openness, though, was identified with positive qualities in private as well as in public life – most importantly, with virility and 'Englishness.' The open ballot was associated with courage, frankness, and honesty, an attitude that crossed ideological lines.[65]

Ancient voting practices therefore informed contemporary political and moral arguments, often on both sides of issues, like Grote's defence of the secret ballot as a modern protection for the common man.[66] Grote's historical and interpretive studies were published during this critical period of national political identity formation and change, where among England's elite, Greek history was being reinterpreted to provide a cultural and political heritage of good government.

At stake for Grote was building support for representational government, especially in advance of the debates connected to the 1867 Reform Bill. In his essays, he reinterpreted the role of the ancient sophists by directly contradicting earlier British historians who associated them with deceit and cunning. To Grote, the sophists made democratic political activity truly possible because they trained the Athenians in the art of rhetoric, championing free discussion and logical argument, free thought, and the value of dissent:

> Democracy in Grecian antiquity possessed the privilege, not only of kindling an earnest and unanimous attachment to the constitution in the bosoms of the citizens, but also of creating an energy of public and private action such as could never be obtained under an oligarchy, where the utmost that could be hoped for was a passive acquiescence and obedience [...] [In the year 500 BC, among the communities of ancient Greece, theories of government] were connected with emotions of the strongest as well as of the most opposite character. The theory of a permanent ruling One, for example, was universally odious; that of a ruling Few, though acquiesced in, was never positively attractive, unless either where it was associated with the maintenance of peculiar education and habits, as at Sparta, or where it presented itself as the only antithesis to democracy [...] But the theory of democracy was pre-eminently seductive; creating in the mass of the citizens an intense political attachment, and disposing them to voluntary action and suffering on its behalf, such as no coercion on the part of other governments could entail.[67]

Grote's radicalism regarded the Homeric monarchs negatively; he called them absolute rulers who allowed the few to run roughshod over the interests of the many. Grote put his faith instead in the ideal of participatory democracy that was promised in the Athenian constitution.

In the book on Plato that Cameron shared with Herschel, Grote wrote that Socratic scepticism was a hallmark of personal and social freedom in the ancient world and provided an essential moral guide that was still relevant to the

Victorian present. Grote's interpretation of Plato advanced the ancient principle of the integrity of an individual's freedom and independence, where 'man is the measure of all things' and possessed an inherent ability to reason and master the complexities of his world. Grote termed this concept 'reasoned truth' and called it the moral foundation from which common people could challenge the elite status of kings, priests, and judges. Socrates embodied such anti-authoritarian principles, wrote Grote; the ancient philosopher was the champion of 'free argumentative discussion', even when facing death:

> Freedom of debate and fullness of search, the paramount value of 'reasoned truth' – the necessity of keeping up the force of individual reason by constant argumentative exercise – and the right of independent judgment for hearer as well as speaker – stand emphatically proclaimed in [the] last words of the dying philosopher [...] His devotion is to 'reasoned truth;' he challenges his friends to the fullest scrutiny by their own independent reason; he recognizes the sentence that they pronounce afterwards as valid for them, whether concurrent with himself or adverse. Their reason is for them what his reason is for him; requiring, both alike (Sokrates here proclaims) to be stimulated as well as controlled by all-searching debate, but postulating equal liberty of final decision for each one of the debaters.[68]

Grote therefore enlisted Plato to attack the orthodox doctrines of the High Church and the interests of the elite in government, two of the dominant social institutions that he considered responsible for crushing the individual under the weight of the group, where tradition and superstition guided the actions of men in power, in opposition to 'reasoned truth'.

Of course Grote had his detractors, including Gladstone, then Chancellor of the Exchequer, and even Benjamin Jowett, who settled into his professorship at Oxford in the wake of the *Essays and Reviews* controversy by focusing almost exclusively on translating and reinterpreting Plato. In 1867, Gladstone followed Grote's lead by looking back to ancient Greece for a model to extend national voting rights, but he also tempered Grote by refusing to challenge the patriarchy embedded in common practice. Gladstone interpreted the Homeric Council, for example, as a kind of benevolent assembly that was characterized by collective decision-making and wise legislation, an interpretation that Grote rejected.[69] By 1869, after the Reform Bill had passed and his first term as Prime Minister had begun, Gladstone extended this historical analysis by uniting the history of the Homeric and British governments. He claimed the best civic institutions produced by both systems had fostered 'the hatred, not only of tyranny, but of all unlimited power; the love and the habit of public in preference to secret action; the reconciliation and harmony between the spirit of freedom on the one hand, the spirit of order and reverence on the other ... Of these elements,' concluded Gladstone, 'whether in ancient or in modern times, great governments have been made.'[70]

Unlike Gladstone, Jowett did not hold a governmental post and was not compelled to find a rationale in ancient Greek philosophy to justify trust in governmental authority. At Oxford, Jowett found in Plato a historical surrogate for his approach to the high moralism of Christianity. According to Frank Turner, 'Jowett and others after him reinterpreted Christianity to mesh with Plato and Plato to mesh with Christianity and both to mesh with polite Anglicanism, moderate social hierarchy, a strong state, and a sense of shared community.'[71] Jowett worked at his translation and interpretation of Plato for almost ten years, finally publishing *Dialogues of Plato, translated into English with analyses and introductions*, in 1871. At Oxford, Jowett helped to educate future leaders of the British government, notably those men who would rule the colonies. His influential comments about the limits and 'proper role' of government are significant, especially in relation to the 1865 rebellion in Jamaica, a conflict that raised deep divisions in England about the nature of imperial rule, the responsibilities of the law in response to civil disobedience, and the relation of the colonized to the imperial centre. In addition, it was Cameron's close friend, Henry Taylor, a regular visitor to the Isle of Wight, who occupied a key position in the Colonial Office at the time, and whose chief role was to oversee the relationship between the island colony and London; he had been one of the architects responsible for making Jamaica a crown colony.[72] In principle, under Taylor's leadership, the Colonial Office maintained high democratic ideals related to Jamaica's governance, but in practice, the laws it imposed helped the small number of European colonists maintain tight economic and social control over the largely Creole population.[73]

It is fascinating to see how Jowett considered the role of the 'ideal statesman' in his book on Plato, written in the aftermath of Morant Bay, and in the context of discussing statesmanship with Henry Taylor during his visits to the Camerons and Tennysons on the Isle of Wight. To Jowett, the role of the statesman was perfectly illustrated by the ancient Greeks' practice that connected their politics to their philosophy; he believed this a suitable model that could provide enlightened moral guidance to present-day Victorians:

> A true statesman is he who brings order out of disorder; who first organizes and then administers the government of his own country; and having made a nation, seeks to reconcile the national interests with those of Europe and of mankind. He is not a mere theorist, not yet a dealer in expedients; the whole and the parts grow together in his mind; while the head is conceiving, the hand is executing. Although obliged to descend to the world, he is not of the world. His thoughts are fixed not on power or riches or extension of territory, but on an ideal state, in which all the citizens have an equal chance of health and life, and the highest education is within the reach of all, and the moral and intellectual qualities of every individual are freely developed, and the 'idea of good' is the animating principle of the whole. Not the attainment of freedom alone, or of order alone, but how to unite freedom with order is the problem which he has to solve.[74]

Like Grote and Gladstone, Jowett also wanted to reinterpret Platonic thought to help legitimize contemporary political positions that extended Britain's imperial reach around the globe. Unlike Grote, however, Jowett used Plato to promote the idea that free thought and action was made possible by benevolent civic law. Social equilibrium could be achieved when those laws maintained order and stability. In this way, Jowett endorsed the principle of providing broad opportunities for everyone in society to prosper. These ideas were consistent with those of others in Cameron's intellectual and artistic circle, especially Matthew Arnold.

Arnold lectured and wrote on matters connected to the neo-Hellenic revival after 1860. As a young man, he was convinced that social discord could be disciplined and tamed when people were in close contact to a nation's dominant culture, or as he framed it, 'the best that has been thought and said in the world'. He advanced these ideas in his essay of 1867 on 'Culture and its Enemies', and after responding to friendly criticism from Henry Sidgwick in Cambridge and Frederic Harrison in Oxford, he broadened these ideas to produce *Culture and Anarchy* in 1869. In this influential volume, Arnold argued that nations like England, composed of a widely different class structure, must strive to attain social harmony; he believed this could be achieved by righting what he called the historic balance of Hellenic (Indo-European) and Hebraic (Semitic) influences in society. *Culture and Anarchy* argued that conscientious reasoning and scepticism (what Arnold called the 'strictness of conscience' found in Platonic thought and Hellenism) must be balanced by civic rules that emphasized constructive conduct and action (what he termed the 'spontaneity of consciousness' associated with Hebraism); in proper balance, he reasoned, democratic institutions would function well in the modern world. For Arnold, achieving this ideal balance (what he also called the 'sweetness and light' of culture) could be realized only when government was trusted to advance the 'best interests' of society. It was in the modern state, according to Arnold, that individuals could find 'the nation in its collective and corporate character, entrusted with stringent powers for the general advantage, and controlling individual wills in the name of an interest wider than that of individuals'.[75] In 1869 in England, where demonstrations and strikes marked an incipient political hostility between wealthy and working classes, many feared that a disastrous social impasse was also emerging. In response, Arnold wrote that the only viable positive solution was to trust government to provide stability.[76] To Arnold, scepticism, free thinking, and 'doing as one likes' ultimately threatened to crush democratic values. Only by vanquishing all threats to cultural instability could he imagine the social order of the status quo maintained.[77]

Unlike Arnold, Julia Margaret Cameron was not entirely bound to the classical ideal; nor was she unreservedly obedient and 'loyal' to the construction of the patriarchal British nation, as demonstrated by her photographs of ancient Greek subjects. Like Jowett's conception of an 'ideal state' that united freedom and order, and Arnold's, which endorsed an idea of 'culture' that could represent all established social interests, Cameron's photographs embodied the moral and social questions that were the focus of this intellectual community. Consequently, she used the ancient Greek myths allegorically to represent the nation's historical identity. But it was chiefly Grote, whose work she discussed with Herschel and very likely her husband Charles, his *History of Greece* outlining the key opposing positions about the ancient legends, who actually described what was at stake for Victorians. Grote stated outright, for example, that the Homeric myths were not to be taken literally at all, but instead were 'stories [to be] accepted as realities ... for the purpose of calling forth sympathy, emotion, or reverence'. As Turner wrote, 'the *Iliad* and the *Odyssey* had furnished the Greeks of the classical age, as the Old Testament had similarly provided later generations of Hebrews, with myths, heroes, and historical narratives wherein lay both a store of moral precepts and the foundation of a sense of cultural unity'.[78] Grote's chief contribution to the identity formation of the nation, then, was to have made sense out of the magical realism of gods and superheroes, helping to differentiate between facts and feelings, rationality and the supernatural, and to have theorized a political reason for their literary creation in the first place. In Grote's words,

> The Aeolic or Ionic colonists, to whom the *Iliad* was addressed, neither saw nor wished to see, in the past, men of their own stature and proportions ... Such narratives presuppose a certain thirst of rational curiosity – a sentiment which had not yet been aroused among the hearers of the ancient epic. To captivate their emotions as well as to win their belief, you must address to them legends, of which the foundation is already laid in their religious feelings; ... legends cast back into an undefined past, the interval between which and the present no one then cares to fathom[79]

Grote's analysis laid an important foundation for analysing the ancient Greek legends as literary forms, historical narratives, and collective memories. He reinterpreted their appearance in various artistic forms as a way to acknowledge their importance to earlier civilizations while interrogating their impact in modern cultural life. Like Grote, Jowett taught lessons from the ancient Greek myths to explain Platonic thought. When he read the 'Vision of Er' to the Tennysons and their guests on New Year's Day 1866, he had to explain this myth in terms of its purpose in the *Republic* as an otherworldly explanation for justice, as his intention was not to scare them with a tale of ghostly reincarnation. Socrates used this myth to teach his listeners that the practice of justice generates great and unexpected rewards for the just, but also to remind them that the practice of just behaviour was not an abstraction; rather, it must be accompanied by practical knowledge. Jowett would have used Plato to express the view that only by pursuing philosophy can individuals reconcile their present lives; only in the present can the soul find peace. Steeped in these intellectual and philosophical

approaches to interpreting the ancient Greek past, Cameron portrayed new interpretations of *Hypatia*, *Balaustion*, and *Ulysses*.

## Platonic redemption: *Hypatia, Balaustion, Ulysses*

Cameron's familiarity with Grote's arguments provided an essential critical and
historical context for her artistic practice, demonstrating how Hellenistic themes
could be projected onto contemporary politics and bring about historical revision
and political change. For Cameron, matters like honour and integrity, the moral
forces that supported enlightened governance, the use of force for peace and
national defence, and the independent feminine role in society, all influenced her
decision to choose specific classical subjects. At the same time, the interpretations
of Plato that emerged during the 1860s by Grote, Jowett, Mill, and Arnold, also
revived enquiries into the historical relationship of Christianity with the earlier
religions and with Platonic philosophy itself. These ideas were embedded in the
subject of the Platonic philosopher *Hypatia* (Cox 469; Figure 4), one of Cameron's
most-reproduced photographs. Although Kingsley's novel *Hypatia* first appeared
in 1853, Cameron's photograph depicting his heroine was not exhibited until
1868. For Kingsley, the novel allowed him to raise a controversial political subject
that drew upon the classical past to comment on the Anglican Church in daily life
as well as the historical legitimacy of modern democratic and educational institutions in England. What was the importance of this classical subject for Cameron
fifteen years after the novel first appeared?

In his novel, Kingsley portrayed a battleground of ideas that fought for prominence rather than the imagined peace and cultural bounty that others believed
flourished during the fifth century. Situating his novel during this period of the
Roman Empire, setting the action in colonized Alexandria, and assigning different
religions and competing ideologies to his characters, Kingsley allowed paganism,
Platonic philosophy, and Christianity to spar like gladiators in the arena. *Hypatia*
re-imagines the intersection of tribes and races co-mingling under the Empire,
where conflict and misunderstanding are commonplace. Kingsley believed that in
these ancient conflicts the seeds of future intellectual and moral disagreements
were first sown, and he believed these differences were still present in Victorian
England:

> Those wild tribes were bringing with them into the magic circle of the Western
> Church's influence the very materials which she required for the building up of
> a future Christendom, and which she could find as little in the Western Empire,
> as in the Eastern; comparative purity of morals; sacred respect for women, for
> family life, law, equal justice, individual freedom, and, above all, for honesty in
> word and deed; bodies untainted by hereditary effeminacy, hearts earnest though
> genial, and blest with a strange willingness to learn, even from those whom they

despised; a brain equal to that of the Roman in practical power, and not too far behind that of the Eastern in imaginative and speculative acuteness.[80]

But Kingsley believed that England's National Church actually fostered positive codes of social order in the present. In fact, *Hypatia* celebrates the role of the Church in downplaying superstition and promoting moral behaviour: 'The very ideas of family and national life – those two divine roots of the Church, severed from which she is certain to wither away into that most godless and most cruel of spectres, a religious world.'[81]

Kingsley's Protestant views stood opposed to those of the converted Catholic, John Henry Newman. The two men had clashed about the ideas expressed in *Hypatia* more than a decade before Cameron made her photograph. Newman responded to Kingsley's *Hypatia* by writing his own novel, which he called *Callista*, in 1855. Both novels were set in an idealized, classical past, both written from conflicting viewpoints that had their origins in the opposition between High Church and Broad Church divisions that would later erupt in the *Essays and Reviews* controversy. Both authors re-imagined an ancient Roman civilization that was marked by senseless violence and the quiet contemplative life of philosophers, a complex multi-ethnic world peopled by Goths, Greeks, Africans, Jews, corrupt Roman prefects, and wild fanatic bishops. While Kingsley's ancient characters portrayed the early Church as a haven of 'light' and 'love', Newman wrote of a period of 'frightful superstition' where non-believers 'go to an eternal Tartarus'.

Almost a decade after the publication of *Hypatia* and *Callista*, Kingsley and Newman continued to spar in print. Kingsley wrote that the Anglican Church provided essential moral direction for how to lead an ethical life, as it offered guidance 'over the ways and works of men – over science, commerce, civilization, colonization, all of which affects the earthly destinies of the race'. Newman countered that life's guideposts were spiritual, not secular; they were marked by adherence to Church doctrine and discipline and centred on the 'saving of souls'.[82] Their public dispute, therefore, was by no means 'settled' when Cameron titled her photograph *Hypatia* in 1868. Rather, *Hypatia* had become a personification of these very debates, because in this subject, the projected beliefs and contradictory meanings of ancient Greek life when Christianity first emerged were embodied historically. The public argument between Kingsley and Newman and the troubled character of their dispute were therefore central to the meaning of Cameron's photograph. As a character in Kingsley's novel, Hypatia was an ascetic teacher of Platonic philosophy who at first regarded the pagan gods and Christianity alike, finding in each faith a common search for meaning and truth. But Hypatia also embodied neo-Platonic worldliness and a rational sensibility that was foreign to, and threatened by, the zeal associated with religious conversion and spiritualism, as she inveighed against irrational superstition and religious mysticism. Her character allowed Kingsley to express his antipathy toward religious orthodoxies and theological rules.

At the very end of the novel, Hypatia is martyred. She is killed not by godless pagans, however, but by a mob of frenzied Christian monks. While it might seem that by portraying a clash between ancient pagan philosophers and early Christian converts Kingsley could have created an effective analogy to the nineteenth-century struggle between doubt and intellectual enquiry, Kingsley instead used his novel to express the need for common ground and to preach redemption in terms of Christian love.[83] In 1868, then, when Cameron displayed *Hypatia* alongside portraits of Benjamin Jowett, Tennyson, and Matthew Arnold in her exhibition, her photograph was able to bring these ancient conflicts into close alignment with the Broad Church beliefs of her contemporaries, again using ancient Greek history to help give historical shape to Victorian questions of identity.

For Cameron, ancient Greece could also embody the importance of cultural memory and the value of historical precedent. In 1871, Robert Browning embraced the allegorical subject of culture's redemptive value in his poem, *Balaustion's Adventure*. That same year, Cameron produced a photograph, *Balaustion*, based upon the poem (Cox 202; Figure 23). Browning's poem in large part retold the story in *Alcestis*, Euripides' historical drama, but in *Balaustion's Adventure*, Browning used the voice of a vibrant young girl from ancient Rhodes to narrate the poem and provide its moral centre. In fact, Browning uses Balaustion rather like the way Socrates uses Er, the Armenian warrior who dies and is reborn to tell of the afterlife of the soul in Plato's 'Vision of Er' myth retold in the *Republic*. In Plato, it is through Er's story that the reader is reminded that one must accept responsibility for every decision one makes in life. In Browning, it is the moral voice of Balaustion which takes on that responsibility for her people: when the Athenians have been defeated by the Spartans on the island of Rhodes and are preparing to swear allegiance to Sparta and renounce their Athenian values, it is the brave young woman, Balaustion, who holds firm and refuses to turn against her history and her nation. To Balaustion, Athens is the only civilization that is 'the life and light / Of the whole world worth calling world at all' (ll. 25–6). Rather than forsake her devotion to her religion, abandon her love of the fine arts, or adopt the godless material culture of the conquering Spartans, she resolves firmly to keep Athenian cultural values alive. As Clyde de L. Ryals writes, '*Balaustion's Adventure* is the young woman's (and Browning's) way of showing to a younger, crasser world that it can be enriched and enlivened when the essence of the culture of the past is imaginatively re-created in the present.'[84]

Also during these years, Tennyson kept the ancient story of Ulysses alive on the Isle of Wight through his poem, *Ulysses* (1842). Emily Tennyson repeatedly recorded in her journal how her husband enjoyed reciting his poem often. In

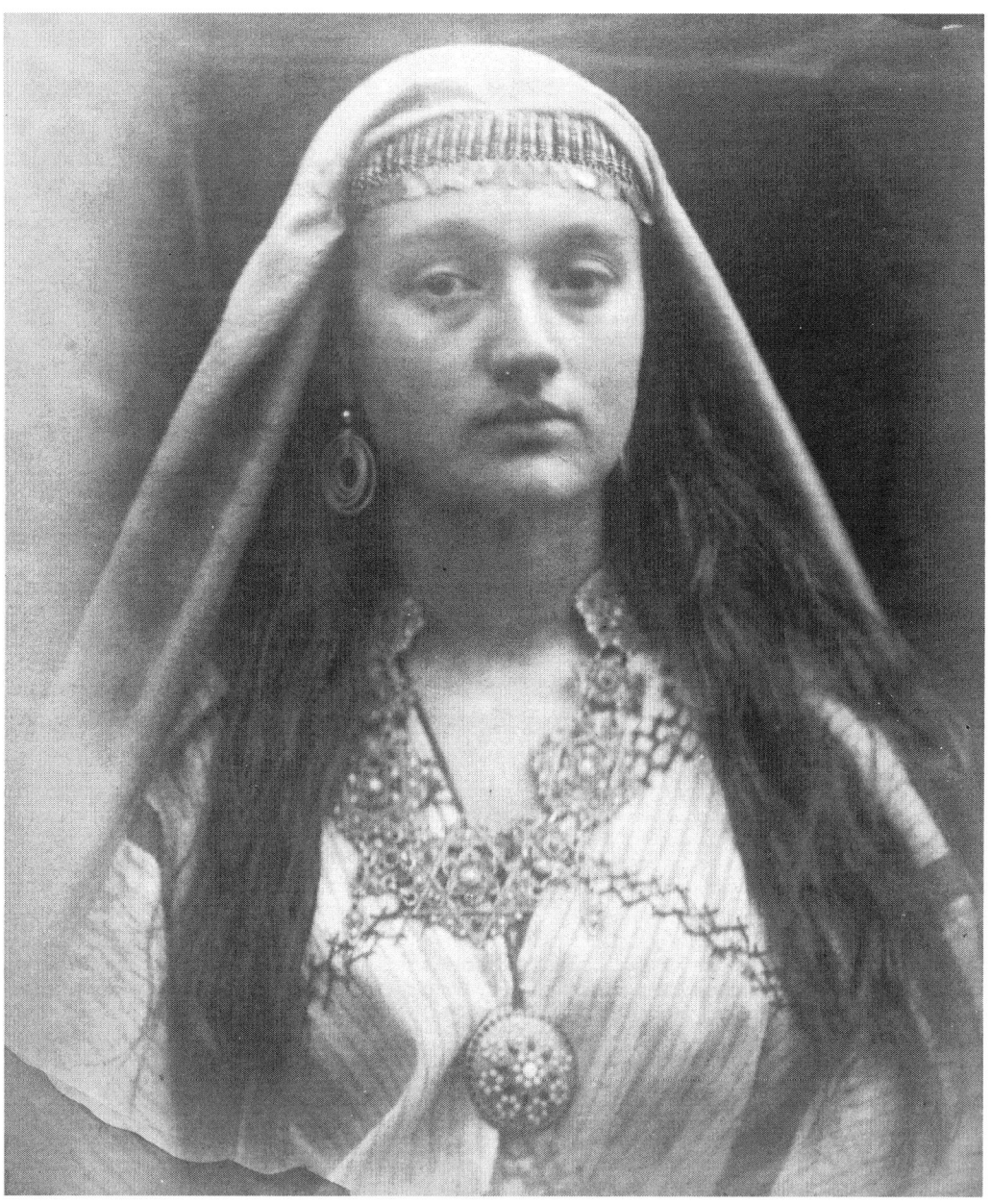

23            Julia Margaret Cameron, *Balaustion* (Cox 202), 1871.
                    Albumen print, 32.7 x 26.8 cm.

*Ulysses*, Tennyson emphasized the confessional character of the warrior-adventurer who pushes forward despite feeling overwhelmed and old, weary and degraded.[85] Like Homer's Odysseus, Ulysses refuses to die; yet he is plainly exhausted. While Odysseus, mindful of Athena's praise for Ithaca, strives to reach the island as a destination, Tennyson's Ulysses is eager to leave it, feeling virtually marooned on what he calls an inhospitable outcropping and at odds with the native people of the island, with whom he is disaffected. In *Ulysses*, the adjectives of the opening lines, 'still', 'barren', 'aged', and 'savage', describe as much the hero's state of mind as the landscape he faces and the ungrateful people he struggles to govern. Yet his story is one of noble perseverance.

Ulysses is also the antithesis to Tennyson's Wellington, the conventional male role model of heroic independence that the poet honoured in 1852 in his poem, *Ode on the Death of the Duke of Wellington*. If Tennyson's Ulysses struggles against old age and exhaustion to find new reservoirs of courage by defying his own inactivity, Tennyson eulogizes Wellington as a leader who was 'Great in council and great in war, / Foremost captain of this time' (ll. 30–1), and who exemplified the vigorous life of heroic action by defeating Napoleon at Waterloo. Vital to the end, Wellington was defined patriotically by forging 'the path of duty' (ll. 202; 210). Having successfully climbed that noble and virtuous 'path upward', wrote Tennyson, Wellington marked his crowning achievement by finding 'the toppling crags of Duty scaled' (ll. 214; 215). By contrast, in Tennyson's hands, Ulysses is ready to leave duty behind, abdicate his rule, and turn over to his son both 'the sceptre and the isle' (l. 34).

Julia Margaret Cameron captured her own allegory of *Ulysses* in 1864–65 in an untitled portrait of her husband Charles (Cox 595; Figure 24). In the photograph, Charles personifies all of the essential elements of the ancient hero: enthroned with a sceptre and an oversized volume, representing a book of laws, Charles Cameron wears a white fur cloak, perhaps ermine, symbolizing kingship. While Cameron's use of the sceptre may symbolize regal power, it also may simply refer to an antique emblem of command, as it did for the ancient Greeks, or even legal influence, as when judges held them to symbolize authority. Cameron's photograph produces a curious mixture of melancholic nostalgia and bright national future, in part because she produced this image just when Britain was debating whether to relinquish control of the Ionian islands and restore them to Greece. In the photograph, Charles Cameron portrays Ulysses as he looks back upon his past glory, just as the restored nineteenth-century Ionians could look back upon ancient Thermopylae as a symbol of their earlier heroic culture, and interpret their modern reunification with Greece as a way to reclaim that greatness. At the same time, because Tennyson's Ulysses surrenders the burdens of power, just as colonial Britain relinquished the Ionian islands, Cameron's Ulysses also looks forward to a future where colonial power is eventually abandoned.[86]

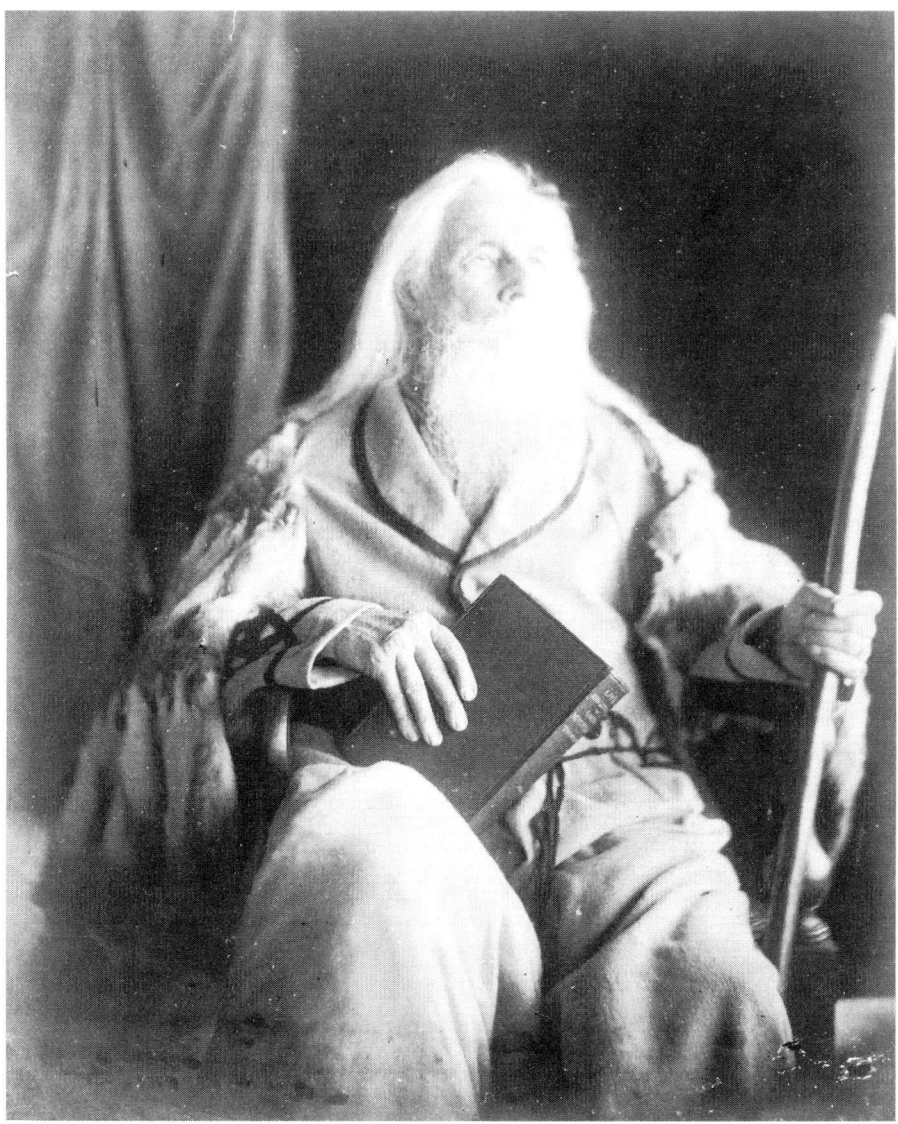

24          Julia Margaret Cameron, *Charles Hay Cameron* (Cox 595), 1864/65.
                        Albumen print, 28.5 x 22.5 cm.

Ironically, in depicting her husband Charles as sceptred ruler, but also as elderly and fatigued, Cameron drew an unexpected personal parallel between her husband and Tennyson's Ulysses, who is bored and wants to leave the island of Ithaca for new adventures. Both Charles Cameron and Tennyson's Ulysses expressed weariness with the tedium of domestic life and longed for the happy undertaking of a long sea voyage. While he gave the impression of being 'settled' on the Isle of Wight, in fact, Charles was apparently always looking ahead and planning his next trip to Ceylon. Tennyson's Ulysses was exhausted, beaten down by the pressures of life, willing to relinquish once ambitious dreams altogether. In 1864, moreover, Charles Cameron was sixty-nine years old, and tired. Fourteen years earlier, when he was turning fifty-five, he decided to leave India and return to England rather than seek a colonial administrative office abroad, though he long hoped to follow in his father's footsteps as a colonial governor; in fact, he had hoped to be posted to the Ionian islands.[87] Not coincidentally, Charles made this resolution just as the Colonial Office began to require its administrators to retire from public service once they had reached that particular age.[88]

Thomas Babington Macaulay, who employed Charles Cameron on the Council of India to impose British laws and establish the colony's penal code, sympathized with the historical oppression of the people of Greece. In 1849, he had celebrated British efforts to restore the country's independence:

> A nation, once the first among the nations, pre-eminent in knowledge, pre-eminent in military glory, the cradle of philosophy, of eloquence, and of the fine arts, had been for ages bowed down under a cruel yoke … Much of [Byron's] most splendid and popular poetry had been inspired by its scenery and by its history. Sick of inaction, degraded in his own eyes … pining for untried excitement and honourable distinction, he carried his exhausted body and his wounded spirit to the Grecian camp … [P]leasure and sorrow had done the work of seventy years … The hand of death was upon him: he knew it; and the only wish which he uttered was that he might die sword in hand.[89]

Although Macaulay did not live to see the Ionian islands restored to Greece, he would have clearly applauded the return. It is not accidental that Cameron's photograph of her husband depicting 'Ulysses' shows him holding a bound volume of the *Life and Letters of Lord Macaulay*. The synchronicity here exposes an uncanny blend of the personal and the political: as a book about Charles Cameron's former mentor, the *Life and Letters of Lord Macaulay* could only symbolize the Camerons' grief at the loss of their dear friend, who died in 1859 and whose one-time energy seemed indefatigable. Moreover, Macaulay and Tennyson were both avid members of the Whig party, sharing a politics that opposed despotism but that was also suspicious of full democracy. Their interests lay in checking the power of the monarchy, preserving the aristocracy, and permitting limited democratic reforms (like the Great Reform Bill, which Macaulay sponsored in Parliament), all toward maintaining social order and the status quo.[90] These were also men of action: Macaulay admired Byron's resolve to 'die sword in hand' as he fought for Greek liberation, while Tennyson's Ulysses likened himself to a dull sword, long out of commission; he regrets the very idea of allowing it to 'rust unburnish'd, not to shine in use!' (l. 23).

Tennyson's *Ulysses* also contains an important literary trope, one that is repeated in other works, like *Tithonus* (1860) and *In Memoriam* (1850), in which he inserts a 'metonymic interchange of beginnings and endings, of early and late. It is the figure of hesper/phosphor, the double star ... and of the mixing of East and West.'[91] In the poem, *In Memoriam*, for example, the split identity of this key symbol plays a significant role:

> Sweet Hesper-Phosphor, double name
> For what is one, the first, the last,
> Thou, like my present and my past,
> Thy place is changed; thou art the same.

(st. 121, ll. 17–20)

Tennyson figuratively used the dawn and the dusk, the morning and the evening star, to convey the passage of time but also the circularity of events. Cameron's photograph of her husband also embodied dual symbolic meanings for the personal and the political: on the one hand, her image of 'Charles-as-Ulysses' represents a backward-looking mind-set one might use when reassessing one's life. This, in turn, is fused together with a forward-looking attitude that searches ahead to find a 'newer world' (*Ulysses*, l. 57) where 'some work of noble note, may yet be done' (l. 52). In her photograph of *Ulysses*, then, Cameron inserted objects like the sceptre and the book to symbolize the dual reality that she believed bound together the East and the West. The photograph embodies these emblematically as dichotomies: pagan and Christian; lawless and lawful; barbaric and civic; passionate and rational; the individual and the nation. *Ulysses* combines Cameron's interest in using the Homeric Greece of myth and legend, and the Platonic Greece of laws and the *Republic*, to create a new synthesis in photography, one that unites two forces. In her photograph, both function together and independently to express the moral code, democratic identity, and heroic voice of the Hellenistic past in the Victorian present.

## Notes

1  Virginia Woolf, 'On Not Knowing Greek', in *The Common Reader* (New York: Harcourt, Brace and Company, 1925), p. 39.
2  Virginia Woolf, *Freshwater: A Comedy* [1935], ed. Lucio P. Ruotolo (San Diego: Harcourt Brace Jovanovich, 1976), p. 40.
3  Thomas Arnold, 'Rugby School', *Quarterly Journal of Education*, 7 (1834), 234–49.
4  Charles Kingsley, *The Heroes* [1856] (London: J. M. Dent and Sons, 1963), p. v.
5  *Lady Tennyson's Journal*, ed. James O. Hoge (Charlottesville: University of Virginia Press, 1981), p. 130.
6  See *The Letters of Alfred Lord Tennyson*, ed. Cecil Y. Lang and Edgar F. Shannon, Jr., vol. 2 (Cambridge, MA: Harvard University Press, 1987), pp. 258 n. 2; 360 n. 2.
7  Yopie Prins, 'Greek Maenads, Victorian Spinsters', in Richard Dellamora, ed., *Victorian Sexual Dissidence* (Chicago: University of Chicago Press, 1999), and Isobel Hurst, *Victorian Women Writers and the Classics: The Feminine of Homer* (Oxford: Oxford University Press, 2006).
8  Lorna Hardwick, *Translating Words, Translating Cultures* (London: Duckworth, 2000), p. 25;

Shanyn Fiske, *Heretical Hellenism: Women Writers, Ancient Greece, and the Victorian Popular Imagination* (Athens, OH: Ohio University Press, 2008).

9  See A. A. Markley, *Stateliest Measures: Tennyson and the Literature of Greece and Rome* (Toronto: University of Toronto Press, 2004), p. 101.

10  *Letters and Papers of John Addington Symonds*, ed. Horatio F. Brown (London: John Murray, 1923), pp. 1–10, quoted in *The Letters of Alfred Lord Tennyson*, ed. Lang and Shannon, vol. 2, pp. 415–21. See also Gerhard Joseph, 'The Homeric Competitions of Tennyson and Gladstone', *Browning Institute Studies*, 10 (1982), 105–15.

11  See 8 December 1865, 'Letters and Papers of John Addington Symonds', in *The Letters of Alfred Lord Tennyson*, ed. Lang and Shannon, vol. 2, pp. 415–21.

12  Frank M. Turner, *The Greek Heritage in Victorian Britain* (New Haven: Yale University Press, 1981); Frank M. Turner, *Contesting Cultural Authority: Essays in Victorian Intellectual Life* (Cambridge: Cambridge University Press, 1993).

13  On the didactic role of the plaster casts and photographs, see Anthony Burton, 'The Uses of the South Kensington Art Collections', *Journal of the History of Collections*, 14:1 (2002), 79–95; on the introduction of reproductive photography in the museum, see Anthony Hamber, '*A Higher Branch of the Art': Photographing the Fine Arts in England, 1839–1880* (London: Gordon and Breach, 1996), pp. 396–414.

14  *Lady Tennyson's Journal*, ed. Hoge, p. 146.

15  Markley, *Stateliest Measures*, p. 29.

16  Woolf, 'On Not Knowing Greek', pp. 54–5.

17  William Hazlitt, *Criticisms on Art and Sketches of the Picture Galleries of England*, 2nd edn, (London: C. Templeman, 1856), p. 245.

18  See Rochelle Gurstein, 'The Elgin Marbles, Romanticism and the Waning of "Ideal Beauty"', *Daedalus*, 131:4 (2002), 88–100; Frederick Cummings, 'Phidias in Bloomsbury: B. R. Haydon's Drawings of the Elgin Marbles', *Burlington*, 106:736 (1964), 323–8; Philip Hunt and A. H. Smith, 'Lord Elgin and His Collection', *Journal of Hellenic Studies*, 36 (1916), 163–372.

19  Caroline Dakers, *The Holland Park Circle: Artists and Victorian Society* (New Haven: Yale University Press, 1999), chapter 2.

20  John Hannavy, 'Roger Fenton and the British Museum', *History of Photography*, 12:3 (1988), 193–204.

21  In a letter from Ruskin to Margaret Bell on 3 and 4 April 1859, quoted in Colin Ford, *The Cameron Collection: An Album of Photographs by Julia Margaret Cameron Presented to Sir John Herschel* (London: Von Nostrand Reinhold and the National Portrait Gallery, 1975), p. 129.

22  *Lady Tennyson's Journal*, ed. Hoge, p. 143.

23  See Ian Jenkins, 'G. F. Watts' Teachers', *Apollo* (1984), 176–81, and Mrs Russell Barrington, ed., *Reminiscences of G. F. Watts* (London: George Allen, 1905).

24  Elizabeth Prettejohn, 'Between Homer and Ovid: Metamorphoses of the "Grand Style" in G. F. Watts', in Colin Trodd and Stephanie Brown, *Representations of G. F. Watts: Art Making in Victorian Culture* (Aldershot: Ashgate, 2004), p. 51.

25  *Ibid.*, p. 56.

26  Dakers, *The Holland Park Circle*, p. 15.

27  Letter dated 21 June 1865 from G. F. Watts to Julia Margaret Cameron, National Portrait Gallery, London, NPG-P125.

28  Letter from Julia Margaret Cameron to Sir John Herschel, dated 31 December 1864, reprinted in Ford, *The Cameron Collection*, p. 141.

29  Letter from Herschel to Julia Margaret Cameron, dated 25 September 1866, quoted *ibid.*, p. 142.

30  Quoted in Prettejohn, 'Between Homer and Ovid', p. 59.

31  See the letter from Watts to Cameron, 21 June 1865, National Portrait Gallery, NPG-P125.

32  Julian Cox and Colin Ford, eds., *Julia Margaret Cameron: The Complete Photographs* (Los Angeles: J. Paul Getty Trust, 2003), p. 175.

33  Quoted in Ford, *The Cameron Collection*, p. 142.

34  As Leonard Barkan explained, the pagan or pre-Christian elements associated with classical mythology were essential for this transformation to occur: 'Pagan stories, and especially tales of metamorphosis, stand squarely between [the arts and the sciences]: their method of interpretation is rhetorical, but their field of reference is nature. As nature itself comes to be seen as full of transformation, so nature becomes a pagan metaphor.' *The Gods Made Flesh: Metamorphosis and the Pursuit of Paganism* (New Haven: Yale University Press, 1986), p. 117.

35  *Lady Tennyson's Journal*, ed. Hoge, p. 191.

36  *William Allingham, A Diary*, ed. H. Allingham and D. Radford (London: Macmillan and Co., 1907), pp. 93–5.

37  Letter from Alfred Tennyson to Martin Farquhar Tupper, dated 17 December 1865, in *The Letters of Alfred Lord Tennyson*, ed. Lang and Shannon, vol. 2, p. 426.

38  Quoted in Markley, *Stateliest Measures*, p. 98.

39  Linda H. Peterson, 'Sappho and the Making of Tennysonian Lyric', *English Literary History*, 61:1 (1994), 121–37; Elizabeth Prettejohn, 'Solomon, Swinburne, Sappho', *Victorian Review*, 34:2 (2008), 103–28; Yopie Prins, *Victorian Sappho* (Princeton: Princeton University Press, 1999).

40  Quoted in Peterson, 'Sappho and the Making of Tennysonian Lyric', 124.

41  See especially Margaret Reynolds, *Fragments of an Elegy: Tennyson Reading Sappho* (Lincoln: Tennyson Society, 2001), pp. 28–9 and n. 5.

42  Prettejohn, 'Solomon, Swinburne, Sappho', 113–15.

43  Prins, *Victorian Sappho*, p. 66, quoting Longinus around AD 250.

44  Quoted in *The Poetical Works of Tennyson*, ed. G. Robert Stange (Boston, MA: Houghton Mifflin, 1974), p. 198.

45  Peterson, 'Sappho and the Making of Tennysonian Lyric', 125.

46  Quoted in Prettejohn, 'Solomon, Swinburne, Sappho', 107.

47  A. Dwight Culler, 'Monodrama and the Dramatic Monologue', *PMLA*, 90:3 (1975), 375.

48  Peterson, 'Sappho and the Making of Tennysonian Lyric', 123.

49  Prins, *Victorian Sappho*, pp. 116–17.

50  See Colin Ford, 'Geniuses, Poets, and Painters: The World of Julia Margaret Cameron', in Julian Cox and Colin Ford, eds., *Julia Margaret Cameron: The Complete Photographs* (Los Angeles: J. Paul Getty Trust, 2003), p. 28. Sylvia Wolf has complained that Cameron's two models 'are not noble icons of godly grace, but two models slouching in sheets', where 'even the drapery looks frumpy, the fabric bunched and twisted rather than wet and revealing of the human form'. See *Julia Margaret Cameron's Women* (Chicago: Art Institute of Chicago, 1998), p. 57.

51  As Joyce Zonana has argued for Swinburne, this imagery joins the real and the ideal by combining 'earthly and heavenly sources of inspiration in a new and stable synthesis', making Cameron's models 'sister-goddesses'. Joyce Zonana, 'Swinburne's Sappho: The Muse as Sister-Goddess', *Victorian Poetry*, 28:1 (1990), 39–50.

52  Christopher Ricks, *Tennyson* (New York: Macmillan, 1972), pp. 52–3, 177, 184–5.

53  Prettejohn, 'Solomon, Swinburne, Sappho', 111.

54  Eva Stehle, 'Sappho's Gaze: Fantasies of a Goddess and Young Man', in Ellen Greene, ed., *Reading Sappho: Contemporary Approaches* (Berkeley: University of California Press, 1996), pp. 193–225.

55  Susan Waller, 'The Artist, the Writer, and the Queen: Hosmer, Jameson, and "Zenobia"', *Women's Art Journal*, 4:1 (1983), 21–8, and Gabrielle Gopinath, 'Harriet Hosmer and the Feminine Sublime', *Oxford Art Journal*, 28:1 (2005), 61–81.

56  T. S. R. Boase, 'The Decoration of the New Palace of Westminster, 1841–1863, *Journal of the Warburg and Courtauld Institutes*, 17:3/4 (1954), 330.

57  Sir Coutts Lindsay, *Boadicea: A Tragedy* (London: W. Clowes and Sons, 1857).

58  Wendy C. Nielsen, 'Boadicea Onstage before 1800: A Theatrical and Colonial History', *Studies in English Literature 1500–1900*, 49:3 (2009), 595–614.

59  For example, in one afternoon in 1863, Sir Coutts Lindsay joined George and Harriet Grote, Arthur P. Stanley, Benjamin Jowett, and Lord Dufferin (then the Commissioner to Syria, and future governor of Canada and viceroy of India) in Holly Lodge, which the earl of Airlie had acquired from Lord Macaulay, for a discussion of the discovery of the source of the Nile, Speke's expedition into Africa, and one of the key misunderstandings that several years later would lead to the Abyssinian conflict. See Dakers, *The Holland Park Circle*, p. 79. In *Lady Tennyson's Journal*, the poet's wife recalled Alfred entertained guests by reading *Boadicea* on five occasions, including 14 February 1859; 27 April 1860; 23 June 1863; 21 October 1868; and 30 June 1871. *Lady Tennyson's Journal*, ed. Hoge.

60  *Lady Tennyson's Journal*, ed. Hoge, p. 241 (written by Emily Tennyson as 'Visions of Ur').

61  Quoted in Ford, *The Cameron Collection*, p. 142.

62  Turner, *The Greek Heritage*, and 'The Triumph of Idealism in Victorian Classical Studies', in *Contesting Cultural Authority*, pp. 322–61.

63  Turner, 'The Triumph of Idealism', p. 335.

64  William Thomas, *The Philosophical Radicals* (Oxford: Clarendon Press, 1979), pp. 406–38.

65  Nadia Urbinati, *Mill on Democracy from the Athenian Polis to Representative Government* (Chicago: University of Chicago Press, 2002), p. 105.

66  Nicolas Haines, 'The Ballot and the Dream: Footnotes to a Century of "Educated Democracy"', *Political Science Quarterly*, 83:4 (1968), 530–50, and Joseph H. Park, 'England's Controversy over the Secret Ballot', *Political Science Quarterly*, 46:1 (1931), 51–86.

67  Quoted in John Stuart Mill, 'Grote's History of Greece', in *Dissertations and Discussions: Political, Philosophical, and Historical*, vol.3 (Boston: William V. Spencer, 1865), pp. 219–20.

68  John Stuart Mill, 'Grote's Plato', in *Dissertations and Discussions: Political, Philosophical, and Historical*, vol. 4 (Boston: William V. Spencer, 1867), pp. 358-9.

69  Turner, *The Greek Heritage*, pp. 237–9.

70  Quoted *ibid.*, p. 243.

71  Turner, 'The Triumph of Idealism', p. 352.

72  Bruce Knox, 'The Queen's Letter of 1865 and British Policy towards Emancipation and Indentured Labour in the West Indies, 1830–1865', *Historical Journal*, 29:2 (1986), 345–67.

73  See Catherine Hall, 'The Nation Within and Without', in Catherine Hall, Keith McClelland, and Jane Rendall, eds., *Defining the Victorian Nation* (Cambridge: Cambridge University Press, 2000), p. 198.

74  Quoted in Turner, 'The Triumph of Idealism', p. 356.

75  Mathew Arnold, *Culture and Anarchy* (New York: Macmillan, 1925), p. 72.

76  *Ibid.*, p. 93.

77  Edward Said wrote: '"the best that is known and thought" must contend with competing ideologies, philosophies, dogmas, notions, and values, and it is Arnold's insight that what is at stake in society is not merely the cultivation of individuals, or the development of a class of finely tuned sensibilities, or the renaissance of interest in the classics, but rather the assertively achieved and *won* hegemony of an identifiable set of ideas, which Arnold honorifically calls culture, over all other ideas in society [...] To be for and in culture is to be in and for a State in a compellingly loyal way. With this assimilation of culture to the authority and exterior framework of the State go as well such things as assurance, confidence, the majority sense, the entire matrix of meanings we associate with "home," belonging and community.' *The World, the Text, and the Critic* (Cambridge, MA: Harvard University Press, 1983), pp. 10, 11.

78   Turner, *The Greek Heritage*, p. 140.

79   George Grote, 'Grecian legends and Early history', in *The Minor Works of George Grote. With critical remarks on his intellectual character, writings, and speeches, by Alexander Bain* (London: J. Murray, 1873), p. 129.

80   Charles Kingsley, *Hypatia; or New Foes with an Old Face* (New York: William L. Allison Co., n.d.), pp. 5–6.

81   *Ibid.*, p. 7.

82   Susan Dorman, 'Hypatia and Callista: The Initial Skirmish Between Kingsley and Newman', *Nineteenth-Century Fiction*, 34:2 (1979), 191, 192, and Raymond Chapman, *Faith and Revolt: Studies in the Literary Influence of the Oxford Movement* (London: Weidenfeld and Nicolson, 1970), esp. chapter 6.

83   Together with a parallel fictional character in the novel, Raphael Aben-Ezra, a Jewish aristocrat who like Hypatia also converts to Christianity, the two figures epitomize the adoption of a code of moral Christian values based upon love and code of civil conduct and mutual responsibility that was associated with St Paul and Augustine, themes that Cameron herself valued and portrayed artistically, as in her photographic series, the *Fruits of the Spirit*. See Dorman, 'Hypatia and Callista', 188; Stanwood S. Walker, '"Backwards and backwards ever": Charles Kingsley's Racial-Historical Allegory and the Liberal Anglican Revisioning of Britain', *Nineteenth-Century Literature*, 62:3 (2007), 339–79.

84   Clyde de L. Ryals, 'Balaustion's Adventure: Browning's Greek Parable', *PMLA*, 88:5 (1973), 1,043.

85   Andrew Elfenbein, *Byron and the Victorians* (Cambridge: Cambridge University Press, 1995), pp. 182–3.Other studies also cite the importance of Byron to Tennyson, especially with respect to *Ulysses*; see for example, Matthew Rowlinson, 'The Ideological Moment of Tennyson's "Ulysses"', *Victorian Poetry*, 30:3–4 (1992), 265-76; James Nohrnberg, 'Eight Reflections of Tennyson's Ulysses', *Victorian Poetry,* 47:1 (2009), 101-50; Martin McKinsey, 'Ulysses Victorianus and the Other Knowledge of Empire', *Ariel* (2004), 99–113; Glyn Davis, 'Ulysses and the Temptation of Idleness: Thinking about Politics through Poetry', *Australian Journal of Political Science*, 38:1 (1998), 73-84; Linda K. Hughes, 'Dramatis and Private Personae: "Ulysses" Revisited', *Victorian Poetry*, 17:3 (1979), 192–203; and Edward Dramin, '"Work of Noble Note": Tennyson's "Ulysses" and Victorian Heroic Ideals', *Victorian Literature and Culture*, 20 (1993), 117–39.

86   Matthew Rowlinson summarizes this doubly inscribed paradox 'as part of the prehistory of a certain ideological construction', in which Tennyson's poem is 'implicated in a colonialist pedagogy that is in its essence nostalgic' because it technically dates 'from before it was possible to speak of a British imperialism, and yet seems peculiarly to speak to and about the twilight of that imperialism'. See Rowlinson, 'The Ideological Moment of Tennyson's "Ulysses"', 270.

87   Charles Cameron senior was governor of the Bahamas from 1804 to 1820.

88   As a result, 'old age' became associated with cultural degradation, 'just as no Westerner needed ever to see himself, mirrored in the eyes of the subject race, as anything but a vigorous, rational, ever-alert young Raj'. Edward W. Said, *Orientalism* (New York: Vintage, 1978), p. 42.

89   Thomas Babington Macaulay, quoted in Nohrnberg, 'Eight Reflections of Tennyson's "Ulysses"', 127.

90   On Tennyson's and Macaulay's affiliation with the Whig party, see Cornelia Pearsall, *Tennyson's Rapture: Transformation in the Victorian Dramatic Monologue* (Oxford: Oxford University Press, 2008), pp. 39–44.

91   Rowlinson, 'The Ideological Moment of Tennyson's "Ulysses"', 270.

# 4

# Byron's 'Beauties':
# national heroines and defenders of liberty

## Byron, Taylor, Cameron

George Gordon, Lord Byron, died in 1824, but among Victorian writers, his legacy and influence were lasting. Among Cameron's circle, William Thackeray, Aubrey de Vere, and Henry Taylor all 'scorned Byron outright', dismissing his enduring popularity because they considered his work vulgar, even offensive.[1] But throughout her decade of photography, Julia Margaret Cameron regularly drew inspiration from Byron's poetry and represented his most popular heroines as 'fancy subjects' in her work. It is clear from her titles and multiple references to Byron that she was familiar with *Childe Harold's Pilgrimage*, *Don Juan*, the *Hebrew Melodies*, and various 'Turkish Tales', like *The Corsair* and *The Bride of Abydos*. For example, she produced at least two versions of *Zuleika* (Cox 200, 201; 1138) and portrayed the heroine of *The Bride of Abydos* (Cox 1138), as well as *Medora* (Cox 499) from *The Corsair*. From Byron's poem *Don Juan*, she represented his heroine Haidée, which Cameron misspelled *Haidie* (Cox 547), and she portrayed Haidée's maid, in a photograph she titled *Zoë* (Cox 542, 543). Cameron even attempted to portray the mysterious female spirit *Astarte* (now an unknown image, but exhibited in 1865 and 1867), a strange literary figure who is conjured from the dead in Byron's dramatic poem, *Manfred*.

Cameron also created several untitled images portraying what we might term Eastern themes, such as a woman with cymbals in an Oriental diadem and costume (Cox 553, 554) and another woman in an Orientalized interior (Cox 209), both clearly meant to invoke the East. Photographs like these may reference interior harem spaces described in works like *The Bride of Abydos*, *The Corsair*, or *Don Juan*. From Byron's poem of Greek liberation, *Maid of Athens, ere we part*, Cameron portrayed an imagined figure she also called *Zoë* (Cox 392). And drawing upon the collection of lyric poetry that Byron published under the title *Hebrew Melodies*, Cameron represented numerous subjects from the Old Testament, selecting individual poems; many of these, in fact, are directly connected to specific lines of poetry. As we shall see, these representations depict women

## Table 2 Cameron's Byronic subjects

(Brackets indicate approximate dates for titles, or unidentified or unknown works; PRO indicates record in the Public Record Office)

| Source poem | Cox ref. no. | 1864 | 1865 | 1866 | 1867 | 1868 | 1869 | 1870 | 1871 | 1872 | 1873 | 1874 |
|---|---|---|---|---|---|---|---|---|---|---|---|---|
| **From The Bride of Abydos** | | | | | | | | | | | | |
| The Bride of Abydos | 1138 | | | | | | | [x] | | [x] | | |
| Zuleika / Rachel at the Well | 200 | | | | | | | [x] | [x] | | | |
| Zuleika | 201 | | | | | | | | [x] | | | |
| **From Don Juan** | | | | | | | | | | | | |
| Woman with Cymbals in Eastern Dress | 553, 554 | | | | | [x] | | [x] | | | | |
| Woman in Harem Scene | 209 | | | | | | | | | | | |
| Haidie / Rebecca | 547 | | | | | | | x | | | | |
| Zoe | 542, 543 | | | | | | | x | | | | |
| Zoe / The East / Rebecca | 548 | | | | | | | [x] | | | | |
| La Donna at Her Devotions (Donna Julia?) | 473 | | | | | x | | | | | | |
| **From Zoe, Maid of Athens** | | | | | | | | | | | | |
| Zoe / Maid of Athens | 392 | | | [x] | | | | | | | | |
| Studies from the Elgin Marbles | 1110, 1111 | | | | x | | | | | | | |
| **From Hebrew Melodies** | | | | | | | | | | | | |
| Jephthah and His Daughter | 168 | | | | | [x | | | | | | |
| King David | 164, 165, 166 | | [x | x | | | | | | x] | | |
| She Walks in Beauty | 333 | | | | | | | | | | | x |

| Source poem | Cox ref. no. | 1864 | 1865 | 1866 | 1867 | 1868 | 1869 | 1870 | 1871 | 1872 | 1873 | 1874 |
|---|---|---|---|---|---|---|---|---|---|---|---|---|
| The Infant Samuel | 953 | | [x] | | | | | | | | | |
| Vision of Infant Samuel | 126 | | [x] | | | | | | | | | |
| **Related:** | | | | | | | | | | | | |
| Rebecca | 547, 548 | | | | | | | x | | | | |
| Rebecca at the Well | 199 | | | | | | [x | x] | | | | |
| Rachel | 513, 514 | | | | x | | | | | | | |
| Rachel at the Well / Zuleika | 200 | | | | | | | [x | x] | | | |
| Boaz and Ruth / [Jacob and Rachel PRO 12 Dec 64] | 163 | [x | x] | | | | | | | | | |
| The Finding of Moses | 58 | x | | | | | | | | | | |
| Pharoah's Daughter | 546 | | | | | | | x | | | | |
| [Leah and Rachel at the Well] | PRO 12 Dec 64 | x | | | | | | | | | | |
| King Ahasuerus and Queen Esther | 167 | | x | | | | | | | | | |
| [Hagar and Ishmael] | PRO 10 Oct 64 | x | | | | | | | | | | |
| **From *Manfred*** | | | | | | | | | | | | |
| Astarte | 251 or 557? | [x | exhib-ited | | exhib-ited | | | | | | | |
| **From *The Corsair*** | | | | | | | | | | | | |
| Medora | 499 | [x | | x] | | | | | | | | |
| **Related imagery:** | | | | | | | | | | | | |
| Maud / Adriana / Clio | 255 | | | [x] | | | | | | | | |

who personify valour, heroism, and national honour. Cameron celebrates their individuality but also their social engagement; she explores their willingness to transgress social taboos; and she portrays their values and behaviour as fitting, and even inspirational, examples for Victorian social life.

Table 2 captures the expansive range of Byronic poetry that inspired Cameron, but broad recognition of these subjects as 'Byronic' is wholly absent from the critical literature about the photographer's work. This absence is consistent with the historical devaluation of her allegorical subjects. Individual 'exotic' photographs have stood out for some scholars, like the photographs titled *Zoë, Maid of Athens* (Cox 392) or *The Bride of Abydos*, but these are described as emblematic of Cameron's interest in depicting 'qualities of innocence, virtue, wisdom, piety, or passion' and epitomize 'a poetic evocation of love and longing'.[2] Framed in this way, these photographs seem caught in the familiar tropes of Orientalism, in which the persistent magnetism of the East is explained in part by its beauty and perceived inferiority, its 'need' for improvement and rehabilitation or protection.[3] Another critical strand regards Cameron's Byronic subjects as part of an effort to expand the 'range of possible models for female behaviour', as if Cameron were working to define an archive of 'Female Subjects' that could be expanded or enlivened by sprinkling 'Byron' into the mix.[4] But by typecasting Cameron as passion-seeking, love-struck, or enamoured of the exotic, we risk turning her into a trivial sentimentalist and diminish her intellectual engagement with these subjects. Despite the evidence of her sustained engagement with Byronic subjects, no surviving written documents establish her thoughts about making and exhibiting these photographs. And to the extent that writers of her time recognized Cameron's personifications of Byron's heroines, critics appear to have reserved their critical judgements about these works. But by way of introducing Cameron's commitment to represent these subjects, it is important to note that one of her closest friends, Henry Taylor, stood firmly against Byron and what he considered the sentimental tendencies of Romantic poetry.

Cameron's personal closeness to Taylor and the extent to which she admired his work must have presented a challenging obstacle to the photographer, one worth exploring in relation to the body of Byronic subjects that she chose to represent. Cameron was an unabashed champion of Taylor's poetry, most especially an enduring fan of Taylor's 1834 drama, *Philip Van Artevelde*. Taylor himself styled his poem a 'dramatic romance', and Cameron praised the work as bursting forth with 'poetic beauty, moral vigour, soundness and elevation of feeling' that was 'second to none but Shakespeare'.[5] She promoted the virtues of *Philip Van Artevelde* to anyone who would listen, even commissioned a German translation of the play, and regularly spoke to Taylor himself by addressing him personally as 'Philip'. Taylor's drama found enough of a literate audience to encourage William Macready to attempt a stage adaptation of *Philip Van Artevelde* at London's Princess's Theatre

in 1847, but the play closed after only five performances. Cameron nevertheless persisted in promoting Taylor's work, holding private readings of *Philip Van
Artevelde* at her home into the 1860s, and even subtitled one of her 1864 portraits
of the author, *Philip Van Artevelde* (Cox 777).[6]

By the date of this portrait, it had been eleven years since *Philip Van Artevelde*
first appeared in print, but in 1864 the play was 'new again' as it was republished
in a second edition. Taylor's dramatic work is notable for its Preface, which
disparages early Romantic poetry, especially the works of Byron. In opposition
to what Taylor called the 'indulgences' and 'luxuries' of Byron, Taylor wrote that
dramatic poetry should embrace timeless 'intellectual' subjects that were both
serious and 'grave' and which induced readers to reflect solemnly and thoughtfully
upon those subjects. *Philip Van Artevelde* was Taylor's effort to reclaim this austere
ground for modern poetry. Given their friendship, one wonders how Taylor toler-
ated his friend's photographic activity in representing characters made famous
in Byron's poems. This chapter offers several explanations, including Cameron's
specific allegorical references, which are indeed serious and 'grave', but also her
photographic depiction of Taylor's anti-Byronic heroine, Adriana, an extraordinary subject that has not been identified previously.

In her photographs of Byronic subjects, Cameron unites two cultures and
depicts an in-between 'zone of intersection' that stresses their commonality.
Stephen Greenblatt has called this space one that calls into question 'all culturally
determinate significations'; by blurring distinctions in this zone, an 'unresolved
and unresolvable hybridity' arises.[7] As a strategy of representation, 'Byron'
helped Cameron combine opposing forces, portraying 'the East' as both alien
and unknown, but also strangely familiar because of its connection to 'the West'.
As we shall see, Cameron's photographs of Byronic heroines capture this hybrid
condition.

How might we define Cameron's 'audience' for her Byronic subjects? Today's
literary scholars typically define Byron's readers in two historical groups, dividing
the readership of *Childe Harold's Pilgrimage* from that of the 'Turkish Tales'.[8] From
the evidence of her chosen subjects, Cameron hoped to engage both segments
of this reading public during the 1860s. Although the production of her imagery
did not follow a chronological pattern, it is useful to examine how Cameron's
Byronic subjects corresponded to the poet's major literary works, especially as
a way to investigate why she chose certain allegorical themes and not others,
and as a means to explore their deeper meanings. Consequently, the first section
considers Cameron's approach to Byron's Eastern heroines in the 'Turkish Tales',
which is followed by Cameron's portrayal of the nationalistic heroes and heroines
of the *Hebrew Melodies*, and Cameron's allegorical treatment of the Greek War
of Independence, which uses Byronic subjects to comment upon contemporary
political affairs then taking place in Britain. By choosing such popular themes,

Cameron capitalized on Byron's enduring reputation and his populist politics to attract and engage a literate audience and contribute to a popular dialogue about issues of national importance.

## East meets West: the 'Turkish Tales'

In pursuing her Byronic subjects, Cameron retitled particular photographs she created over time to give them new purpose, status, or meaning – a strategy that she used in her religious and classical imagery as well. When the same image possesses two different titles, it might be said to occupy two identities at once. For example, in a photograph that depicts her model in Eastern robes and headscarf, holding a vase on a pedestal that is supposed to represent a well, she assigned two different titles: one image is called *Zuleika* and the other *Rachel at the Well* (Cox 200; Figure 25). Another photograph occupies a similar dual status: one print is marked *Rebecca* and its identical twin is titled *Haidie* (Cox 547; Figure 26). Cameron's working method was too precise, too deliberate, and above all, too intellectual to attribute these different titles to the same image by chance or personal idiosyncrasy. Because she repeated this practice again and again, it is worth exploring some of the likely reasons she gave multiple titles to the same image. The photographic pair *Zuleika/Rachel*, for example, may have resulted from an idea that a literary thread linked the two subjects together (in their original narrative sources, for example, both women experience moments of discovery at a well that foretell their futures, or perhaps, as in Byron's poem as well as the Old Testament story, both women are daughters of unscrupulous and untrustworthy fathers). Or possibly Cameron drew upon familiar Western stereotypes and considered the subjects interchangeable, and therefore chose her model to possess a physiognomy that could work equally well as an Oriental 'type', a suitable model for a subject of Egyptian, Palestinian, or North African origins.

In the second example, *Rebecca/Haidie*, the Old Testament story of Rebecca and the Byronic story of Haidée suggest opposing narratives that confound any attempt to link the two. Perhaps Cameron had other reasons for using these two titles for this image. Both could be called 'ideal types' having ancient ethnic lineages: Haidée, the Greek maiden in *Don Juan*, discovered the shipwrecked Juan and nursed him back to health. And in the Old Testament, Rebecca becomes the wife of Isaac. Perhaps Cameron simply disregarded these differences in favour of uniting the two images as Oriental subjects. Or perhaps these photographic pairs correspond to the familiar cultural duality made popular by Matthew Arnold, one that linked the two based on ideas of cultural inheritance: in *Culture and Anarchy*, Arnold described the Hellenic (Haidée) and the Hebraic (Rebecca) as evidence of two complementary historical traits that form what he called the uniquely English character of the nineteenth century.

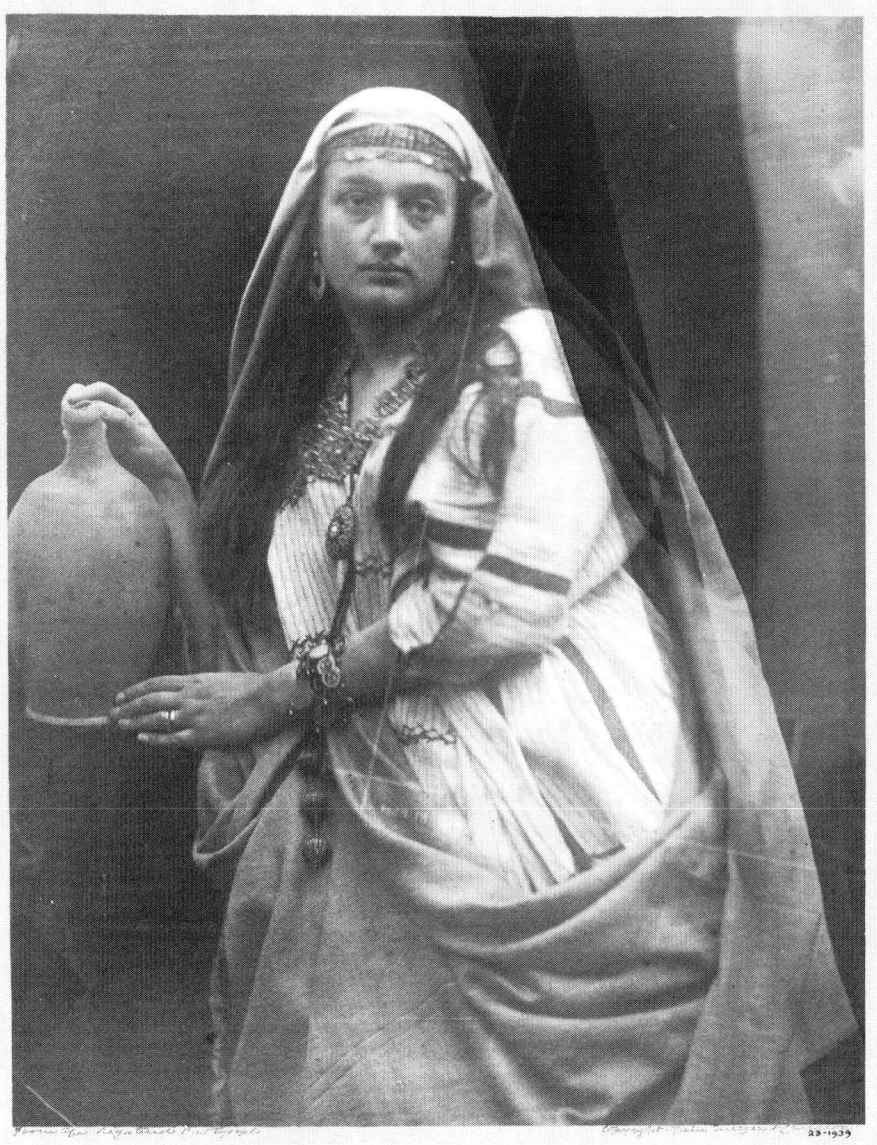

Julia Margaret Cameron, *Zuleika / Rachel at the Well*     25
(Cox 200), c. 1864–66. Albumen print, 34.1 x 26 cm.

An exceptional example of Cameron's representational strategy may be found in an uncanny photograph that she actually titled *three* different ways: *Rebecca*, *Zoë*, and *The East* (Cox 548; Figure 27). In this singular image, Cameron's distinct titles reference a Byronic heroine (*Zoë*), a prominent Old Testament figure (*Rebecca*), and a figurative allusion to an immense geographic area and

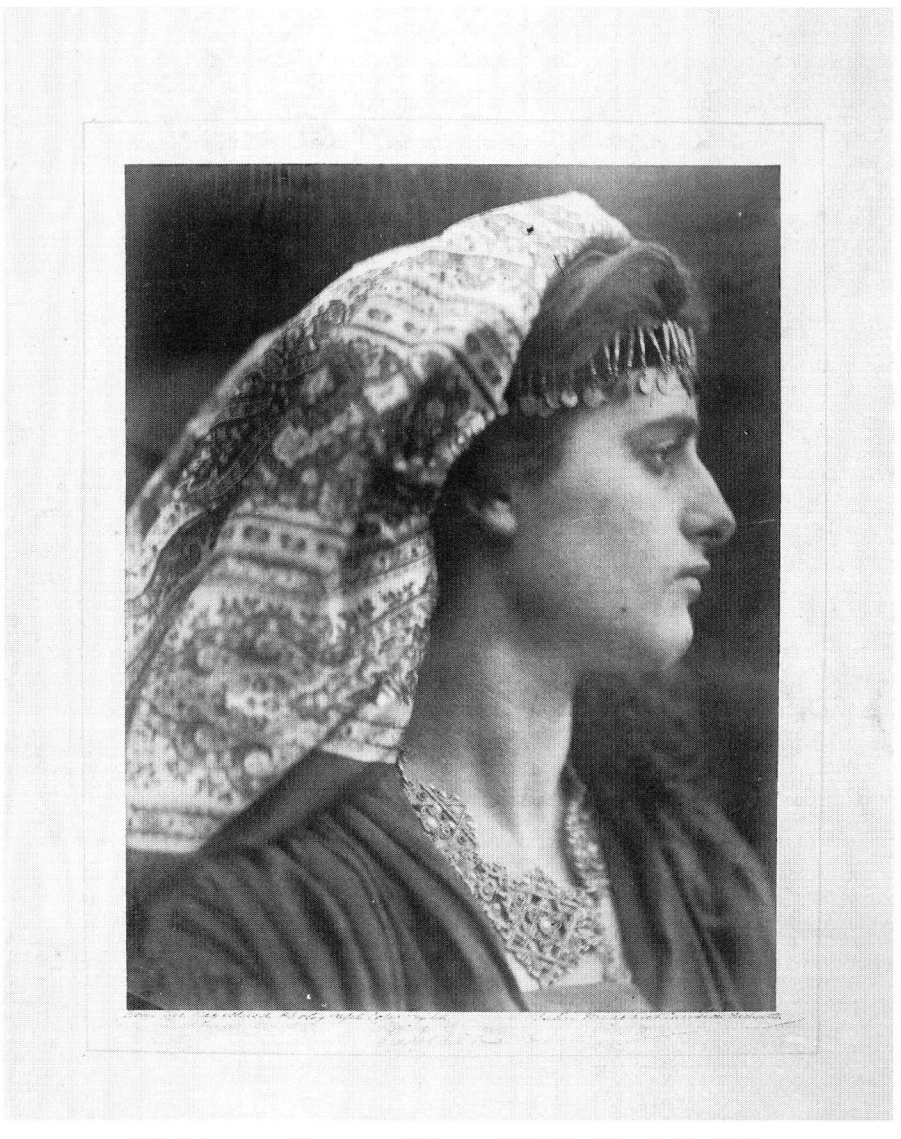

26          Julia Margaret Cameron, *Rebecca / Haidie* (Cox 547), 1870.
                      Albumen print, 34.6 x 28.4 cm.

indefinable cultural symbol (*The East*). Why did Cameron invest such complexity
in a single image? In order to engage multiple audiences, perhaps, she expanded
the hybrid nature of the image: in this case, the duality *Zoë/Rebecca* could blend
the particular Greek/Jewish and Hellenic/Hebraic identities of the subjects in
Arnoldian terms, but the addition of *The East* to the duality *Zoë/Rebecca* brings
with it a vast and ambiguous point of reference that suspends or denies history,

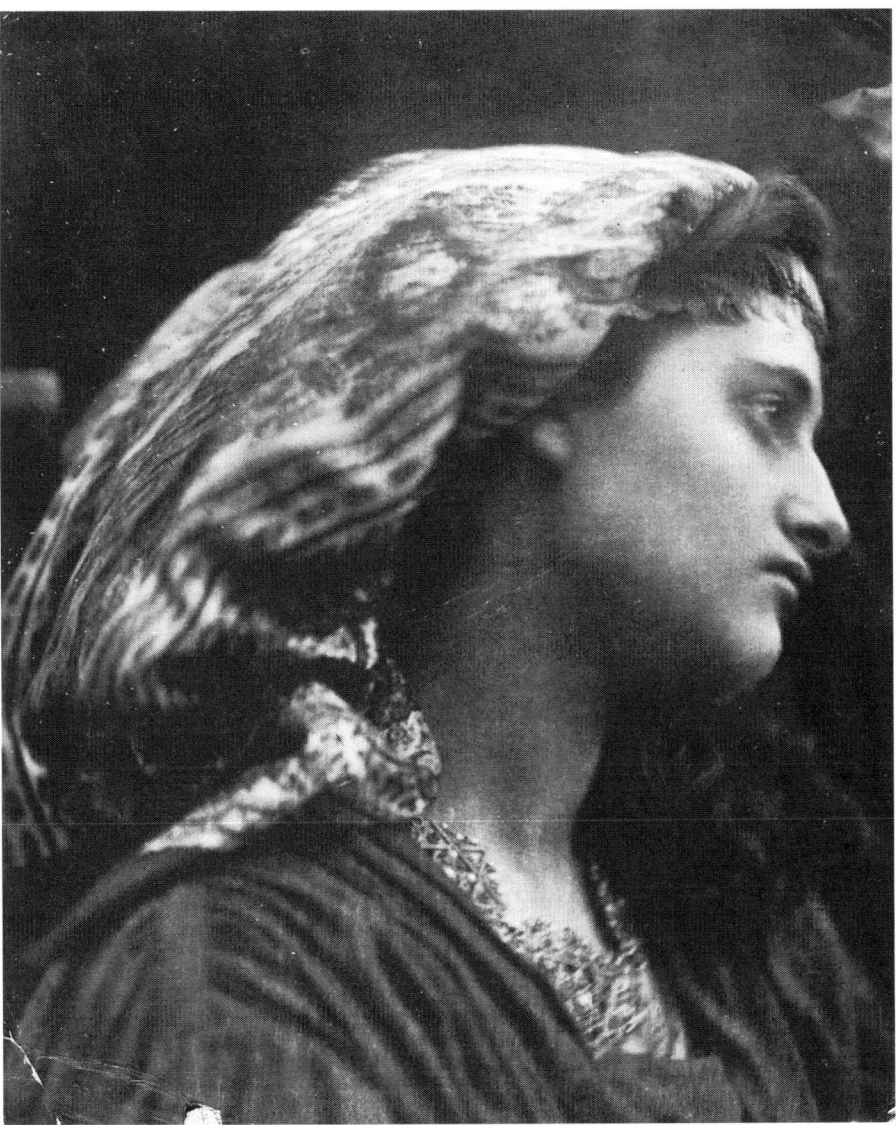

Julia Margaret Cameron, *Rebecca / Zoë / The East* (Cox 548), c. 1870.
Albumen print, 34.1 x 27.7 cm. 7

27

because framed in this way, 'The East' represents the eternal and timeless Orient, while in political and geographic terms, 'The East' stands in cultural opposition to 'The West'.

Roland Barthes described the European impulse to portray 'The East' as alien as a strategy of representation embedded in the discourse of British colonialism. He wrote: 'By appending to Eastern realities a few positive signs which mean "native," one reliably immunizes them against any responsible content. A little "situating," as superficial as possible, supplies the necessary alibi and exempts one from accounting for the situation in depth … In any case, the main thing is to deprive [the East] of its history.'[9] Consequently, Cameron's title, *The East*, disconnects the image from history and from Zoë/Rebecca. In addition, Cameron's photograph resists a one-dimensional interpretation because of these multiple references. As a hybrid work, the image cannot simultaneously portray Rebecca *and* Zoë; an ancient story of the Old Testament *and* a modern war of liberation; an Old Testament Jew *and* a modern Greek. Moreover, in Cameron's photograph the East/West dichotomy is up-ended, because each title has redefined the discursive space of East and West, and one narrative cancels out the others. As a result, the instability and indeterminacy of a hybrid work like this cannot be resolved. Whether we consider the image a triad or three individual works, *Rebecca/Zoë/ The East* remains unstable because one cannot tear apart the intertwined identity of the intermixed narratives. We also might consider that Cameron intended to blend the genealogy of different cultures and histories in this image. If so, Cameron may be said to have 'transposed' the subject of Byron's heroines in her photography: by fusing together the 'Eastern heritage' of the Hebrew Rebecca and the Greek Zoë, Cameron figuratively could have portrayed a united Eastern heroine who could stand in resistance to the dominance and authority of Europe.[10]

Cameron's circle would have recognized in the titles to photographs like *Zuleika* or *Medora* clear references to the heroines of Byron's 'Turkish Tales', in particular, *The Bride of Abydos* and *The Corsair*, respectively. Both poems had been popular in England since they were first published between 1814 and 1818. Their popularity was sustained by literary reviews that appeared for many years. Thomas Carlyle, for example, read *The Corsair* and *The Bride of Abydos* at the same time that he read reviews of each work in the *Edinburgh Review*.[11] When Byron published *Don Juan* in 1819, sales of the 'Turkish Tales' flourished again. William St Clair has shown that during the 1820s, Byron first captured a middle-class reading public which was enthusiastic about *Don Juan* but relatively indifferent to *Childe Harold*. Numerous pirated editions of *Don Juan* flooded the market in response its popularity. By 1830, *Childe Harold* and the Tales had saturated the middle- and upper-class markets and finally reached the literate but less-prosperous 'second-hand market'. During the next decade, Byron's publisher John Murray started producing low-cost reprints of the individual poems for a few pence each, extending the reach of Byron's work: 'The price of all of Byron, not just *Don Juan*, was by the 1840s well below the price of bread, and well within the reach of clerks, artisans, and even carpenters, and we know that demand was brisk and that turnover was high.'[12] The popularity of *Don Juan* made this possible, as it helped to drive down prices and increase the accessibility of Byron's works, and the rise of an educated readership meant that 'Byron' could continue to generate ever new revenues, whether on stage in dramatic adaptations or in printed illustrations made for a growing mass market.

The Oriental character 'Zuleika' gained fame as a literary persona that was particularly well suited to the Victorian stage. To many Victorians, Byron meant Oriental luxury mixed together with Oriental despotism, and the harem came to symbolize the stereotype of a closed society marked by transgressive sexuality and feminine submissiveness. On the English stage, the poetic Byron was recreated as a dramatic phenomenon, where colourful fantasy-inspired sets and dramatic encounters between richly costumed pashas, giaours, giaffres, and slaves tantalized audiences across London. Because the Orient was gendered female, this fascination almost always turned on the exotic visual display of women's bodies. As Edward Ziter explained: 'Actresses in pink fleshings or draped in diaphanous material helped deliver the East to English audiences.'[13] Harem imagery and Byron's heroines, in particular, transfixed audiences and kept attendance high. In 1818, for example, William Diamond produced an adaptation of *The Bride of Abydos* in the Drury Lane; his stage directions for a scene in 'Zuliaka's' apartment combined music-playing female slaves, dancers and flower girls, and glittering veils, all thrown in a swirl of frenzied movement that ended with the actors floored in an exhausted sprawl: as Ziter observed, 'Diamond evoked tropes that had only begun to emerge in orientalist painting and would come to dominate stage depictions of the harem: native instruments and music that intensify the sensualisation of female bodies, Sapphic play that reads as both innocent and provocative, a central figure who begins or concludes the dance reclined on a couch or litter, and scarves or a canopy that act as props in the dance but ultimately serve to frame the central figure – the languorous odalisque.'[14] In play after play, the submissive female and mysterious harem were transposed from Byron's poetry to visual sensations on the stage: in 1822, for example, *Don Juan* was revised for the stage and emerged as *The Sultana; or, a Trip to Turkey*. Produced at a minor theatre, it began with a revised opening that starts with Haidée's discovery of the shipwrecked Juan. In 1827, Mozart's *The Abduction from the Seraglio* was produced at the Covent Garden, keeping harem imagery popular. The following year, *Don Juan* was adapted for the Adelphi. In 1837, *The Corsair* was produced as both a ballet and a stage performance (King's Theatre), and its popularity extended its run in 1844 to the Drury Lane and in 1856 to the Théâtre Impérial de l'Opéra.[15] *Sardanapalus* was produced in London in 1834, and revived in 1853.[16] Ziter notes how the build-up of these dramatic performances reinforced the Eastern stereotype that the harem was an exotic place of excess, sensuality, and timelessness, and that these qualities added to the popular confusion about which elements were factual and which fictitious in works featuring such imagery.[17]

Popularized in this way, Zuleika became a character so well known in England as Byron's heroine from *The Bride of Abydos* that Thackeray could take her name entirely out of context in conversation and in print. In his book, *Notes of a Journey from Cornhill to Grand Cairo* (1846), Thackeray used Zuleika to symbolize his despair at the loss of the 'authentic' Orient, where the Turks had lost their 'ferocious vitality', and the picturesque and the sublime had become overrun by the ordinary and the commonplace. To the author, the romance of travel evaporated because the aura of experiencing 'the original Orient' had also disappeared: 'A Londoner is no longer a spittoon for true believers', he complained, 'and now that dark Hassan sits in his divan and drinks champagne, and Selim has a French watch, and Zuleikha perhaps takes Morrison's pills, Byronism becomes absurd instead of sublime, and is only a foolish expression of cockney wonder.'[18] To Thackeray, the archaic could still be found in the modern world, but the West's penetration across the globe had punctured the 'mystery' of the East. Nevertheless, encouraged by the sight of 'dark eyes' peering out behind 'flirting fans' of Spanish ladies and the veiled faces staring from latticed windows in the East, the author reassured readers that the picturesque and exotic Orient still existed. Toward the end of his journey, Thackeray wrote how 'there is a picture in every street' which, back in England, one could experience vicariously by viewing the paintings of John Frederick Lewis. In his book, Thackeray also imagined travel in the East as an erotic tour for Europeans to procure trophies: 'There was a certain tattooed girl', he wrote, 'with black eyes and huge silver earrings, and a chin delicately picked out with blue, … whose likeness I longed to carry off.'[19] One suspects that Thackeray would have liked to make off with something more than her mere likeness alone.

The theme of representation as a symbolic act of possession is a commonplace in visual art, and John Frederick Lewis's status as an English expatriate living in Cairo allowed him to claim cultural familiarity and authority over his subject matter. To a trusting British public, his pictures of harem interiors seemed realistic and believable. Lewis's watercolour, *The Hhareem*, offers a perfect example: following the exhibition of Lewis's painting in 1850, the critic for the *Illustrated London News* described the painting in the same terms used to describe Zuleika in one of William Diamond's stage directions, in which the harem girl in her apartment is surrounded by extravagance and material goods:

> A female slave, of exquisite symmetry, and of beauty too (in the Eastern notion of the term), is brought into the hhareem, and the heavy drapery in which she was wrapped has just been removed by a female attendant. What scene is now before her! The lord of the seraglio is seated, and surrounded by his women, who lie in Eastern repose at his feet. Wherever the eye rests all is Oriental luxury and ease: flowers and fruit and rich dresses lend fresh variety and colour to the scene. How gracefully, how modestly she stands, while surveyed by the lord and ladies of the hhareem; and how unconscious she is of the laughter of the black attendants of the palace. The rich, full lazy eyes of the ladies are exquisitely caught.[20]

From 1851, when he returned to London, Lewis focused almost exclusively on depicting harem interiors. Familiar themes embrace the Orientalist trappings of *The Hhareem*, including heavy drapery juxtaposed with partial nudity, hidden seclusion giving way to revealed exhibitionism, incongruous modesty amidst outright violation and mockery, and male voyeurism joining in Sapphic pleasure, all taking place within a cluttered and enclosed interior that overwhelms the senses. Around 1860, Lewis sat for his own photograph in the dress he wore for almost a decade in Cairo; this self-portrait allowed him to create his own persona as an authority on representing the East. Lewis won critical praise from the critics of the *Art Journal* and *The Times*, and John Ruskin thought Lewis's claims to authenticity in Cairo were on par with the Pre-Raphaelites' attention to authentic detail. Despite his success, Mary Roberts has shown how Lewis deceived his audience by exaggerating his broad access to the harem and exploiting his expatriate status.[21]

The market for mass produced prints mirrored the activity of the London stage in promoting Byron's imagery. As early as 1814, for example, the London print market capitalized on Byron's popularity by reproducing Thomas Phillips's painting of Byron in an Albanian costume, which Byron's publisher Murray first engraved and used as a frontispiece in several editions.[22] St Clair examined how additional artists came forward to take advantage of Byron's popularity. In the spring of 1814, for example, an artist named Thurston produced a series of line-drawings illustrating *The Corsair*, and another named Stodhart created a set of twelve engravings for Murray's other editions. In 1819, after these illustrations attracted favourable review, Murray commissioned another set of prints by Richard Westall.[23] That same year, the French lithographic printer Lasteyrie, together with the artist Horace Vernet, responded to the growing international demand for printed illustrations of Byron's work; the two collaborated in creating French editions of *Don Juan*, *Manfred*, *The Bride of Abydos*, *The Corsair*, and *Mazeppa*.[24]

At this point it is necessary to contextualize the popularity of these graphic works, first in relation to an important earlier project organized to illustrate the works of Shakespeare, and second, to explain the persistence of this graphic art (representing both Shakespeare's and Byron's texts) into the 1860s, coinciding with Cameron's most active years. The Shakespeare project, in which art, commerce, and nationalism coalesced, was instigated in 1789 in London by John Boydell's enterprise known as the Shakespeare Gallery; the business lasted until 1805.[25] Boydell commissioned a series of paintings inspired by Shakespeare's plays as a way of reinvigorating history painting. These paintings were intended to serve double-duty as both prominent display pieces in the Gallery and models for reproductive engravings. Boydell issued his prints in folio-sized editions as collectibles, and later again in smaller dimensions that could function as book illustrations. The project's high-minded ambitions were undermined, however, when the art market grew to favour portraiture and genre works instead of history paintings. Boydell's painters understandably responded to the pressures of the marketplace: 'Entrusted with creating a school of history painting that could rekindle feelings of civic virtue, [the painters] instead produced naturalistic scenes of private virtue in mixed modes – "historical portraits," "domestic histories," and "fancy pictures" – that were better suited to the nineteenth-century image of England.'[26] Cameron's circle was deeply connected to the Arundel Society, which also sought to popularize paintings by means of graphic reproductions, and the activity of the graphic arts marketplace undoubtedly sharpened her awareness of the commercial popularity of such 'fancy pictures'.

Because Shakespeare was considered one of England's most important historical national figures, Cameron chose several scenes from Shakespeare's plays during this time.[27] During the 1860s, 'Shakespeare' was also drawn into opposing political camps, as his works were equally able to represent the interests of 'free thinkers' and conservative aristocrats alike. According to Anthony Taylor, 'Shakespeare's centrality to the literary canon, and the claim that he represented the true wellspring of English creative genius, meant that by 1800 there was already a strong tradition of attributing to him political ideas and notions that were anachronistic in early nineteenth-century terms, but which benefited from his associations with Englishness, the landscape, and the nation.'[28] Unfortunately, Boydell's engraved prints were of poor quality, and in order to satisfy complaints, he created a lottery to meet the large demand for redress. As late as 1816, just as new prints illustrating Byron's poetry hit the market, Boydell was still exchanging prints for the vouchers he issued.[29]

Mass-produced prints illustrating Byron's works appeared in this context, accompanied by yet another novel publishing enterprise, the literary anthology called the 'Beauty'. 'Beauties' were famous excerpts taken from much longer poems. The 'Beauties of Byron' therefore reprinted selected stanzas and lyric songs drawn from Byron's most popular long poems. They were extracted from their original context, often illustrated, and published as 'the best of' selected reading. The 'Beauties' also helped revive Byron for a large reading public because they suppressed the erotic or carnal scenes that might have shocked or offended some readers. To help guard sensitive and impressionable eyes, publishers enlisted clergymen to bless these anthologies as 'safe'.[30] By 1861, when Palgrave's anthology of lyric poetry, *The Golden Treasury*, was published, anthologies of this kind had become extremely popular. They appealed to a wide audience that was largely female, reprinting favourite passages of romantically inspired yearning and sentimental episodes where heroes mourned their beloved and died nobly for a national cause.

In 1833–34, two brothers, William and Edward Francis Finden, exploited Byron's popularity by creating illustrated volumes as visual counterparts to these

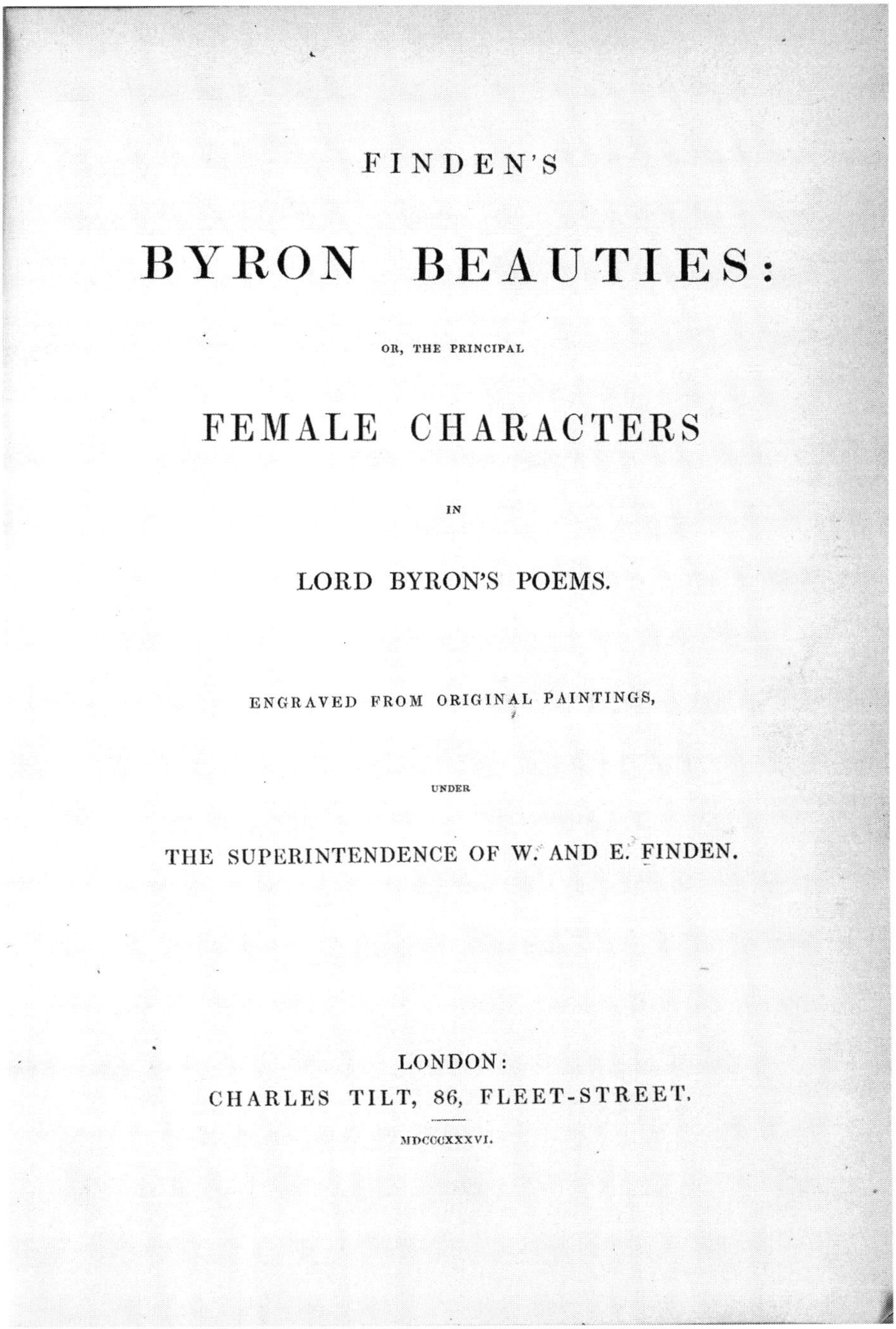

FINDEN'S

# BYRON BEAUTIES:

OR, THE PRINCIPAL

## FEMALE CHARACTERS

IN

### LORD BYRON'S POEMS.

ENGRAVED FROM ORIGINAL PAINTINGS,

UNDER

THE SUPERINTENDENCE OF W. AND E. FINDEN.

LONDON:

CHARLES TILT, 86, FLEET-STREET.

MDCCCXXXVI.

*Finden's Byron Beauties: or, the Principal Female Characters in Lord Byron's Poems,*    **28**
*engraved from original paintings, under the superintendence of W. and E. Finden,*
title page (London: Charles Tilt, 1836).

anthologies. Their first graphic editions were called *Finden's Illustrations of the Life and Works of Lord Byron, With Original and Selected Information on the Subject of the Engravings*; this collection of reproductive engravings was made after paintings and drawings by artists like J. M. W. Turner, George Cattermole, and John Frederick Lewis, among others. In their first edition, the prints almost entirely portrayed picturesque topographic views, allowing viewers to situate themselves in the landscape, a familiar formula that the Findens repeated two years later in their *Landscape Illustrations of the Bible*. In 1836, the two brothers realized their ultimate commercial success when they created *Finden's Byron Beauties; or, the Principal Female Characters in Lord Byron's Poems* (Figure 28). This volume emerged in England 'as one of a series of projected standards for female beauty', as Andrew Elfenbein explained, because 'Byron had become so closely associated with respectable culture that his characters could stand for his poetry.' As a measure of that respectability, even the Brontë sisters copied Finden's engravings to practise their drawing.[31] The success and popularity of *Finden's Byron Beauties* gave rise, several years later, to *The Book of the Boudoir; or, The Court of Queen Victoria* (1842), a work illustrating fashionable ladies of the court who, not incidentally, were portrayed to look remarkably like one another. In *Bleak House* (1853), Dickens satirized Finden's graphic publications as *The Divinities of Albion, or The Galaxy Gallery of British Beauty*. His characters Mr Guppy and Mr Weevle effusively admire, and become self-consciously embarrassed by, the copperplates of these beautiful women, solemnly calling them examples of 'truly national work'.[32] Ironically, to the modern eye, 'Victoria's Court' closely resembles 'Byron's Beauties', no doubt revealing the narrow range of physical features for women that constituted 'Victorian beauty'.

The thirty-nine engravings that comprise *Finden's Byron Beauties* are certain precursors to Cameron's photographs of Byron's heroines. Both draw upon a common storehouse of stereotypes that situate the women in a vaguely Eastern locale, reflecting Byron's settings through the costume and jewellery worn by his heroines. But particularly for the Finden brothers, poses, expressions, and gestures were used to emphasize a romantic state of mind for their viewers, these attributes belonging to the tradition of popular 'fancy pictures'. As the volume's Preface claimed:

> In truth, it is not from the glowing back-grounds from whence they emerge, nor from the quaint or antique form of their draperies, nor from the pomp by which they are surrounded, nor from the dramatic action in which they are engaged, that the female characters of Byron derive their enchantment: their charm exists in their intensity of individual feeling, in their 'naked power of passion', or in their 'reposing energy of grief'.[33]

In Finden's volume, Zuleika's hands are clasped together over her breast in a gesture of humility; Astarte is portrayed ghostly and angelic as she self-consciously

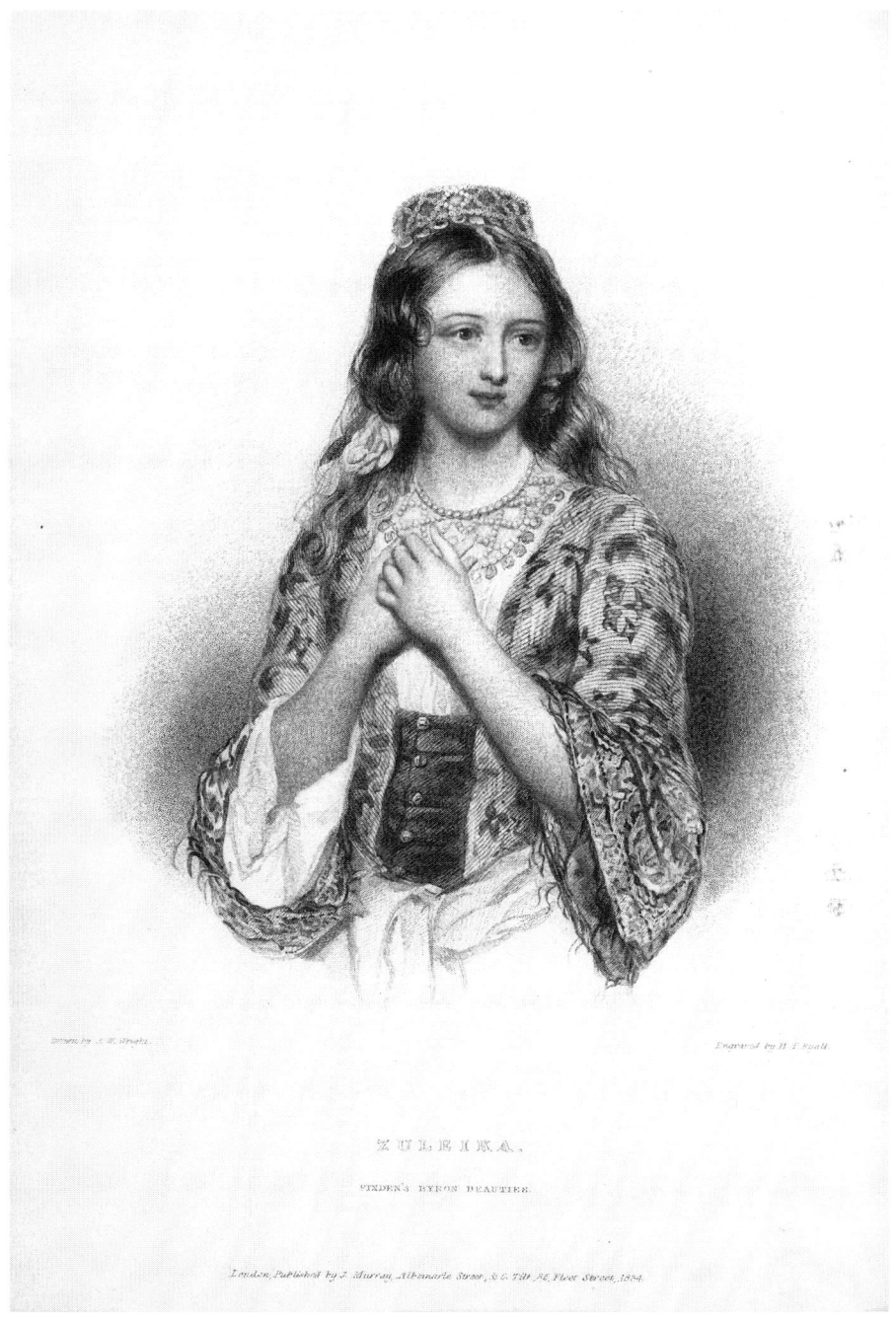

'Zuleika', engraving, from *Finden's Byron Beauties: or, the Principal Female Characters in Lord Byron's Poems, engraved from original paintings, under the superintendence of W. and E. Finden*, not paginated (London: Charles Tilt, 1836).

29

fingers her ringlets of hair; Medora clinches her hands together almost coquettishly under her chin as she gazes upon the setting sun; and Haidée delicately holds a rose between her right thumb and forefinger as she turns to face a stiff wind, which billows her scarves and headdress behind her. They all draw upon the familiar tropes of the sentimental fancy subject. When Cameron represented these very same characters in photographs, however, she portrayed them in scenes of arrested action. Although her models were obliged to remain still and obey her stage directions to avoid creating a photographic blur, Cameron's Byronic heroines are not passive and self-absorbed as they are in Finden's volume.

As an example, Zuleika appears meek and childlike in Finden's volume (Figure 29). The accompanying text helps explain to the reader the artist's visual interpretation: 'Scarcely passed the age of childhood, and brought up in the seclusion of the Harem, the life of Zuleika was but a history of the affections.' Cameron, by contrast, represented Zuleika photographically (Cox 200; Figure 25) with a ceramic urn as a prop, apparently referencing the following lines of action from *The Bride of Abydos*:

> Thrice paced she slowly through the room,
> And watch'd his eye – it still was fix'd;
> She snatch'd the urn wherein was mix'd
> The Persian Atar-gul's perfume,
> And sprinkled all its odours o'er
> The pictured roof and marbled floor;
> The drops, that through his glittering vest
> The playful girl's appeal address'd,
> Unheeded o'er his bosom flew,
> As if that breast was marble too.
>
> (Canto I, X, ll. 15–24)

In Cameron's version, Zuleika is purposeful rather than submissive. A self-possessed young woman, she acts upon her own circumstances to determine her fate. As Byron describes it, she is playful as she paces the room, watches for her opportunity, snatches the urn, and sprinkles its perfume.

Byron's Medora, in contrast to Zuleika, embodies heartbreak, sorrow, and loss, and Finden's illustrator depicts her accordingly, gazing mournfully into the sun from the deck of Conrad's ship. Rather than focusing on this sunset scene of loneliness and abandonment, however, Cameron chose to represent the moment when hope confronts despair. In Cameron's photograph (Cox 499), Medora's actions are arrested by what Byron describes as a rush of feeling that overwhelms her temporarily. Cameron chose the moment in *The Corsair* when Conrad separates from Medora, which Byron uses to emphasize his heroine's fair features (pale face; blue eyes) and her overwhelming grief and sadness:

> But still her lips refused to send – 'Farewell!'
> For in that word – that fatal word – howe'er
> We promise, hope, believe, there breathes despair.
> O'er every feature of that still, pale face,
> Had sorrow fix'd what time can ne'er erase:
> The tender blue of that large loving eye
> Grew frozen with its gaze on vacancy,
> Till – Oh? How far! – it caught a glimpse of him,
> And then it flow'd, and phrensied seem'd to swim
> Through those long, dark, and glistening lashes dew'd
> With drops of sadness oft to be renew'd.
>
> (Canto I, XV, ll. 7–17)

Cameron used the actress Ellen Terry to model Medora, posing her in a gesture similar to that of her better-known image, *Sadness* (Cox 497), with her left hand, as opposed to her right, tugging at the necklace at her throat, wearing a heavy-lidded mournful expression. But the Terry of *Medora* is a mature woman, unlike the childlike girl of *Sadness*. And ever so subtly, in *Medora* Terry looks upward and out, while in *Sadness*, the emotion is confined inward and down.

When Alfred Edward Chalon of the Royal Academy depicted *Haidée* for the Findens, he drew upon Byron's description from *Don Juan* to portray the details just right:

> Her brow was overhung with coins of gold,
>     That sparkled o'er the auburn of her hair –
> Her clustering hair, whose longer locks were rolled
>     In braids behind;
>
> (Canto II, CXVI, ll. 921–4)

Cameron, too, instructed her model to wear a strand of gold coins on her forehead to help signify Haidée's distinguishing crown, and added a scarf or shawl above and behind her model to serve as the headdress that encircled her hair (Figure 26). Chalon portrayed Haidée as statuesque against the shoreline breeze as Byron described her in *Don Juan* (Canto II, CXVIII). By contrast, Cameron's *Haidie* exhibits none of the feminine markers of innocence, desolation, and isolation depicted by Chalon. Rather, Cameron portrays Haidée indoors and in profile, suggesting her character's interaction with some unknown presence outside the image. In addition, Cameron's model wears an expression that is self-assured and resolved rather than diffident and demure, as if portraying Haidée in the poem's fourth canto when she confronts her father Lambro, whose territorial power she and Juan had usurped in his absence, and whose physical return to the island spells an end to their idyllic world. With a focus on the 'dark eyes' of the East, Byron described the altercation between Haidée and Lambro as starting off with a terrible showdown of fierce, warlike gazes:

> He gazed on her, and she on him;'twas strange
>> How like they looked! the expression was the same;
> Serenely savage, with a little change
>> In the large dark eye's mutual-darted flame;
> For she, too, was as one who could avenge,
>> If cause should be – a Lioness, though tame.
> Her father's blood before her Father's face
> Boiled up, and proved her truly of his race.

(Canto IV, XLIV)

Cameron's confidence in interpreting Byron's heroines according to her own lights, departing significantly from her predecessors in Finden's volume, is revealed by an additional example. The engraving of Aurora Raby, another character in *Don Juan*, epitomizes the approach taken by the Findens. In this case, the viewer is positioned as a voyeur who peers into Aurora's private interior, where he finds her in private devotion. She is seen from behind and unaware of being observed. In front of a makeshift prie-dieu, she has propped up a wooden cross and clasped her hands together in prayer; absorbed internally, she looks heavenward through arched windows. By contrast, Cameron's photograph *La Donna at Her Devotions* (Cox 473) inverts this scene by empowering her character. The image, previously unattributed, portrays Donna Julia from the first canto of *Don Juan*.[34] Julia is portrayed by Marie Spartali, who is represented in a seated pose under a Spanish black veil that covers the back of her head; one hand holds a small crucifix while the other holds rosary beads and a folded Spanish fan. Unlike the submissive portrayal of Aurora Raby, Cameron's *Donna Julia* gazes out directly at the viewer with penetrating black eyes: 'Her eye (I'm very fond of handsome eyes) / Was large and dark, suppressing half its fire / Until she spoke' (*Don Juan*, Canto I, LX, ll. 473–5).

Yet Cameron's image is also left intentionally ambiguous. On the one hand, the photograph reveals the tortured moments Julia experienced in the first canto when she resisted her growing attraction to Juan:

> Poor Julia's heart was in an awkward state;
>> She felt it going, and resolved to make
> The noblest efforts for herself and mate,
>> For Honour's, Pride's, Religion's, Virtue's sake:
> Her resolutions were most truly great.

(Canto I, LXXV, ll. 593–7)

On the other hand, Cameron's photograph might equally well represent Julia at the moment immediately following the exposure of her illicit liaison with Juan. In the letter she sent to Juan following her confinement in a convent, Julia described her repentance and isolation, mixed at the same time with acceptance for the forbidden love they shared. She also expressed her ultimate indifference to her present state, effectively disavowing the social stigma that now stains her reputation:

> all is o'er
> For me on earth, except some years to hide
>    My shame and sorrow deep in my heart's core:
> These I could bear, but cannot cast aside
>    The passion which still rages as before.
>
> (Canto I, CXCV, ll. 1554–8)

Cameron's inclination to create photographs that carry hybrid meanings seems to characterize her approach to Byron's poetry, as described in these examples. She extended this practice in portraying explicitly patriotic and nationalistic subjects when she chose figures from Byron's *Hebrew Melodies*.

## Family meets nation in the *Hebrew Melodies*

'I must tell you of one of my present avocations', wrote Lord Byron in 1814 to his fiancée Annabella Milbanke, about his newest project 'to write words for a musical composer who is going to publish the *real old undisputed Hebrew Melodies* which are beautiful & to which David & the prophets actually sang the "songs of Zion"– & I have done nine or ten – on the sacred model – partly from Job &c. & partly my own imagination'. Byron added that his project was an ironic undertaking because he had been 'abused as "an infidel" [by his critics in the press] – Augusta [Byron's sister] says "they will call me a Jew next"'.[35] Like many members of the English elite at the time, Byron might have sympathized with the plight of England's Jews and felt compassion for their historic wandering and suffering, but privately he considered their character 'vile' and held them in the same low opinion in which he held modern Greeks.[36] Paradoxically, at the same time that he championed the cause of Greek liberation and was sympathetic to the call to release Middle Eastern Jews held in captivity, he was indifferent to the condition of actual London Jews. During the nineteenth century, English Jews could not participate in civic life, and the poet never advocated for restoring those rights. Rather, Byron drew upon Old Testament figures for their symbolic and literary value, not in sympathy with the plight of London Jews.[37] In fact, wrote Tom Mole, 'importing Hebraic words to *Hebrew Melodies* reprised Byron's technique of deploying Oriental words in his [Turkish] tales, and archaisms in *Childe Harold's Pilgrimage*'. These literary devices helped to convey the work's credibility. Mole concluded: 'Byron's Jewishness was generally seen as just another costume for the poet to try on.'[38] But during the 1860s, Cameron could not ignore how the political cause of Jewish nationalism became closely associated with British foreign policy and the nation's own cultural identity. The alignment of these interests helps us contextualize the long-standing popularity of Byron's *Hebrew Melodies* and connect the popularity of this work to Cameron's photographs that were based upon Byron's poems.

Because sales of *The Corsair*, *The Bride of Abydos*, and the first two cantos of *Childe Harold* made up the bulk of early sales, historians have concluded that, prior to 1816, Byron's popularity rested on his reputation as 'a poet of romance' rather than on his standing as a champion of liberal and democratic causes.[39] But Byron's *Hebrew Melodies* was first printed in April 1815 and appealed to a distinctly different public from those who purchased the early romances. Byron's new audience was more educated and enjoyed the fashion of celebrating different 'national melodies'. They purchased translations of ancient texts in their original language and bought books that combined text and music – sometimes ancient lyrics and traditional song – and especially works that were religiously inspired. Byron's publisher, Isaac Nathan, recognized the value of the new market and modelled his collaboration with Byron on Thomas Moore's *Irish Melodies*, which was produced in 1808. (Cameron's own familiarity with Moore's *Irish Melodies* could very well have inspired her to create her *Minstrel Group* series in 1866 (Cox 1099–104), a series of photographs that depict travelling troubadours.) However, Byron's *Hebrew Melodies* came on the market in two versions that were published almost simultaneously. One edition was an ornate, expensive, folio-sized volume. This work included only twelve lyric poems that were accompanied by musical scores connected to each verse; it sold for the costly sum of one guinea. Byron's regular publisher Murray released the other edition shortly thereafter, in May 1815. This was a much smaller volume of the same work and was designed to sell at less than half that price, but which contained twenty-four poems and no music.[40]

The two different formats of Byron's *Hebrew Melodies* are significant with regard to the meanings associated with Byron's poetry, as the design of the larger, ornate volume focused readers' attention on the relationship of the verses to sacred music. This association, however, did not transfer to the smaller format. Whereas the larger volume stressed the sacred elements from Scripture, the smaller publication emphasized the lyrical qualities expressed in the romantic, nostalgic, and Oriental motifs that readers had found in the 'Turkish Tales' and *Childe Harold*.[41] Joseph Slater analysed Byron's market for these editions, and found that 'Pious persons who bought the *Hebrew Melodies* in the expectation of finding sacred poetry by Lord Byron found instead a book almost as secular as *The Bride of Abydos*. Nine of the poems are Biblical in subject but Byronic in treatment; two are love songs; five are reflective lyrics, neither Jewish nor Christian; and five are expressions of what might be called proto-Zionism.'[42]

In creating this wide range of photographs from *Hebrew Melodies*, Cameron allegorically represented the nationalistic themes of the ancient Hebrew people by using the currency of Byron to represent Old Testament figures. That is, rather than relying on the Old Testament as a 'primary source' for her imagery, Cameron inserted Byron as an intermediary, using his poetic narratives to help shape meaning in her photographs. Framed in this way, we may perceive Cameron's Old Testament subjects as both Byronic and biblical, rather than typological.[43] In writing the *Hebrew Melodies*, Byron said he drew heavily upon inspirational and historically significant biblical narratives. In 1814, he wrote: 'Of the Scriptures themselves I have ever been a reader & admirer as compositions, particularly the Arab-Job – and parts of Isaiah – and the song of Deborah.' Thomas L. Ashton called Byron's use of these liturgical sources important for their ability to extend beyond Scripture and to comment on his own political identity: '"Arab" Job for the infidel Calvinist, Isaiah for its nationalism, and Deborah for its defiance and archaic expression. These were just the strains to be interwoven in the *Hebrew Melodies*, where the sacred would be sacrificed to the political and the political to the romantic.'[44] Joseph Slater has gone further, suggesting the overarching theme of *Hebrew Melodies* was the political cause of Jewish nationalism. Byron's *Hebrew Melodies* provides another example of cultural hybridity, fusing together the sacred, the political, and the romantic. In nineteenth-century England, the question of assimilation conflicted with the Jews' physical separation from others in society, and the persistence of this disenfranchised minority became an embarrassment to the larger goal of creating an inclusive and modern nation.[45]

By reconnecting Cameron's Hebrew subjects to the broader cultural representation of Jews in nineteenth-century London, both in relationship to the construction of 'Jewish history' and to the dominance of the Anglican Church, we may reclaim Cameron's Hebrew subjects as a subset of her larger interests. As Tamar Garb has written, 'in British imperial discourse the Jew could be embraced in the construction of a Judeo-Christian "common culture" whose mission it was to civilize the world and, simultaneously, could be figured as its dark other, the savage within European consciousness'.[46] Because the civilized/savage dichotomy was inherently unstable, the stereotype needed to be repeated in various contexts. For example, in satire, journalism, and printed cartoons, Jewish men were depicted as overly materialistic, on the one hand, and supremely intellectual, on the other. Among women, Jewesses were styled as warm, sensual, and embracing, but also repressed, untrustworthy, and seductive, especially in contrast to their virtuous and chaste Christian counterparts. Because they were reviled in racial terms, English Jews could also be portrayed as if they were trapped inside their own bodies: men were depicted as effeminate or decrepit, and women idealized as exotic and erotic, alluring yet dangerous.[47] While Christianity was said to have 'transcended' Judaism, actual English Jews and their pre-Christian religious practice still endured in nineteenth-century Britain. Consequently, evangelical Christians were reminded that society had not advanced substantially. Indeed, Jews – especially those who resisted assimilation in their dress and language – were considered archaic remnants of 'the East' living in modern Western culture.[48]

This polarizing language posed a contradiction: although England's Jews did not possess political power, Victorian society was deeply invested in its own 'reputation for religious tolerance and political liberty that made the issue of intolerance toward the Jews so vital a concern to conceptions of English national identity', as Michael Ragussis has argued.[49] During the 1840s and 1850s, Parliament took up the question of whether to grant the Jews basic civic rights. In 1848, Bishop Samuel Wilberforce argued against Jewish emancipation, claiming 'the Jews have no home for which to fight, no nation for which to feel, no literature by which to be lifted up, no hope and hardly a God'.[50] In contrast, as Foreign Secretary during the 1840s, Lord Palmerston instructed the British consul in Jerusalem to protect the Jews from persecution there and tried to persuade the Sultan in Constantinople to accept the emigration of English Jews.[51] Others in the National Church had written about the importance of the Hebraic foundation of Christianity, insisting upon the English debt owed the Hebrews, who had first embraced the concept of the eternal divinity of God and the importance of his laws. Matthew Arnold separated ancient Judaism from what he considered modern forms of Hebraic culture, which he associated with positive actions in the world that were moral and true.[52] But Arnold also argued that society's debt to the Jews had limits, because, as he explained, contemporary English Jews had stubbornly held on to their archaic Oriental roots: 'Hellenism is of Indo-European growth, Hebraism is of Semitic growth; and we English, a nation of Indo-European stock, seem to belong naturally to the movement of Hellenism.'[53] In using the term 'we English', Arnold clearly intended to exclude Britain's Jews.[54] At the same time, however, Arnold insisted that the double-sided nature of English culture, which rested on both Hellenic and Hebraic foundations, required of English national identity a complicated balancing act that embraced two complementary cultural forces simultaneously. As Arnold wrote,

> For *the days of Israel are innumerable*; and in its blame of Hebraising too, and in its praise of Hellenising, [British] culture must not fail to keep its flexibility, and to give to its judgments that passing and provisional character which we have seen it impose on its preferences and rejections of machinery. Now, and for us, it is a time to Hellenize, and to praise knowing; for we have Hebraised too much, and have over-valued doing. But the habits and discipline received from Hebraism remain for our race an eternal possession; and, as humanity is constituted, one must never assign to them the second rank to-day, without being prepared to restore to them the first rank to-morrow.[55]

A coherent national culture required both sides to coexist, argued Arnold, because the nation's internal conflicts and divisions were established historically in equal parts.[56]

Cameron also portrayed the double nature of the ancient Jew in English culture. In her allegorical representations and fancy subjects, she fused together

East and West, faith and reason, religion and civic life. For example, Cameron chose the subject of *King David* (Cox 164, 165) from Byron's *Hebrew Melodies* because of its enduring symbolic value as a personification of the House of David, under whom the ancient Jews were once united politically as a nation. In depicting an enthroned and pensive King David, who averts his eyes and tips his head down, holding his hands together in a gesture of contemplation or worry, Cameron created a complex image of a weakened, despondent, once-mighty ruler. Allegorically, King David represents an emblem of ancient messianic religious devotion and Jewish national and historical identity. In Cameron's photograph, *King David* embodies something essential about the ancient Hebrews; she depicts his historical failure as well as his physical weakness and decline. Four of Byron's poems in *Hebrew Melodies* refer to the legacy of David; drawn from the two Books of Samuel, the poems, *Saul, My Soul is Dark, The Harp the Monarch Minstrel Swept*, and the *Song of Saul Before His Last Battle*, tell interconnected narratives of David's story, and run throughout the *Hebrew Melodies*. Historians have described how these poems humanize the egotism and pride of rulers and tyrants, and express humility for their arrogance and self-importance.[57] The four short poems provide depth to Cameron's portrayal of David, who was heir to Saul but also, in his old age, a feared and shunned autocrat. Cameron effectively represents Byron's political allegory that 'tyrants provide for their own decay'.

The harp is an apt metaphor for David's reign, since under his rule, music was first brought into Jewish sacramental rites. However, in Byron's interpretation, all four poems are permeated by a lyrical melancholy, since David's great triumphs were followed by a disastrous fall.[58] Cameron's image extends this ominous portrayal photographically, as David's dark demeanour corresponds to the poet's lines that once the harp 'told the triumphs of our King' (*The Harp*, l. 11), but since then, song is 'heard on earth no more' (*The Harp*, l. 16). Consequently, no instrument appears in David's hands. Similarly, in Byron's poem, *My Soul is Dark*, Saul urges David to take up the harp once again as a way to soothe his 'heavy heart':

> But bid the strain be wild and deep,
>   Nor let thy notes of joy be first:
> I tell thee, minstrel, I must weep,
>   Or else this heavy heart will burst.
>
> (ll. 9–12)

In dramatizing the biblical lines from I Samuel 16: 14–23, Byron explains Saul's melancholy as a response to Samuel's prophecy of Saul's later doom, a foretelling that had been uttered when the prophet was a small child and again later, from the grave, when Saul conjured back Samuel as an otherworldly spirit. Cameron represented the prophet as infant – *The Vision of the Infant Samuel* (Cox 126), and again later, representing Samuel as a small child – *The Infant Samuel* (Cox 953). Cameron connected her photograph of *Samuel* to that of *King David* because in his melancholic state David could only attempt to produce 'sounds that seem as from above, / In dreams that day's broad light can not remove' (ll. 19–20). Indeed, this poem, *The Harp the Monarch Minstrel Swept*, is steeped in melancholy. On at least one occasion in 1865, Cameron exhibited the two photographs *King David* and *The Infant Samuel* together. The two versions of *Samuel* appear in the album she presented to Lord Overstone in 1865, and the cropped version of her image of King David appear in the album she presented to Sir John Herschel (Cox 164) in 1867. By 1868, at Cameron's German Gallery exhibition, all three photographic interpretations of David and Samuel appeared together.

Cameron's print of *King David* was made from a photographic negative that originally depicted two individuals rather than a solitary person. In the actual negative, Cameron represented Henry Taylor as David and Mary Hillier as Bathsheba (Cox 166). Although Cameron printed the full image at least once, she ultimately disregarded the idea of using the full composition of David and Bathsheba together, favouring instead the cropped version of David alone (Cox 164, 165). Perhaps Cameron insisted on producing these cropped versions because there were no references to Bathsheba in her Byronic source material, or perhaps she found David's worldly and spiritual denigration too explicit and degrading in the biblical tale of Bathsheba. As recounted in 2 Samuel 11–12, this story embodies the most extreme example of David's dictatorial rule, describing how David took Bathsheba by force and then sent her husband to war, where he was sure to be killed in battle. Denounced for his murderous actions, David was vilified socially and politically. After Bathsheba gave birth to their son, the boy died unexpectedly. This was interpreted as a divine sign punishing David for his transgression; the events conspire to deepen his melancholy.[59] It is significant, therefore, that Cameron literally cut out Bathsheba from her composition: indeed, Bathsheba's absence allowed Cameron to present David's lament as symbolic of the lost political unity of his people, rather than as a personal or family drama. In *The Harp the Monarch Minstrel Swept*, Byron used David's harp and the power of song as a special emblem for the presence of the divine in sacred music.[60] But in Cameron's portrayal of King David, she has severed the inspirational role of lyric poetry from the now-quiet harp, just as religion has been separated from civic life.

Literally split apart from Bathsheba in the photograph (Cox 164, 165), David's apparent despondency may express regret for his nation's lost glory, for his separation from his son Absolom, or for his moral failures in his pursuit of Bathsheba. In the Old Testament, David's old age melancholy is connected to all three of these events. In Cameron's photograph, King David, the 'monarch minstrel', corresponds to the related weeping musicians who lament the loss of the Jewish nation in the *Hebrew Melodies*, especially in Byron's poems titled *Oh! Weep for Those* ('weep for the harp of Judah's broken shell'), *By the River of Babylon We Sat Down and Wept* ('We sate down and wept by the waters / Of Babel, and thought of the day / When our foe, in the hue of his slaughters, / Made Salem's high places his prey'), and *In the Valley of Waters* ('we wept o'er the day / when the host of the stranger made Salem his prey'). In each poem, the voice and the harps of the Jews lie 'mute'. The poem *Oh! Weep for Those* goes even further with respect to articulating the nationalist cause, asking in the second verse:

> And where shall Israel lave her bleeding feet?
> And when shall Zion's songs again seem sweet?
> And Judah's melody once more rejoice
> The hearts that leaped before its heavenly voice?
>
> (ll. 5–8)

The state of mourning experienced in these poems is also directly connected to Byron's poem about Jewish exile in *Hebrew Melodies*, called *On Jordan's Banks*. In this poem, the poet asks two more direct questions of God and then explicitly chastens God to awaken from his sleep so that he might deliver his people into freedom: 'How long by tyrants shall thy land be trod? / How long thy temple worshipless, Oh God?' (ll. 11–12). Susan Spector has noted that Byron worked together with Isaac Nathan to unite *On Jordan's Banks* to the song *Ma'oz Tsur*; an incongruous pairing as the song expresses a joyful melody of deliverance. As a result of this coupling, the poem 'exposes the fundamental question underlying Zionism: should the Jews believe literally in Zionism, or should they transform their belief into a metaphorical interpretation of a return to Jerusalem, and actively build a life in the Diaspora?'[61] George Eliot took up this very question in 1876 in *Daniel Deronda*.

Cameron's image of King David is directly related to her other images of Old Testament figures discussed above, as each character chosen by the photographer bears an important historical role in representing the human cost of exile and banishment, or in delivering the Jews from bondage, or with respect to their perpetual wandering without a stable homeland. For example, the biblical figures of Rebecca and Rachel are each represented 'at the well', a site that is symbolic of their generosity to strangers and of their fertility as historical matriarchs. According to the Old Testament, Rebecca was the wife of Isaac and mother of Esau and Jacob. Rachel's son, Joseph, led the Jews during their exile, and when Rachel wept for her children (as described in Jeremiah 31: 15) it was in grief over the destruction of the Temple by the Babylonians. In 1867, Cameron photographed Rachel at the well (Cox 513, 514) and in 1870, portrayed Rachel in an Eastern headdress (Cox 200). Esther was a descendant of Rachel as described in the Apocrypha (Esther 15: 7). When she was accused of treason and brought before King Ahasuerus, Esther defended the honour of her people, imploring the

King to preserve their lives, resist false accusations made against them, and secure their freedoms. In a photograph of 1865, Cameron portrayed Esther's supplication before Ahasuerus (Cox 167), using Henry Taylor, whom she used to portray King David, as the model for King Ahasuerus. Another biblical subject, Pharaoh's daughter, who found Moses in the bulrushes, also symbolizes the deliverance of the Jews, and was photographed by Cameron around 1866 or 1870 (Cox 546). A founding narrative of Jewish identity, Pharaoh's daughter's selfless actions helped liberate the Jews from Egyptian bondage. Another 'daughter of Pharaoh' was the twice-exiled Hagar, the second wife of Abraham, who was banished not only from Egypt but also from her own home, together with Ishmael, her son by Abraham. Although no extant print survives of *Hagar and Ishmael*, on 10 October 1864, Cameron registered a photograph by this title for copyright protection, suggesting her steadfast interest in representing another Old Testament matriarch who endured the pain of exile. And, like the symbolism present in her images of Rebecca and Rachel, Cameron's photograph of *Boaz and Ruth* (Cox 163) represents Boaz sharing the fruits of his harvest with Ruth. This is significant, since in the Book of Ruth, Boaz married Ruth as an act of redemption to preserve their tribal heritage, another symbolic hallmark of national identity that was represented in the Old Testament. Because Ruth was one of David's ancestors, who later, when king, united the disparate tribes of Israel, Cameron's choice of Old Testament subjects turns full circle.

In poetry and photography Byron and Cameron also told the biblical story of Jephthah and his daughter (Cox 168), a tale from Judges 11: 30–40, in which Jephthah of Gilead, recruited to lead the Jews in battle against the Ammanites, made a fateful bargain with God. In order to assure his victory on the field, Jephthah promised to sacrifice the first living thing he saw upon his return from war. To Jephthah's great distress, his daughter – his only child – appeared to him first, but she yielded obediently to Jephthah's vow and agreed to pay her father's debt with her life. Jephthah's daughter has no name, but Byron wrote his lyric entirely from her perspective. In each stanza of the poem, Jephthah's daughter offers her consent, agreeing to put nation above family. After returning from a self-imposed seclusion, she prophesies that her story will become a symbol of duty and national honour after her death.[62] In his poem, Byron openly questions the Hebrew God's love for his own people, as he did in *On Jordan's Banks*. By incriminating a vengeful God who would not only demand but actually accept such a terrible sacrifice, the poet questions the national celebration that was supposed to accompany the girl's sacrifice with bitter and ironic words, 'And my Father and Country are free!' (l. 16).

Prior to Cameron's photographic treatment of this subject, several Victorian poets and artists had also represented Jephthah and his daughter. The same sense of duty that bound daughters to their fathers under ancient rabbinic law was

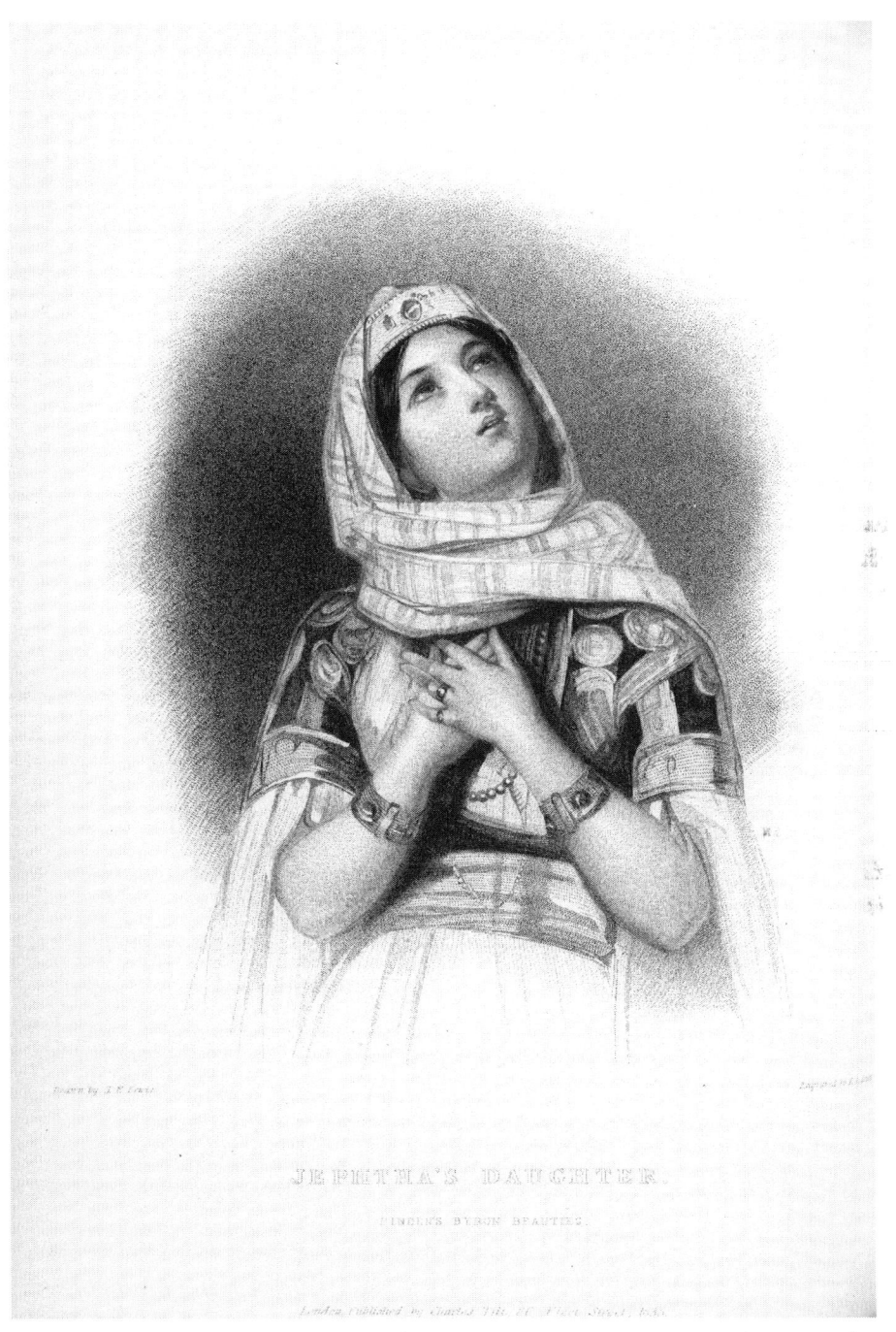

'Jephthah's Daughter', engraving, from *Finden's Byron Beauties: or, the Principal Female Characters in Lord Byron's Poems, engraved from original paintings, under the superintendence of W. and E. Finden*, not paginated (London: Charles Tilt, 1836).

**30**

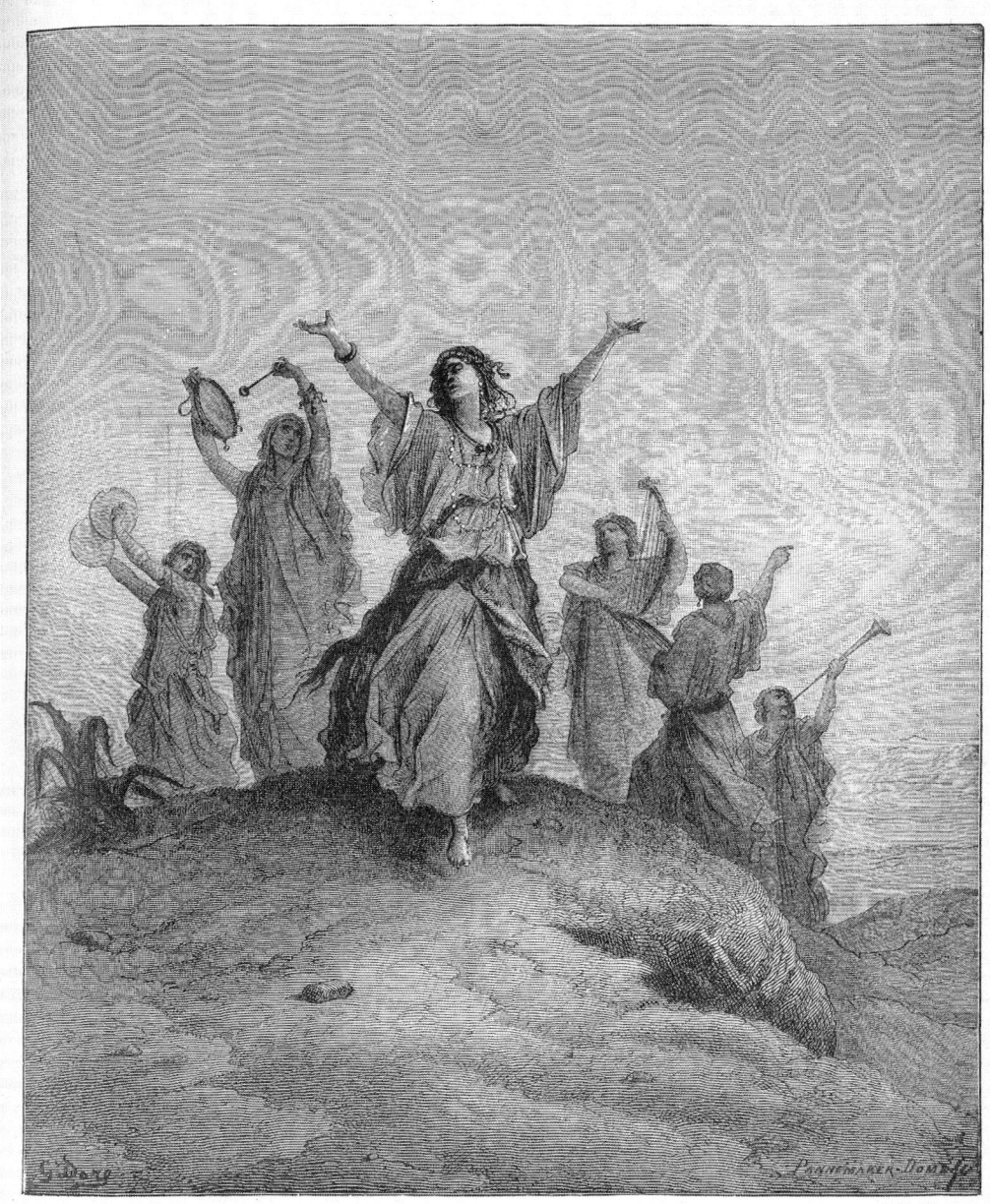

JEPHTHAH MET BY HIS DAUGHTER.

**31**      Gustave Doré, *Jephthah's Daughter Coming to Meet Her Father*, 1866.
Woodcut, reprinted in *The Bible Gallery illustrated by Gustave Doré
with memoir of Doré and descriptive letter-press by Talbot W. Chambers*
(New York: Cassell Publishing Company, 1880).

also expected of well-behaved women under Victorian patrimony. In his *Byron Beauties*, Finden included a graphic depiction of *Jephthah's Daughter* by John Frederick Lewis to accompany his other representations (Figure 30). As with the other illustrations in this folio, Finden selected Byronic subjects that mapped well to accepted ideas about Victorian women's proper roles and moral character. But *Jephthah's Daughter* was the *only* poem from *Hebrew Melodies* selected to appear along with Byron's other heroines in *Byron Beauties*. Consistent with Finden's preferred format, Jephthah's daughter stands alone, but in representing her in this way, Lewis isolated the young woman as the only subject in the story. Clutching her hands to her breast and looking heavenward, as if imploring God to intercede on her behalf and save her, or, in the act of pledging her unquestioning faith, Jephthah's daughter is portrayed as the tragic heroine. Only in Finden's accompanying text does the reader learn about the absent father and the daughter's sacrifice to assure her people's freedom and national honour.

John Everett Millais, who exhibited a painting of *Jephthah's Daughter* at the Royal Academy in 1867, also typifies the representation of the loyal and devoted daughter. But Millais's composition depicts mourning and despair, as opposed to Lewis, who represented his character's stoic virtue: Millais depicted Jephthah as a weary victor, seated heavily in his chair after the battle, his shield at his side. But Millais also reverses narrative roles: it is Jephthah who hangs his head in misery and regret while holding his quiet and composed daughter's hands. Not only does Jephthah's daughter accept her fate in silent grace, she comforts her father by holding him in *her* arms, while the women in their company huddle together to weep and pray. In yet another contemporary interpretation of this story, Gustave Doré represented *Jephthah's Daughter Coming to Meet Her Father* in 1866. In this high-spirited woodcut, Doré portrayed the young woman just prior to the unexpected moment of learning her future was tied to her father's ill-conceived vow. She is an exuberant and light-hearted young girl caught in the act of greeting her father in dance and song upon his return from war (Figure 31).

Like Byron and Doré, Tennyson was also inspired by this particular episode in the biblical narrative. In his poem, *A Dream of Fair Women*, which enjoyed enduring popularity throughout the century, Tennyson celebrated the purity and exuberance of the high-spirited girl:

> The daughter of the warrior Gileadite,
>     A maiden pure; as when she went along
> From Mizpeh's tower'd gate with welcome light,
>     With timbrel and with song.

(ll. 197–200)

As a reflection of Victorian values, and in a faint echo of Byron, Tennyson praised Jephthah's daughter's selflessness and obedience. He ignores, however, any mention of the ultimate sacrifice she made to keep her country free:

> How beautiful a thing it was to die
> For God and for my sire!
>
> It comforts me in this one thought to dwell,
>     That I subdued me to my father's will,
> Because the kiss he gave me, ere I fell,
>     Sweetens the spirit still.
>
> (ll. 231–6)

In first selecting an earlier moment when Jephthah's daughter welcomed her father 'with timbrel and with song', Tennyson reprises the moment of her sacrificial death as if it were a surrender made for God and father (and *not* for country). In Tennyson's narrative, it is the now-deceased spirit of Jephthah's daughter who recounts her final actions and thoughts, a macabre poetic device that makes sense only as a dream recounted in the poem. In Byron's poetic interpretation, by contrast, Jephthah's daughter narrates the action in the present tense and has no benefit of the hindsight Tennyson gave her. Yet for both Byron and Tennyson, the experience of God's wrath upon Jephthah and his daughter does not ultimately end up redeeming his people, since unlike the Isaac of Genesis, Jephthah's daughter received no last-minute reprieve, and by extension, the wandering of the Jews finds no end or deliverance.

Rather than portray Jephthah's daughter alone, Cameron used two models, still unknown, in her photograph, *Jephthah and His Daughter* (Cox 168; Figure 32). Her interpretation of the story also strays farthest from its biblical source and departs from Byron and Tennyson; visually, it is also unlike its contemporaries in the art of Millais or Doré. In Cameron's photograph, both Jephthah and his daughter appear neither resigned nor inspired, but rather, she has portrayed the two as if dazed and stunned. Their eyes are struck wide, expressing surprise that Jephthah's impetuous bargain with God would actually be accepted. In Cameron's interpretation, God is neither forgiving nor compassionate. While Jephthah holds a small book, perhaps a hymnal, and reflects on his actions and his promise, his daughter stares off into the distance. The impression is of sheer bewilderment rather than joyful submission or sorrowful resignation. Cameron's image portrays the flip side of God's redemption of his people, an interpretation that contemporary English Jews might well have imagined. Isaac Nathan, for example, articulated this view as early as 1815:

> When these beautiful lines were composed by Lord Byron, I was anxious to ascertain his real sentiments on the subject, hinting my own belief that it might not necessarily mean a positive sacrifice of the daughter's life, but perhaps referred to a sentence of perpetual seclusion, a state held by the Jews as dead indeed to society, and the most severe infliction that could be imposed.[63]

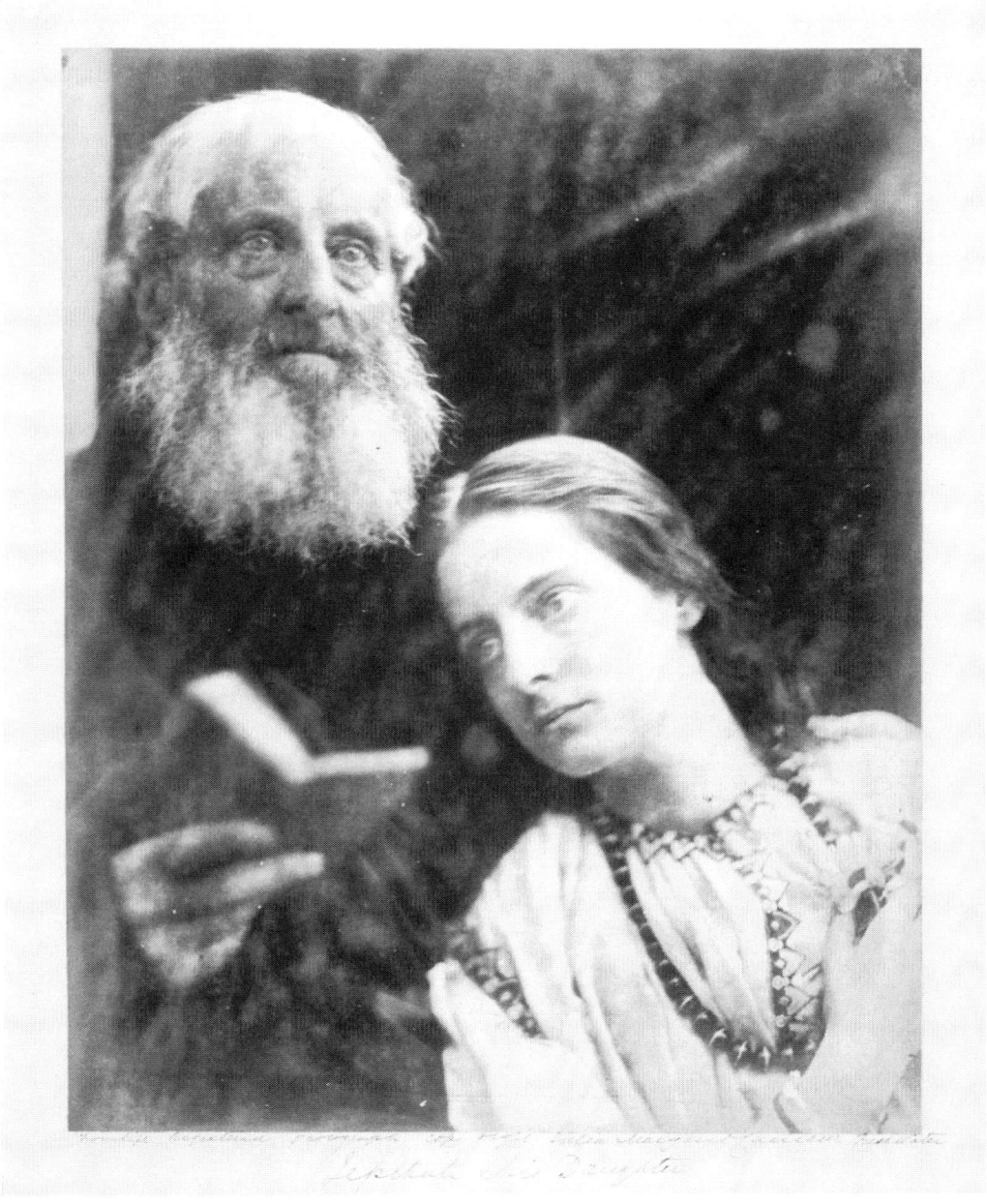

Julia Margaret Cameron, *Jephthah and His Daughter* (Cox 168), c. 1868. **32**
Albumen print, 36.1 x 28.1 cm.

Cameron's photograph of *Jephthah and His Daughter* visually conveys the tragedy of the 'perpetual seclusion' of nineteenth-century English Jews. She has portrayed Jephthah and his daughter as if they have been 'inflicted' with a numbing malady, rendering them unable to take positive action, looking into a bleak future of displacement and exile. In Cameron's photograph, the two subjects seem to represent a dawning realization of their condition that has made them 'dead indeed to society'.[64]

In a final example, Cameron borrowed the title of Byron's short poem, *She Walks in Beauty*, directly from its source in *Hebrew Melodies*. She used this title for a photograph depicting her niece, Julia Duckworth, in 1874 (Cox 333). In 1870, Duckworth endured the sudden death of her second husband, Herbert. Because of Julia Duckworth's close family ties and Cameron's own sentimental attachment to her niece, this image has been interpreted almost exclusively as a personal commemoration of Duckworth's beauty and her stoic character. We know this photograph was made some four years after Herbert Duckworth's loss and several years prior to Julia's remarriage to Leslie Stephen.[65] These biographical facts turn the image into an allegory of loneliness and personal sorrow.

But that this photograph also bears the title to Byron's evocative poem of wandering and exile in *Hebrew Melodies* makes sense in relation to Cameron's use of Byronic subjects as allegories of familial and national bonding. In Nathan's edition of the *Hebrew Melodies*, he set Byron's verse *She Walks in Beauty* to a musical score known in messianic Judaism as *Lekha Dodi*, an ancient Hebrew song that focused on the archaic symbol of the *Shekhinah*. According to legend, the *Shekhinah* represented the 'feminine divine' who had been exiled by the Fall of Man and condemned to wander in exile, much as the Jews of the Old Testament were cast out from their homeland into the wilderness. The song *Lekha Dodi* celebrates the reunification of the *Shekhinah* to the Messiah. Byron's text, read in the context of this song to which it was paired in *Hebrew Melodies*, becomes a parable of the fragmented, wandering, and unsettled ancient Hebrews and a corresponding allegory of divine grace.[66] Photographs do not easily take on such mystical references, but Cameron evidently believed her titles could focus such attention. By detaching the photograph from Cameron's biography and reconnecting it to its Byronic context, the allegorical references become less personal. In *Hebrew Melodies*, *She Walks in Beauty* refers to 'the nameless grace' of Woman as it is expressed in the concept of the 'divine feminine'; in other words, Byron's text connects this image to the female dwelling place of God. These are themes that Cameron explored earlier in another context: in the *Fruits of the Spirit*, for example, she represented the timeless moral truths written about by Paul; they are a Christian counterpart to the same virtues represented by Byron in *Hebrew Melodies*.

By using her cherished niece as the model for this image, it is certainly possible that Cameron might have transferred her personal attachment to Julia Duckworth into her personification of divine grace, a happy by-product and memento of the photographic activity itself. But also in 1874, Cameron reconceived the image once again and used a different model entirely, portraying Isabel Bateman in Julia Duckworth's role (Cox 170). It would seem, then, that Cameron's decision to make this additional image with the same title separates the iconography from the personal and biographical and argues instead for a larger allegorical interpretation. Both photographs portray solitary women, standing in isolation, starkly lit against dark backdrops; while Duckworth stands against an ivy-covered wall, Bateman is bathed in ethereal light against an empty void. Both stare out impassively at the viewer. By returning these images to their allegorical context, we might reframe them both in relation to Cameron's interest in representing divine grace in the face of distress, dispossession, and exile.

## Ionian nationalism

In 1836, twelve years after the death of Byron and more than a quarter-century since Byron first travelled to Greece, Finden included a youthful and idealized *Maid of Athens* among his *Byron Beauties*. An excerpt from the poem of the same title accompanied the image, an ode to Byron's love for Theresa Macri, the young woman to whom he had dedicated the poem when it was first published in 1812. Finden's was not a political volume; his strategy was to capitalize on Byron's popularity as a means to sell 'exotic' female imagery that could have broad appeal in the market; consequently, he chose this subject because it focused attention on a young woman's physical features and her youthful beauty, as with the other women represented in the volume:

> By those tresses unconfined,
> Wooed by each Aegean wind;
> By those lids whose jetty fringe
> Kiss thy soft cheeks' blooming tinge;
> By those wild eyes like the roe,
> *Zoë mou, sas agapo* [My life, I love you].
>
> (st. 2, ll. 7–12)

But Finden appended a brief narrative to these lines that inserted an unexpected note of sadness and nostalgia: 'We are sorry to dim the images of loveliness and grace conveyed by [Byron's] verses; but four-and-twenty years have passed since they were written, and a recent traveller has assured us, that he saw Theresa Macri last year, without a vestige of her former beauty, struggling with poverty, but striving, in the sacred character of wife and mother, to obtain a scanty subsistence for her numerous children.'[67] What motivated Finden to destroy the illusion of his idealized maiden by introducing a description of her hard-bitten, real-life experience? Beauty and perfection could indeed be tarnished by time, fatigue, and poverty, but noble sacrifice lies at the heart of Romantic sentiment, and its illusions are not often broken by reality.

Cameron's photograph of c. 1865–66, *Zoë/Maid of Athens* (Cox 392) closely resembles Finden's in its sentimental footprint. She portrayed her heroine with downcast eyes, her head tilted slightly in a pensive manner, resting on her hand. Unlike Finden, however, Cameron placed her photograph into a different kind of discursive space altogether, one that was inflected by history and politics. By titling her photograph *Zoë/Maid of Athens*, she once again chose a hybrid allegory to personify a personal and political subject. On the one hand, *Zoë/Maid of Athens* depicts a young woman who embodies both love of country and the will to unite her people. As *Zoë*, Cameron's model personifies a brave nationalistic partisan who fights for Greek independence against invading Ottoman forces. Toward this end, Cameron personified Byron's *Maid of Athens* by giving her the female name Zoë, which is also Greek for 'life' and not the name of an actual person. At the same time, by using a vibrant model to represent the *Maid of Athens*, Cameron commemorated Britain's 1864 cession of the Ionian islands to the newly constituted Kingdom of Greece, an extraordinary and unique contraction of the British Empire that dominated parliamentary debate throughout 1863.[68] We know that the Camerons followed the political fortunes of the Ionian islands closely in Parliament, since for many years Charles expected to be appointed governor of the islands.[69]

The Treaty of Paris of 1815 established the United States of the Ionian Islands as a protectorate of Great Britain. The union comprised the islands of Corfu, Paxo, Cephalonia, Ithaca, Santa Maura, Zante, and Cerigo. Venice had long controlled the islands until 1797, when Bonaparte took that republic by force. The Treaty ended the subsequent struggle between France and Russia from 1797 to 1814 for control of the islands. Nominally independent under the British, the Ionian Islands formed its own constitution but was established as a dominion in the Colonial Office. As a *de facto* colony, the Islands provided an eastern port to shelter the Royal Navy, which helping ease British fears about Russian or Ottoman expansion. Under British rule, participation in the Ionian legislature was restricted to the wealthy, but in 1849, a populist movement agitated for reunification with Greece, causing Palmerston to dispatch Gladstone in 1859 to recommend a viable course of action. Gladstone was against relinquishing control of the colony, arguing that Britain's dominant role in world affairs was based on uniting Christian moral principles with Hellenic order and culture, and that this union produced a superior common law and common heritage that bound together the two peoples.[70] Within the Colonial Office, Herman Merivale, Sir Frederick Rogers, and the Cameron's friend Henry Taylor also resisted Britain ceding its control.[71] In order to bring this awkward public debate to a close, Disraeli extracted strategic military concessions from the Greek Provisional Government in exchange for returning the Islands to Greece.

After Britain closed this embarrassing political chapter in 1864, many in England expressed interest in helping Greece reclaim its past glory. For Byron, of course, this theme had been the great cause of the nationalist sentiments that he expressed in poetry, from the second canto of *Childe Harold's Pilgrimage* to the wistful song, 'The Isles of Greece', which he published in *Don Juan* at the start of the Greek War of Independence.[72] For Byron, only genuine national liberation could guarantee the truest kind of personal and political salvation. In *Childe Harold*, for example, he wrote:

> When Grecian mothers shall give birth to men,
> Then may'st thou be restored; but not till then.
> A thousand years scarce serve to form a state;
> An hour may lay it in the dust: and when
> Can Man its shattered splendor renovate,
> Recall its virtues back, and vanquish Time and Fate?
>
> (Canto II, st. 84, ll. 795–800)

*Don Juan* also promotes the return of Greece to its past glories. In the poem, a Greek troubadour sings a heart-wrenching ballad that laments his countrymen's lost freedom and honours the past excellence and beauty of Greece when it 'was young':

> Must we but weep o'er days more blest?
>   Must we but blush? – Our fathers bled.
> Earth! render back from out thy breast
>   A remnant of our Spartan dead!
> Of the three hundred grant but three,
> To make a new Thermopylae!
>
> (Canto III, st. 86, 7, ll. 725–30)

Byron could count on his readers' knowledge from Herodotus that Thermopylae was the location of the famous Greek battle of 480 BC, where a small and outnumbered Greek army held off a much larger force of invading Persians. In 1858, George Rawlinson published a new translation of Herodotus' *History* for British readers, capitalizing on broad interest in ancient Greek history and the continued English fascination with Greek culture. As represented in Byron's poem, the much-awaited political, cultural, and moral rejuvenation of modern Greece could take place, especially for philhellenes like Byron, only if it were accompanied by a spirited cultural restoration, one that was comparable to the zeal with which ancient Thermopylae was defended. After Greek reunification with the Ionian islands, Cameron's contemporary, Matthew Arnold, used the event to represent the synthesis of Hellenism and Hebraism that expressed his ideal model of cultural harmony. In his pursuit of this ideal balance, Arnold wrote that the ancient Athenians successfully united what he called the severe and righteous culture of the Dorians to the tolerant and undisciplined 'Asiatic Greeks of Ionia'. In

1865, Arnold used this historical example to claim that cultural harmony could be recovered and war redeemed.[73] Around the same time, Cameron portrayed *Zoë/ Maid of Athens* as a Greek liberator. This image both allegorically restores Byron's appreciation of Greece's past greatness and introduces Arnold's position about cultural harmony, because, in the photograph, the once childlike and demure Theresa Macri has been reinvented as a robust and mature 'Zoë', a self-confident figure who now personifies a modern combatant in the Greek War of Independence. In undergoing this figurative transformation, the youthful romantic object of Byron's fascination has not only undergone an identity change but also taken on new a symbolic role as heroic warrior, political liberator, and cultural saviour.

Cameron has transformed the Greek heroine from the blushing adolescent who inspired Byron's *Maid of Athens* into an intense and mature woman: her photograph depicts in 'Zoë' an image of womanhood that could equally portray the Maid of Saragossa of the Peninsular War. Byron invoked this heroine in *Childe Harold's Pilgrimage*: the Maid of Saragossa 'Stalks with Minerva's step where Mars might fear to tread' (Canto I, st. 54, l. 566).[74] Cameron's allegorical image therefore embeds yet another subject of nationalistic pride for England, namely, the heroism of the Duke of Wellington, who defeated France and liberated Iberia during the Napoleonic Wars. Byron's political poetry served as a perfect foil for Cameron's photography because it combined the heroic mythology of liberation associated with both the Maid of Athens and the Maid of Saragossa. At the same time, by symbolically drawing upon the national heroism associated with the Duke of Wellington, Cameron helped to rewrite this historical chapter in relation to Britain's role of restoring national honour to those lands from which it had once been stripped away.

## Picturing Adriana

Byron scholars have emphasized that the poet wrote during an exceptional historical moment: Napoleon's influence was in decline, Russian power in the eastern Mediterranean was on the rise, and British expansion into India was accelerating. At the same time, the balance of power in the Balkans was shifting, as the Ottoman Empire showed signs of weakening. In response to these political events, Byron's characters express many noble virtues. But they have also been 'Orientalized' under the thumb of despotic regimes, and many of them revolt against autocratic forces or imperialistic domination. [75] In *The Giaour*, for example, Byron represented two empires in conflict: the Christian and Venetian (personified by the Giaour), stand in diametrical opposition to the Islamic and Ottoman (personified by the character Hassan). The male actors in the poem represent the two opposing political and religious factions, and both vie for the affections of the hapless female slave, Leila. Once their actual conflict erupts, Leila is executed, Hassan is ambushed and killed, the Giaour is secluded in a monastery, and the reader is left to ponder the futile conflict between East and West in the struggle for Greece. Despite Byron's close connection to the Whig leader, Lord Holland, to whom Byron dedicated *The Bride of Abydos*, and his denunciation of Lord Elgin, the Tory who pilfered the Parthenon Marbles, in *Childe Harold*, Byron's political interests were apparently class-bound, his politics nostalgic, and his imagery intentionally popularized for its exotic appeal and 'Orientalism'. As Marilyn Butler has cautioned, 'Byron cannot be turned into an exemplary modern political preacher.'[76]

Nor can Cameron. She also seems to have produced photographs that embraced an overt political iconography, but their association with Byron's poetry marked them as exotic and 'Oriental'. Moreover, they contained stereo- typed archaic allusions to 'The East' (Cox 548) and the harem (Cox 209, 553, 554), and portrayed visionary prophets (*The Vision of Infant Samuel*, Cox 126; *The Infant Samuel*, Cox 953), deposed kings (*King David*, Cox 164), and female liberators who were revered for their beauty as much as for their efforts to redeem and unify the nation (*Rebecca*, Cox 548; *Zoë / Maid of Athens*, Cox 392; *She Walks in Beauty*, Cox 333). Cameron found in Byron's poetry a reservoir of subjects that allowed her to embed potent symbols in each vivid character, using his figurative imagery to form a larger narrative of women who were inspired by, and who fought for, liberty and national independence.

By her careful selection of subjects and her serious photographic treatment of them as personifications of patriotism, Cameron embraced Byron's 'poetry of sensation', which Henry Taylor had condemned in his Preface to *Philip Van Artevelde*. Taylor repudiated Byron because he did not accept the poet's ability 'to infer and to instruct', seeing instead only raw passion and exaggerated sentiment- ality. He denounced Byron's Romantic poetry because he thought it stood 'aloof from everything that is plain and true', or that, like music, it acted only 'upon the fancy, the affections, the passions, but scarcely connected with the exercise of the intellectual faculties'.[77] Taylor linked Byron to Shelley and then dispar- aged Shelley's dream-filled poems, calling them 'seats of anarchy and abstrac- tion, where imagination exercises the shadow of an authority, over a people of phantoms, in a land of dreams'.[78] In contrast, wrote Taylor, modern poets must try to overcome that which the Romantics had destabilized by reasserting the authority of reason against sensation and the primacy of logic over irrationality.

Inspired by Byron, however, Cameron's photographs invoked the pain of wandering, the hardship of exile, and the aching of isolation, offering sombre allegorical representations of these conditions. At the same time, she also repre- sented the honour of national sacrifice, the duty of political resistance in the face of injustice, and the moral righteousness of defending personal liberation and political independence. Cameron therefore took Byron's 'fancy subjects' earnestly and used them to construct a larger narrative of nationalism and liberation. As hybrid images, her photographs exploited Oriental otherness, but they also offered a subtle critique of contemporary British politics. In creating such complex imagery that connected figures of the Old Testament and ancient Greece to Victorian Britain, Cameron probably fell into some critical accord with Taylor about her use of Byron.

Were it not for this solidarity, it seems unlikely that Taylor would have supported Cameron's interest in representing his character Adriana Van Merestyn, the principal female protagonist in his drama, *Philip Van Artevelde*. But in 1866, Cameron indeed personified Taylor's *Adriana* in photography (Cox 255; Figure 33). She accomplished this feat by retitling a pre-existing image of 1866 of Mary Hillier, which she had also titled, at one time, both *Maud* and *Clio*. In a print conserved by the Ashmolean Museum, Cameron framed the new photograph of *Adriana* in an arched top. Some years ago, Mike Weaver thought this photograph represented a character of the same name in Jean Boncoeur's forgotten novel *Adriana*, but this small domestic tale was out of print and obscure even then, and not likely to have interested Cameron.[79] In contrast to this character, Cameron's *Adriana* is true to Henry Taylor's drama: elegant and refined, made even larger than life and dignified regally in the new arched frame. She exhibited *Adriana* in 1868 and again in 1873, both times accompanied by an earlier portrait of Taylor that she titled *Philip Van Artevelde* (Cox 777).

And yet, it would also seem that by imagining Mary Hillier as Adriana Van Merestyn and Taylor as Philip Van Artevelde, Cameron disregarded Taylor's chief criticism of the role of imagination in the art of representation. Why did Taylor go along with Cameron in this way, or did he not regard it a provocation? In 1864, when *Philip Van Artevelde* was reissued as part of the first volume of the author's *Collected Poems*, the author's censorious views about Byron gained new readers. In May 1865, for example, Anthony Trollope reviewed the new edition of Taylor's work in the *Fortnightly Review* and devoted more than half his column's space to the play, which no doubt delighted Cameron because of her abiding affection for Taylor and his work.[80] But *Adriana* is a curiosity, in part because of its connection to Taylor and in part because it was a repurposed image. Indeed, the photograph is a kind of Janus figure that contains antithetical symbols about the role of the imagination and the nature of art, precisely because it is connected to other photographs that have the same image but different titles. By re-inscribing identical prints *Adriana*, or, in one instance of reverse printing, *Maud*, Cameron exercised her authority – and her authorship – to re-imagine her allegorical subject in different identities. This singular portrait, then, seems the ultimate *tabula rasa*, as nothing about the model, in her attitude, dress, or manner is particular to the Muse Clio, or Tennyson's character Maud, or Taylor's character Adriana. What seems clear, however, is that Cameron printed the negative of Mary Hillier to face in opposite directions in the final photographs of *Adriana* and *Maud*, while she apparently discontinued titling prints *Clio* after 1866. While *Adriana* shows the model's left profile to the viewer, *Maud* shows the right (Figure 34). Cameron knew the literary sources of these references well, and it is certain that she understood the oppositional symbolic attributes of these two fictional characters because of her close connections to Taylor and Tennyson.

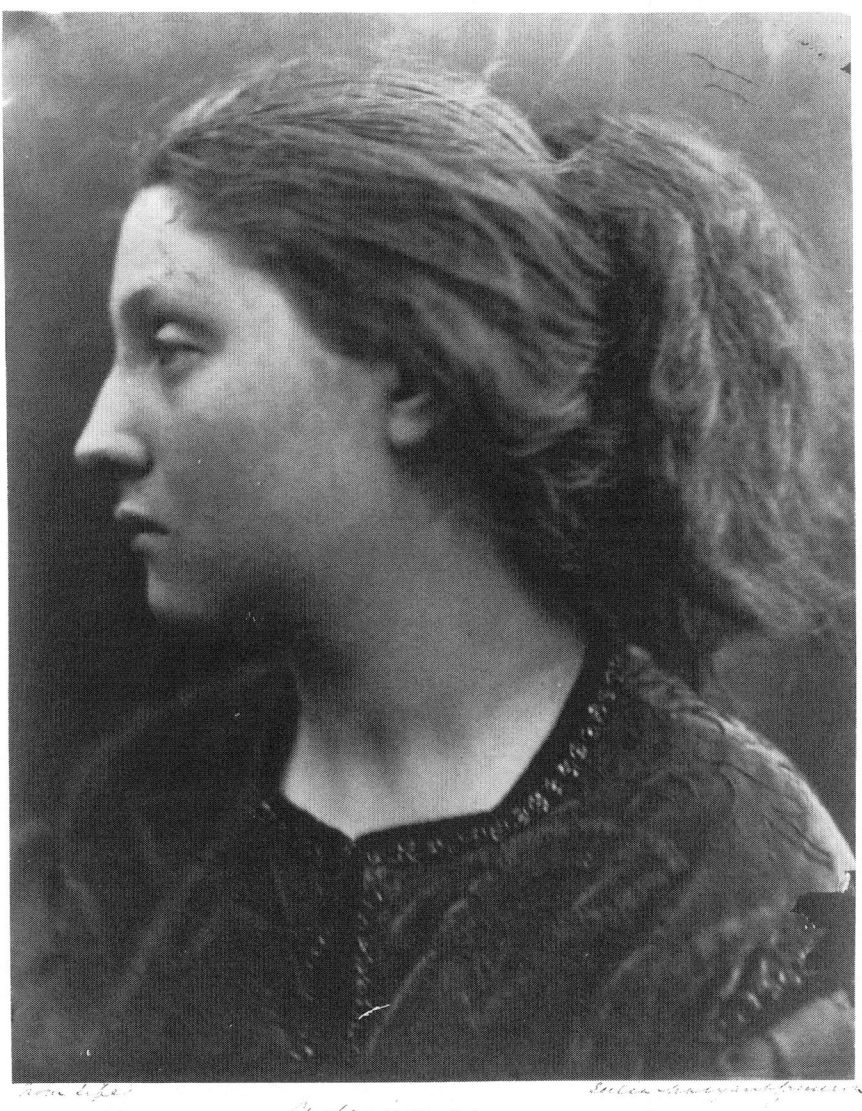

Julia Margaret Cameron, *Clio / Adriana* (Cox 255), 1866.     **33**
Albumen print, 34.6 x 27 cm.

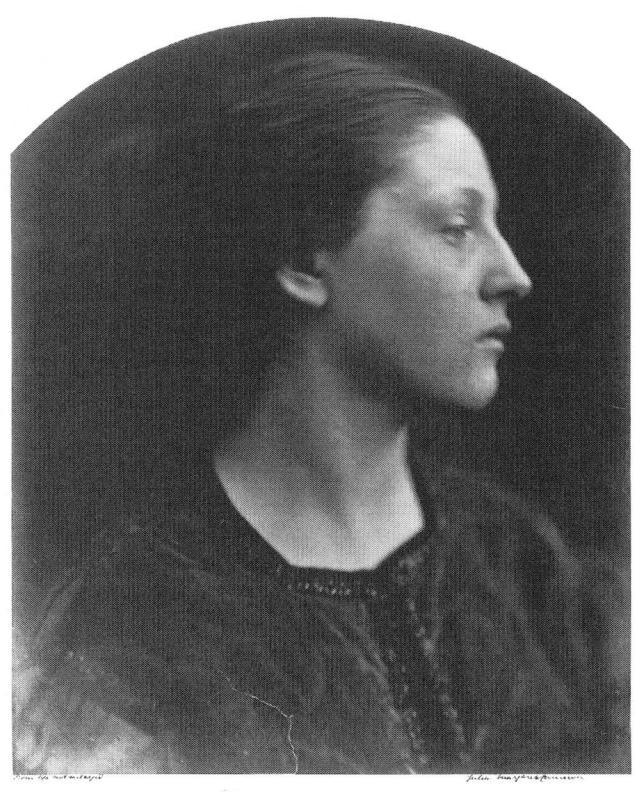

34          Julia Margaret Cameron, *Maud* (reverse printing of Cox 255), 1866.
                        Albumen print, 36.3 x 29.1 cm.

This allegorical opposition reveals another aspect of Cameron's creative process: on the one hand, she portrayed a personification of rationality; on the other, sensation. To Taylor, Byron was a negative example in poetry. In *Philip Van Artevelde*, Taylor described his hero, Philip, as a contemplative man, devoted to his family, the memory of his father, and the family's historical legacy. As Lawrence Poston described, '[Philip] is most alive when musing on the nature of illusion and reality, of moral growth and decay.'[81] In the drama, Philip asks his fiancée, Adriana, to reflect deeply on the burden of being married to such a sombre and serious man, and to deliberate earnestly and solemnly on her decision before giving her final consent. As described earlier, Taylor wrote that poetry was a means to express 'grave' subject matter. As a result, in *Philip Van Artevelde*, Philip and Adriana are bound separately and together by rationality, tradition and history, and a firm moral code, as the warrior-turned-statesman Philip is duty-bound to conduct himself with honour and dignity and obliged to uphold the laws of chivalry and rules of warfare as a measure of his status and position.

Tennyson's melodramatic and erratic Maud stands in opposition to Taylor's subdued and rational Adriana. In the structure of Tennyson's poem, the reader experiences abrupt changes that reflect the unstable character and the animated mood of his narrator. In representing this emotional instability, Tennyson repeatedly shifts the state of feeling suddenly in the poem, a technique that was understood well by his contemporaries: in 1856, for example, Robert J. Mann described the poem in his pamphlet, *Maud Vindicated*, in these terms: 'Every utterance, whether it be of sentiment, passion, or reflection, is an impulsive outburst … The syllables and lines of the several stanzas actually trip and halt with abrupt fervour, tremble with passion, swell with emotion, and dance with joy, as each separate phase of mental experience comes on the scene.'[82] Nothing could be further from Taylor.

But Byron's influence on Tennyson is apparent, especially in the sensationalism and narrative elements drawn from the Turkish Tales. As Elfenbein observed: '*The Bride of Abydos* contains, like *Maud*, lovers raised in a brother-sister relationship, a hero's father destroyed by the heroine's father, a heroine nearly forced to wed an unworthy man, a violent confrontation between the lover and the heroine's relatives, and the death of the heroine from grief.'[83] In paying homage to both of her literary idols, Henry Taylor and Alfred Tennyson, Cameron's Janus-like photograph, *Adriana/Maud*, seems like an attempt to fix in a stable form two divergent narrative and poetic approaches. At the same time, Cameron's multiple titles seem to acknowledge that such a tenuous equilibrium could only be false and artificial. In *Adriana/Maud* (Figures 33 and 34), Cameron represents both of these opposing yet twinned poles in a single hybrid photograph: left-profile *Adriana* and right-profile *Maud* are one.

## Notes

1   Andrew Elfenbein, *Byron and the Victorians* (Cambridge: Cambridge University Press, 1995), p. 88.

2   '"Men Great thro' Genius … Women thro' Love": Portraits by Julia Margaret Cameron', *Metropolitan Museum of Art Bulletin*, New Series, 56:4 (1999), 37.

3   Edward W. Said, *Orientalism* (New York: Vintage , 1978).

4   See Sylvia Wolf, *Julia Margaret Cameron's Women* (Chicago: The Art Institute of Chicago, 1998), p. 54.

5   Letter from Julia Margaret Cameron to Sir John Herschel, 1 November 1849, quoted in Victoria C. Olsen, *From Life: Julia Margaret Cameron and Victorian Photography* (New York: Palgrave Macmillan, 2003), p. 81.

6   Colin Ford, *Julia Margaret Cameron: A Critical Biography* (London: National Portrait Gallery, 2003), p. 74.

7   Stephen Greenblatt, *Marvellous Possessions: The Wonders of the New World* (Oxford: Clarendon Press, 1991), p. 4

8   William St Clair, 'The Impact of Byron's Writings: An Evaluative Approach', in Andrew Rutherford, ed., *Byron: Augustan and Romantic* (New York: St Martin's Press, 1990), p. 19.

9   Roland Barthes, 'The Lost Continent', in *Mythologies*, trans. Jonathan Cape (New York: Hill and Wang, 1972), p. 96.

10  Homi Bhabha called such a transposition 'the inappropriate Other' in 'Of Mimicry and Man: The Ambivalence of Colonial Discourse', in *October: The First Decade*, ed. Annette Michelson, Rosalind Krauss, and Douglas Crimp (Cambridge, MA: MIT Press, 1987), p. 318.

11  Elfenbein, *Byron and the Victorians*, p. 93.

12  St Clair, 'The Impact of Byron's Writings', p. 20.

13  Edward Ziter, *The Orient on the Victorian Stage* (Cambridge: Cambridge University Press, 2003), p. 65.

14  *Ibid.*, p. 67.

15  *Ibid.*, pp. 65, 70, 74.

16  Samuel C. Chew, *Byron in England: His Fame and After-Fame* (New York: Charles Scribner's Sons, 1924), p. 275, n. 1.

17  Ziter, *The Orient on the Victorian Stage*, p. 211, n. 36.

18  M. A. Titmarsh [Wm. Makepeace Thackeray], *Notes of a Journey from Cornhill to Grand Cairo*, [1846] (New York: George P. Putnam, 1848), p. 54.

19  Robert Hampson, 'From Cornhill to Cairo: Thackeray as Travel-Writer', *Yearbook of English Studies*, 34 (2004), 228–9.

20  *Illustrated London News*, 4 May 1850, quoted in Mary Roberts, *Intimate Outsiders: The Harem in Ottoman and Orientalist Art and Travel Literature* (Durham, NC: Duke University Press, 2007), pp. 35–6.

21  Roberts, *Intimate Outsiders*, pp. 30–1.

22  Pirated copies helped to disseminate this image widely; see Robert Beevers, *The Byronic Image: The Poet Portrayed* (Abingdon: Olivia Press, 2005).

23  St Clair, 'The Impact of Byron's Writings', pp. 20–1.

24  Beatrice Farwell, *The Charged Image: French Lithographic Caricature, 1816–1848* (Santa Barbara: Santa Barbara Museum of Art, 1989), p. 178.

25  Winifred H. Friedeman, *Boydell's Shakespeare Gallery* (New York and London: Garland, 1976); *The Boydell Shakespeare Gallery*, ed. Walter Pape and Frederick Burwick (Bottrop, Germany: Peter Pomp, 1996); for the impact of Shakespeare, see Jonathan Bate, *Shakespeare and the English Romantic Imagination* (Oxford: Oxford University Press, 1986).

26  Christopher Rovee, '"Everybody's Shakespeare": Representative Genres and John Boydell's *Winter's Tale*', *Studies in Romanticism*, 41: 4 (2002), 510.

27  Ronald Paulson, *Book and Painting: Shakespeare, Milton, and the Bible. Literary Texts and the Emergence of English Painting* (Knoxville: University of Tennessee Press, 1982).

28  Anthony Taylor, 'Shakespeare and Radicalism: The Uses and Abuses of Shakespeare in Nineteenth-Century Popular Politics', *Historical Journal*, 45:3 (2002), 362.

29  Winifred H. Friedeman, 'Some Commercial Aspects of the Boydell Shakespeare Gallery', *Journal of the Warburg and Courtauld Institutes*, 36 (1973), 400.

30  Elfenbein, *Byron and the Victorians*, p. 55; St Clair, 'The Impact of Byron's Writings', p. 20.

31  Elfenbein, *Byron and the Victorians*, pp. 55, 129.

32  Dickens wrote that the volumes depicted 'ladies of title and fashion in every variety of smirk that art, combined with capital, is capable of producing'. Charles Dickens, *Bleak House* [1853; 1868 edn] (New York: Bantam, 1992); pp. 265, 416, 521.

33  *Finden's Byron Beauties: or, the Principal Female Characters in Lord Byron's Poems* (London: Charles Tilt, 1836), 'Address', n.p.

34  This work is called 'La Donna' without specifying Donna Julia; Cameron's entries in Public Record Office registers offers a number of possibilities, all copyrighted on 15 September 1868. Public Record Office, Kew, COPY 1/14.

35  Quoted in David Ben-Merre, 'Reading *Hebrew Melodies*', *Shofar*, 24:2 (2006), 13, original emphasis.

36  Wrote Byron: 'I love the cause of liberty, which is that of the Greek nation, although I despise the present race of Greeks, even while I pity them, I do not believe they are better than the Turks, nay, I believe that in many respects the Turks surpass them ... I am nearly reconciled to St. Paul, for he says, there is no difference between the Jews and the Greeks, and I am exactly of the same opinion, for the character of both is equally vile.' Quoted in Thomas L. Ashton, *Byron's Hebrew Melodies* (Austin: University of Austin Press, 1972), p. 74.

37  See N. I. Matar, 'The English Romantic Poets and the Jews', *Jewish Social Studies*, 50:3/4 (1988), 231.

38  Tom Mole, 'The Handling of *Hebrew Melodies*', *Romanticism*, 8:1 (2002), 24, 25, 26.

39  St Clair, 'The Impact of Byron's Writings', p. 10.

40  On the *Hebrew Melodies*, see: Sheila A. Spector, 'The Liturgical Context of the Byron-Nathan *Hebrew Melodies*', *Studies in Romanticism*, 47:3 (2008); Ben-Merre, 'Reading *Hebrew Melodies*'; Mole, 'The Handling of *Hebrew Melodies*'; Ashton, *Byron's Hebrew Melodies*; Joseph Slater, 'Byron's *Hebrew Melodies*', *Studies in Philology*, 49:1 (1952), 75–94.

41  Mole, 'The Handling of *Hebrew Melodies*', 27–29.

42  Slater, 'Byron's *Hebrew Melodies*', 86.

43  Mike Weaver, *Julia Margaret Cameron, 1815–1879* (Southampton: John Hansard Gallery, 1984), p. 90.

44  Ashton, *Byron's Hebrew Melodies*, pp. 67–8.

45  Spector, 'The Liturgical Context ', 397.

46  Tamar Garb, 'Introduction: Modernity, Identity, Textuality', in Linda Nochlin and Tamar Garb, eds., *The Jew in the Text: Modernity and the Construction of Jewish Identity* (London: Thames and Hudson, 1995), p. 25.

47  Sander Gilman, *The Jew's Body* (New York: Routledge, 1991), chapter 2.

48  On the cultural separation of Judaism from Jewishness, see Hannah Arendt, *The Origins of Totalitarianism* (London: George Allen and Unwin, 1958). On Jewish assimilation in relation to Victorian representations, see Reina Lewis, *Gendering Orientalism: Race, Femininity, and Representation* (London: Routledge, 1996), pp. 212–20. On the importance of the Jews to English imperial policy, see Frances Knight, 'The Bishops and the Jews, 1828–1858', in *Christianity and Judaism*, ed. Diana Wood, *Studies in Church History*, 29 (1992), 387–98; Abigail Green, 'The British Empire and the Jews: An Imperialism of Human Rights?', *Past and Present*, 199 (2008), 175–205; David Aberbach, 'Nationalism and the Hebrew Bible', *Nations and Nationalism*, 11:2 (2005), 223–42; and Eitan Bar-Yosef, 'Christian Zionism and Victorian Culture', *Israel Studies*, 8:2 (2003), 18–44.

49  Michael Ragussis, 'The "Secret" of English Anti-Semitism: Anglo-Jewish Studies and Victorian Studies', *Victorian Studies*, 40:2 (1997), 295.

50  Quoted in U. R. Q. Henriques, 'The Jewish Emancipation Controversy in Nineteenth-Century Britain', *Past and Present*, 40 (1968), 137–8.

51  Palmerston wanted to persuade the Sultan 'of the very great benefit [that] would accrue to the Turkish Government if any considerable number of opulent Jews could be persuaded to come [from Britain] and settle in the Ottoman Dominions', which also could be regarded an effort to rid Britain of this question through emigration. Quoted in Salo W. Baron, 'The Jewish Question in the Nineteenth Century', *Journal of Modern History*, 10:1 (1938), 63.

52  Lionel Gossman, 'Philhellenism and Antisemitism: Matthew Arnold and His German Models', *Comparative Literature*, 46:1 (1994), 1–39; and Michael Ragussis, *Figures of Conversion: 'The Jewish Question' and English National Identity* (Durham, NC: Duke University Press, 1995), chapter 5.

53  Matthew Arnold, *Culture and Anarchy* (New York: Macmillan, 1933), p. 141.

54  This point is also argued by Michael Ragussis, *Figures of Conversion*, p. 224.

55  *Ibid.*, p. 32.

56  Robert J. C. Young, *Colonial Desire: Hybridity in Theory, Culture and Race* (London: Routledge, 1995), pp. 82–9.

57  Ashton, *Byron's Hebrew Melodies*, pp. 76–7.

58  *Ibid.*, p. 139, n. 1.

59  On the David and Bathsheba story, see Marshall Berman, 'A Little Child Shall Lead Them: The Jewish Family Romance', in Nochlin and Garb, *The Jew in the Text*, pp. 256–7.

60  Jeremy Davies, 'Jewish Tunes, or *Hebrew Melodies*: Byron and the Biblical Orient', in Peter Cochran, ed., *Byron and Orientalism* (Newcastle-upon-Tyne: Cambridge Scholars Publishing, 2006), p. 220.

61  Spector, 'The Liturgical Context', 405.

62  *Ibid.*, 407.

63  Isaac Nathan, *Fugitive Pieces*, quoted by Spector, 'The Liturgical Context', 407.

64  Because Hagar was doubly exiled from her own people and her husband's family, the Victorian era considered her story among the harshest of all the biblical punishments. See Daniel A. Harris, 'Hagar in Christian Britain: Grace Aguilar's "The Wanderers"', *Victorian Literature and Culture*, 27:1 (1999), 143–69.

65  See the chronology of Julia Jackson's life in Diane F. Gillespie and Elizabeth Steele, eds., *Julia Duckworth Stephen: Stories for Children, Essays for Adults* (Syracuse: Syracuse University Press, 1987), pp. xix–xx.

66  Spector, 'The Liturgical Context', 405–6.

67  *Finden's Byron Beauties*, 'The Maid of Athens', n.p.

68  C. C. Eldridge, 'The Myth of Mid-Victorian "Separatism": The Cession of the Bay Islands and the Ionian Islands in the Early 1860s', *Victorian Studies*, 12:3 (1969), 331–46.

69  Letter from Charles to Julia Margaret Cameron, dated 28 January 1851, Cameron Papers, J. Paul Getty Museum, Box 11.

70  David Hannell, 'The Ionian Islands under the British Protectorate: Social and Economic Problems', *Journal of Modern Greek Studies*, 7:1 (1989), esp. 107–9; Harold Temperley, 'Documents Illustrating the Cession of the Ionian Islands to Greece, 1848–70', *Journal of Modern History*, 9:1 (1937), 48–55.

71  Rogers was then the Permanent Under-Secretary for the Colonies; Merivale had left that position in 1859 to become Permanent Under-Secretary for India; and Taylor occupied the position of Senior Clerk in the West Indian Department. See Eldridge, 'The Myth of Mid-Victorian "Separatism"', 340.

72  See, for example, Bernard Blackstone, 'Byron's Greek Canto: The Anatomy of Freedom', *Yearbook of English Studies*, 4 (1974), 172–89.

73  See Gossman, 'Philhellenism and Antisemitism', 28.

74  Diego Saglia, '"O My Mother Spain!": The Peninsular War, Family Matters, and the Practice of Romantic Nation-Writing', *English Literary History*, 65:2 (1998), 363–93.

75  Nigel Leask, *British Romantic Writers and the East: Anxieties of Empire* (Cambridge: Cambridge University Press, 1992), pp. 4, 59; Marilyn Butler, 'Byron and the Empire in the East', in Rutherford, *Byron: Augustan and Romantic*, pp. 68–9; Cochran, *Byron and Orientalism*, pp. 76–9.

76  Butler, 'Byron and the Empire in the East', p. 80.

77  Henry Taylor, *Philip Van Artevelde: A Dramatic Romance in Two Parts* (London: Kegan Paul, Trench & Co., 1883), p. viii.

78  *Ibid.*, p. xv; see also, Isobel Armstrong, *Victorian Poetry: Poetry, Poetics and Politics* (London: Routledge, 1993), pp. 97–101.

79  Weaver, *Julia Margaret Cameron, 1815–1879*, p. 121.

80  Norris D. Hoyt, '"Can You Forgive Her?": A Commentary', *Trollopian*, 2:2 (1947), 60.

81  Lawrence Poston, 'Philip Van Artevelde: The Poetry and Politics of Equipose', *Victorian Poetry*, 18:4 (1984), 386.

82  Quoted in A. Dwight Culler, 'Monodrama and the Dramatic Monologue', *PMLA*, 90:3 (1975), 378.

83  Elfenbein, *Byron and the Victorians*, p. 196.

# 5

# Overstone's 'Negromania': justness and justice at home and abroad

## 'Negromania'

On 30 May 1868, the satiric journal *Punch* published an item of shrewd political commentary that joined together two seemingly unique recent events, the Jamaican rebellion of 1865 and the Abyssinian War of 1868. This brief notice appeared in the regular column it called *'Punch's* Essence of Parliament', a running commentary on the current affairs of state, and it forced the connection of these two overseas conflicts as a provocative indictment of the way both incidents were being interpreted in the British media. Using proper names that would have been widely recognized by the journal's readers, the column referred simply to the role of three men: 'Sir Robert Napier', the Field Marshall who led the 1868 war, was used as shorthand for the British military invasion of Abyssinia; 'Mr Eyre', the embattled ex-governor of Jamaica, personified the 1865 native uprising that he had suppressed; and 'Lord Overstone' substituted for the concerned British public at large, especially public individuals who were largely uninterested in these outcomes but drawn nevertheless into choosing sides – in support of or in opposition to the colonial conflicts abroad.

By May 1868, Napier's war had generally been regarded a 'just' encounter, a fight to release British missionaries held captive after numerous appeals to the Abyssinians to release them had been rejected, whereas Eyre's conflict, on the other hand, was still unresolved. Three years after the Jamaican rebellion, in fact, the question of Eyre's legacy was being fought daily in the court of public opinion, chiefly on two counts: first, whether Eyre was 'just' in quashing the rebellion by using military force, and second, in using such force, whether Eyre should stand trial and 'face justice' for violating basic human rights. *Punch* framed it this way:

> CAPTAIN ARCHDALL put into a Question *Mr Punch's* suggestion last week, that Negromania might induce a prosecution of SIR ROBERT NAPIER, for the same reason that it had induced a prosecution of MR. EYRE. Two military gentlemen also adverted to the subject; but on the whole, we think their advocacy of MR. EYRE had better be confined to an imitation, according to their means,

of LORD OVERSTONE, the typical dispassionate man, who has come forward with a subscription of £200 to the Eyre Defence Fund, and a dignified intimation that the pecuniary ruin of that brave and good officer 'can never be permitted'.[1]

In 1867, when Julia Margaret Cameron was planning her solo exhibition at London's German Gallery to take place the following year, she made sure that examples of both the Jamaican conflict and the Abyssinian War were present and on display. Rather than simply regard these two events as if they were incidental to the exhibition, she sought out sitters and made allegorical photographs that were specifically designed to trade on these timely events, right up until the moment the exhibition opened.

Cameron presented more than two hundred photographs in this exhibition, which took place in January and February 1868 (Figure 1): she listed 130 under the category 'Fancy Subjects', the largest group, called 80 photographs 'Portraits', and described twelve among the 'Fancy Subjects' as 'Life-sized heads', principally comprising untitled pictures of children.[2] Eyre himself appeared among the portraits, along with two images of Thomas Carlyle, Eyre's chief public defender as head of the 'Eyre Defence and Aid Fund'. Because of his association with these two men, Cameron also included her portrait of Anthony Trollope, who vividly described the economic life of Jamaica in his 1859 book, *The West Indies and the Spanish Main*, and portrayed the social life of the British landowner on the island in his short story of 1860, 'Miss Sarah Jack, of Spanish Town, Jamaica'. Cameron possessed limited copies of Trollope's portrait, Colin Ford speculates, because she had damaged the original glass negative.[3] After the exhibition had closed, Cameron added several portraits of Captain Speedy to her *Priced Catalogue*. Speedy was a mercenary British soldier who fought with Sir Robert Napier during the prosecution of the war and returned to England with the young Prince Alamayou, son of the deposed Abyssinian king. She sent these photographs to Colnaghi's, her print dealer, along with others that also depicted the African child and the Prince's African attendant, with instructions to display them in the dealer's window and begin taking orders (Cox 1119).

The interconnected narratives that bind together the diverse elements in Cameron's photographs of 1867 and 1868 are the focus of this chapter; they include the Eyre controversy, the aftermath of the Abyssinian War, and the expanding role of covert British interventions in both sovereign states and colonial territories. These narratives centre on the attitudes of the British toward less powerful countries like Abyssinia and colonies like Jamaica, and expose contrasting views toward those distant lands, including opposing notions of cultural and racial superiority, competing approaches toward economic development and social order in the colonies, and differing views about the use of military force as expressions of political power. These attitudes were represented in polemical essays by Thomas Carlyle and John Stuart Mill; in travel narratives by Austin Henry

Layard and Richard Francis Burton; in the short fiction of Anthony Trollope; in the fundraising activities of the groups wanting to prosecute or defend Governor Eyre; in the official correspondence of colonial administrators like Henry Taylor and Herman Merivale; in graphic representations that were printed in the *Illustrated London News* and *Punch*; and in the various narrative forms that Cameron applied to her allegorical photographs of the Abyssinian refugees.

By 1868, what *Punch* called 'Negromania' did not need to be explained to the journal's readership. Unlike *Punch*'s preposterous term 'Crinolineomania', which it invented in 1856 to ridicule women and their expanded roles in public life,[4] British 'Negromania' was used blatantly as a denigrating and hostile term, and embodied the long-standing racial conflict between white colonialists and one-time African slaves of the colonies who still suffered economic hardship and harboured deep resentments long after having been emancipated in 1833, when the British abolished slavery. Since the late seventeenth century, after all, Jamaica had been a large and active slave market; by the early nineteenth century, more than 300,000 slaves worked its plantations.[5] As used by *Punch*, 'Negromania' referred to abolitionists and others in British society who sympathized with the plight of the former slaves and worked to improve their condition. The term also carried pejorative connotations for their opponents, who saw in the African sympathizers both hypocrisy and false grievance because, in turning their attentions to perceived injustice in the colonies, they ignored social inequality and economic misery at home. Sometimes, 'Negromania' was stripped of its associations with either slavery or colonialism and used a strictly racial and economic term. In *Bleak House* (1853), for example, Dickens satirized those well-meaning British philanthropists in the character of Mrs Jellyby, a naive woman who writes endless letters to raise funds on behalf of the African children of 'Borrioboola-Gha' while ignoring the evident squalor surrounding her own family. In March 1865, *Punch* satirized the same impulse in a cartoon called 'Telescopic Philanthropy', portraying Britannia's rapt attention to the plight of black men and women abroad, and her blind eye for her own children, who beg at her feet for care and attention, crying 'ain't we black enough to be cared for?' Also embedded here is ridicule for the sentimentality that would cry for the innocent and hungry child of the streets, in what is essentially a mean-spirited caricature about two dispossessed groups (Figure 35).

But *Punch*'s use of the term 'Negromania' is also elusive, because in explicitly centring on racial difference as the focus of British philanthropic activity, the original drive to colonize Africa, which helped cause those very hostilities, has been minimized or erased. By contrast, Cameron directly confronted the history of slavery in the colonies and British interventions abroad in her photography: in her portraits of Eyre and his supporters, in her allegorical photographs depicting the submission of Abyssinia to the will of the British, and in her photographs

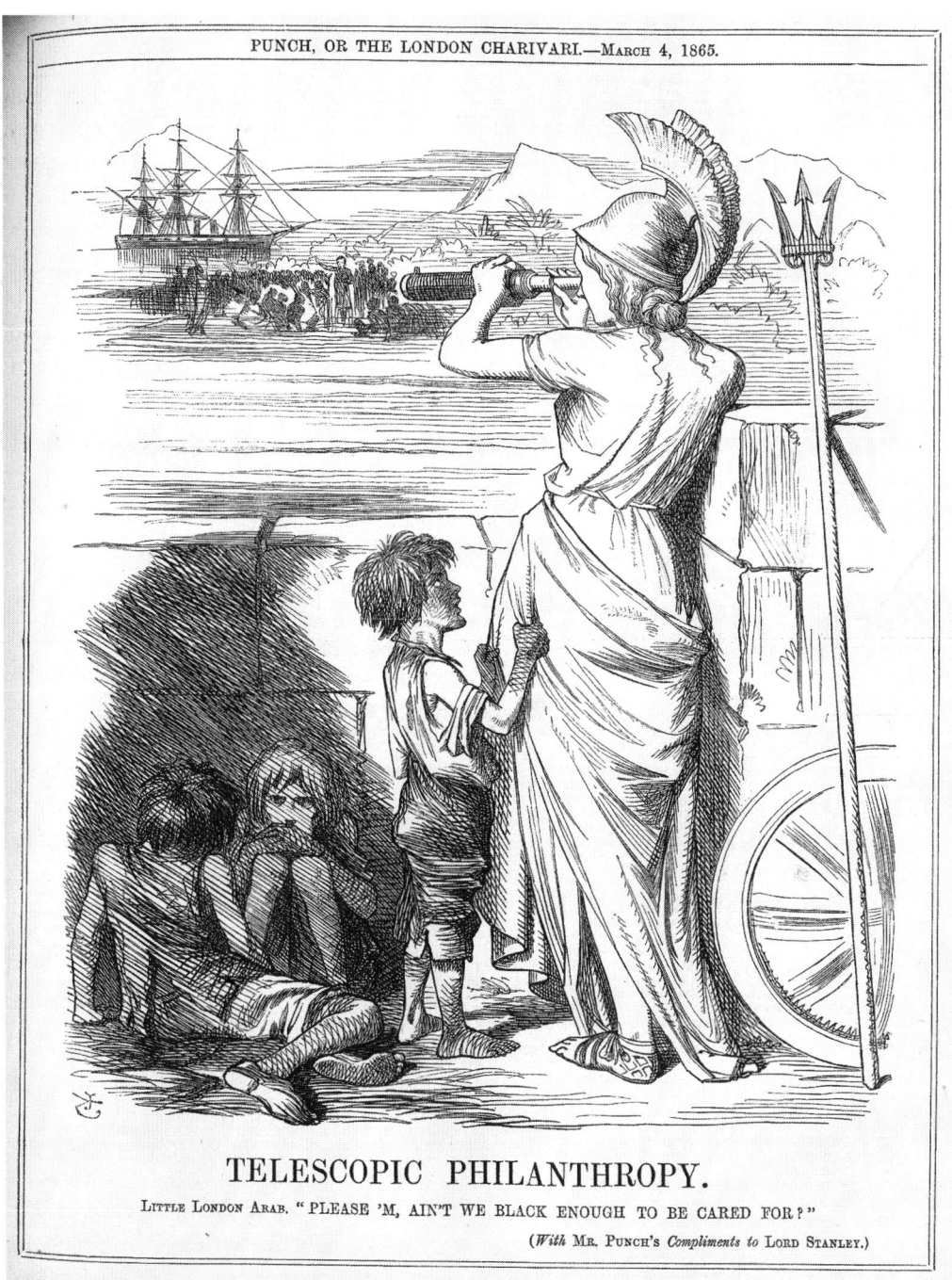

TELESCOPIC PHILANTHROPY.

Little London Arab. "PLEASE 'M, AIN'T WE BLACK ENOUGH TO BE CARED FOR?"

(*With* Mr. Punch's *Compliments to* Lord Stanley.)

Telescopic Philanthropy, cartoon in *Punch, or the London Charivari*, 4 March 1865.    **35**

of British explorers who covertly entered protected areas that were forbidden to Westerners, Cameron represented subjects that were connected directly to events in the Caribbean islands, North Africa, and the Middle East. When she created this imagery, she embedded a viewpoint that recognized Britain's domination of other people and other lands as an historical fact of colonialism.[6] Yet, in both her exhibition space and within the symbolic terrain of her allegorical photographs, she also created contested, unstable, and indeterminate spaces, places of ambivalence and displacement that created opportunities for her public to question this dominant worldview. Ambivalence characterizes Cameron's choice of subjects, the selection of images, and the context and timing of her photographic exhibition. One measure of her ambivalence is the context in which she displayed her work; another is the repetitive quality of this imagery, a fact that often annoyed many of the art critics who covered her exhibitions. Significantly, instead of segregating these works apart from other portraits and fancy subjects in her exhibition, she displayed them all together along with her life-size heads, religious images, and literary subjects, allowing her audience to assign various possible meanings to her photography.

In representation, ambivalence maybe apparent when a selection of works is reduced to a stock house of stereotypes, because the impact of typecast imagery is diminished with each repetition, and only through repeated efforts can an artist attempt to create a more powerful image.[7] Cameron's celebration of the members of the Eyre Defence Committee as 'heroic' individuals, for example, helps us establish her conscious political position in relation to the new approach to photographic portraiture that she pioneered. In these portraits, starkly illuminated men emerge dramatically from darkened shadows behind them. In the photographs she made of the orphaned Prince Alamayou of Abyssinia and his attendants, which make use of an evenly lit studio set, rather than her vivid approach using raking light, Cameron manipulated her subjects in carefully staged poses that represented modern allegories. And in portraits that she made of disguised political operatives in the weeks and months after her exhibition closed, Cameron relied upon similar techniques of camouflage and doubling in her photographs to those used in the field by these men. When these 'British subjects' donned Oriental costumes to become 'colonial subjects', they skilfully shifted the sites of inscription that defined their outward appearance.

Cameron's 1868 exhibition included examples of portraits and allegories that made use of the same individuals in multiple roles, even though she knew that this practice disturbed her critics in the press, who could not abide such blurring of the artistic boundaries in photography.[8] For example, she made portraits of Alfred, Lord Tennyson as 'himself' and as *The Dirty Monk* (Cox 796); Sir Henry Taylor as 'himself' and as *King David* (Cox 165), *Prospero* (Cox 780), and *Philip Van Artevelde* (Cox 777); and George Frederick Watts as 'himself' and as the inspired artist in *Whisper of the Muse* (Cox 1086, 1087). In her representations of women, she displayed May Prinsep as 'herself', and as *The Maid of Athens* (Cox 392), *Beatrice* (Cox 408), and *Christabel* (Cox 396); Cyllena Wilson as 'herself', in profile, and as *Rachel* (Cox 513); Mary Ryan as 'herself' and as *Irish Mary* (Cox 453). Freddy Gould, a young boy of the Isle of Wight, appears as *Astyanax* (Cox 955), *Cherub and Seraph* (Cox 872), and simply as *Freddy* when titled as one of the 'Life-sized heads of Fancy Subjects'. By 1868, this pattern was well established: when she assembled these works in albums or for exhibition, Cameron often included both the portrait and allegorical versions.[9] The Overstone Album, for example, includes three categories: Portraits, Madonna Groups, and Fancy Subjects for Pictorial Effect, while the 1868 exhibition includes Fancy Subjects (with a subcategory of Groups and another of Life-sized heads) and Portraits. But the extent to which Cameron clearly enjoyed blurring the lines that separated her 'portraits' from her 'fancy subjects' has not been considered previously as a conscious decision, despite the fact that her handwritten additions to the 1868 *Priced Catalogue* include both conventional portraits and allegories that she apparently appended indiscriminately across the three pages of the brochure. She understood intuitively that, as Arthur Danto reminds us, 'pictures which *use* models are rarely pictures *of* models', meaning that the visual metaphors used by artists are representational and emblematic; they personify important historical figures, prophets and characters from the Old Testament, heroes and gods from myths and legends, native or foreign individuals representing different social strata, even abstract political ideas.[10]

Cameron also included new and older work together in the exhibition, displaying several photographs that had been previously validated in the marketplace, such as her portraits of Alfred Tennyson and Sir John Herschel.[11] But Cameron chose also to include what we may recognize as imagery that was fraught with potential political conflict, such as her portraits of Edward John Eyre and Thomas Carlyle. Perhaps she intended the larger exhibition to provide a noble context to these photographs, because the majority of the 'fancy subjects' on display included allegories of virtue, goodness, and justice, and these associations could help lend support to the 'justice' of Eyre's cause or the 'justness' of spreading British influence across Africa and the Middle East. Within the context of this exhibition, Cameron's photographs also depicted mythological heroines who sacrificed themselves for honour, duty, and patriotic causes, which, within the context of the exhibition, could also have been intended to support the besieged Eyre or to justify British expansion. As Carlyle had argued, and as Dickens, Ruskin, and Tennyson would later echo, Eyre's suppression of the Jamaican rebellion was 'just', because in saving British lives and property on the island, he preserved and even strengthened colonial rule across the Empire, all while selflessly putting his own life in danger, and as Sir Stratford Canning argued in the House of Lords and Sir Henry Bulwer demanded in the *Pall Mall Gazette*, 'the country and the world' expected the British to 'exercise justice' by punishing the Abyssinian king for resisting Britain's diplomatic overtures and refusing to release his captives.[12]

In the previous chapter, we examined how Orientalism was present in Cameron's depiction of scenes from Byron's poems, such as *The Bride of Abydos* or *Don Juan*, and how these works signified cultural difference about 'the East' and expressed those differences as Oriental exoticism, mystery, or weakness. As viewed from London, the Orient preserved remnants of primitive cultures that were defined as economically and culturally inferior to Britain; because Britain wielded superior economic and military power across the globe, the vectors of influence were once thought to be a one-way street.[13] But many historical representations of the East actually permeated important cultural foundations in the West, and over time cultural activity in the colonies effectively diminished the cultural gaps that separated them from London.[14] In the complex narrative gap that occupies the space separating image and text, journals notable for their graphic works, like *Punch* and the *Illustrated London News*, appended captions that created additional contradictions and ambiguities.[15] In *Punch's* illustration, 'Telescopic Philanthropy', for example, the English child begging for food is identified as a 'Little London Arab'. Earlier terminology described itinerant children as street urchins, scamps, or guttersnipes, but 'Street Arabs' gained favour during this time as a way to focus on the nomadic habits of the children, a particularly 'Eastern' quality that made them far more dangerous to society than did the hardships and difficulties of surviving poverty and homelessness on the streets alone.

Cameron filed for copyright protection for her Abyssinian photographs on 23, 27, and 29 July 1868. During the intervening months, she was not likely to have missed *Punch's* caustic commentary of May 1868 using 'Negromania' to describe British responses to the Jamaican and Abyssinian affairs, in large part because the notice emphasized the fact that Cameron's friend and patron, Lord Overstone, had jumped into the fray. Samuel Jones Loyd became Baron Overstone in 1850 and inherited a banker's social position and vast wealth.[16] Years earlier, he had formed a close bond with Charles Cameron and George Warde Norman when they were members of London's Political Economy Club. During the 1850s and 1860s, the Loyds, Normans, and Camerons formed a close bond that lasted a lifetime. Lord Overstone helped to support the family financially for many years; he was named godfather to Charlie Hay Cameron, Julia Margaret's second-youngest son, and later helped Charlie purchase land in Ceylon when he grew to be a young man.[17] In gratitude for his enduring support, Julia Margaret took his portrait in 1865 and presented him with a beautifully crafted photographic album. But she also continued to supply him with additional photographic imagery, noting on 5 November 1867, just two months prior to her German Gallery opening, that she expected to hear back from him shortly with an assessment of her recently printed photographs:

> I am anxious that you should see to what point I have now been able to bring photography. Our English artists tell me that I can go no farther in excellence, so I suppose I must suppress my ambition & stop – but it is an art full of mystery & beauty & I long to hear your and Harriette's opinion abt. my pictures which you will give me when they reach you.[18]

Lord Overstone was a patron of the arts and a valued friend to the Camerons, but in 1868 he emerged a reluctant partisan in the Eyre affair. Uncharacteristically for Overstone, he did this in a most public way. Unlike others who supported Eyre anonymously or quietly, Lord Overstone chose to publish a letter in *The Times* announcing his £200 pledge to the Eyre Defence Fund and his desire to recruit others to the cause of supporting Eyre.[19] Overstone's friend, Roderick Murchison, wrote to the baron enthusiastically after his letter was published, indicating that his open support had stimulated additional contributions from many others that amounted to several hundred pounds.[20] Lord Overstone clearly did not define himself strictly as the disinterested collector and impartial banker that recent biographers have made him out to be.[21] In fact, by his siding with Eyre and against the 'Negromaniacs' in 1868, *Punch* derided Lord Overstone's claims to be 'above' the dispute, mocking him as 'the typical dispassionate man'. These extraordinary events, the journal seemed to admit, demanded that even dispassionate men take sides.

## Heroes – and anti-heroes – on Bond Street

William Allingham, a poet and friend of Cameron in the circle of the Tennysons and the Thackerays, visited the German Gallery in Bond Street, London, on 4 February 1868 and discussed his visit on 7 February with Anne Thackeray. In his diary entry of that date, he wrote: 'Mrs Cameron's Exhibition—"I blew the trumpet for it in the *Pall Mall* [*Gazette*]"', a reference to the unsigned review that appeared in that journal on 29 January 1868.[22] Although Cameron's photographs of Eyre and Carlyle, for example, might be taken as among the most unambiguously 'political' of her photographic portraits, she chose to cloak these photographs in an ambivalent frame, exhibiting them 'in plain sight' on the walls of her very public exhibition. The context in which these photographs were taken and where they first appeared in public are important in reconstructing their complex levels of meaning.

In the first week of June 1867, Cameron arranged a sitting with Thomas Carlyle, whom she had known for almost a decade after having met him at Little Holland House (Cox 629; Figure 36). The circumstance of their meeting has always been framed as an example of Cameron's efforts to photograph her heroes, illustrating her dogged pursuit, or the happy result of her persistence,

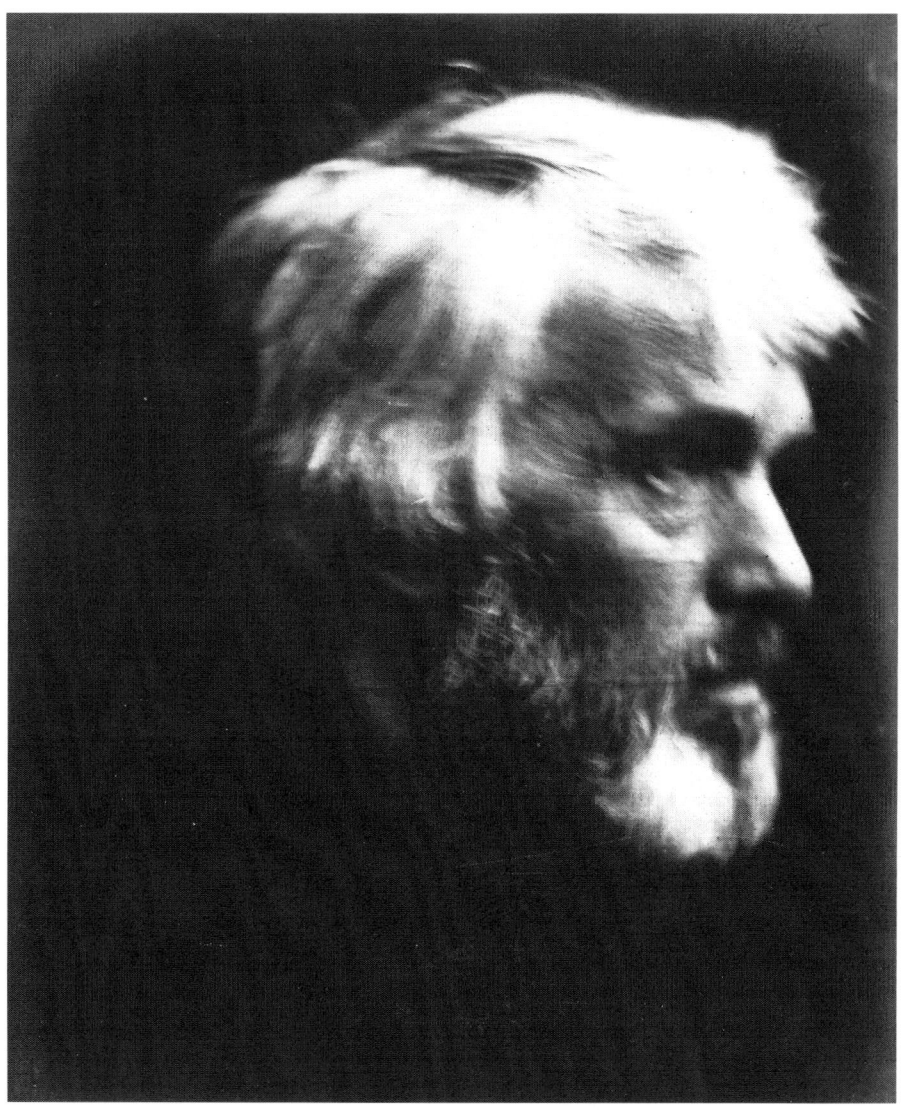

**36**     Julia Margaret Cameron, *Thomas Carlyle* (Cox 629), 1867.
Albumen silver print, 30 x 24.1 cm.

as if Carlyle had finally relented after being pursued for so long.[23] But this was a planned meeting: she took her photographic apparatus and developing equipment from her home in Freshwater and travelled to Kensington, London, to take this photograph, a full day's journey by coach, ferry, and train.[24] On 8 June, Cameron again travelled to London, this time to register her copyright for not one, but two extraordinary portraits, one portraying Edward John Eyre, the ex-governor of Jamaica (Cox 661; Figure 37), and another of Thomas Carlyle, then Eyre's

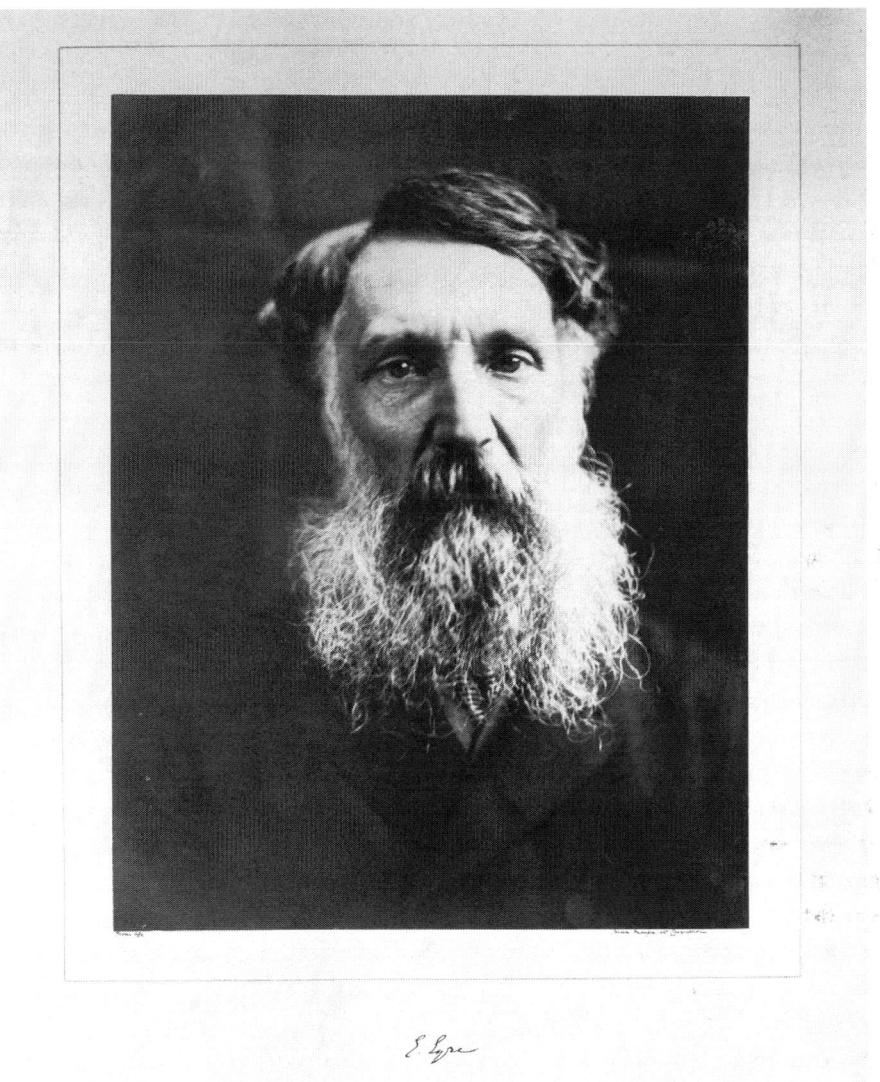

Julia Margaret Cameron, *Edward John Eyre* (Cox 661), 1867.     **37**
Albumen print, 34.2 x 25.7 cm.

most visible public supporter as Vice-President of the Eyre Defence and Aid Fund
(Cox 627, 629). Helmut Gernsheim noted that Eyre autographed his portrait and
dated it 4 June 1867, but because the copyright register suggests that both images
were taken on the same day prior to 4 June, it is likely that Carlyle invited Eyre to
accompany him to Little Holland House for the sitting.[25] Although the ex-governor's notoriety made him a valuable subject for Cameron, his actions in Jamaica
made him one of the most polarizing figures of the day.

Eyre had been recalled from Jamaica, his governorship withdrawn by the Colonial Office pending the inquiry of a Royal Commission into the circumstances of his brutal reaction to riots in Morant Bay in October 1865. After Eyre imposed martial law, British troops killed more than four hundred native islanders, flogged more than six hundred men and women, and burned more than a thousand homes, principally of the island's poor black population. Most historical accounts agree that the extreme violence took place *after* the insurrection had actually been suppressed, meaning the carnage was dispensed as punishment.[26] Eyre's most egregious retaliation took the form of court-martialling and executing a native islander, George William Gordon, who had been an effective and outspoken critic of his administration. When news of these reprisals reached England late in 1865, John Stuart Mill helped to organize a 'Jamaica Committee' and worked hard to recall Eyre to London with the eventual aim of prosecuting him for unlawful actions that condemned Gordon 'without a jury or any adequate security for justice'.[27] Thomas Carlyle, by contrast, wrote of Eyre as a 'Hero who had, with such promptitude, sagacity and intrepidity, trampled out *fire in the powder-room*, and saved the whole West Indies *ship* from flying aloft amid the deep seas'.[28] In his caustic reaction to Mill's Jamaica Committee, Carlyle spoke crudely against what he called 'a small loud group ... of Nigger-Philanthropists, barking furiously in the gutter', sentiments which reflected his well-documented racial intolerance and disdain.[29] In this example of Carlyle's racist phrasing, he extended *Punch*'s 'Negromania', itself an offensive term intended to disparage sympathy for former African slaves in Jamaica, to repudiate the very idea that justice under the law extended to all races. By contrast, in its statement Mill's Jamaica Committee aimed 'to arouse public morality against oppression generally, and particularly against the oppression of subject and dependent races' and to uphold the lawful course of due process to all British subjects, irrespective of race.[30] By slandering the activists connected to Mill who thought that Jamaicans' human rights had been trampled, Carlyle and his group hailed Eyre a modern-day hero.

During mid-century and for several decades thereafter, the cult of hero-worship and honouring of men of power was associated with Carlyle's lectures and his influential book, *On Heroes*.[31] In Carlyle's essays on his heroic types, he attached a great deal of importance to their physical attributes as they were expressed in their portraits, thinking that a portrait could confirm his ideas about the strengths and weaknesses of historical figures. During the nineteenth century, physiognomy referred to the outward features of men, and associated moral and character traits with an individual's physical features. This practice gained prominence as a pseudo-science, but Carlyle applied it as a matter of course.[32] In fact, Carlyle connected the portraits of his heroes to those substantial attributes about them which he admired: as Paul Barlow has written, Carlyle's rationale for working with a portrait by his side was to afford him 'a permanent reminder that language, whether historical or pictorial, is tied to the fact of the bodily and psychological presence of those about whom it is written'.[33] As a consequence, Carlyle found valuable 'any representation made by a faithful human creature of that face and figure which he saw by his own eyes'.[34]

Cameron shared Carlyle's faith in heroism and belief that a portrait revealed something essential about the sitter. Of her photographs of Carlyle and others whom she also considered heroic, Cameron herself wrote: 'When I have had such men before my camera my whole soul has endeavoured to do its duty towards them in recording faithfully the greatness of the inner as well as the features of the outer man.'[35] But Carlyle even went further: 'Every student of history', he wrote, who strived to comprehend the deepest motivations of men, must 'search eagerly for a portrait – for all the reasonable portraits there are; and [should] never rest till he had made out, if possible, what the man's natural face was like'.[36] For Carlyle as for Cameron, photographs were valued because of their direct connection to the sitter: Cameron's photographs (many of which were printed life size or larger than life) were always about the excellence of those men as individuals. And Carlyle and Cameron both shared ideas about the indexicality and symbolic importance of photography: as Carlyle wrote, a photographic portrait revealed its status as an index, because it was literally 'that face and figure which [a photographer] saw by his own eyes'. But he also recognized that photographic portraits acquired symbolic value, that they could stand emblematically for an individual's worldly accomplishments and even represent his ideas or universal appeal.[37]

Six months after copyrighting her portraits of Carlyle and Eyre, Cameron readied them for display at the German Gallery. The timing of Cameron's session with both Carlyle and Eyre in June 1867 and their exhibition at the beginning of the following year is highly significant, since during the intervening period two prominent events fuelled outrage and public debate concerning the Eyre affair: first, in August 1867, Carlyle's pamphlet, *Shooting Niagra: And After?* was published,[38] and second, in February 1868, Carlyle finished writing and submitted to Parliament the petition of the Eyre Defence Committee.[39] This period, in other words, was one of persistent visible activity for the defenders of Edward John Eyre and the cause of British imperialism. It also marked the beginning of a backlash of public sentiment on Eyre's behalf and against John Stuart Mill, the Liberal Member of Parliament from Westminster who led the efforts to prosecute Eyre.

Carlyle and Mill had faced off earlier in *Fraser's Magazine* in 1849–50 over questions of racial dominance and imperialism. Carlyle's political essay of 1849, 'Occasional Discourse on the Nigger Question', addressed what he regarded as the disastrous effects of emancipating black Africans in the British West Indies. To Carlyle, the domination of blacks by whites was a 'natural' phenomenon; he regarded whites as 'wiser' than blacks, their 'born lords'. Carlyle's hostility to blacks was based upon an unquestioned belief in European superiority; he considered the black man effeminate and primitive and therefore unworthy of self-determination. It was only the effect of European influence, he claimed, that allowed the Caribbean islands to realize their 'true potential' in economic or social terms. Finally, Carlyle deplored what he regarded as the black man's unreasonable refusal to work for the European plantation owners.[40] In Mill's impassioned response, 'The Negro Question', he condemned Carlyle for his racist language along with the island's plantation owners for their inept moral defence in claiming it was just to live off the labour of others, as well as their apparently shared belief that 'one kind of human beings are born servants to another kind'.[41] If Carlyle's offensive use of the term 'nigger' was a lone voice in 1849, the term gained more common usage in England by 1857, the year of the Sepoy rebellion.[42] By 1865, news of the American Civil War had polarized English society even more; while Carlyle supported the South and idealized the slaves' actual living conditions, Mill decried any effort to legitimize slavery as an affront to liberty and law-abiding citizens.[43]

Carlyle's essay supported the racist views of his friends in the Holland Park circle as well as members of Cameron's own family. In the *demi-monde* of 1860s London, for example, Cameron's nephew Val Prinsep attended boxing matches as 'entertainment' that featured black men fighting each other in bare-knuckle confrontations. Prinsep attended these matches with Dante Gabriel Rossetti; both men apparently mocked the combatants in the ring as less than human specimens. As Prinsep recalled:

> we took our places among a lot of sporting 'bungs,' *en evidence* of about as low an audience as could be found even in London. Rossetti reclined on his chair and hummed to himself in his usual absent manner as he looked at the roughs around him ... Presently there stepped forward a negro. After his round he sat in his corner and was attended to by his friends, who fanned and otherwise refreshed him. While he was being fanned the 'nigger' assumed a seraphic expression which was most comic. 'Look,' cried Rossetti in a loud voice, 'Uncle Tom aspiring to heaven, by Jove!' The whole house 'rose' with delight. One of the 'patrons' seated by us wanted to stand us a pint apiece.[44]

In 1867, Carlyle defended Eyre's actions in Jamaica in part by insisting that the enslaved condition of the Negro race was a permanent condition. In his pamphlet, *Shooting Niagra: And After?*, he reasserted an earlier position from the 'Occasional Discourse': 'One always rather likes the Nigger; ... he is the only Savage of all the colored races that doesn't die out on sight of the White Man; but can actually live beside him, and work and increase and be merry. The Almighty Maker has appointed him to be a Servant.'[45] Eyre himself maintained this racist point of view: in his own defence to the charges brought by the Jamaica Committee before the Royal Commission, Eyre justified his actions with the following statement, declaring, as if it were incontrovertible evidence,

That the negroes form a low state of civilization and being under the influence of superstitious feelings could not properly be dealt with in the same manner as the peasantry of a European country ... That as a race the negroes are most excitable and impulsive, and any seditious or rebellious action was sure to be taken up by and extend amongst the large majority of those with whom it came in contact.[46]

Finally, Carlyle wrote in his petition to the House of Commons in support of Eyre that the Governor actually deserved commendation rather than scorn, that 'Governor Eyre, by his courageous, prompt, and skilful conduct, quenched down a Savage Insurrection in Jamaica, which threatened to envelope that Island in nameless horrors; and which, many judge, might have kindled into conflagration all our West Indian Possessions together.'[47] To Carlyle, Eyre was a certifiable Hero for preserving English rule, for suppressing anarchy, for maintaining the overlord-servant relationship, and for putting himself in harm's way to destroy any claims to self-determination on the island. As Catherine Hall has documented, both Carlyle's Defence Committee and Mill's Jamaica Committee manufactured their own stunts at manipulating public opinion: 'They set up meetings, wrote to the newspapers, published pamphlets, organized lecture tours, established committees with official positions, organized finances, sent delegations to the appropriate places, kept up pressure in Parliament, and generally made themselves as publicly prominent as they could.'[48]

With her fresh portraits of Eyre and Carlyle now added to her pantheon of great men, Cameron's January–February 1868 exhibition at the German Gallery may be regarded as one such public-relations effort to promote Eyre's cause, and helps to explain why the portrait-taking session involved both men at Little Holland House. In addition, the exhibition included Cameron's photographs of other prominent members and subscribers of the Eyre Defence Committee, whose published list included such literary figures as Alfred, Lord Tennyson, the jurist and entrepreneur Henry Thoby Prinsep (Cox 736–40) and his son Val Prinsep (Cox 741–3), and the author Anthony Trollope (Cox 823). Their public positions on matters such as race and colonial politics were well known: during this time, Henry Thoby Prinsep served on various internal committees of the India Office, notably that of the Political and Secret Department, arguing repeatedly on behalf of conservative causes.[49] Beyond his status as a former member of the East India Company and the Council of India, Prinsep was also Julia Margaret Cameron's brother-in-law, married to her sister Sara.[50] Alfred Tennyson lent perhaps the greatest legitimacy to the aims of the Eyre Defence Committee once he released his name as a supporter of Eyre's cause; Carlyle's committee published Tennyson's comments widely: 'I sent my small subscription as a tribute to the nobleness of the man [Eyre], and as protest against the spirit in which a servant of the State who has saved to us one of the islands of the Empire, and many English lives, seems to be hunted down. In the meantime the outbreak of an Indian mutiny remains as a warning to all but madmen against the want of vigour and swift decisiveness.'[51]

In his book, *The West Indies and the Spanish Main* (1859), Trollope expressed his agreement with Carlyle's views about the 'debased nature' of the black man, but went even further in explicitly contradicting the sentiments of the abolitionist movement in Britain. Since the late eighteenth century, the graphic image of a kneeling African slave in chains, accompanied by the phrase, 'Am I not a man and a brother?', had been associated with the anti-slavery movement in Britain.[52] Trollope impugned the abolitionists by calling them uninformed philanthropists whose compassion blinded them to the Jamaicans' widespread refusal to accept wages in exchange for working in the fields of British landowners. At stake was the economic crisis that would result from their refusal to work:

> And now, just at this moment, philanthropy is again busy in England protecting the Jamaican negro. He is a man and a brother, and shall we not regard him? Certainly, my philanthropic friend, let us regard him well. He is a man; and if you will, a brother; but he is the very idlest brother with which a hardworking workman was ever cursed, intent only on getting his mess of pottage without giving us anything in return.[53]

In Trollope's short story of 1860 about life in Jamaica, he connected these racist theories to the economic hardships he witnessed during his travel. Transforming poverty into 'decadence', Trollope justified British control of the island as a kind of charitable by-product of its civilizing mission: 'There is nothing so melancholy as a country in its decadence, unless it be a people in its decadence. I am not aware that the latter misfortune can be attributed to the Anglo-Saxon race in any part of the world; but there is reason to fear that it has fallen on an English colony in the island of Jamaica.'[54]

Accompanying the portraits of Carlyle, Eyre, the Prinseps, and Trollope, were many prints depicting Henry Taylor. Although Taylor was not listed a subscriber to the Eyre Defence Fund, he nevertheless was an articulate spokesman for the Colonial Office's pro-slavery position in his debates against Mill and the Benthamites.[55] Moreover, Taylor had long been associated with Jamaica specifically, because in 1865 he authored the so-called 'Queen's Letter' to British colonists of the island, which denied their appeals for small land grants and other forms of economic relief.[56] Prior to the rebellion that would take place later that year, Taylor shared his belief with others in the Colonial Office that the island's emancipated slaves would continue to show subservience toward the British:

> [It was] fortunate that the Negroes … have shown themselves to be of a nature not prone to serious or atrocious offences. They are avaricious, litigious, and quarrelsome … and they are immoral and unsteady in the relations between the sexes, but they are a sober people, and there is no great depth of malignity in them. Their faults partake of the shallowness of their nature.[57]

During these critical years, Taylor developed policies that would import 'coolie labour' to Jamaica from India and elsewhere specifically to counter the native Jamaican's resistance to work for wages for British plantation owners.

In the German Gallery, Cameron did not confine her imagery to portraits of her heroes. She also displayed allegories of authoritarian men, who were, as Mike Weaver noticed, also 'compulsive and compelling in the manner of Carlyle's heroes'. In fact, Weaver astutely claimed that the allegories displayed there 'consciously displayed the dark side of male authority'.[58] In the context of Cameron's portraits of heroic men, we might even extend the observation and suggest that these allegories represented anti-heroes: all of them involve harsh, severe, or callous father figures who have placed their virtuous and pure daughters in uncompromising predicaments, or whose overbearing and inflexible character stand in stark contrast to their daughters' kindness and compassion. They included *Beatrice* (Cox 406) modelled on Beatrice Cenci created by Percy Shelley, who plotted her father's murder after having been cruelly abused by him; *Christabel* (Cox 396), from an unfinished poem by Samuel Taylor Coleridge, the heroine struck by a demon's spell only to be ignored by her obtuse father, Sir Leoline; *Prospero and Miranda* (Cox 1093) from Shakespeare's play *The Tempest*, the daughter shielded from the world as a reflection of her father's repressive control; and *Friar Laurence* (Cox 1089) who Cameron depicted with Juliet from Shakespeare's *Romeo and Juliet*, the monk the agent of the two youths' destruction.

Other representations of women displayed in 1868 in these allegories fare equally poorly by their absent or neglectful fathers as well as those who take their place: *Rosalba* (Cox 509) for example, a character from Thackeray's children's fairy tale, *The Rose and the Ring* (1854), becomes a lost, forest-dwelling and nameless orphan when her father abandons her as a toddler to fight off one of his rebellious vassals; later in the story, the young child is taken into royal society as a beggar-maid, but is once again cast out of society by courtiers jealous of her growing beauty. When the grown-up Rosalba ultimately confronts the new king who killed her father, Thackeray calls him a 'ruffian and usurper, who had such a bad cause, and who was so cruel to women'.[59] In a similar vein, Cameron portrayed the story of King Cophetua and the Beggar Maid, a popular tale mentioned in Shakespeare's *Romeo and Juliet*, *Richard II*, and *Love's Labour's Lost*, and taken up as a subject by Tennyson in his 1842 poem, *The Beggar Maid*. In Cameron's photograph *King Cophetua* (Cox 1188), she portrayed the stern monarch who transformed the menial life of yet another beautiful and impoverished servant girl.[60] Ultimately, in these stories, men's social status and their domestic control over women are portrayed as the ultimate force with which women must reckon, and the frequently nameless women fare well only when, as Tennyson says, they are 'more beautiful than day'.

Weaver came to terms with the recognition that Cameron chose female subjects whose male counterparts were unthinking and callous, brutish and coarse. He charitably excused her artistic representations of the 'dark side' of these men as little more than human nature: 'With the insight of genius as well as affection, she recognized dark forces in the greatest of men.'[61] But ironically, Weaver was referring her to *allegorical* representations of men. The public and atrocious 'dark side' of Cameron's 'real heroes', on the other hand, might seem extreme.[62] To what extent did Cameron leave open the possibility for her audience to re-inscribe the portraits of her male heroes as anti-heroes? Cameron's portrait subjects, like the male allegorical figures described above, are also fair and intolerant; humanized and barbaric; strong and unfit; caring and selfish; able and inept. But in her photographs of literary subjects, the emblems of male power have been undermined by fictional characters who deny their humanity ('Friar Laurence'); are wilfully cruel to their children ('Beatrice'); perpetuate a dominant and controlling relationship with others ('Rosalba', 'King Cophetua'); or who neglect the urgency to combat the evil that flourishes in their midst ('Christabel', 'Prospero').

In Cameron's 1868 exhibition, a fascinating amalgam of heroes and anti-heroes emerges: rather than displaying selected portraits of public figures who were heroic in her sights or arranging allegorical photographs that depicted male brutality or intolerance, she instead combined the two forms, effectively presenting a complex interplay between the forces of virtue and vice – both purity *and* sinfulness; duty *and* betrayal; innocence *and* evil – in her literal portraits and allegorical studies. As a consequence, both extremes were cancelled out. Published essays about the exhibition reflected this critical ambiguity, with the result that Cameron was again advised to separate her portraits and fancy subjects rather than intermingle them on display. Writing in the *Athenaeum*, for example, one art critic dismissed the allegories and literary personifications that she called her 'Fancy Subjects': 'Of these [photographs] we dismiss at once such as bear "fancy" names, and pretend to subjects of the poetic and dramatic sorts.'[63] Yet another took the opposite approach; writing in the *Court Circular*, he praised Cameron for her emblematic 'Fancy Subjects' of innocent children and for the first time aligned her efforts to the historical paintings of Sir Joshua Reynolds, the acknowledged master of the fancy picture: 'No person that we know of has ever photographed children as Mrs Cameron has done. Raffaelle, Correggio, and Sir Joshua Reynolds have been the painters of children par excellence; and what they did with the brush Mrs Cameron has done with the camera.'[64]

At the same time, however, Cameron evidently blurred the boundaries that defined portraits and allegories, especially in photography, although she attempted to distinguish the two in her printed catalogue for the exhibition. As a consequence, the public role of men depicted in formal portraits affected the interpretation of the fancy subjects, and the presence of Cameron's allegories weakened the independence of the portraits. In short, the evident artificiality of each form stained the other. Staining, the leaving of a resistant trace, is an apt metaphor for the resilient 'mark' of that which has become destabilized.[65]

## The double face of infiltration and war

In the months following her German Gallery exhibition, Cameron's interest in depicting colonial subjects broadened to include photographs of key diplomats at the Colonial Office, British emissaries who infiltrated distant lands on behalf of the Empire, and foreign visitors and refugees from the war in Abyssinia. That is to say, she abandoned much of the domestic imagery associated with her family albums during this time, including her Madonna studies and images of children posed asleep or in prayer. These were replaced by new compositions that were unambiguously related to current and world events. But rather than adopting a new approach to represent these subjects, Cameron captured the essence of these conflicts by creating new allegories.

The Abyssinian War of 1868 was the linchpin of this diverse photographic activity. Initially a conflict of words and misunderstandings between the Abyssinian king, Theowodrus II (whom the English called Theodore), and British diplomats in the Foreign Office, the 'Abyssinian difficulty' began in 1865. The two countries had similar political and economic goals given the particular geography of the region, now Ethiopia, then widely called the Horn of Africa: King Theodore saw an alliance with the British as a way to consolidate power, an opportunity to use British clout to hold off Muslim incursions from the Sudan and French influence from Egypt while keeping important trade routes open on the Red Sea. At the same time, the British looked to Abyssinia as a way to counter French influence by establishing a commercial partner on the Red Sea. Ever since Napoleon's invasion of Egypt at the turn of the century, in fact, Britain had sought ways to hold off French colonial expansion and secure a shortened route to India, and regarded Abyssinia's geography its most distinctive advantage in forging any alliance. The alignment of these economic and political interests gave way to a lengthy diplomatic correspondence during the 1860s between Britain and Abyssinia to establish mutual consulates, but this unhappy story is one of miscommunication and failed diplomacy.[66]

In short, important letters between King Theodore and Queen Victoria were apparently lost and their respective envoys delayed because of travel difficulties and the great distance between the two countries. Misinterpretations in the Colonial Office were followed by perceived insults on both sides, and in the end, mutual economic and political interests lost to pride and competition. When the Abyssinian king imprisoned the Queen's envoy, Charles Duncan Cameron (no relation to Charles and Julia Margaret), the misunderstandings became a diplomatic crisis. Austen Henry Layard, then parliamentary under-secretary, sent yet another messenger, Hormuzd Rassam, to seek the release of the Queen's envoy, hoping to bring about a peaceful resolution. For Layard and his colleagues, the cost of threatening war against Abyssinia was considered too great: not only were there extreme geographical obstacles and manpower questions to overcome, Theodore was considered unpredictable, meaning that any hostile action could jeopardize the captives' safety. Additionally, there was growing public disillusion in Britain with the nation's expansionist policies and a growing reticence to engage in conflicts that could provoke yet another revolt of the kind that had erupted in Jamaica and further humiliation.

Rather than release the British consul and his entourage, King Theodore imprisoned Rassam along with the others. A long drumbeat for war emerged in Parliament and in the popular press, urging Britain to end the political stagnation and overcome its resistance to declaring war.[67] As a result, the Abyssinian War became a 'popular' war in England, designed to 'save face' by rescuing the British captives by force, thereby teaching the insolent Africans 'a lesson'.[68] The campaign itself was also an overwhelming display of military power, logistical skill, and outright determination, as Robert Cornelis Napier, then the most decorated Field Marshall of the Royal Engineers, was commissioned to command an army of almost four thousand English and Indian soldiers by sea and over rough terrain to release the British captives.[69] Throughout 1867, the progress of Napier and his forces was chronicled in regular dispatches in *The Times* and in pictorial reports in the *Illustrated London News*. In 1868, the *Illustrated London News* also assembled a luxuriously bound commemorative volume of excerpts and field reports, illustrated with folio-sized engravings of Napier and his forces crossing rivers, traversing deep gorges, and forging ahead to the mountain stronghold where the King was waiting for the military expedition to arrive.[70] The newspaper's illustrations were based on photographs taken by a dedicated war photographer brought along specifically to record Napier's progress.

Napier's final push at Magdala left King Theodore dead by his own hand. The conquest itself left his son, the child-prince Alamayou,[71] orphaned and his country occupied. Under the patronage of Queen Victoria herself, young Alamayou, the British officer Captain Speedy, and one of the Prince's servants were brought to England, first settling on the Isle of Wight in July 1868.[72] Cameron's Abyssinian subjects therefore unwittingly came directly to her: she made a formal portrait of Napier on the occasion of his visit to the Queen at Osborne House (Cox 717), and nine photographs of the Abyssinian refugees in July and August (Cox 1114–15, 1117–23). In spite of the fact that Queen Victoria, Emily Tennyson, William Allingham, and others recorded the presence of her subjects on the Isle of Wight that summer, the narrative of the Abyssinian Expedition and its aftermath on Freshwater Bay has been considered incidental to Cameron's photography.[73]

Cameron devoted considerable time and attention to these subjects. She took numerous photographs of the young Prince Alamayou of Abyssinia, the Prince's African attendant, and the Prince's appointed guardian, Captain Tristram Speedy, on at least two separate occasions. The three visitors stayed at Afton Manor, the home of Mrs Cotton, Captain Speedy's mother-in-law. Speedy attained some celebrity during the war as Napier's translator and trusted aid. Prior to this military role, however, he actually lived in Abyssinia as a hunter, mercenary, and 'adventurer', and at one point was even pressed into serving King Theodore as *his* translator.[74] As a multilingual man of imposing size who was also fond of wearing a native Abyssinian costume, Speedy was depicted in reports and images published in the *Illustrated London News* as a colourful figure serving Napier.[75] Once they relocated in England, Speedy and Alamayou frequently visited Queen Victoria at her summer palace, Osborne, and called upon the Tennysons at Farringford and the Camerons at their home, Dimbola. The Prince caused 'something of a sensation' among the island's residents, according to Captain Speedy's notebooks: 'everyone was very interested in the Abyssinian Expedition and wanted to catch sight of Alamayehu'.[76]

Cameron copyrighted her photographs of Alamayou in July and quickly sent them off to London, there to be displayed in the window of her print dealer, P. & D. Colnaghi's, in anticipation of taking orders. One image, marked 'Study No. 2', for example (Cox 1119), depicting the Prince and Captain Speedy, bears the inscriptions, 'From life registered photograph taken at Freshwater 20 July 1868', 'Copyright registration of 23 July 1868', and 'For the window immediately orders will be taken.' These activities reflect both Cameron's business-like approach and her ambitious goals; they stake an immediate, if not urgent, claim over her imagery, suggesting a desire to assert her priority to the works and control their dissemination, revealing a personal investment in the success of her project (see Cox 1114–22). She also made a reduced-size *carte de visite*, suitable for collecting in its own right, or as a way to generate sales for her larger photographs.

Cameron's investment was of a political nature, too, as she was not simply content to confine her imagery of the Abyssinian group to the few portraits sent to Colnaghi's in July. In fact, the following month, she organized another portrait session with the same subjects. In his diary entry of 21 August 1868, William Allingham wrote of witnessing the preparations for these photographs. Although he himself never sat for Cameron, Allingham's narrative reveals telling observations that shed light on the photographer's working methods as well as the fascinating series which resulted:

> Mrs Cameron's: Captain Speedy opens the door. Little Alamayu, pretty boy, we make friends and have romps, he rides on my knee, shows his toys. His Abyssinian attendant. They dress to be photographed by Mrs C., the Prince in a little purple shirt and a necklace, Captain Speedy in a lion-skin tippet, with a huge Abyssinian

sword of reaping-hook shape ('point goes into your skull'). Photographing room—Speedy grumbles a little, Mrs C. poses them. Photograph of Tennyson's maid as 'Desdemona.'[77]

The three photographs of the Abyssinian group that resulted from this sitting were not formal portraits, but instead posed allegorical representations of her subjects acting out defined and prescribed roles. If the first session of July resulted in three closely cropped arrangements with the Prince as the primary subject, the August session shunned conventional portraiture in favour of producing three dramatic figure groups, much in the same way Tennyson's maid was said to have been transformed into a character from *Othello*, Desdemona, around the same time. Moreover, props surrounding the figures, who were arranged in front of a curtained stage, are prominent in the results of the second sitting, suggesting a new approach to social relationships or emphasis on some metaphoric association; these are not at all present in the formal portraits of July (Cox 1114). As Allingham indicated, this image (1114) also includes the figure identified as Alamayou's 'Abyssinian attendant'. Although this individual's origins and actual identity are uncertain, Roger Fry and Virginia Woolf identified him as 'Casa'.[78] There is a discrepancy between the dates of Cameron's actual copyright registrations and Allingham's apparent witnessing of the photographic session, which might be reconciled by the poet's recording the events after the fact, or by his confusion over yet another session of August, when Cameron's model, Mary Kellaway, posed in an Abyssinian costume.[79] Interestingly, neither 'Desdemona' nor the image of the costumed Kellaway have been identified or now survive, and it is intriguing to speculate what titles Cameron might have given these photographs and whether or not she conceived their making in relation to her other photographs of Abyssinian subjects.

The most unusual and perplexing photograph of the entire series is the one depicting Speedy, the costumed soldier, and the Prince's African attendant, which has come to be known by the suggestive title, *Spear or Spare* (Cox 1115; Figure 38).Cameron apparently first called it by that name in the hand-written appendix she made to the printed checklist of her 1868 exhibition (Figure 1), although this actual title does not appear on the print itself. In the photograph, the child, Prince Alamayou, is not present. Instead, Cameron has depicted an image of arrested conflict between two grown men, one British, the other Abyssinian: she has positioned Speedy hierarchically above Casa, his right foot placed on Casa's hip, forcing Casa into a supine position. In addition, Cameron has instructed Speedy to act as if he is pushing back against Casa's head with his left hand and directed the reclining man to stare up at Speedy. A spear held in Speedy's right hand is positioned near the throat of the bug-eyed Casa, and yet, in contrast to his expression of extreme alarm, the prostrate man offers no apparent resistance. Rather, he lies loosely in Speedy's grasp, his right arm draped limply over an Abyssinian shield, which is used for decoration rather than defence.

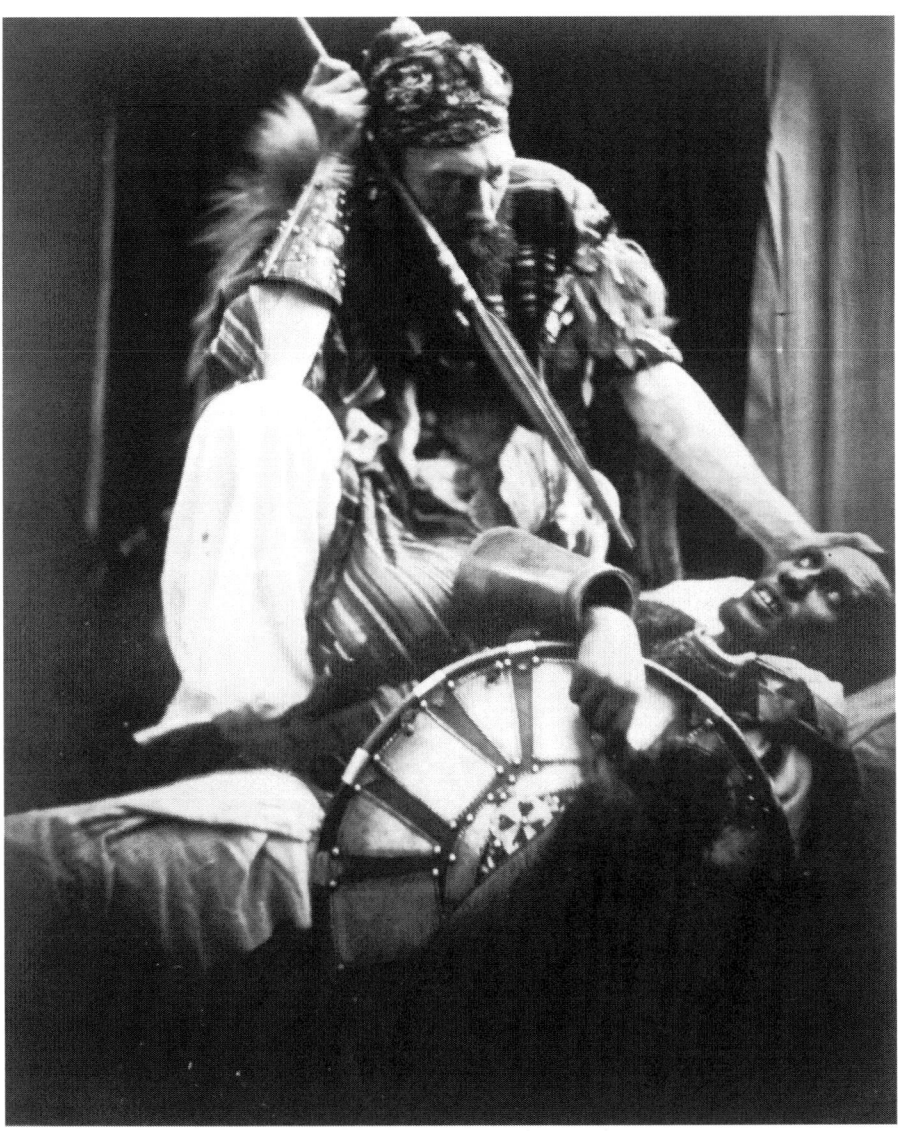

Julia Margaret Cameron, *Spear or Spare* (Cox 1115), 1868.     **38**
Albumen print, 31.2 x 25 cm.

In this image, Cameron has constructed her version of the Abyssinian conflict, depicting a standstill of sorts in the relations between white European and black African. It is helpful to contextualize the particular time period in which this photograph was conceived and produced to help explain its impact. Allingham's diary provides some background about the photograph's staging and production, while the portrait photographs she produced simultaneously provide another important context. During this period, Cameron made portraits of celebrated

African and Middle Eastern explorers, including Richard Francis Burton (Cox 845), Austen Henry Layard (Cox 700), and William Gifford Palgrave (Cox 733). Other portraits of important colonial figures, like Henry Taylor, Anthony Trollope, and Henry Thoby Prinsep, had already been exhibited in Bond Street, along with her well-known study of *William Holman Hunt in an Arab Dress* (Cox 685–7) that she had taken several years earlier.

All of these photographs were available for purchase at Colnaghi's. But while Cameron's portraits of these men praise their cultural importance, the new portraits taken in the summer of 1868 and afterward owed much to the Orientalist tradition in portraiture that she had pursued in her representations of Byronic subjects. In those photographs, however, Cameron represented exclusively female protagonists: Donna Julia and not Don Juan; Haidée and not Lambro; Medora and not Conrad. But in 1868, she exhibited portraits of men who were associated directly with disguise, subterfuge, and infiltration, men whose public identities were called 'Orientalist' because they had penetrated into foreign lands and passed as native Arabs while living abroad. As mentioned, William Holman Hunt had been photographed in the costume he wore while in Egypt and Palestine, his attire chosen, according to the painter, the better to fit in, but also as a kind of spiritual identification with his subjects. Similarly, in her 1868 exhibition, Cameron displayed a photograph she titled *Henry Taylor in Arab Dress*, a curious matter-of-fact image that does not represent Taylor personifying King David and does not recreate a period of his life abroad, like her portrait of Hunt, but in its literal form, awkwardly represents Taylor as a camouflaged official in the Colonial Office. Or perhaps Cameron dressed him in this way to honour his colonial activities, as she did for Hunt.[80]

In June 1868, Cameron portrayed William Gifford Palgrave in his Eastern disguise, depicting him in the turban he used while crossing Arabia in 1862–63. Disguised as a Syrian doctor and merchant, Palgrave was paid in part by Napoleon III, to whom he reported on the attitude of the Arabians toward the French.[81] In this regard, he acted as a kind of double agent, especially as France and Britain jousted for influence in the region. In a similar vein, Cameron photographed another British agent, Richard Francis Burton, who became famous as the first Westerner to penetrate into the Great Mosque of Mecca. The Royal Geographic Society subsidized Burton's exploits, although he reported officially to the military. As a celebrated linguist, he won fame in 1853 for translating the *Arabian Nights*. But as a disguised Arabian, Burton entered the popular imagination for his infiltration. His account of this accomplishment, called *A Personal Narrative of a Pilgrimage to El-Medinah and Meccah*, was first published in 1855 but was revised in four subsequent editions during Burton's lifetime, and again in four later editions after his death.[82] Burton's usefulness to the Empire was well chronicled, as he informed the British army against planned revolts, and his field reports functioned as avant-garde military updates.[83]

Austen Henry Layard, too, hoped to serve the Empire beyond his status as a Member of Parliament. Much as Edward John Eyre had first been known as an explorer and adventurer in Australia prior to governing Jamaica, Layard also acquired an explorer's reputation for his voyage into ancient Assyria and his archaeological treatise on the ruins of Nineveh and Babylon. In political life, however, Layard declined the post of Consul-General of Egypt that he was offered in 1853 for a career in Parliament and the Foreign Office, where he helped Britain confront France, Russia, and Turkey over the control of Jerusalem, and later, the Crimea.[84] Years later, in 1865, Layard and Palgrave both tried to help resolve the emerging conflict in Abyssinia, with Layard, now under-secretary in the Foreign Office, instrumental in sending Palgrave to Egypt as a stopover on the way to Abyssinia.[85] And in 1867 Anthony Trollope, who then edited the *Saint Paul's Magazine*, attempted to secure from Layard a literary contribution about the confrontations between the Ottoman East and the British West, as Trollope knew his readers wanted to understand this long-standing conflict, especially during the run-up toward the popular war in Abyssinia.[86]

Fixed in Cameron's portraits of these men is the twin reality of the undercover operator: when portrayed in their costume as a disguised Eastern subject of the British Empire, Palgrave, Prinsep, Taylor, Burton, and Holman Hunt are all presented as active agents but also passive objects, or, in Edward Said's memorable phrase, representing 'both exhibit and exhibitor, winning two confidences at once, displaying two appetites for experience'.[87] The very construction of personal and social identity informs Said's comment as much as it does Cameron's portraits of these men. Their 'Eastern costumes' become signifying emblems of their identity, and as a result, they occupy an ambiguous middle ground. Public revelations about the 'true identity' of these men could produce hot-tempered responses. For example, in Palgrave's book of 1865, *A Narrative of a Year's Journey through Central and Eastern Arabia*, the author explicitly censured Burton's deceit in Arabia as a malicious act of dishonesty:

> To feign a religion which the adventurer himself does not believe, to perform with scrupulous exactitude, as of the highest and holiest import, practices which he inwardly ridicules, and which he intends on his return to hold up to the ridicule of others, to turn for weeks and months together the most sacred and awful bearings of man towards his Creator into a deliberate and truthless mummery, not to mention other and yet darker touches – all this seems hardly compatible with the character of a European gentleman, let alone that of a Christian.[88]

In response, Burton attacked Palgrave, who then found himself on the defensive: Burton noted that Palgrave, who was born Protestant but was of Jewish descent, had become a Jesuit priest; how he worked as a French secret agent even though he was a sworn British officer; how upon returning to Protestantism he violated

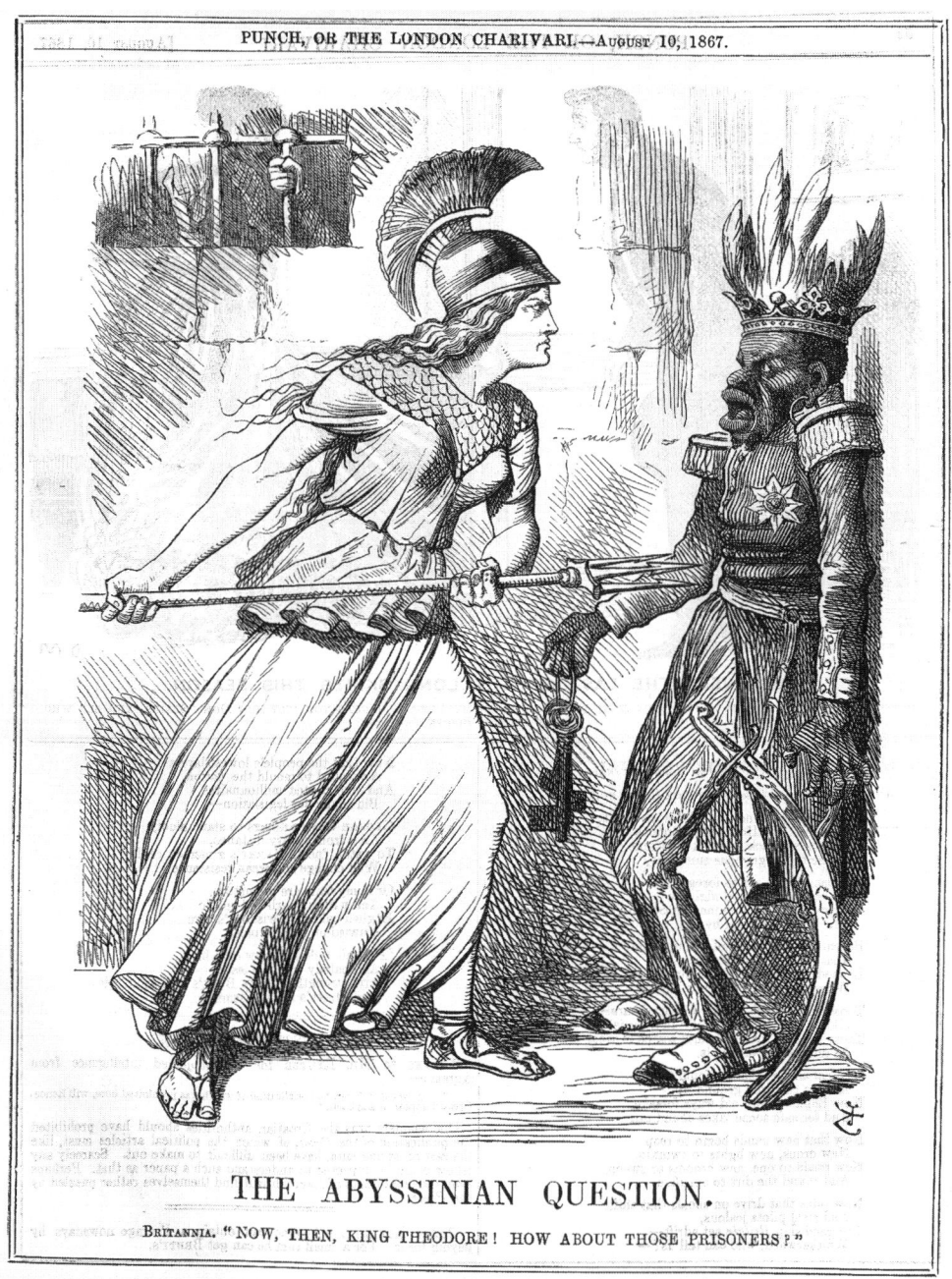

THE ABYSSINIAN QUESTION.

BRITANNIA. "NOW, THEN, KING THEODORE! HOW ABOUT THOSE PRISONERS?"

39    The Abyssinian Question, cartoon from *Punch, or the London Charivari*, 10 August 1867, p. 57.

the sanctity of his Catholic vows; in short, how there were multiple layers to his duplicity and deception.[89]

In Cameron's portrayals of Burton and Palgrave, the subterfuge commemorated photographically has already past, and the image marks its aftermath, its successful finale. Cameron's photographs of these men, along with Prinsep, Taylor, and Holman Hunt, actually perform a double function as distinguished portraits of celebrated men in that they conceal the violence of their infiltration while commemorating the success of their deception.[90] Unlike the actor who in a dramatic role may take on the physical characteristics of his part, Cameron's costumed explorers credibly portray the in-between state occupied by these men because they embody two identities at once. But while they may occupy this unstable middle ground, these portraits are also anti-heroic in the sense used earlier to describe the absent or negligent fathers in Cameron's allegorical photographs of Rosalba, Christabel, and Beatrice. Palgrave's and Burton's mutual accusations and personal smears betrayed how the two explorers tarnished and dishonoured 'both sides' of their double identities in equal measure.

The political collaboration that brought together Layard and Palgrave in 1865 as would-be settlers of the Abyssinian dispute was understood two years later in the British press as a kind of political ultimatum. A cartoon from *Punch* expressed this arrogant confrontation, with a bold, gladiator-like personification of Britannia as the imperial army portrayed threatening a cowering and fearful Abyssinian king (Figure 39). Outside an imagined prison holding Britain's consul and its envoys, Britannia holds a spear to Theodore's torso, and cries: 'Now, then, King Theodore! How about those prisoners?'[91] Once war had actually been declared in 1868, the editors of *Punch* brashly speculated on what Britain might do should Field Marshall Napier actually succeed in capturing King Theodore, although this outcome was never articulated as an *official* goal of the war. In order to recompense the British taxpayer for the trouble of subduing him, they reasoned, the 'African Negus' should be turned literally into a 'circus African'.[92] By capturing the Abyssinian king and making him the centrepiece of a live exhibition that would tour the country, Britain could raise funds as a way of restocking the financial coffers of the Royal Army:

> First catch your Negus, of course; but having caught him, bring him away and constitute him an exhibition. In so doing there would be no need to keep him in a cage or den; he might be made perfectly comfortable, only open to public inspection during certain hours daily at the Egyptian Hall, Piccadilly, or some other place equally commodious. Admission on the five days out of the six … might be one shilling, the sixth day being a half-crown day, for the accommodations of the superior classes. After having been shown in London, … he might be conveyed throughout the rest of the United Kingdom.[93]

Two months later, on 18 July 1868, another cartoon appeared, mocking the 'King of the Lion Kingdom', the historical title that Theodore claimed for himself. The lion's jail keepers were portrayed as the British Royal Court, on one side, and on the other, in the person of the moustachioed Field Marshall Napier, the imperial army. Cameron capped her own telling of the Abyssinian Expedition with her own portrait photograph of Napier (Cox 717), an image she produced to capitalize on the enduring popularity of the General and to compete against the popularity of *cartes-de-visite* produced by others.

In Cameron's photograph of the white, costumed soldier and the black, African attendant that she called *Spear or Spare*, she enlarged upon these pictorial and discursive strategies that depicted the struggles and frustrations of the Abyssinian conflict. This photograph makes sense as a kind of reaction to *Punch*'s satire 'Negromania', which mocked the idea that British compassion to Jamaicans or Abyssinians could have forestalled those conflicts, because in Cameron's image, intimidation and aggression replaces compassion and empathy. This photograph also makes sense in terms of Cameron's ambiguous attitude towards the Abyssinian campaign as represented by her anti-heroic portraits of Palgrave and Layard, who both failed to resolve the Abyssinian crisis diplomatically, and her heroic portrait of Napier, who ultimately succeeded militarily. Casting her white and black subjects in opposing roles, Captain Speedy, the British officer, is portrayed threatening the life of his captive, holding a spear to the throat of Casa, Prince Alamayou's dark-skinned African attendant. The black man lies prostrate, gazing up, alarmed, a portrayal of fear and powerlessness effectively resembling the exaggerated representation satirized in *Punch*'s cartoon of Britannia menacing King Theodore.

By August 1868, this photograph referred unambiguously to the armed combat in Abyssinia, but it also revealed hybrid references that allow us to question Cameron's commitment to that war and to the larger conflict between East and West, and her attitude regarding race relations between Europeans and Africans in general. Fear and control, threat and violence, vanquished and conqueror, death and life: all are represented here, as we are confronted symbolically with a powerful instance of colonialist discourses of power as they are both expressed and denied. The presence of both attributes is marked allegorically by the hybrid quality of the photograph, a result of the instability and displacement found in the shifting ground that characterizes this image.[94] The hybrid is therefore a site of multiple inscriptions and continuing interpretation, where meaning, inherently unsettled and shifting, requires continued inscription – that is, continued narrative explanation – in order to make sense over time.

Cameron's photograph became just such an example of continuing multiple inscriptions. First called *Spear or Spare* in 1868, Cameron inscribed at least one print of the image *Báshá Félika*, which was the Amharic name taken by Captain Speedy in Abyssinia. When titled in this way, the photograph of the two men obscures or conceals the black man's identity, or perhaps the presence of the African is invisible or beneath notice; he is not identified because he is not truly seen. It is also possible that the inked signature was appended by Speedy himself, just as, in a different context, Cameron had Thoby Prinsep write his own name in Urdu underneath his own portrait (Cox 737). On the mount of the print containing the inscription 'Báshá Félika', a line was drawn and an additional inscription penned: 'Captn. Speedy', perhaps by a different hand. Other photographs from this series are also given inscriptions in Amharic, the native language of Abyssinia used by Prince Alamayou and his father, King Theodore. This ancient language was mastered by Speedy, but also belongs to Alamayou, giving these multi-dimensional images further marks of their status as multi-inscribed, culturally hybrid works of art.

Additional marks of hybridity are embedded in this photograph and discernible in at least three ways: first, we have a representation of conflict and of difference, embodying for Cameron's audience a narcissistic attachment to the foreign-costumed Speedy, the white British officer, and a mistrustful fear of the black African, Casa. But because hybridity subverts the narratives of superiority and colonial power, the markers of cultural authority are undermined in the photograph. Cameron's placement of the two major actors, her excessive use of exotic props, and her creation of a scene of power and domination, cannot operate as a faithful sign of the historical memory concerning Abyssinia, because the photographic encounter reduces the British war with Abyssinia into a static one-on-one conflict between two men.

If the re-imagined tableau attempted to substitute her sitters for the complicated political, territorial, and cultural warfare they supposedly represent, it falls short of convincingly narrating that power relationship and instead appears artificially constructed, a product of a distanced abstraction because of its inanimate, motionless encounter. When Queen Victoria received Alamayou at Osborne House, she accepted the young Prince as a child, a powerless, foreign-born potentate who was literally dependent upon her largesse; his future lay in an English boarding school, there to be 'civilized' in the mould of the British, as he had been stripped from his language of origins, his land, and his history; ill health unfortunately cut his life short in adolescence. 'Casa', on the other hand, could be represented only as dominated, subservient, supine. There is no mistaking the hostility, controlled rage, and even blood lust lying thinly veiled behind the surface of this image.

Second, *Spear or Spare* endorses a narrative of decadence and melancholy that may be traced to Trollope and Carlyle, whose fiction and political essays describe in racist terms the two authors' views about the inferiority of the conquered black Africans, whether former slaves in Jamaica or native Abyssinians. Made sometime after the Jamaica rebellion, which ended very differently, Cameron's photograph represents a proxy for the proud and victorious West, now able to present a different morality tale that signifies its racial, economic, and military superiority. Importantly, Casa offers no defiance in his confrontation with Speedy: his docile demeanour may symbolize for Cameron's audience the despondency of his capture, or more broadly, his inferiority, indolence, or decadence as it might have been framed by Trollope or Carlyle. But as a hybrid image, the staged passivity of this photograph also contains its opposite meaning, as Casa also symbolizes the latent seed of forthcoming armed resistance. Because there is no justness to the domination pictured, justice demands the tables be turned some future day, the wounds healed and the injustice atoned for or remedied.

Third, Cameron's photograph of staged conflict unwittingly re-enacts another narrative altogether, a celebrated story that was central to at least one version of Abyssinian history. According to this legend, it was King Theodore who ended Abyssinia's historical civil war and unified the country's warring chieftains.[95] In Cameron's photograph, it is Captain Speedy, the mercenary once employed by Theodore prior to Napier's landing, who is represented subduing a 'native son' of Abyssinia. Importantly, he holds a spear rather than a rifle, symbolically re-enacting his subversive warfare on behalf of, rather than in resistance to, King Theodore. Like Cameron's other costumed explorers discussed above, Captain Speedy has concealed his 'true' British identity under the cloak of camouflage, thereby manifesting yet another type of hybridity. This dual role – in the photograph, Speedy is not always immediately recognized as European, much less British – is emblematic of the hybrid nature of the image. The Speedy represented here is *both* King Theodore's covert agent *and* Field Marshall Napier's valued soldier.

Finally, the British war with Abyssinia is also represented in this photograph, with the imperial forces represented by Speedy, who occupied the land, released the British captives, and deposed the African monarch, his one-time sovereign. Rather than depicting an act of explosive violence, however, Cameron's characters are represented as strangely lethargic, even passive. Her desire to represent the dramatic immediacy of armed combat is undermined by her actors' obvious resignation and perhaps even her uninspired direction. We might even say the image is overdetermined in its artificiality, a consequence of Cameron's own ambivalence more than the need to keep the actors still in the making of the image. In *Spear or Spare*, a photograph of conflict between Captain Speedy as Báshá Félika and Prince Alamayou's Abyssinian attendant, Casa, Cameron could not escape the still-unsettled questions of justness and justice that are embedded in her allegory. In the photograph, it remains unsettled whether Speedy should kill or save his captive, a symbolic impasse that also described Britain's attitude toward Abyssinia in the aftermath of the war. Having punished Theodore for his affront to the Empire, in the end, Britain resolved to stay out of Abyssinia and ultimately withdrew its military forces. However, when she made this photograph, Britain's decision to do so was far from settled.

*Spear or Spare* embodies Cameron's unsettled condition. The Jamaican insurrection and lead-up to the Abyssinian War gave shape to her German Gallery exhibition, to which this work was connected, as these conflicts also drew into the public arena her neighbour Tennyson, her brother-in-law Thoby and nephew Val Prinsep, and her patron Lord Overstone, forcing him to declare his position as a defender or opponent of Eyre. The photographic subjects she pursued during this time provide a historical context for her portraits and a new allegorical framework upon which her fancy subjects took on complex new meanings. *Spear or Spare*, as with the photographs she assembled in 1868 for exhibition in the German Gallery, exposed Cameron's interest in representing the troubling questions of justness and justice, questions that were unsettled in the British West Indies as much as in Parliament, and unresolved in the Foreign Office, even after the conclusion of the Abyssinian War. It is because of these unresolved conflicts that Cameron's photography expressed uncomfortable dilemmas: where she attempted to portray the prevailing Orientalist stereotypes of her time, she made hybridized images instead; where she attempted to create a convincing dynamic struggle representing the war in Abyssinia, she could only create tenuous and unstable sites of inscription, creating photographs with compound titles, multiple storylines, and differing narratives, all subject to competing and overlapping interpretations.

## Notes

1  'Punch's Essence of Parliament', *Punch, or the London Charivari*, 30 May 1868, p. 233.
2  Julian Cox estimated approximately 235 photographs exhibited; see Julian Cox and Colin Ford, eds., *Julia Margaret Cameron: The Complete Photographs* (Los Angeles: J. Paul Getty Trust, 2003), pp. 539–40.
3  Colin Ford, *The Cameron Collection: An Album of Photographs by Julia Margaret Cameron Presented to Sir John Herschel* (London: Von Nostrand Reinhold and the National Portrait Gallery, 1975), p. 124. Trollope's *West Indies and the Spanish Main* went into a second edition in 1860 (London: Chapman and Hall); his short story in the 3 November and 10 November 1860 issues of *Cassell's Illustrated Family Paper. Anthony Trollope: The Complete Short Stories, Vol. 3, Tourists and Colonials*, ed. Betty Jane Slemp Breyer (Fort Worth: Texas Christian University Press, 1981), p. 25.
4  See Julia Thomas, *Pictorial Victorians* (Athens, OH: Ohio University Press, 2004), pp. 77–103.
5  See Bernard Semmel, *The Governor Eyre Controversy* (London: MacGibbon and Kee, 1962), p. 32.
6  Homi K. Bhabha, *The Location of Culture* (London and New York: Routledge, 1994), p. 44.
7  Ambivalence may be detected, wrote Bhabha, when imagery vacillates uneasily 'between what is always "in place", already known, and something that must be anxiously repeated ... [which] can never really, in discourse, be proved'. Homi Bhabha, 'The Other Question, ...', *Screen*, 24:6 (1983), 18.

 8  See Joanne Lukitsch, *Cameron: Her Work and Career* (Rochester, NY: International Museum of Photography at the George Eastman House, 1986), pp. 47–66.

 9  See the printed pamphlet, 'Mrs. Cameron's Photographs, Priced Catalogue, 1868', reprinted in Cox and Ford, *Julia Margaret Cameron*, p. 3.

10  Danto called this the 'non-extensionality' of metaphors. Arthur Danto, *Beyond the Brillo Box: The Visual Arts in Post-Historical Perspective* (Berkeley: University of California Press, 1992), pp. 76–80.

11  Herschel's portrait won 'honorable mention' at the Universal Exhibition of 1867 in Paris ('Photography at the French Exhibition', *Photographic News*, 11 (21 June 1867), 278–9.)

12  See Canning in *Hansard*, CLXXXVII, p. 239; Bulwer in the *Pall Mall Gazette*, 11 June 1867, p. 3. The controversy and public opinion campaign for Abyssinia is examined in Nini Rogers, 'The Abyssinian Expedition of 1867–1868', *Historical Journal*, 27:1 (1984), 143.

13  See Edward W. Said, *Orientalism* (New York: Vintage, 1978) and *Culture and Imperialism* (New York: Vintage, 1993).

14  Julie Codell and Diane Sachko Macleod, eds., *Orientalism Transposed* (Aldershot: Ashgate, 1998), and Margaret Cohen and Carolyn Dever, eds., *The Literary Channel* (Princeton: Princeton University Press, 2002).

15  Julie Codell, 'Imperial Differences and Culture Clashes in Victorian Periodicals' Visuals: The Case of *Punch*', *Victorian Periodicals Review*, 39:4 (2006), 410.

16  Walter Eltis, 'Lord Overstone and the Establishment of British Nineteenth-Century Monetary Orthodoxy', *University of Oxford Discussion Papers in Economic and Social History*, 42 (2001), 4–32.

17  Letter from Julia Margaret Cameron to Lord Overstone, dated 5 November 1867, Overstone Correspondence, University of London Library, 1853/1–5, a.

18  *Ibid.*

19  *The Times*, 23 May 1868, p. 12, issue 26,132, col. F.

20  Letter from Sir Roderick Impey Murchison, dated 25 May 1868, Overstone Correspondence, University of London Library, 1374.

21  See Mike Weaver, *Whisper of the Muse: The Overstone Album and Other Photographs by Julia Margaret Cameron* (Malibu: J. Paul Getty Museum, 1986), pp. 15–21, and Victoria C. Olsen, *From Life: Julia Margaret Cameron and Victorian Photography* (New York: Palgrave Macmillan, 2003), p. 179.

22  *Pall Mall Gazette*, 29 January 1868, p. 10; William Allingham, *William Allingham's Diary*, introd. Geoffrey Grigson (Fontwell, Sussex: Centaur Press, 1967), p. 171.

23  Cameron's son, Henry Herschel Hay Cameron, perpetuated these stories after his mother's death; in an article in *Windsor Magazine*, reprinted on 12 May 1896 in the *Sacramento Daily Union* (91:75) under the title 'Photographing Thomas Carlyle', the story is related how she caught sight of him 'in the street' and bribed a street urchin to badger him until he relented.

24  This visit is noted by Cameron herself in her 'Annals of My Glass House' (1874), reprinted in Beaumont Newhall, ed., *Photography: Essays and Images* (New York: Museum of Modern Art, 1980), p. 137. At the time, Carlyle was regularly visiting Little Holland House for portrait sessions with George Frederic Watts; see M. S. Watts, *George Frederic Watts*, 3 vols. (New York: Hodder and Stoughton, c. 1903), vol. 1, pp. 248–50.

25  Helmut Gernsheim, *Julia Margaret Cameron: Her Life and Photographic Work* (New York: Aperture, 1975), pp. 189, 190.

26  On the Governor Eyre controversy, see Bernard Semmel, *Jamaican Blood and Victorian Conscience* (Boston: Houghton Mifflin, 1963); Gillian Workman, 'Thomas Carlyle and the Governor Eyre Controversy: An Account with Some New Material', *Victorian Studies*, 18:1 (1974), 77–102; George H. Ford, 'The Governor Eyre Case in England', *University of Toronto Quarterly*, 17:3 (1948), 219–33; Catherine Hall, 'The Economy of Intellectual Prestige:

Thomas Carlyle, John Stuart Mill, and the Case of Governor Eyre', *Cultural Critique*, 12 (1989), 167–96; and Howard W. Fulweiller, 'The Strange Case of Governor Eyre: Race and the "Victorian Frame of Mind"', *CLIO*, 29:2 (2000), 119–42. The relation of the controversy to debates surrounding the 1867 Reform Act has been analysed in Catherine Hall, Keith McClelland, and Jane Rendall, *Defining the Victorian Nation* (Cambridge: Cambridge University Press, 2000), esp. chapter 4.

27  On the Jamaica Committee, see John Stuart Mill, *The Collected Works of John Stuart Mill, Volume 21: Essays on Equality, Law, and Education*, ed. John M. Robison (Toronto: University of Toronto Press, 1984), Appendix E: 'Jamaica Committee: Public Documents' (1866, 1868).

28  Letter from Carlyle to Charles Kingsley, 3 September 1866, reprinted in Workman, 'Thomas Carlyle and the Governor Eyre Controversy', 93, original emphasis.

29  Quoted in Ford, 'The Governor Eyre Case in England', 223.

30  'Statement of the Jamaica Committee' (1868), in Mill, *The Collected Works*, vol. 21, ed. Robison, Appendix E.

31  Thomas Carlyle, *On Heroes, Hero-Worship, and the Heroic in History* [1841], ed. Michael K. Goldberg (Berkeley: University of California Press, 1993).

32  *Ibid.*, p. xxxvii. Watts and Carlyle apparently debated the physiognomies of the figures portrayed on the Elgin Marbles, as recounted by Watts's wife and biographer, Mary S. Watts, *George Frederic Watts*, 3 vols. (New York: G. Doran, 1913), vol. 1, p. 249.

33  Paul Barlow, 'The Imagined Hero as Incarnate Sign: Thomas Carlyle and the Mythology of the "National Portrait" in Victorian Britain', *Art History*, 17:4 (1994), 523.

34  *Ibid.*, 522.

35  Cameron, 'Annals of My Glass House', p. 137.

36  Quoted in Barlow, 'The Imagined Hero as Incarnate Sign', 522.

37  Carlyle's familiarity with this dual status was revealed in an exchange with his wife Jane when she recognized her portrait in a shop window and recognized its status as index and as emblem: 'The greatest testimony to your fame', she wrote, 'seems to me to be the fact that my photograph is stuck up in Macmichael's window … It proves the interest, or curiosity, you excite; for being neither a "distinguished authoress," nor a "celebrated murderess," nor an actress, nor a "Skittles," it can only be as Mrs Carlyle that they offer me for sale.' Quoted by Gernsheim, *Julia Margaret Cameron*, p. 58.

38  Thomas Carlyle, *Shooting Niagra: And After?* (London: Chapman and Hall, 1867).

39  See 'Document 7' in Workman, 'Thomas Carlyle and the Governor Eyre Controversy', 98–100.

40  Thomas Carlyle, 'Occasional Discourse on the Nigger Question', in *Critical and Miscellaneous Essays,* 16 (Boston: Dana Estes and Charles E. Lauriat, 1884), pp. 299, 302, 317.

41  Quoted in Hall, 'The Economy of Intellectual Prestige', 181.

42  See Victor Kiernan, *The Lords of Human Kind* (London: Weidenfeld and Nicolson, 1969), pp. 48–9.

43  Hall, 'The Economy of Intellectual Prestige', 181–2; Simon Gikandi, *Maps of Englishness: Writing Identity in the Culture of Colonialism* (New York: Columbia University Press, 1996), pp. 50–83.

44  Quoted in Marcus Wood, *Blind Memory: Visual Representations of Slavery in England and America, 1780–1865* (New York: Routledge, 2000), pp. 141–50.

45  Thomas Carlyle, 'Shooting Niagra: And After?', in *Critical and Miscellaneous Essays*, 16, pp. 424–5.

46  Quoted in Catherine Hall, 'The Economy of Intellectual Prestige', 189.

47  'Petition to the House of Commons by Thomas Carlyle', in Workman, 'Thomas Carlyle and the Governor Eyre Controversy', 98, Document 7.

48  Hall, 'The Economy of Intellectual Prestige', 184.

49  Donovan Williams, *The India Office, 1858–1869* (Hoshiarpur: Vishveshvaranand Vedic Research Institute, 1983).

50  Caroline Dakers, *The Holland Park Circle: Artists and Victorian Society* (New Haven: Yale University Press, 1999), chapter 2.

51  Quoted in William Francis Finlason, *The History of the Jamaica Case*, 2nd edn (London: Chapman and Hall, 1869), p. 368bbb; Hamilton Hume, *The Life of Edward John Eyre, Late Governor of Jamaica* (London: R. Bentley, 1867), p. 291.

52  The seal of the Society for the Abolition of the Slave Trade, or SEAST, was established in 1787; Josiah Wedgwood fashioned the graphic image of a man in chains surrounded by the phrase, which was mass-reproduced in many different media throughout nineteenth-century England and America. See Wood, *Blind Memory*, pp. 22–3.

53  Anthony Trollope, *The West Indies and the Spanish Main*, 2nd edn (London: Chapman and Hall, 1860), pp. 65–6.

54  Anthony Trollope, 'Miss Sarah Jack, of Spanish Town, Jamaica' [1860], in *Anthony Trollope: The Complete Short Stories, Vol. 3, Tourists and Colonials*, ed. Breyer, p. 1.

55  See Leslie Stephen and Sidney Lee, eds., *Dictionary of National Biography* (London: Oxford University Press, 1964), vol. 19, p. 410.

56  Bruce Knox, 'The "Queen's Letter" of 1865 and British Policy towards Emancipation and Indentured Labour in the West Indies, 1830–1865', *Historical Journal*, 29:2 (1986), 345–67.

57  Quoted *ibid.*, 366.

58  Weaver, *Whisper of the Muse*, p. 58.

59  William Makepeace Thackeray, *The Rose and The Ring* [1854] (Pennsylvania State University: The Electronics Classic Series, 2000–13), p. 69. In *Julia Margaret Cameron's Women* (Chicago: Art Institute of Chicago, 1998), p. 233, Sylvia Wolf identified Rosalba as a character in Henry Taylor's play, *The Virgin Widow* (1849). However, Taylor's play was never performed and did not receive any positive critical review, while Thackeray's volume was first issued as a popular Christmas edition in 1854, and Thackeray's daughters were close friends of the Camerons.

60  Cameron returned repeatedly to these themes after 1868. Victoria C. Olsen, 'Idylls of Real Life', *Victorian Poetry*, 33:3–4 (1995), 371–89.

61  Weaver, *Whisper of the Muse*, p. 58.

62  As Homi Bhabha wrote, 'To be the father and the oppressor; just and unjust; moderate and rapacious; vigorous and despotic: these instances of contradictory belief, doubly inscribed in the deferred address of colonial discourse, raise questions about the symbolic space of colonial authority. What is the image of authority if it is civility's supplement and democracy's despotic double?', *The Location of Culture*, p. 96.

63  Quoted in Lukitsch, *Cameron: Her Work and Career*, p. 65.

64  Quoted in Gernsheim, *Julia Margaret Cameron*, p. 65.

65  Bhabha, *The Location of Culture*, p. 49.

66  Nini Rogers, 'The Abyssinian Expedition of 1867–1868: Disraeli's Imperialism or James Murray's War?', *Historical Journal*, 27:1 (1984), 129–49.

67  The *Pall Mall Gazette* pressed for such a resolution as early as 1865. Rogers, 'The Abyssinian Expedition of 1867–1868', 138–9.

68  Williams, *The India Office, 1858–1869*, p. 30.

69  Darrell Bates, *The Abyssinian Difficulty* (Oxford: Oxford University Press, 1979), Appendix B, pp. 224–5; T. J. Holland and H. M. Hozier, *Record of the Expedition to Abyssinia* (London: Her Majesty's Stationery Office, 1870).

70  Roger Acton, *The Abyssinian Expedition and the Life and Reign of King Theodore, with engravings from the Illustrated London News* (London: Illustrated London News, 1870).

71  'Alamayou' is a phonetic rendering of the Prince's name; this spelling is adopted here because of its common use. The Prince's name may also be found in English sources as Alámáyou, Alamayehu, Alamayu, and Alameeo.

72  'Prince of Abyssinia on His Way to England', *The Times*, 2 July 1868, p. 10, col. 2. See also: Darrell Bates, 'The Abyssinian Boy', *History Today*, 29 (1979), 816–23; Lord Amulree, 'Prince Alamayou of Ethiopia', *Ethiopia Observer*, 13:1 (1970), 8–15; Richard Pankhurst, 'Captain Speedy's "Entertainment": The Reminiscences of a Nineteenth Century British Traveller to Ethiopia', *Africa* (Rome), 38:3 (1983), 428–48; Jean Southon, 'Prince Alamayou and Captain Speedy', in Bahru Zewde, Richard Pankhurst, and Taddese Beyene, eds., *Proceedings of the Eleventh International Conference of Ethiopian Studies*, Addis Ababa, 1–6 April 1991, vol. 1 (Institute of Ethiopian Studies: Addis Ababa University, 1994), pp. 251–63.

73  Gernsheim mistook one of these photographs as an outtake from Cameron's illustrations of Tennyson's *Idylls of the King* in *Julia Margaret Cameron*, p. 194.

74  See John M. Gullick, 'Captain Speedy of Larut', *Journal of the Malayan Branch of the Royal Asiatic Society*, 26:3, 3–103.

75  See Pankhurst, 'Captain Speedy's "Entertainment"', and Southon, 'Prince Alamayou and Captain Speedy'.

76  Quoted by Southon, 'Prince Alamayou and Captain Speedy', p. 257.

77  Allingham, *William Allingham's Diary*, pp. 185–6.

78  Virginia Woolf and Roger Fry, eds., *Victorian Photographs of Famous Men and Fair Women* (London: Chatto and Windus, 1992), p. 32. The identity of 'Casa' is unclear; apparently only two Abyssinians left the country on 11 June 1868 as attendants to the Prince: Gabra Medin, identified as a eunuch, and the boy's tutor, Alaca Zarat. They both accompanied Speedy and Alamayou (and Napier and his command) aboard the HMS *Feroze*, but at the Suez Canal, Napier dismissed both tutor and eunuch, sending them back to Mombassa. Lord Amulree, 'Prince Alamayou of Ethiopia', 9.

79  Cameron registered the following photographs for copyright protection on 17 August 1868: 'Mary Kellaway full face in Abyssn. Costume, No. 1'; 'Mary Kellaway ¾ face in Abyssn Costume, No. 2'. Copyright registrations, Public Record Office, Kew, COPY 3 / 108.

80  No specific photograph has been directly connected to this title; it is possible that it was applied to one of the portraits of Taylor from 1865 in which he wore the 'Eastern costume' used to portray King David and King Ahasuerus (Cox 783, 784 and Cox 164–167).

81  Stephen and Lee, *Dictionary of National Biography*, vol. 15, pp. 109–10.

82  Edward Rice, *Captain Sir Richard Francis Burton: A Biography* (Cambridge, Da Capo Press, 1990), p. 285.

83  See Rana Kabbani, *Europe's Myths of Orient* (Bloomington: Indiana University Press, 1986), p. 91.

84  On Layard, see Gordon Waterfield, *Layard of Nineveh* (New York: Frederick A. Praeger, 1968).

85  *Ibid.*, p. 301.

86  *The Letters of Anthony Trollope, Vol. I, 1835–1870*, ed. N. John Hall (Stanford: Stanford University Press, 1983), letters of 7 November 1867 and 30 November 1867, pp. 399, 403.

87  Said, *Orientalism*, p. 160.

88  Rice, Captain Sir Richard Francis Burton, p. 287.

89  *Ibid.*

90  On the role of the infiltrator, see Mireille Rosello, 'The Infiltrator Who Came In from the Inside: Making Room in Closed Systems', *Canadian Review of Comparative Literature*, 22:2 (1995), 241–54.

91  'The Abyssinian Question', *Punch, or the London Charivari*, 10 August 1867, p. 57.

92  Bernth Lindfors, 'Circus Africans', *Journal of American Culture*, 6:2 (1983), 9–14.

93  'An Abyssinian Exhibition', *Punch, or the London Charivari*, 2 May 1868, p. 192.

94  Bhabha, *The Location of Culture*, p. 112.

95  Bates, *The Abyssinian Difficulty*, chapter 2.

# 6

# Tennyson's nationalism:
# epic and lyric in *Idylls of the King*

> Why take the style of those heroic times?
> For nature brings not back the Mastodon,
> Nor we those times; and why should any man
> Remodel models? These twelve books of mine
> Were faint Homeric echoes, nothing-worth,
> Mere chaff and draff, much better burnt.
>
> (Alfred Tennyson, *The Epic* [1842], ll. 35–40)

## Arthur's return

In Tennyson's poem, *The Epic*, a group of dejected literary men discuss the unfortunate destruction of a friend's poem, the loss made worse by the fact that the damage was inflicted by the author's own hand. This lost work is described as an epic narrative, a twelve-volume 'King Arthur'. A member of the group recounts that this poet agreed with contemporary nineteenth-century attitudes that old-fashioned epic narratives had run their course, their ability to tell a fresh story exhausted. To these other literary men, however, this view was surely mistaken. As discussed by the group, it could only be a flawed conclusion borne of misguided arrogance 'that nothing new was said, or else / Something so said 'twas nothing – that a truth / Looks freshest in the fashion of the day'.[1] When he wrote *The Epic*, Tennyson conceived it as a frame for his *Morte d'Arthur*, to provide a context for readers to allow them to imagine Arthur's return from Avalon as a way to redeem the moral centre of modern England. In the tale of Arthur's return, Tennyson used medieval ethics as a kind of historical model for honourable and virtuous action that could stand in opposition to the forces of deceit, treachery, and decadence. *The Epic* sets this stage well, drawing upon the medieval past to provide guidance and direction for the confused and disoriented present.

When Tennyson put the above rhetorical questions in the poem to his readers, letting them know he intended to bring back the epic form – and King Arthur's legendary world – in a brand new incarnation, he proposed joining the distant medieval world to contemporary Victorian England. As one reviewer of the day enthused, Tennyson's poems about Arthur were sure to make the 'British king … more ubiquitous in his resuscitation than even in the days of his mortality'.[2] While paintings based upon Tennyson's *Idylls*, like Watts's *Sir Galahad* (1862), added lustre to the legend's reputation, beginning in 1859, Tennyson sought broader popular acclaim for his poetry and allowed new illustrated volumes of the *Idylls* to appear.[3] By 1874, he also knew that the narrative possibilities of using photography to illustrate his tale would appeal greatly to his neighbour on the Isle of Wight, and in early autumn of that year he approached Cameron asking if she would be interested in illustrating *Idylls of the King* for publication. The photographer jumped at the offer. She recounted this conversation in a letter later that year to Sir Edward Ryan, where she reported replying to Tennyson: 'Now *you* know, Alfred, that *I* know that it is immortality to me to be bound up with you'.[4]

When Tennyson's many volumes of poetry were published during his lifetime, his works were reviewed in the periodical press and discussed critically in relation to their use of classical metre, their religious and moral commands, their melodramatic sentiments, and their gendered conflicts, but *Idylls of the King* had long been interpreted in literary journals as an epic poem that dared to narrate a tale of the nation's origins.[5] Consequently, modern scholars have tried to identify the mythical and historical time frame in which Tennyson's King Arthur reigned; they have connected the poet's epic narrative to the so-called Arthurian revival of the early nineteenth century, to the author's public role as Poet Laureate, and more broadly, to England's anxieties about its status as a colonial power during the second half of the nineteenth century. Only more recently have literary scholars examined Tennyson's representation of national identity in relation to the poet's own uncertainty about the suitability of the epic form as an effective narrative strategy, questioning his motivations as much as the effect of his literary choices.[6]

But in December 1874, when Cameron's photographic volume, *Illustrations to Tennyson's Idylls of the King and Other Poems*, first appeared in time for the Christmas buying season, numerous editions of Tennyson's poetry, of the *Idylls* in particular, were available to the public. If the various instalments of the *Idylls of the King* offered Tennyson's readers an ever-enlarging myth of England's medieval history, the serial nature of its publication accentuated that perspective.[7] In fact, King Arthur's death and return in subsequent instalments over a thirty-year period not only rejuvenated the story, it also helped Tennyson's audience extend its metaphors of moral redemption and patriotism over time. To many readers, the legend of Arthur – his chivalry and religious fervour, his rejection of moral relativism, and his insistence on principles of good government – was accepted as a kind of historical guidepost for Victorians who applauded, in turn, Britain's self-appointed mission to bring Christianity to foreign lands, its efforts to cement political and economic alliances with neighbouring European powers, and its commitment to defend its borders and possessions by the use of force.[8] Tennyson famously described his *Idylls* as 'the world-wide war of Sense and Soul, typified by individuals', stressing their moral lessons. But Tennyson also inhabited a world of political conflict, having written militaristic and patriotic poems about the Napoleonic Wars (*Ode on the Death of the Duke of Wellington*), the Crimean War (*The Charge of the Light Brigade*), and various nationalistic verses about imagined future conflicts (*Hands All Round*; *Britons, Guard Your Own*; *The War*). As a result, Tennyson's seemingly innocent phrase has also been interpreted as a useful metaphor for the essential conflict between 'civilization and barbarism, which had a powerful hold on the European and above all the British mind' since 'empire meant in ideal terms the bringing of order and peaceful progress to lands beyond the pale'.[9]

Despite the popular worldwide acclaim Tennyson received and the handsome income he enjoyed from the poem's multiple editions, his early critics did not consider *Idylls of the King* an unqualified literary success. For example, Swinburne, Elizabeth Browning, and Edward FitzGerald found the poet's narrative of moral conflict unconvincing and often unsatisfying.[10] Cameron herself offered a singular interpretation of the *Idylls* in her photographs and two-volume publication illustrating the poem. As we shall see, her version could also be considered a critique and reinterpretation of Tennyson. Like other illustrators before her, she was compelled to select specific scenes to represent, as it was impossible to recreate the entire text visually. But by examining how and why Cameron chose specific verses to illustrate photographically as well as the overall context in which her volumes appeared, we will see how she modified Tennyson's epic according to her own narrative design: this chapter examines how Cameron created allegorical photographs that used both a didactic approach to depict scenes of nationalism and power and a dramatic style of performance-based imagery to express anxiety about the state of the nation, its imperial course, and in particular, its effect on modern women.[11]

Cameron's photographs were calculated to achieve two additional aims: first, by illustrating women's lyric songs present in the poem, they actively displaced the otherwise strong 'homosocial bond'[12] that linked together the male protagonists in the *Idylls*, disrupting their repeated and relentless cries to wage war by striking hard against 'the heathen', and to bring about a form of national rejuvenation that was based upon patriarchy as much as patriotism. At the same time, Cameron's photographs gave voice and female identity to what Tennyson had called 'the temperate qualities' of English civilization that are present in the *Idylls*; qualities that simultaneously could hold war in check on the one hand, and at the same time provide the world with England's moral guidance and principled direction on the other. The fruit of such activity would be met, wrote Tennyson in his *Ode on the Death of the Duke of Wellington*, by guarding against any external threat to imperial power and by keeping 'our noble England whole'. Cameron's photographic strategies appear in two distinct ways, and this chapter analyses her contributions to Tennyson's *Idylls of the King* by examining the formal visual approach she employed to represent the epic poem photographically. It will be useful to compare Cameron's artistic method directly to Gustave Doré in his illustrations of the *Idylls of the King* that he produced in 1869, not only because Cameron did so herself, but because each set of formal strategies also suggests important ideological points about the approach of the other. The first section accordingly compares Cameron's 'epic' approach to Doré's 'descriptive' style. From this foundation, the second section examines the 'epic' versus 'lyric' strategies of the text itself and compares these differences to the strategies Cameron employed in her representations. Finally, the third section makes the case that Cameron chose her allegorical subject matter because of its political associations – both in terms of patriarchy and in terms of patriotism – in order to examine how her photography confronted the ideological contradictions in the narrative, leading to a new visual interpretation of the legend of King Arthur.

## Narrate or describe

In 1874, when Cameron embraced Tennyson's proposal to illustrate a new edition of *Idylls of the King*, she did not know that her works would be reduced drastically in scale to cabinet size and transformed into crude woodcuts for Edward Moxon's mass-produced and inexpensive 'people's edition' of his poetry.[13] One of these woodcuts, *Elaine* (based upon Cox 1165), appeared in 1874 as the frontispiece to Volume 6 of the ten-volume work. Two others appeared in 1875: *Arthur* (based upon Cox 1174) was included in Volume 7 and *Maud* (based upon Cox 1195) in Volume 9. The small scale obviously blunted the impact of her work, and the visual effect of the woodcut gave thick and hard outlines to what would otherwise have appeared as Cameron's soft-focus photographic style. Other frontispiece illustrations to this popular edition included a wide array of imagery: the first volume reproduced a portrait of Tennyson taken by Mayall and Collins that was reproduced in Woodburytype; the next two volumes depicted two of Tennyson's personal residences, Aldworth and Farringford, reproduced as woodcuts. Two engravings were included as well: one represented a scene from *The Princess*, depicting Princess Ida holding Psyche's Babe on her hip; the other portrayed Arthur Henry Hallam, whom Tennyson eulogized in his poem, *In Memoriam*. In a letter to his publisher, Tennyson disparaged these illustrations, particularly the references to his homes, thinking they promoted a vulgar, bourgeois interest in property and worldly goods, when instead he had hoped for evocative illustrations drawn from the poems themselves.[14]

Cameron's views about this publication were equally harsh; to the photographer, the work was poorly produced and illustrated pitifully: 'I have worked for three months putting all my zeal and energy into my high task', she wrote in a letter to Sir Edward Ryan, complaining that the small size blunted the impact of her photographs. In response to her objections, Tennyson asked her, 'Why don't you bring them out their actual size in a big volume at your own risk?'[15] The result was a new photographically illustrated book that Cameron titled *Illustrations to Tennyson's Idylls of the King and other Poems*. The first volume of this two-part work was issued at Christmas time, 1874, the second in May 1875. Each contained a frontispiece portrait of Tennyson and twelve additional albumen prints illustrating his poetry. These photographs were interposed by excerpts of the poems that were chosen by Cameron, written in her own florid hand and signed at the bottom by Tennyson himself, all reproduced by means of lithography. Together they made a slender volume, but as one that contained hand-made prints in folio sized dimensions, it was a handsome book that made a perfect gift for the Christmas season. Indeed, Cameron's Christmas-time release was chosen to take advantage of up-to-date marketing and promotion tactics that Tennyson's publishers had employed successfully since 1865.[16]

From 1875, it was Tennyson's new publisher, Henry S. King, who issued both of Cameron's photographic volumes, as well as the small cabinet edition described above.[17] By the time of their almost simultaneous publication that year, they entered the marketplace joining earlier unsold volumes of the *Idylls* produced by the Moxon firm, notably the luxury illustrated edition containing Gustave Doré's engravings. Although Doré's work was published just five years earlier, a large number of unsold editions remained on the market, and the publication failed to receive the enthusiastic response that Tennyson and his publishers had hoped it would receive.[18] Cameron believed her illustrations were not only comparable to Doré's artistically, but in fact superior. She made these claims in a letter to Sir Edward Ryan:

> Doré got a fortune for his *drawn* fancy Illustrations for these Idylls – Now one of my large photographs, take one for instance illustrating Elaine who is May Prinsep (now Hitchens) at her very best would excite more sensation and interest than all the drawings of Doré – ... – the Elaine of May Prinsep and the Enid of another lovely girl are as all agree *not* to be surpassed as Poems and Pictures, and the King Arthur all say is a magnificent Mystic mythical a real embodiment of conscience – with piercing eyes and a spiritual look and air.[19]

With Cameron's photographic publication, the marketplace now contained three 'new' illustrated editions of Tennyson's *Idylls of the King*. These editions included: a) Doré's richly printed volume containing thirty-six illustrations of the four 'original' *Idylls* (*Enid, Elaine, Vivien*, and *Guinevere*), which featured an ornate frontispiece depicting a sculpted medallion of Tennyson surrounded by his characters along with Tennyson's *Dedication* to the late Prince Albert; b) the ten-volume 'people's edition' of the complete poems, containing all of the more recently issued sections of the *Idylls*, including *The Coming of Arthur*, *The Holy Grail*, *Pelleas and Ettarre*, *The Passing of Arthur*, *The Last Tournament*, and *Gareth and Lynette*, as well as the concluding verse, *To the Queen*; and c) Cameron's two folio-sized volumes of photographs, hand-made editions that illustrated selected *Idylls*, featuring poetic selections excerpted from the larger work, much like Byron's 'Beauties', and that included illustrations to several additional poems, chosen by Cameron, that were not poems included in the *Idylls of the King*.

Whether or not Cameron's complimentary assessment of her own imagery in comparison to Doré was overstated matters less than the substantive differences between these illustrations and their choice of subject matter and manner of presentation. In volume one, all twelve of Cameron's photographs are devoted to representing selections from the *Idylls*, but volume two contains just three photographs illustrating additional *Idylls* scenes from *Lancelot and Elaine* and *The Passing of Arthur*, with the remaining nine prints illustrating other poems. Cameron's approach is consistent throughout the two volumes: she fills the frame with her models posed in tight compositions, focusing on a head, a torso, or a tightly assembled couple or clustered group. All subjects are posed close to the front of the picture plane in little or no depth of field. As we have seen, these formal qualities were consistent with her preferred stylistic choices. The point-of-view of these images never varies; they are always taken from a position directly in front of the subjects, unerringly level with their figures' line of sight, as if the viewer were in the same room or occupied the same theatrical space as the subject.

Doré's illustrations differ from Cameron's photographs in more ways than simply artistic style, creative licence, or differing views about the role of illustration: each artist has actually interpreted the principal subject of the poem differently. As Meyer Schapiro once observed, it is often difficult to discern the actual degree of correspondence between word and picture in illustrated texts, as artists will often emphasize certain elements of the text while restraining or displacing others.[20] In descriptive illustrations, and in cases where a story being depicted visually is not well known, details become quite important, whereas, for more symbolic or allegorical representations, only a few elements from a known text might be required. In this case, Schapiro says, 'the text is often so much fuller than the illustration that the latter seems a mere token, like a pictorial title'.[21]

Schapiro's breakdown of the two approaches is a useful starting point to compare Doré and Cameron: on the one hand, Doré's visual approach appears to be more descriptive than emblematic, a characterization which becomes plain if we compare the way each illustrated Tennyson's poem, *Enid*, for example. In the woodcut in which *Yniol shows Prince Geraint his ruined castle*, Doré has placed the two central figures in the visual centre of the image, but the viewer's attention is also riveted by other scenes of action in the composition (Figure 40). Although they are bathed in light, the two central figures are hardly the exclusive centre of

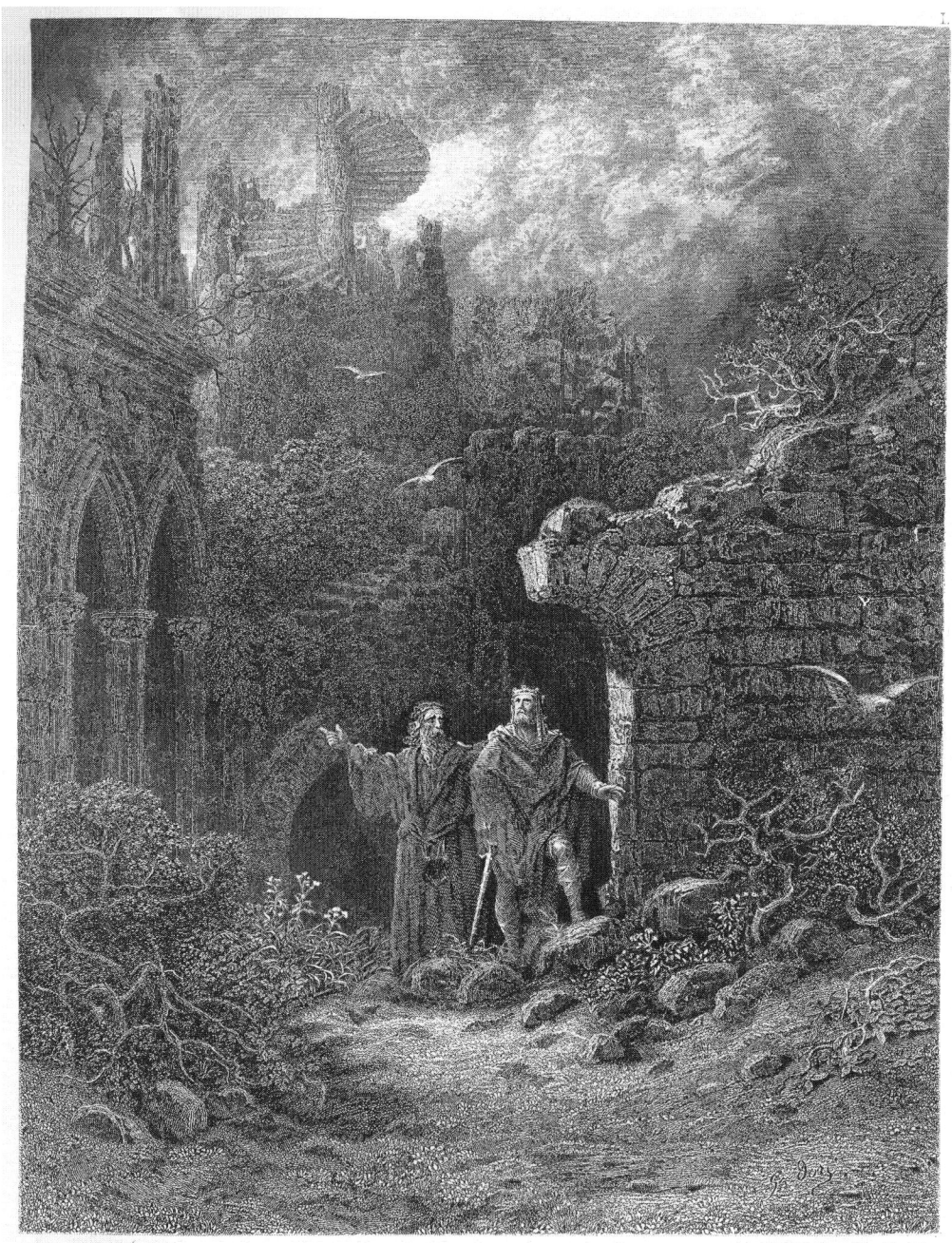

**40**    Gustave Doré, *Yniol shows Prince Geraint his ruined castle*, 1859.
Woodcut, reprinted in *The Story of Enid and Geraint, retold from Ancient Welsh,
Norman, German, and Scandinavian legends and modern poetic versions,
with 9 illustrations by Gustave Doré* (London: E. Moxon and Son, 1879).

attention. Rather, Doré has represented the ruined castle with a feast of imaginative details and highly specific renderings, so much so that were Tennyson to have described verbally all that we see, he would have taken pages to do so rather than just two lines of text. In Schapiro's terms, Doré has 'enlarged the text' by adding specific details to the setting that are not originally described in the poem, including, importantly, a visual perspective that renders this scene from below, thereby opening up numerous lines of sight and creating a grand pictorial scale. Moreover, the scene's dramatic lighting permits Doré to draw beams of light falling provocatively on the shocked face of Prince Geraint, but also on the crumbling stones, gnarled roots, and broken walls of the setting. And in the upper-left part of the scene, Doré has created a moment of visual astonishment, in which the artist has dramatically imagined Tennyson's words, 'And high above a piece of turret stair, / Worn by the feet that now were silent, wound / Bare to the sun' (*Marriage of Geraint*, ll. 320–2). The wide array of added details, the use of dramatic lighting, and the focused moment of visual clarity are all elements that characterize Doré's illustrations to *Enid*. To describe two other examples, in *Geraint Charges the Bandits*, a scene that illustrates the lines, 'But at the flash and motion of the man / They vanish'd panic-stricken, like a shoal / Of darting fish' (*Geraint and Enid*, ll. 467–9), Doré interprets the forest scene as dark and foreboding by starkly foreshortening his rendering of the overpowered bandits, vividly portraying their surprise, powerlessness, and hasty flight. And in *Geraint Slays Earl Doorm*, Doré depicts an interior hall in the Earl's castle, imagining numerous witnesses to the grisly scene. In representing the shock expressed by each witness to the sudden decapitation of the Earl, Doré twists and arches their bodies and turns their heads about to gaze in disbelief at the severed head lying on the floor some few yards away from the Earl's body, the surprise accentuated by its proximity and lighting and the head's shocked expression, which still registers incredulity and bewilderment.

In contrast to Doré's descriptive approach, Cameron's interpretations of the poetic text are symbolic and emblematic, the hallmark elements of her allegorical style of making fancy pictures. While it was clearly important for her to dress her models in the appropriate clothes, jewellery, and hairstyles and to give them an appropriate expression to match the scene depicted, Cameron's illustrations of Tennyson's text largely avoid excessive details or wide variations in lighting or pictorial effect. Instead, Cameron's photographs centre on the model's expression and pose. Pushed to the front of the picture plane, Cameron's models leave little extra pictorial space for depicting situational details, such as a room's interior decorations or lighting. In fact, her illumination is always held at a constant value, unlike the stark raking light she used for portraits. This diffused lighting and shallow depth of field flattens her subjects even more owing to the low contrast. The overall effect is to dampen overall description in favour of accentuating facial expressions and symbolic gestures.

Cameron illustrated two scenes from *Enid*; both photographs depict the title character at a crucial reflective moment in the poem. One depicts Enid at the 'cedarn cabinet' where she stores the ragged dress that she wore when she first met Prince Geraint (Cox 1158–60); the other portrays her in isolation, when she sings a forlorn song to Fortune and the Wheel of Chance (Cox 1161). In the first image, the cabinet is used as a metaphoric vehicle, a device alluding to the internal conflict of the heroine: Enid holds the cabinet door with two hands, as if one pulls the door while the other pushes to keep it shut, the psychological weight so great and the ambiguous or contradictory feelings so strong that it takes the strength of two arms to open. As viewers, we are barred from peering into the cabinet itself, a useful symbolic device for Cameron: the flattened space piques the viewer's interest and simultaneously withholds details about the cabinet's contents. But such details are not important here. Symbolism in this image is not found in the interior or exterior of the cabinet doors but is expressed by the internal psychological conflict depicted on Enid's face. Enid's internal debate is further reinforced by the visual opposition of the dark, closed cabinet on the right contrasting with the fair, white-clad woman on the left. As a result, Cameron has effectively represented a moment of psychological distress that is affirmed by the despair registered on Enid's face. Cameron clarifies the tension and ambivalence embodied in this conflicted relationship in her chosen excerpt from the poem:

> And thou, put on thy worst and meanest dress
> And ride with me.' And Enid ask'd, amazed,
> 'If Enid errs, let Enid learn her fault.'
> But he, 'I charge thee, ask not, but obey.'
> Then she bethought her of a faded silk,
> A faded mantle and a faded veil,
> And moving toward a cedarn cabinet,
> Wherein she kept them folded reverently
> With sprigs of summer laid between the folds,
> She took them, and array'd herself therein,
> Remembering when he first came on her
> Drest in that dress, and how he loved her in it,
> And all her foolish fears about the dress,
> And all his journey to her, as himself
> Had told her, and their coming to the court.
>
> (*Marriage of Geraint*, ll. 130–44)

Because the internal state of Enid's 'remembering' defines the scene, Cameron uses an economy of details to portray Enid's moment of uncertainty in her moment of flashback and reflection.

Cameron's second image from the *Idylls*, *And Enid Sang* portrays Enid holding a stringed instrument vertically against her right shoulder (Cox 1161, Figure 41). Although she holds the instrument's neck in her left hand, she appears unready

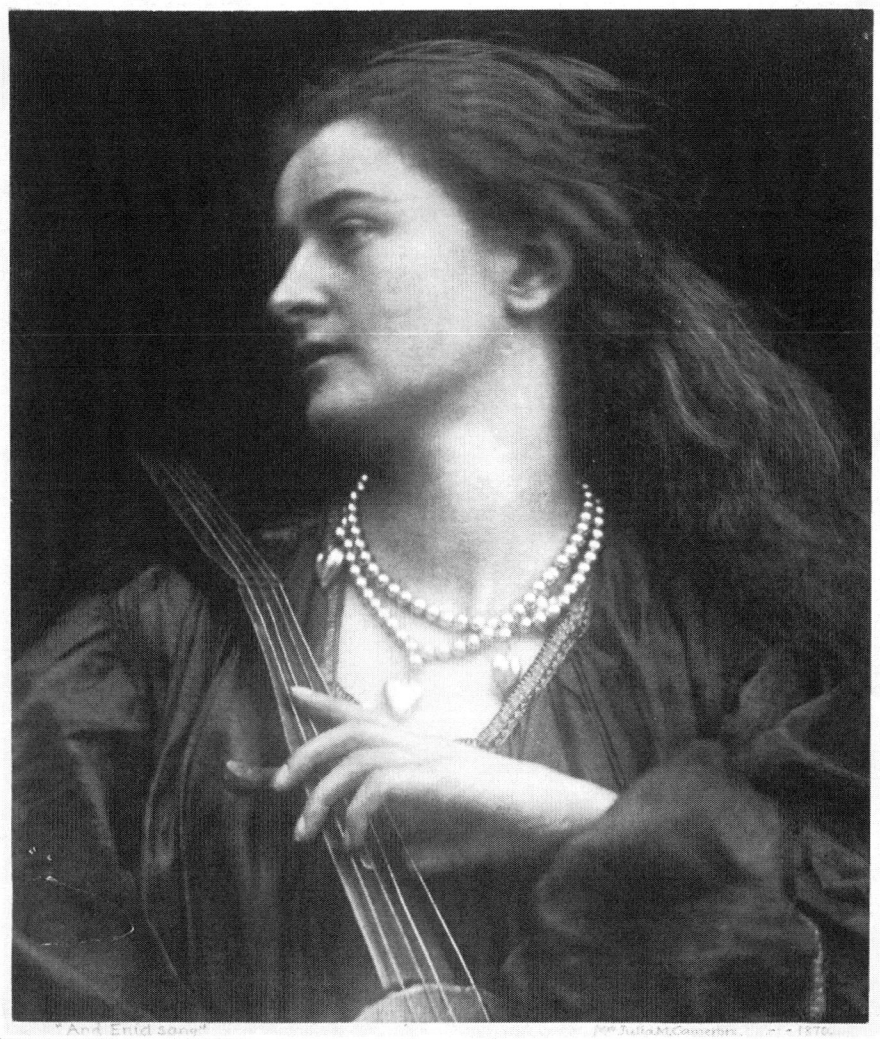

Julia Margaret Cameron, *And Enid Sang* (Cox 1161), 1874.        **41**
Albumen print, 34.3 x 27.3 cm.

to play it. Pressed close to and nearly filling the picture plane from the waist up, with her head turned in near-profile to the viewer, Cameron's model appears to occupy a space of solitary introspection. In the text chosen to accompany this image, Cameron reproduced Tennyson's lines leading up to the song as well as the song itself:

> So fared it with Geraint, who thought and said,
> 'Here, by God's grace, is the one voice for me.'

> It chanced the song that Enid sang was one
> Of Fortune and her wheel, and Enid sang:
>
> 'Turn, Fortune, turn thy wheel, and lower the proud;
> Turn thy wild wheel thro' sunshine, storm and cloud;
> Thy wheel and thee we neither love nor hate.
>
> 'Turn, Fortune, turn thy wheel with smile or frown;
> With that wild wheel we go not up or down;
> Our hoard is little, but our hearts are great.
>
> 'Smile and we smile, the lords of our many lands;
> Frown and we smile, the lords of our own hands;
> For man is man and master of his fate.
>
> 'Turn, turn thy wheel above the staring crowd;
> Thy wheel and thou are shadows in the cloud;
> Thy wheel and thee we neither love nor hate.'
>
> (*Marriage of Geraint*, ll. 343–58)

Cameron's emblematic portrayal suggests Enid's pure and noble character, indomitable faith, and inner moral strength, a state of mind that is reinforced by the lyrical text. As Schapiro observed, 'one or two figures and some attribute or accessory object, seen together, will evoke for the instructed viewer the whole chain of actions linked in that text with the few pictured elements, unless an incompatible detail arrests the interpretation'.[22] And *In Enid Sang*, Cameron has given the viewer no such distraction.

Given these wide differences between the artistic methods of the two artists, it might seem unfair to compare Doré and Cameron. Tennyson, in fact, complemented *both* artists for their efforts, seemingly oblivious to the formal differences and visual strategies of the two or the fact that these approaches reflected fundamental disparities in how the two artists interpreted his poem: 'It seems to me', he wrote to Doré of his wood engravings, 'that their dark and noble beauty accords perfectly with the genius of the old legends.'[23] And according to Cameron, Tennyson visited her regularly to see how her project was progressing: 'Alfred Tennyson himself is very much interested in my work and has been up here perpetually to see how I am going on', she wrote again to Ryan, continuing, 'He approved of my King Arthur greatly.'[24] Apparently Tennyson was obtuse to the correspondence of these visual approaches to the literary practice of narration and description. Ironically, when Tennyson offered comments to others about the shortcomings of illustration – disparaging its ability to represent 'poetic feeling' or to portray an author's textual references – he made them believe he was a thoughtful observer about the complex ways that words and images worked independently and together to represent ideas and visual images in poetry.[25]

When Cameron's second volume appeared on the market in 1875, the *Times'* critic accepted her photographs for their allegorical value, writing that they conveyed 'something vague and sweet, and mythical, or ... by some cipher intelligible only to the imaginative a portion of the meanings which the scene recorded was itself intended to illustrate'.[26] Cameron's symbolic approach allowed her to select one or two essential elements – among all the other possible meanings, 'a portion of the meanings', in the words of the *Times* critic – in her photographic illustrations of Tennyson's *Idylls*. To what extent, we might ask, did Cameron and Tennyson consider this symbolic approach appropriate to the epic narrative? In his historical essay about this difference in creative method, 'Narrate Or Describe?' (1936), Georg Lukacs wrote that an author's decision to use narration or description was less a conscious choice than it was an expression of deep-seated ideological points of view that were embedded in the author's relationship to his place in society. To Lukacs, terms like narration and description were useful to connect works of art to broader social issues, specific historical moments, and to the personal and political forces that surround and give shape to an author's activities. Lukacs's insights about the role of the epic form shed particular light on Cameron's allegorical approach.

As Tennyson's biographers have demonstrated, the poet devoted a great deal of time and thought to the question of whether his poem, *Idylls of the King*, was an epic narrative; he had expressed such doubts in his 1842 poem, *The Epic*, but also in a letter to his American publishers in 1858, in which he asked them to 'disabuse in your own minds, and those of others, as far as you can, that I am about an Epic of King Arthur. I should be crazed to attempt such a thing in the heart of the 19th Century.'[27] Years later, Tennyson's son Hallam called the *Idylls* an epic narrative in spite of his father's evident disavowal. Indeed, he used the term to indicate the significant literary weight of the endeavour as well as the intended seriousness of the project.[28] Lukacs insisted that an epic narrative 'consists in discovering the significant and vital aspects of social practice'. Descriptive art, by contrast, occupied the opposite pole, as it was hindered by social disengagement and apathy. If description was dispiriting, the epic form, by contrast, was positive and uplifting. To Lukacs, it provoked readers to expect rich symbolism and emblematic thinking:

> From epic poetry men expect a clearer, sharper mirror of themselves and of their social activity. The art of the epic poet consists in a proper distribution of emphasis and in a just accentuation of what is essential. A work becomes impressive and universal according to how much it presents the essential element – man and his social practice – not as an artificial product of the artist's virtuosity but as something that emerges and grows naturally, as something not invented, but simply discovered.[29]

By the end of 1874, Tennyson apparently recognized the impressive epic scale that was present in Cameron's symbolic approach to his narrative. Using the language of allegory, Tennyson described her illustrations to his *Idylls* in epic terms, at least according to Cameron. In her letter to Ryan, she wrote, 'He always says that his Arthur is an embodiment or I might say Incarnation of *Conscience*. That he was "the principle of conscience moving among his knights."'[30] Accordingly, Cameron's image of *King Arthur* (Cox 1174) unites the visually symbolic and the epic narrative forms. Like the approach she used in her photograph, *And Enid Sang*, Cameron confined her illustration to a lone figure who displays a simple identifying attribute and is portrayed in arrested action, the figure isolated against a dark void, pressed to the front of the picture plane. For Cameron, *King Arthur* possessed 'eyes that search into one and is *mythical* and spiritual in the highest degree'.[31] As an emblematic image representing Arthur's nobility, moral courage, and spiritual strength, this photograph corresponds well to Lukacs's thoughts about the role of the epic in literature. Cameron's photograph also embodies elements that we might call instructive and idealized: didactically, the photograph presents the King in his role as sovereign and symbolically expresses an idealized moment from the 'national heroic past'. Grasping the hilt of his sword, Arthur appears ready for battle, a hero poised and ready to act. Epic narrative, according to Bakhtin, was perfectly suited to the glorification of nationalism – that is symbolized in this image – because it simultaneously emphasizes tradition: 'The epic past, walled off from all subsequent times by an impenetrable boundary, is preserved and revealed only in the form of a national tradition. The epic relies entirely on this tradition.'[32]

## Epic versus lyric

Cameron confronted the symbolic potential of the epic form when she chose specific episodes to illustrate *Idylls of the King*. The fifteen photographs from this project (all twelve from volume one and three from volume two), suggest that Cameron displaced the overtly 'epic' qualities of the narrative with selected moments that interrupt the text. These narrative breaks in the poem are filled with scenes that we might call lyric pauses. When Tennyson inserts songs and dramatic asides as punctuating literary devices, he emphasizes a break in the narrative drive and a temporary halt to the action. As a result, the reader can breathe and enjoy a moment of reflection. As Monique Morgan writes, 'lyric is a suspended moment that stops the time of narrative and focuses instead on the "now" of composition and reception'.[33] This strategy also gives Tennyson's readers an opportunity to pause and reflect on the narrative action then taking place. Tennyson fills these open spaces with voices of his female protagonists – typically in the form of song – that reflect their innermost thoughts. For the most part, these songs are contemplative, reveal the motives of others, or speculate on a future encounter or an anticipated event.

But as strategies of narrative control, Tennyson's lyric insertions may also be described as dialogical interruptions to the 'monologism' of the epic, which are all the more significant (in literary terms, but also to Cameron and her audience) precisely *because* they are spoken by female protagonists. One of the consequences of this strategy for Cameron's illustrations is that in selecting lyric songs over epic moments of action, she has simultaneously undermined, in a manner of speaking, the universal and optimistic qualities that Lukacs associated with imagery that he termed 'narrative' rather than 'descriptive'. But Cameron constructed her photographs to embody allegorical motifs, and as a result, we may see them as doubly constructed, possessing both epic and lyric elements. How did Cameron achieve this hybrid quality?

In *Idylls of the King*, Tennyson inserted his lyric songs as opportunities for new voices to be heard during the course of the long narrative. While these narrative breaks occur outside the chief action centred on the quests of King Arthur's knights, Tennyson's lyrical moments are not insignificant. As John R. Reed has written, 'Arthur and his knights are mainly inarticulate because their deeds speak for them'; though, toward the end of the *Idylls*, 'as deeds fail to embody the ideal, Arthur and others fall back more and more upon the use of language to explain'.[34] Narrative, after all, is driven by plot and action, but Cameron's photographs seem to emphasize the interruption of that narrative drive. By selecting scenes of reflection over plot, by giving attention to those voices which articulate meditative feeling over mortal combat and physical struggle, Cameron has called her readers' attention to the voices in *Idylls* that appear in the interstices of the poem, around the edges of the great quest. Herbert Tucker wrote that Tennyson constructed the fabric of *Idylls of the King* to include such narrative breaks deliberately, believing they originated from his incomplete 'borrowing' of source material from earlier renditions of the King Arthur story: 'Renovating and perfecting the "old imperfect tale" obliges the poet to refine away what is impure in the Arthurian matter handed down by scribal tradition, and thus to leave his own version "imperfect" by opening narrative gaps for the reader to fill.'[35] Just as Tennyson filled the unanswered or unexplained from his sources in Mallory or Geoffrey, through the poem's narrative gaps and lyric pauses, so these in turn provide an opportunity for Cameron to 'fill the gap' with her own interpretive voice.

Cameron established a pattern that allows the viewer to connect the chosen illustration to the particular lines of poetry that inspired it. In images throughout volume one, for example, Cameron was consistent in her lyric selection. Similarly to *Enid*, *Elaine*, who is depicted alone in her room with Lancelot's shield, embroidering a coverlet to protect it, is portrayed at the moment when she sings 'The Song of Love and Death' (*Lancelot and Elaine*, l. 998). In 1874, Cameron subtitled this image *Elaine the Lily-Maid of Astolat* (Cox 1165). Years earlier, in 1867, seeking a title for a different photograph entirely (Cox 257), she chose the concluding line of the poem, 'Call and I follow, I follow,' ['let me die!'] (*Lancelot and Elaine*,

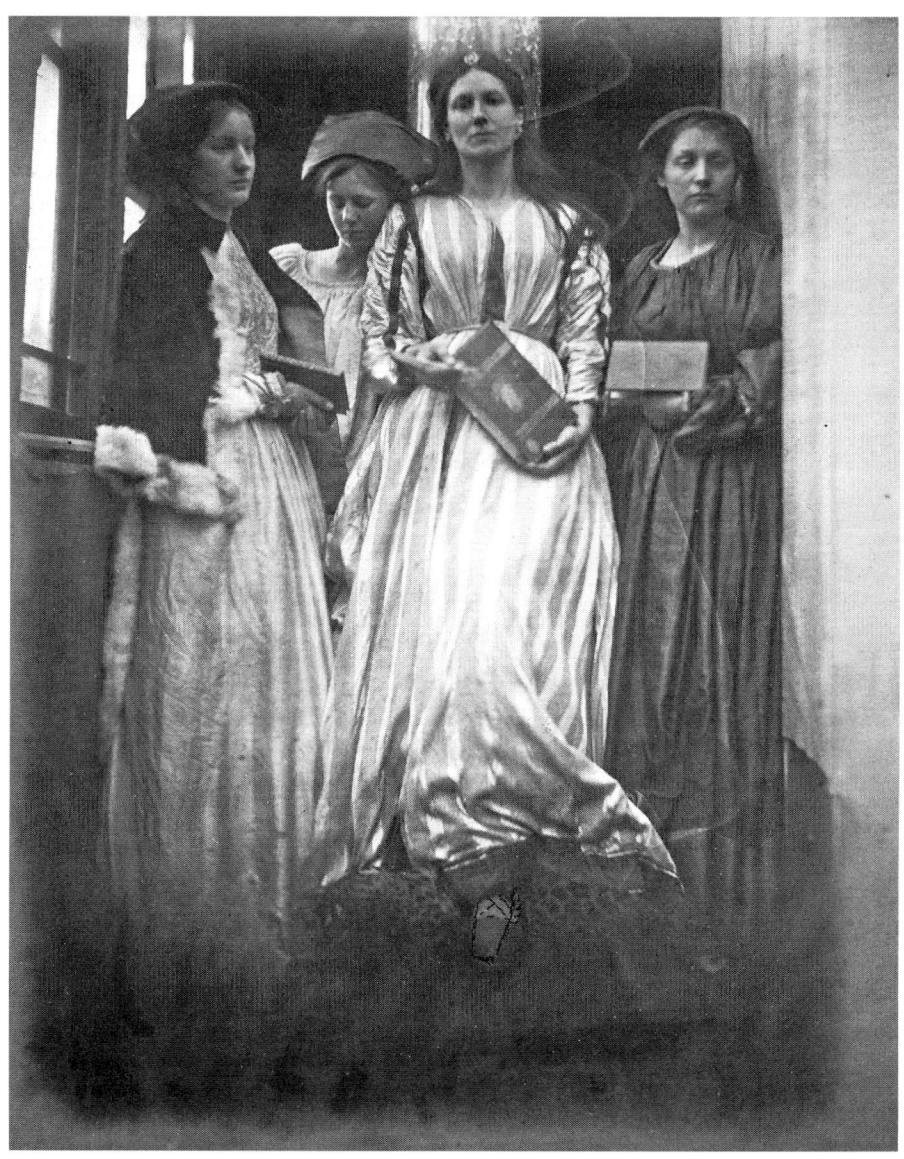

42

Julia Margaret Cameron, *The Princess* (Cox 1181), 1875.
Albumen silver print, 33 x 25.7 cm.

l. 1011). Cameron's newer photograph is yet another instance of her return to earlier imagery of the same narrative source (*Elaine*) to interpret the subject for a new purpose or with a different dramatic emphasis. Within the context of the poem's structure, Elaine's 'song' also interrupts the plot. The moments selected are significant in Tennyson's *Idyll*, as they give the reader insight into his character's state of mind and chillingly foretell her later demise.

In volume two, Cameron added further songs to these lyric representations: three photographs are used to illustrate *The May Queen* to correspond to the three parts of this poem (Cox 1176, 1177, 1180).[36] The repeated lines, the canting verse, and the allusions to 'the blessed music' of the emotions all reinforce the lyricism of the poem. *The Princess: A Medley*, is also represented by three photographs (Cox 1181, Figure 42; Cox 1182 and 1185). In this poem, Tennyson expounds upon the role of women and the importance of song as a literary device. As we have seen, he interjects lyric song to disrupt the primary narrative with an explicit purpose. Early in *The Princess*, Tennyson outlined how he would assign these roles in the course of narrating the poem itself:

> And let the ladies sing us, if they will,
> From time to time, some ballad or a song
> To give us a breathing-space.'
>
> So I began,
> And the rest follow'd; and the women sang
> Between the rougher voices of the men,
> Like linnets in the pauses of the wind:
> And here I give the story and the songs.
>
> (*The Princess*, Prologue, ll. 233–9)

Two of the three images created by Cameron to illustrate this poem present such ballads. The image captioned '*O hark O hear how thin and clear / And thinner, clearer, farther going*' (Cox 1182) makes sense only in the context of the poem as a whole. This fragment, in other words, is somewhat unusual because it is not framed as a song in the poem. Nor is it introduced as a kind of narrative break by the photographer: instead, Cameron's illustrations depict three stanzas of a song, each bearing a final couplet with variations on the lines 'Blow, bugle, blow, set the wild echoes flying, / And answer, echoes, answer, dying, dying, dying' (*The Princess*, Part III, ll. 348–65). Cameron has essentially invented these scenes, as Schapiro might have said, virtually creating the entire narrative context for the photograph: she has chosen the model and her instrument, the lighting and focus, the pose and expression. Her choice of these elements not only conforms to her established style, but they express the sentiments and feeling of the song symbolically through her own allegorical interpretation. The image that she captioned, '*Tears from the depth of some divine despair, / Rise in the heart and gather to the eyes*' (Cox 1185, Figure 43) is drawn from the first song of the poem, which the verse describes as having been set to music and accompanied by a harp, occurring at the beginning of Part IV of the poem.

Tennyson's songs and Cameron's approach to illustrating those songs intentionally break the flow of the main narrative, but these interruptions are essential to provide opportunities for Tennyson's characters to interact with each other

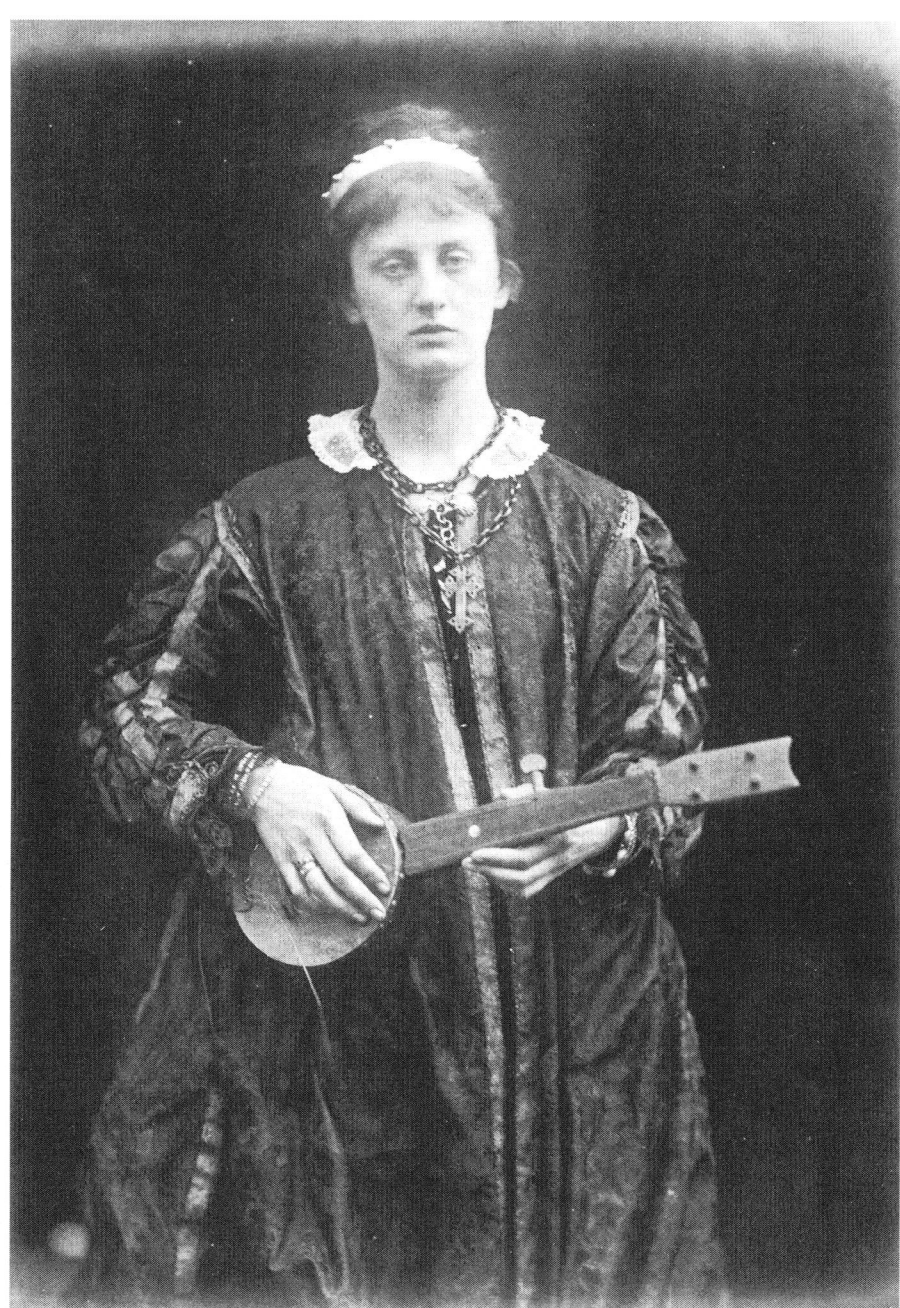

43    Julia Margaret Cameron, *'Tears from the depth of some divine despair, / Rise in the heart and gather to the eyes'* (Cox 1185), 1875. Albumen print, 33 x 22.5 cm.

discursively. For example, both Enid's song and Elaine's song are integral to the text *because* they are integrated *into* the text. According to Bakhtin,

> The words of the author that represent and frame another's speech create a perspective for it; they separate light from shadow, create the situation and conditions necessary for it to sound; finally, they penetrate into the interior of the other's speech, carrying into it their own accents and their own expressions, creating for it a dialogizing background.[37]

Like Tennyson, Cameron also exploited the idea of isolating the speech of her female protagonists, as she did in illustrating the songs of *Enid* and *Elaine*. These are scenes where the action is halted and female songs are heard, where women break into a dialogic relationship with their male counterparts and assertively communicate an independent voice of their own. Consequently, these figures visualize the lyrical discontinuities of the poem itself. In *Idylls of the King*, Tennyson used his female characters to represent Camelot's purity and its evil, its honour and its destruction. In Cameron's photographic illustrations, she uses Enid and Elaine to represent 'The True' half of the dichotomy posed earlier by Tennyson, who in 1859 published the first four books of the poem as *The True and The False*. The other two characters, Vivien and Guinevere, represent negative examples for women. While Enid and Elaine endure pain for their goodness, Vivien and Guinevere conspire and sin and, as a result, suffer for their actions.

Cameron's illustrations for *Vivien* and *Guinevere* do not represent them in song, but instead isolate them in some kind of arrested action or participating in a deceptive discourse. For example, Cameron depicts Vivien cajoling Merlin twice (Cox 1163, 1164); in one, she portrays Vivien conniving against Merlin and coaxing him to give up his secrets, and in the other, she represents the aftermath of his betrayal. Guinevere, too, is depicted with others: first with Lancelot in a scene of their parting (Cox 1170), and subsequently with the Little Novice (Cox 1173; Figure 44). In these photographs, Cameron represents Tennyson's two anti-heroines at the moment when they give voice to their moral or social transgressions, with the text chosen precisely at the point where these women actually speak the fateful words of betrayal that deny Arthur his pure, idealistic kingdom. Significantly, at these moments, the male protagonists do not, or cannot, speak. For example, Cameron depicts Vivien bewitching Merlin precisely at the point where 'he was mute' (*Merlin and Vivien*, l. 227). After this episode, in fact, Merlin turns away from her, and utters the grave lines, 'Who are wise in love / Love most, say least' (ll. 245–6). Cameron's illustration of Merlin's entrapment in the oak tree also is a selected key moment, representing exactly the point when an exhausted, impotent Merlin again becomes speechless: 'For Merlin, overtalk'd and overworn, / Had yielded', begins Cameron's excerpt of the *Idyll* for this scene (ll. 963–4). Charles Cameron, who represented Merlin in this image, is captured with his eyes closed, which Cameron invented as an effective visual metaphor for his character's muteness. *The Parting of Lancelot and Guinevere*, in Cameron's rendition (Cox 1170), captures the scene when Guinevere voices the auspicious line, 'O Lancelot, if thou love me get thee hence' (*Guinevere*, l. 94). This statement, the most overt line in the poem that exposes Lancelot and Guinevere's transgression, is heard by one person only: 'Vivien, lurking, heard' (l. 97). Significantly, Cameron included *both lines* of text to accompany this photograph. In the scene of *The Little Novice with the Queen Guinevere in the Holy House at Almesbury*, Guinevere is forced to endure the guileless song of the girlish nun, who unwittingly echoes Guinevere's earlier lines from her flight to the convent, where 'in herself she moan'd "Too late, too late!"' (l. 129) (Figure 44).Of course, having asked the novice for a song to help console her and unbind her emotions, she must endure listening to the novice's 'foolish prattle' in complete silence, a consequence that further implicates her feelings of guilt.

In her illustrations to the four principal female characters in *Idylls of the King*, then, Cameron offered her readers the poignant lyrical songs of Tennyson's heroines and the key dialogues that expose the motives of his anti-heroines. By choosing to represent a mixture of dissonant voices, Cameron portrayed the blending of song and listeners together with representations of stifled, exhausted, or suppressed speech, and in this way offered her readers another visual interpretation of *Idylls of the King*. When dissonance of this kind articulates potentially contradictory points of view, Bakhtin called this competing mixture of voices a 'hybrid discourse'.[38] Cameron created these hybrid discourses in two familiar ways: through scene selection and the titles she used.

As hybrid images that relied upon a textual source, Cameron's illustrations also re-stabilize the epic context of the narrative, as it would have been untrue to the larger poem had she tried to represent the *Idylls* only as a series of 'women's songs'. To avoid this possibility, Cameron linked together dynamic opposites in her two volumes, stitching together a new structure that supported the epic narrative: Cameron focuses closely on the themes of honour and betrayal, harmony and discord, good and evil, and song and silence. In doing so, she has formally 'rebalanced' Tennyson's epic, modifying its narrative drive with a new equilibrium.[39] These twin but opposing forces are most clearly represented in the poem, *The Last Tournament*, the most action-filled and warlike of the *Idylls*. Ironically, however, Cameron chose not to represent any elements of this particular poem in her *Illustrations*. In Tennyson's *The Last Tournament*, the rival moral forces that vie for prominence in King Arthur's Camelot are exposed by the overt threats of the Red Knight, whose verbal assault shocks his listeners in an effort to provoke Arthur:

> 'Tell thou the King and all his liars that I
> Have founded my Round Table in the North,
> And whatsoever his own knights have sworn
> My knights have sworn the counter to it – and say

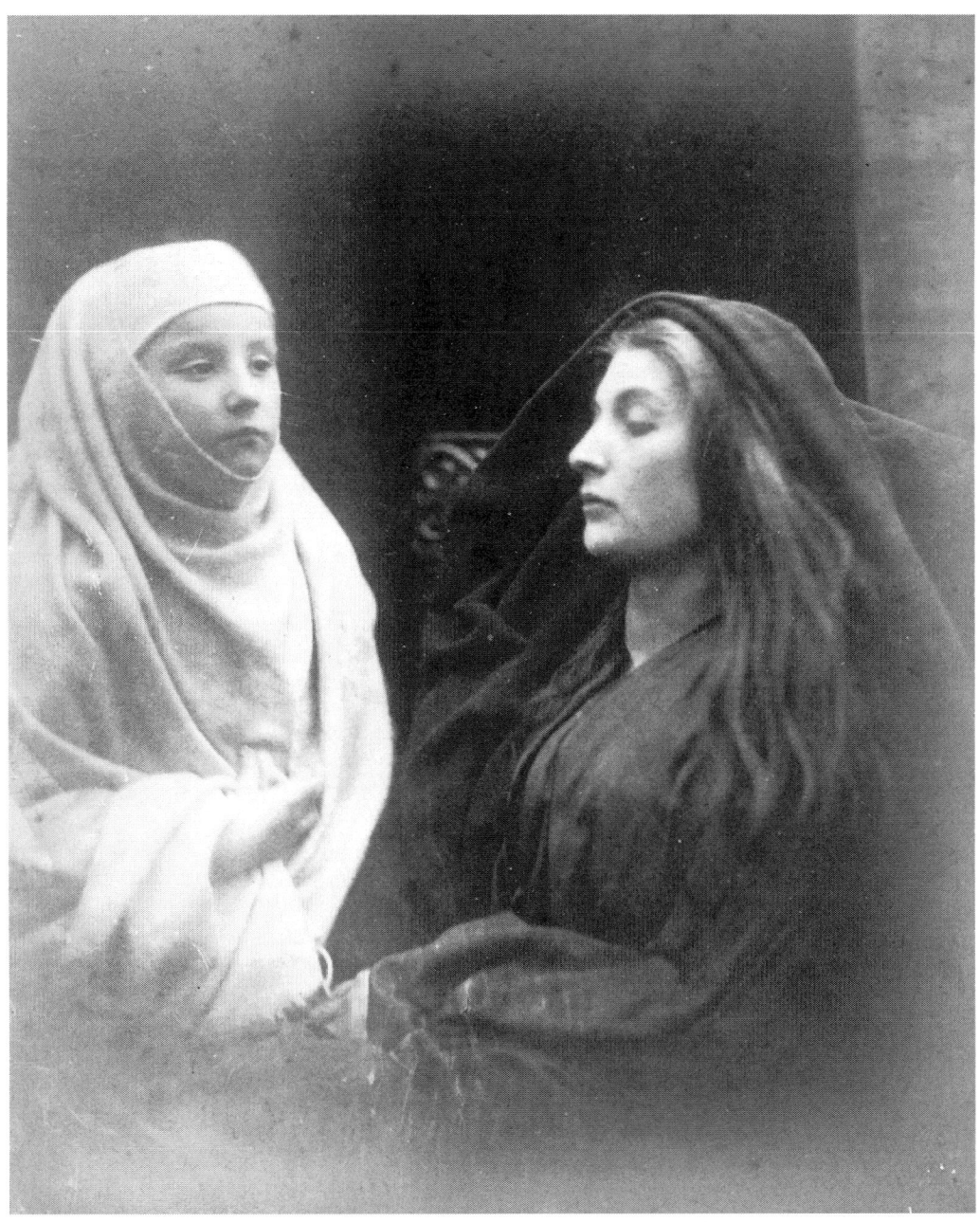

Julia Margaret Cameron, *The Little Novice with the Queen Guinevere
in the Holy House at Almesbury* (Cox 1173), 1874.
Albumen print, 34.8 x 28.4 cm.                                          **44**

> My tower is full of harlots, like his court,
> But mine are worthier, seeing they profess
> To be none other than themselves – and say
> My knights are all adulterers like his own,
> But mine are worthier, seeing they profess
> To be none other; and say his hour is come,
> The heathen are upon him, his long lance
> Broken, and his Excalibur a straw.'
>
> (*The Last Tournament*, ll. 77–88)

Significantly, Arthur interprets the Red Knight's tirade as a threat posed by 'the heathen'. He calls this menace an 'ever-climbing wave' that 'hath lain for years at rest', but which now, along with other traitors and deserters, 'make their last head like Satan in the North' (*The Last Tournament*, ll. 91–7). When the reader has left *The Last Tournament* and passed on to *Guinevere*, the moral, religious, and political stakes are clear. Tennyson has built a powerful counter-narrative to Arthur's idealized realm that threatens its metaphorical boundaries as surely as its internal integrity. Arthur disregards the signs at every turn; his tragedy is that he cannot truly see both sides. By avoiding the alternative paths that are sung for him in the lyrical breaks of the poem, Arthur is set up to fall hard.

In volume one of her *Illustrations*, Cameron faithfully stayed close to Tennyson's text. But it is clear that she also disagreed with Tennyson's characterization of Arthur, disliking the King's smug self-satisfaction and lack of compassion for the suffering of others. In 1874, Cameron asserted the validity of her own interpretation in a letter to Sir William Gregory, who had recently been appointed governor of Ceylon:

> *I for* one think King Arthur very *imperfect* – 'The frailty of a Man' & the 'Security of a God' describes the perfect man but King Arthur seems to have had no frailty but that of *self* righteousness & certainly his neglect of his lovely young Wife ought to have brought on *self* reproach instead of the morbid harangue of his farewell. I know what a heretic I am & that the *Nation* (like Gladstone) think this the finest thing in the English language – I wholly differ & have always told Alfred Tennyson so & I believe he *half* thinks I am right. [40]

Styling herself a friendly iconoclast in Tennyson's midst, Cameron took new liberties in volume two to express these conflicting feelings about Tennyson's poetry and emphasize her own visual interpretations of the poem.

During the years Tennyson wrote the twelve episodes of *Idylls of the King*, he endured a great deal of criticism. Critics called it archaic, old-fashioned, retrograde. In 1859, for example, Ruskin suggested that Tennyson forgot the present and misplaced his emphasis on a remote and inaccessible past.[41] Later, in 1872, Swinburne provoked Tennyson by calling his epic a trivial domestic spat, 'rather a case for the divorce court than for poetry'. In the same essay, he mocked the *Idylls* as if it were an updated 'Morte d'Albert', a play on words that elided Thomas Mallory's fifteenth-century title with the name of Albert, Queen Victoria's deceased husband.[42] But by recognizing modern domesticity and marital fidelity to be inadequate as  metaphors for a nation, Swinburne viewed Tennyson as unpersuasive and his reinterpretation of the Arthurian legend unconvincing because he misrepresented minor shortcomings as if they were profound and meaningful events.[43]

Cameron also endured criticism that disparaged her photographs. Usually these were directed against her sometimes-imperfect photographic techniques or her soft-focus style. But the common thread that linked together Tennyson and Cameron was their representation of medieval rather than contemporary subjects. Tennyson's critics faulted him for choosing a feudal subject like Arthur to represent contemporary life and disagreed with his interpretation that the present was marked by moral and structural decline.[44] In Tennyson's version of the mythical past, traditional elements of society are simple and uncomplicated, heroes are unassailable, and national borders are known and secure. In the 1870s, by contrast, men and women clashed on the social front and in courts of law, 'heroes' fell victim to their extreme fears and poor judgement, national allegiance could not be taken for granted, and diplomatic uncertainties between competing nations that were seeking economic expansion and political influence caused widespread discontent across society.

As Cameron knew, Gladstone, the Liberal Prime Minister, wrote about Tennyson's *Idylls of the King* in 1859 enthusiastically: 'It is national; it is Christian', he exclaimed. 'Though highly national,' he continued, 'it is universal; for it rests upon those depths and breadths of our nature to which all its truly great developments in all nations are alike essentially and closely related.'[45] Instead of accepting Gladstone's almost jingoistic assessments, Tennyson expressed wary reservations for interpretations that tried to apply specific allegorical references to his literary figures. For example, he took issue with those critics who claimed that the Three Queens who appear at Arthur's coronation represent Faith, Hope, and Charity. About these critics, Tennyson said:

> They are right, and they are not right. They mean that and they do not. They are three of the noblest of women. They are also those three Graces, but they are much more. I hate to be tied down to say, '*This* means *that*,' because the thought within the image is much more than any one interpretation.[46]

In this way, Tennyson maintained open-ended literary allusions and effectively denied explicit or implied references to modern political or social events. By situating all action in the mythical-historical past, he insisted, even overt symbolism must be read through a lens that is deliberately archaic and abstract (one might think of the mystical gate, for example, on the margins of Camelot, with its obscure meanings and its 'secret code').

In *To the Queen*, Tennyson described his epic narrative using such abstract language, invoking the late Prince Albert and imploring the Queen: 'For one to whom I made it o'er his grave / Sacred, accept this old imperfect tale, / New-old, and shadowing Sense at war with Soul, / Ideal manhood closed in real man' (ll. 35–8). In our own time, scholars have reinterpreted Tennyson's abstractions as a kind of disavowal that afforded him distance from the imperial activities of the British Empire. Colin Graham noted that *Idylls of the King* 'works by attempting to undercut the evaluative connotations of the "modern" with the promise of resurrection from the past (Arthur is thus the perfect figure – the once and future king, he is forever past and always potentially contemporary)'.[47] Cecily Devereux wrote persuasively that the poem's epilogue, *To the Queen*, manifested Tennyson's anxiety about the dissolution of the British Empire, calling the epic narrative a direct appeal to preserve 'the imperial centre as it is with the fostering of the "bond" between Canada and England'.[48] For Linda Hughes and Michael Lund, the poem lies 'in between the expression of hope and of doubt for the British realm, suggesting that the Arthuriad has a bearing on these issues of empire and leadership'.[49] Did Cameron's two-volume *Illustrations* affirm or deny these interpretations?

## Preserving the castle walls: she who told the tale

Throughout *Idylls of the King*, Tennyson interspersed a repeated variation of the phrase, 'he who tells the tale'. As a rhetorical device, this stylistic element acquired increasing significance as the narrative unfolded. We might interpret this expression as the author's own retelling of the legend that has its roots in Mallory and Geoffroy or as a self-reflexive statement in which his own voice reiterates the act of narration. Tennyson, of course, was known to enjoy reciting his own poetry. But the phrase also separates the tale from the teller, redirects the narrative source, and accords authority to any subsequent reader who also might recite the poem aloud. In his poem of 1855, *Ode on the Death of the Duke of Wellington*, Tennyson claimed the telling and retelling of national stories was essential to the larger process of forming national identity: '*We have a voice* with which to pay the debt / Of boundless love and reverence and regret / To those great men who fought, and kept it ours' (VII, ll. 6–8, emphasis added). In the concluding lines to *Gareth and Lynette*, Tennyson reiterated the point, emphasizing the transformative act of reciting the narrative: 'And he that told the tale in older times / Says that Sir Gareth wedded Lyonors, / But he that told the tale later says Lynette' (*Gareth and Lynette*, ll. 1392–4).

In taking up the legend of King Arthur *after* Tennyson, Cameron exercised a new authorial voice in the act of her own retelling, much like the structure of recitation and reiteration that Tennyson built into the poem itself . For example,

Cameron illustrated episodes from *Idylls* that were meaningful to her, but included additional poems as well (these included *The Princess, The Beggar Maid, Mariana,* and *Maud*). Unexpectedly, in her second volume, she blended these photographs with additional selections from *Idylls of the King.* Cameron announced this new authorial voice on the dedication page: in 1874 she wrote: 'Dedicated by gracious permission to Her Imperial and Royal Highness Victoria, The Crown Princess of Germany and Prussia and Princess Royal by Julia Margaret Cameron.'

Although the precise connection between Cameron and Queen Victoria's eldest daughter in 1874 is still largely unknown, Victoria Adelaide, the Crown Princess of Prussia, had written to Tennyson some twelve years earlier about the personal impact that *Idylls of the King* had made upon her from the moment she first heard it. Significantly for the importance of the idea of a dramatic recitation, Tennyson's epic poem was apparently read *to* Victoria Adelaide, rather than having been read *by* her as a personal and silent activity. In a letter to Tennyson from the Crown Princess, dated 25 February 1862, Tennyson received these lines, coming just two months after Prince Albert's untimely death:

> The first time I heard [the *Idylls*] was last year, when I found the Queen and Prince quite in raptures about them. The first bit I ever heard was the end of 'Guinevere', the last ten pages, the Prince read them to me, and I shall never forget the impression it made upon me hearing those grand and simple words in his voice! He did so admire them, and I cannot separate the idea of King Arthur from the image of him whom I most revered on Earth![50]

Earlier, at the time of her father's illness, when she was pregnant and confined in Berlin, Victoria Adelaide had worked on some drawings inspired by the *Idylls* to give her father as a Christmas present. According to Hannah Pakula, 'Prince Albert was proud of her artistic talent and had asked her to try illustrating Tennyson's "Idylls of the King," which they had read together during the summer [of 1861].'[51]

When the Crown Princess suggested that Tennyson modify the order of the four central *Idylls* by placing *Morte d'Arthur*, the earlier poem, to follow *Guinevere* in sequence, the poet responded negatively. Tennyson offered two reasons: first, he 'could scarcely light upon a finer close than that ghostlike passing away of the King and the other that the Morte is older in style and suggestive of a less modern social state'.[52] This supports the idea that *Idylls* embedded an allegory about the nation during a critical moment of its social and moral development. His admission also supports Kiernan's contention that Tennyson regarded Camelot a land 'marshalled by an Arthur turned into a Victorian gentleman, refined and rarefied, but a muscular Christian too, a king on horseback; a type of the heroes like General [Charles George] Gordon, who were building the empire, liberating its peoples supposedly from the darkness of bondage and superstition'.[53] For Victoria Adelaide, a staunch supporter of Britain and advocate for its global strength, *Idylls of the King* successfully expressed the 'civilizing mission' of its empire. In subsequent years, Tennyson remained on good terms with the Crown Princess and visited her at Osborne House again in 1871, at the conclusion of the Franco-Prussian War, when she came to visit the Queen's summer palace on the Isle of Wight.[54] Victoria Adelaide's visit was as much a vacation as it was an effort to make amends with her brother, the Prince of Wales, who sympathized with France during the war.[55]

Royal marriages between European nobility had long cemented political and economic alliances between the states, and the sons and daughters of kings and queens were the commonly accepted currency. Victoria Adelaide, Prince Albert and Queen Victoria's eldest daughter, knew that her role on the world stage included bringing unity between England and Prussia. Before she wed on 25 January 1858 at the age of seventeen, her father had prepared her as much as possible by sharing his political interests in establishing a modern constitutional government in Prussia and in unifying the future German States. Albert understood the complex strategic role of Germany's place in world affairs: writing to his future son-in-law, who was at the time attending the coronation of Czar Alexander II in Russia, he observed, 'I understand that your future alliance is looked on askance in Russia ... The German stands in the centre between England and Russia; his high culture and his philosophic love of truth drive him towards the English conception, his military discipline, his admiration of the Asiatic greatness ... which is achieved by merging the individual into the whole, drives him in the other direction.'[56] By the time the Crown Princess was twenty-one years old, having lost the guiding influence of her father, she emerged an important ally to her husband, Frederick III, in supporting his opposition to Bismarck's efforts to restrict the free press.[57] When Prussia formed the North German Confederation in 1867, many in London grew alarmed at what they perceived to be Germany's empire-building and fretted over Britain's seeming paralysis, focusing attention once again on the question of the nation's relationship to the continent and toward its colonies across the globe.[58]

British imperial expansion after 1870 was on Tennyson's mind as he wrote further instalments to the *Idylls of the King*.[59] King Arthur seems to have been written as a mythical forerunner in the nation's mission to spread Christianity across the globe, his benevolence an extension of imperial Britain's self-proclaimed altruism toward its colonies. Tennyson's friend, James Spedding, a former colleague of Henry Taylor in the Colonial Office, wrote in the *Westminster Review* in 1870 against Britain giving up its colonies, warning against actions that could lead to 'curtailment of trade; ... diminution of supplies of raw staples; ... deprivation of ports of refuge in case of war; ... loss of national prestige; ... loss of nationality by all outgoing English people; ... loss of territories where the army ... can be kept; loss of openings where the youth of England can find ample scope for their business aptitudes'. As Spedding cautioned, 'should America, Prussia, or any other rising power take a helpless but abandoned colony under its protection, England's loss will be the other nation's gain'.[60] Elliot Gilbert and Deirdre David have argued that Arthur's moralizing tone in the *Idylls* was more consistent with high-minded Victorian idealism than it was with blood-soaked references to past military glory of the kind found in *Boadicea*, since the female Boadicea voices fury and rage while the male Arthur offers a tame and measured expression of national honour. Arthur acts by means of moral reproach and the example of steady virtue. Such relative coolness, they argue, was consistent with the Colonial Office's view that colonial lands should be managed not by means of intimidation and tyranny, but rather 'by the victories of mind over brute matter and blind mechanical obstacles'.[61]

Victoria Adelaide and her mother, Queen Victoria, wrote letters to each other almost daily, covering every subject from family worries and gossip to important matters of state and governmental policy. While she described herself as feeling more and more Prussian as the years went by, the Crown Princess also affirmed her admiration for, and defence of, Britain's global imperial ambitions. Her language accepts the 'civilized and uncivilized' divide that split East and West and that infused the speeches of Macaulay and Merivale, the letters of Taylor and Spedding, and the poetry of Tennyson. For example, in a letter to Queen Victoria, dated 6 July 1873, she wrote:

> England is the only country at present which devotes all its energies to the cause of 'culture' and real civilization. How much is being done in India since your Reign and how much more might still be done; it is always my dream that England should release the whole of the East from the yoke of barbarity, by exerting its wise humanising influence, not through missionaries and by trying to convert the people to Christianity against their will and without the great principle of loving one another being understood by them, but through giving them by degrees as many of the advantages of our ways and customs as possible. I am sure you think and feel as I do. There are such grand resources in the East. Neither France nor Germany could ever do what England can in this direction.[62]

Tennyson cheered the fall of Gladstone's ministry in February 1874. At this time, the British government was still undecided whether it wanted to expand into islands of the South Seas, the Malay States, and even portions of West Africa. When Britain finally absorbed the Fiji Islands, the Crown Princess congratulated her mother on their acquisition: 'How glad I am that England has them', she wrote, continuing as a gratified daughter of the Empire: 'We now form a belt right round the globe which is a proud thing for us and a blessing for civilization.'[63]

In December 1874, when Cameron dedicated her book to the Crown Princess, she was able to claim a number of personal and political relationships: first, by invoking the eldest daughter of the royal sovereign, she was able to

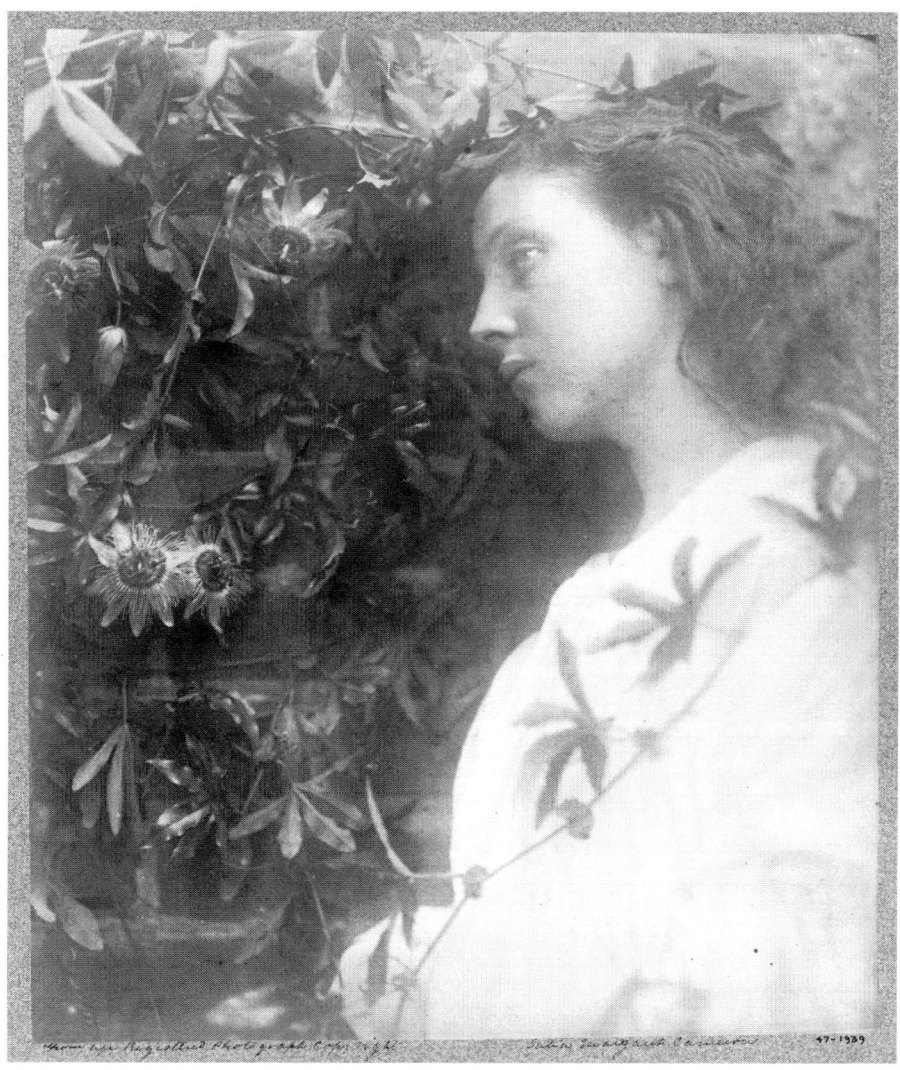

**45**     Julia Margaret Cameron, *Maud* (Cox 1195), 1875. Albumen print, 32 x 27 cm.

connect her photographs to Tennyson's own prologue, the *Dedication* to Prince Albert, and his epilogue, *To the Queen*. In doing so she could also claim equally familiar terms with the royal family. Cameron's dedication also emphasizes the royal ties that bound Great Britain to the new German Empire. This new unity was a significant political symbol and expression of support and allegiance on the eve of Disraeli's Conservative government. Although the British queen was quick to reassure her daughter that the government's transition was good for the nation and would enhance the stability of Europe,[64] Cameron's dedication emphasized the common bond between the two nations and placed faith in the prosperity of their shared future. As a result, she followed Tennyson's lead in praising the royal family as inspired and just.

Under the first several years of Disraeli's government, Britain's foreign policy expanded; Disraeli addressed the relationship between the imperial centre and the nation's Eastern dominions by strengthening Britain's relative position in world affairs, actions that the Crown Princess regarded positively. First, Disraeli orchestrated the purchase of Suez Canal shares, assuring Britain's free access to sea routes to India and the Pacific colonies, which the Crown Princess interpreted as yet another success for her mother's reign: 'This will mark in History among the many great good and useful things done in your reign', she wrote to her mother, 'and that makes me so proud and happy.'[65] Second, Disraeli helped to organize a tour of India by the Prince of Wales, a public relations event designed to reassert Britain's claims over its crown colony in the eyes of the world, especially Russia. And third, the Prime Minister supported the Royal Titles Bill of 1874, which crowned Queen Victoria Empress of India, another occasion symbolizing the inevitability of British colonial expansion; this last public event met with the Crown Princess's equally high approval.

As we have seen, Cameron's second volume contained additional photographs beyond those she selected from *Idylls of the King*. Briefly, volume two opens with three illustrations for *The May Queen*, followed by three photographs for *The Princess*, and then additional images depicting *Mariana* and another, *King Cophetua and the Beggar Maid*. Three more illustrations to *Idylls of the King* occur next in the sequence: two photographs depict scenes from *Lancelot and Elaine* and one from *The Passing of Arthur*. Finally, the second volume concludes with a rendering of *Maud*, depicting 'the passion-flower at the gate' (Cox 1195; Figure 45). What principle or narrative coherence holds this seemingly random group of photographs together?

Contemporary scholars have stressed that virtually all of Cameron's photographs in the second volume depict women in varying states of extreme despair (*Mariana*, *The May Queen*), as personifications of imminent death (note the transient echoes of the horns of Elfland and earliest sounds of half-awakened birds, as represented in *The Princess*), or as actually deceased, like Elaine, having died from a broken heart (Cox 1190). But Tennyson rarely expressed despair in his poetry without also offering some rays of hope, suggesting that joy followed sadness and that peace followed pain and suffering. For example, of the grief-filled poem, *In Memoriam*, Tennyson said,

> It is rather the cry of the whole human race than mine. In the poem altogether private grief swells out into thought of, and hope for, the whole world. It begins with a funeral and ends with a marriage – begins with a death and ends in promise of a new life – a sort of Divine Comedy, cheerful at the close.[66]

Similarly, in the context of volume two, Cameron's protagonists express morbid thoughts and hopelessness but also profess faith in the future. The organization of the volume itself reveals the complexity of Cameron's reinterpretation of Tennyson. First, she has chosen dying characters that are ignorant of Christian beliefs. In *Idylls of the King*, Tennyson represented their innocence by having Arthur call them primitive, uncivilized, or heathen, but through their actions and by means of their purity and virtuous death, they demonstrate Christian faith in 'life-after-death'. This dual condition apparently appealed to Cameron, because in volume two she represented simultaneously antithetical personifications of both Christian and pagan approaches to death.

In particular, of the twelve illustrations to the poems in volume two, the first six photographs represent her characters' expressions of longing for death. In *The May Queen*, Cameron represents the Christian idea of life-after-death, but in *The Princess*, she relied upon the iconography of Orientalism to represent a non-Christian understanding of death. As Kerry McSweeny explained,

> One reason Tennyson's classical personae [like Oenone, but also the two Marianas] are able to give full voice to their longing for death is that they live in a pagan world which has not experienced the Christian revelation of a life beyond the grave: 'Death closes all,' as Tennyson's Ulysses insists; 'Death is the end of life' as his mariners chant in 'The Lotos Eaters.' That the classical setting allowed Tennyson to indulge feelings otherwise unacceptable to a Christian culture should not be construed to mean ... that Tennyson sought poetically to indulge his 'impulse to suicide.'[67]

Knowing that her purity and goodness will lead to an eternal life in heaven, the May Queen dies sure that her soul will have a safe place to go and that she will experience eternal peace: she expresses this belief confidently: 'a blessed home – / And there to wait a little while till you and Effie come – / To lie within the light of God' (*The May Queen, Conclusion*, ll. 56–8). Mariana, by contrast, has no such rosy or hopeful outlook. Instead, Tennyson says that 'She could not look on the sweet heaven, / Either at morn or eventide' (ll. 15–16).

In 1875, Cameron devised new compositions to illustrate *The May Queen* (Cox 1176, 1177, 1180), returning once again to a familiar subject that she explored years earlier in photographs copyrighted in November 1864 (Cox 1068), January 1865 (Cox 1069), and May 1866 (Cox 1098).[68] This return (or repetition) is significant, because Cameron apparently felt the need to create new photographs for this subject, whereas, she did include an older photograph (of 1867) representing *King Cophetua* in volume two. *King Cophetua* is the eighth photograph in the sequence of volume two, which immediately precedes her return to subjects from *Idylls of the King*.[69] The organization of volume two, then, reveals Cameron's structural use of *King Cophetua* to serve as a kind of thematic bridge, one that links the pagan imagery of *Mariana* to the Christian chivalry in *Idylls of the King*.

Cameron's three illustrations for *The Princess* lie between *The May Queen* and *Mariana*. King Cophetua, whose character is empowered by a Christian moral code, 'steps down' to the beggar maid in order to 'raise her up' into a kind of Christian enlightenment. But in *The Princess* Tennyson describes Princess Ida's situation as far more difficult (and certainly not nearly as patriarchal). Princess Ida also wants to liberate women from their low social status, but she finds her own abilities thwarted. Seeking a worldly metaphor to explain Ida's predicament, Tennyson compared her situation to Britain's political and economic challenge to improve material conditions in the Fiji Islands, those colonies in the South Pacific that Britain had recently acquired:

> 'No doubt we seem a kind of monster to you;
> We are used to that; for women, up till this,
> Cramp'd under worse than South-sea-isle taboo,
> Dwarfs of the gynaeceum, fail so far
> In high desire, they know not, cannot guess
> How much their welfare is a passion to us.
>
> (The Princess, Part III, ll. 259–64)

Cameron's illustration for *The Princess* expresses Ida's deep frustration. Posed in a tight space, symbolically representing the cramped potential of their lot, Ida and her retinue are confined and unable to move (Cox 1181; Figure 42).

In keeping with her strategy to represent the 'dual nature' of Tennyson's heroines, Cameron continued her illustration of *The Princess* by adding two photographs expressing the finality of death. Both are pagan deaths shrouded in ritual and mystery. In the first of the two, Cameron depicted her model with a kind of lyre, an odd choice for an accompanying instrument to illustrate a song of death. Moreover, this song contains the refrain, 'Blow, bugle, blow, set the wild echoes flying, / And answer, echoes, answer, dying, dying, dying' (Part III, ll. 364–5). But this instrument is not the lyre of ancient Greece, but instead is equipped with a resonator called a chordophone, a musical fusion derived from historical roots in the Congo.[70] Consequently, the image, *'O hark, O hear'* (Cox 1182) contains elements that Victorian audiences would have associated with primitivism or paganism because of the African instrument's curved neck, irregularly spaced strings, and stretched animal skin resonator. Even if her readers could not place the instrument's origins specifically in Africa, its unrefined and non-Western characteristics would nevertheless associate it, like the strand of thick beads worn by her model, with the 'South-sea-isle taboo' of non-Christian music and song that is alluded to in Tennyson's poem.

Cameron's third illustration of *The Princess* also represents the finality of death, as Oenone and Mariana, whose characters were ignorant of the Christian faith, expressed it in verse. Accordingly, in the photograph, *'Tears from the depth of some divine despair'* (Cox 1185; Figure 43), Cameron has replaced the 'harp' of the poem with a different stringed instrument that resembles a folk lute or banjo. Although of unknown origins, its associations are also connected to primitivism because it was used in the context of a pagan ritual. Cameron's model may indeed wear a crucifix held by a chain around her neck (unlike the model with the African chordophone), but the caption to this photograph also alludes to the fateful final line of the song: 'O Death in Life, the days that are no more!' (Part IV, l. 40).

In contrast to *The Princess*, King Arthur's story is Christian, where the souls of the virtuous heroes and heroines of Camelot live on forever because the Christian faithful live beyond death. Elaine, for instance, dies with the lily of purity clutched in one hand and a letter held in the other, but her words are spoken after death. Cameron illustrated her death witnessed by King Arthur (Cox 1190, 1191). Before dying, she requests of her listeners, 'Pray for my soul, and yield me burial' (*Lancelot and Elaine*, l. 1272). In lines that echo the biblical last words of Christ on the Cross,[71] King Arthur also articulates his fervent belief in life after death:

> My God, thou hast forgotten me in my death:
> Nay – God my Christ – I pass but shall not die.
>
> (*The Passing of Arthur*, ll. 27–8)

The organizational structure of volume two therefore reflects Cameron's extraction of themes embedded in Tennyson's poems. She presents a complex weave that joins allegories of the pagan and feminine East, where religious life was considered backward and unenlightened and where death was ritualized and final, with photographs illustrating hopeful expressions of life after death, which are made possible by Christian belief.

Volume two ends with *Maud*, but a convincing explanation remains to be made about why this image anchors a book dedicated to *Idylls of the King*. How did Cameron regard this poem, first published some twenty years earlier, in the context of Tennyson's great epic, and what were the thematic or allegorical elements that influenced her decision to use an illustration of *Maud* to conclude the volume? In the photograph, she posed her model against a garden wall with climbing flowers, illustrating the lines, 'There has fallen a splendid tear / From the passion-flower at the gate' (I, x, ll. 1–2) (Cox 1195; Figure 45). Although *Maud* is a complex poem that contains a wide range of verse, including lines of dramatic monologue and introspective soliloquy, Cameron selected some of the most lyrical lines from *Maud* to illustrate the poem:

> She is coming, my dove, my dear;
> She is coming, my life, my fate.
> The red rose cries, 'She is near, she is near;'
> And the white rose weeps, 'She is late;'
> The larkspur listens, 'I hear, I hear;'
> And the lily whispers, 'I wait.'
>
> (*Maud*, I, x, ll. 910–15)

Finally, Cameron's photograph is a curious choice: for one thing, Tennyson's *Maud* lacks the lyric or epic qualities present in the other poetry she selected for the *Illustrations*. Tennyson called *Maud* 'a Monodrama', and the poem accosts readers with a relentless march that for the most part lacks narrative breaks or songs to allow the action to pause, to offer a different voice, or to balance the verse harmonically. In fact, the only 'interruption' from the narrator's extended rant are the two stanzas chosen by Cameron, verses which readers and critics have long admired.[72] In *Maud*, the narrator is male, and the character 'Maud' the object of his fixation. Since the male narrator in *Mariana* also speaks irrationally from an isolated world that is cut off from any positive connection with others, Cameron might have selected *Maud* as a kind of counterpoint to her photograph of *Mariana*.

But Tennyson used the poem to denounce the rising materialism of his time. The poem's narrator condemns Maud's 'millionaire' father and her *nouveau riche* suitor, a 'new-made lord'. In flight from having rashly killed Maud's brother, Tennyson's unstable narrator decides to flee England by enlisting and fighting in the Crimean War. Tennyson uses this overseas conflict as if it were an epic battleground where his narrator can find meaning and salvation, redemption for his meaningless actions. 'Ironically', writes Deirdre David, the Crimean War was 'a conflict not exactly fought for the Arthurian British heroism he seeks but rather a war in defence of British interests in India, and elsewhere, against the advances of the Russian bear'.[73] Written after the fact of the war, *Maud* actually commemorated Britain's Crimean War victory, and therefore its glorious military past, but also, by implication, the nation's potential for a glorious future. Critics recognized these qualities in the poem as early as 1855. In *Saturday Review*, for example, Goldwin Smith wrote that the poem displaced 'more real motives' with a bloodlust for war: 'What [the narrator] wants is not a just and necessary war, but war in itself – war, as a cure, first for the Mammonism of a nation which has still enough of the spiritual left in it to produce and honour a great poet, and secondly, for the hysterical mock-disease of a heart-broken and, one must add, guilty man.'[74]

The poem embodies longing for past national greatness, an expression of Tennyson's fear that it might be lost or slipping away. *Maud* also insists upon the need to defend imperial greatness and patriarchal honour, values that must be reinforced and secured because they are fugitive and perhaps not entirely justifiable, especially to the vanquished. Cameron's illustrated volume two appeared in May 1875, just three months prior to renewed political conflict with the Ottoman Empire, when Britain found itself again responding to domestic calls to wage war against the threat of Russian expansion, a threat referred to in Parliament as the 'Eastern Question'. In 1875, the rise of the 'Eastern Question' returned Britain to a global problem that had only been postponed, one that had not been truly resolved by the earlier Crimean War. Responding to renewed cries for combat on the one hand and for establishing a new colonial federation on the other,

Cameron's *Illustrations* make the case that the spiritual rebirth of the nation could emerge only when a restored 'King Arthur' could rise, like a phoenix, from the ashes of Sebastopol. The photograph of *Maud* closes Cameron's *Illustrations to Tennyson's Idylls of the King* because it calls, like the *Idylls* themselves, for a national rejuvenation of the British nation through war.[75] At the same time, this hybrid image acts as a counterbalance to Tennyson's militarism by recalling the lyric voices of his heroines and their personification of moral guidance and restraint.

## Notes

1  Tennyson, *The Epic*, first published in 1842 in *English Idylls and other Poems*, lines 30–2.

2  W. Lucas Collins, 'King Arthur and His Round Table', *Blackwood's Edinburgh Magazine*, September 1860, p. 311.

3  Julia Thomas, *Pictorial Victorians: The Inscription of Value in Word and Image* (Athens, OH: Ohio University Press, 2004), chapter 2. Tennyson's June 1859 edition turned out to be extremely popular: no less than 40,000 copies were printed in the first edition and 10,000 were sold within six months; in August, a second edition was published. See June Steffensen Hagen, 'Tennyson's Troubled Years with Moxon & Co.: A Publishing Relationship', *Browning Institute Studies*, 7 (1979), 25–6.

4  Quoted by Helmut Gernsheim, *Julia Margaret Cameron: Her Life and Photographic Work* (New York: Aperture, 1975), p. 42.

5  See, especially, Roger Simpson, *Camelot Regained: The Arthurian Revival and Tennyson, 1800–1849* (Cambridge: D.S. Brewer, 1990); John D. Rosenberg, *The Fall of Camelot: A Study of Tennyson's 'Idylls of the King'* (Cambridge, MA: Belknap Press of Harvard University Press, 1973); Robert H. MacDonald, *The Language of Empire: Myths and Metaphors of Popular Imperialism, 1880–1918* (Manchester: Manchester University Press, 1994); Elton Edward Smith, *Tennyson's 'Epic Drama'* (Lanham, MD: University Press of America, 1997); William E. Buckler, *Man and His Myths: Tennyson's Idylls of the King in Critical Context* (New York: New York University Press, 1984); Mark Girouard, *The Return to Camelot: Chivalry and the English Gentleman* (New Haven: Yale University Press, 1981); Debra Mancoff, *The Arthurian Revival in Victorian Painting* (New York: Garland, 1990).

6  Colin Graham, *Ideologies of Empire: Nation, Empire and Victorian Epic Poetry* (Manchester: Manchester University Press, 1998); Herbert F. Tucker, 'The Epic Plight of Troth in Idylls of the King', *English Literary History*, 58:3 (1991), 701–20; V. G. Kiernan, 'Tennyson, King Arthur, and Imperialism', in *Poets, Politics and the People*, ed. Harvey J. Kaye (London: Verso, 1989); Michael C. C. Adams, 'Tennyson's Crimean War Poetry: A Cross-Cultural Approach', *Journal of the History of Ideas*, 40:3 (1979), 405–22; Cecily Devereux, 'Canada and the Epilogue to the *Idylls*: "The Imperial Connection" in 1873', *Victorian Poetry*, 36:2 (1998), 223–45.

7  Linda Hughes and Michael Lund, *The Victorian Serial* (Charlottesville: University Press of Virginia, 1991), p. 128, and June Steffensen Hagen, *Tennyson and His Publishers* (London: Macmillan, 1979).

8  Adams, 'Tennyson's Crimean War Poetry', 405–22.

9  Kiernan, 'Tennyson, King Arthur, and Imperialism', p. 137.

10  For Swinburne's criticism, see John D. Jump, ed., *Tennyson: The Critical Heritage* (London: Routledge and Kegan Paul, 1967), pp. 318–21, and Kerry McSweeney, *Tennyson and Swinburne as Romantic Naturalists* (Toronto: University of Toronto Press, 1981). For criticisms by FitzGerald, Elizabeth Browning, Hopkins, Meredith, and Bridges, see Kiernan, 'Tennyson, King Arthur and Imperialism', esp. pp. 137–8.

11  Homi K. Bhabha, 'DissemiNation: time, narrative, and the margins of the modern nation', in *The Location of Culture* (London: Routledge, 1994), pp. 145–6.

12  The term is borrowed from Eve Kosofsky Sedgwick, *Between Men: English Literature and Male Homosexual Desire* (New York: Columbia University Press, 1985), see esp. chapter 7, 'Tennyson's *Princess*: One Bride for Seven Brothers'.

13  Joanne Lukitsch, 'Julia Margaret Cameron's Photographic Illustrations to Alfred Tennyson's "The Idylls of the King"', *Arthurian Literature*, 7 (1987), 145–57. On Tennyson's publishers, see Hagen, *Tennyson and His Publishers*, and Jim Cheshire, 'The Fall of the House of Moxon: James Bertrand Payne and the Illustrated Idylls of the King', *Victorian Poetry*, 50:1 (2012), 67–90.

14  Leslie Howsam, *Kegan Paul: A Victorian Imprint* (London: Kegan Paul International, 1998), p. 37.

15  Quoted in Gernsheim, *Julia Margaret Cameron*, pp. 45–6.

16  See Cheshire, 'The Fall of the House of Moxon', 72–3.

17  King took over for Alexander Strahan as described in the letters between Tennyson and James Thomas Knowles, in *The Letters of Alfred Lord Tennyson*, ed. Cecil Y. Lang and Edgar F. Shannon, Jr., vol. 3 (Oxford: Clarendon, 1990), pp. 26, 37, 59. See also, Hagen, *Tennyson and His Publishers*.

18  See Tennyson's letter thanking Doré and complementing him on his illustrations in *The Letters of Alfred Lord Tennyson*, ed. Cecil Y. Lang and Edgar F. Shannon, Jr., vol. 2 (Cambridge, MA: Harvard University Press, 1987), p. 452; Gordon Ray, *The Art of the French Illustrated Book, 1700–1914*, vol. 2 (New York: Pierpont Morgan Library and Cornell University Press, 1982), pp. 326–48; and Cheshire, 'The Fall of the House of Moxon', 68–9.

19  Quoted in Lukitsch, 'Julia Margaret Cameron's Photographic Illustrations to Alfred Tennyson's "The Idylls of the King"', 147, original emphasis.

20  Meyer Schapiro, *Words and Pictures: On the Literal and the Symbolic in the Illustration of a Text* (The Hague: Mouton, 1973).

21  *Ibid.*, p. 9.

22  *Ibid.*

23  See letter from Tennyson to Doré, 16 February 1867, in *The Letters of Alfred Lord Tennyson*, ed. Lang and Shannon, vol. 2, p. 452 (original in French).

24  Letter dated 4 December 1874, quoted in Lukitsh, 'Julia Margaret Cameron's Photographic Illustrations to Alfred Tennyson's "The Idylls of the King"', 153. In another letter, dated 15 December 1974, she wrote, 'Tennyson is himself very much pleased with this ideal representation of his Idylls.' Quoted in Gernsheim, *Julia Margaret Cameron*, p. 48.

25  See Thomas, *Pictorial Victorians*, pp. 54–5.

26  'Photographic Illustrations of Tennyson', *The Times*, 14 October 1875, p. 4.

27  Quoted in A. Dwight Culler, *The Poetry of Tennyson* (New Haven: Yale University Press, 1977), pp. 223, 269, n. 5.

28  Hallam writes that his father 'founded his epic', and wrote an 'earliest fragment of an epic', refers to 'the epical King Arthur', and to the poem's 'Epic unity'. Quoted in Buckler, *Man and His Myths*, p. 10.

29  Georg Lukacs, 'Narrate Or Describe: A Preliminary Discussion of Naturalism and Formalism' [1936], in *Writer and Critic and Other Essays*, ed. and trans. Alfred D. Kahn (New York: Grosset and Dunlap, 1970), p. 126.

30  Quoted in Lukitsh, 'Julia Margaret Cameron's Photographic Illustrations to Alfred Tennyson's "The Idylls of the King"', 153.

31  *Ibid.*, original emphasis.

32  See M. M. Bakhtin, *The Dialogic Imagination*, trans. Caryl Emerson and Michael Holquist, ed. Michael Holquist (Austin: University of Texas Press, 1981), pp. 15–16.

33  Monique Morgan, *Narrative Means, Lyric Ends: Temporality in the Nineteenth-Century Long Poem* (Columbus: Ohio State University Press, 2009), p. 4. Years ago, Cora Kaplan made a similar observation in introducing Elizabeth Barrett Browning's poem *Aurora Leigh. Aurora Leigh and other poems* (London: The Women's Press, 1978); my thanks to Griselda Pollock for this reference.

34  See John R. Reed, 'Tennyson's Narrative on Narration', *Victorian Poetry*, 24:2 (1986), 198.

35  Tucker, 'The Epic Plight of Troth in Idylls of the King', 716.

36  Cameron's interest in the poem had been a long-standing source of inspiration; she made two images of the May Queen in 1864 (Cox 1068, 1069).

37  Bakhtin, *The Dialogic Imagination*, p. 358.

38  *Ibid.*, p. 361.

39  Rosenberg, *The Fall of Camelot*, pp. 64–5.

40  Quoted in Victoria C. Olsen, *From Life: Julia Margaret Cameron and Victorian Photography* (New York: Palgrave Macmillan, 2003), p. 236; original emphasis.

41  Quoted in Elliot L. Gilbert, 'The Female King: Tennyson's Arthurian Collapse', *PMLA*, 98:5 (1983), 876, n. 2.

42  Algernon Charles Swinburne, 'Under the Microscope', in *Swinburne Replies*, ed. Clyde K. Kyder (Syracuse: Syracuse University Press, 1966), p. 57.

43  Isobel Armstrong noted that some conservative reviewers of the 1860s interpreted the *Idylls* positively for the poem's 'depoliticized Englishness' that celebrated pastoral life, domesticity, and simplified roles for men and women; *Victorian Poetry: Poetry, Poetics, and Politics* (London: Routledge, 1993), pp. 500–1, n. 27.

44  *Ibid.*, pp. 270–83; Deirdre David, *Rule Britannia: Women, Empire and Victorian Writing* (Ithaca, NY: Cornell University Press, 1995), pp. 167–81.

45  Quoted in Jump, *Tennyson: The Critical Heritage*, p. 250.

46  Quoted in Rosenberg, *The Fall of Camelot*, pp. 21–2.

47  Graham, *Ideologies of Empire*, p. 30.

48  Devereux, 'Canada and the Epilogue to the *Idylls*', 224.

49  Hughes and Lund, *The Victorian Serial*, p. 151.

50  Quoted in *The Letters of Alfred Lord Tennyson*, ed. Lang and Shannon, vol. 2, p. 297, n. 3.

51  Hannah Pakula, *An Uncommon Woman: The Empress Frederick, Daughter of Queen Victoria, Wife of the Crown Prince of Prussia, Mother of Kaiser Wilhelm* (New York: Simon and Schuster, 1995), p. 158.

52  Letter from Tennyson to the Duke of Argyll, [25] February] 1862, in *The Letters of Alfred Lord Tennyson*, ed. Lang and Shannon, vol. 2, p. 297.

53  Kiernan, 'Tennyson, King Arthur and Imperialism', p. 136.

54  Letter from Alfred Tennyson to Emily Tennyson, dated 9 July 1871, in *The Letters of Alfred Lord Tennyson*, ed. Lang and Shannon, vol. 3, p. 8.

55  *The Letters of the Empress Frederick*, ed. Sir Frederick Ponsonby (London: Macmillan, 1929), p. 128.

56  Quoted in Pakula, *An Uncommon Woman*, pp. 72–3.

57  *Ibid.*, pp. 188–90.

58  Charles Wentworth Dilke, *Greater Britain: A Record of Travel in English-Speaking Countries in 1866–7* (London: Macmillan, 1869).

59  C. C. Eldridge, *England's Mission: The Imperial Idea in the Age of Gladstone and Disraeli, 1868–1880* (London: Macmillan, 1973), p. 111.

60  James Spedding, 'The Future of the British Empire', *Westminster Review*, American edn, 94 (July–October 1870), 30.

61  Eldridge, *England's Mission*, p. 238; Gilbert, 'The Female King', 865ff.; David, *Rule Britannia*, pp. 173–5.

62   Letter from the Crown Princess Victoria to Queen Victoria, 6 July 1873, in Roger Fulford, ed., *Darling Child: Private Correspondence of Queen Victoria and the Crown Princess of Prussia, 1871–1878* (London: Evans Brothers, 1976), p. 101.

63   Letter from the Crown Princess to Queen Victoria, 11 November 1874, in Fulford, *Darling Child*, p. 161.

64   Robert Blake, *Disraeli* (London: Eyre and Spottiswoode, 1966), p. 540.

65   In a letter to Queen Victoria from Berlin on 30 November 1875, the Crown Princess wrote: 'I must congratulate you on the newest deed of your Government, the buying of half the shares of the Suez Canal; it sent a thrill of pleasure and pride, almost of exultation through me. It is a delightful thing to see the right thing done at the right moment. Everybody is pleased here and wishes it may bring England good.' Fulford, *Darling Child*, p. 199.

66   In James Knowles, 'Aspects of Tennyson, II', *Nineteenth Century* (January 1893), p. 182, quoted in Jump, *Tennyson: The Critical Heritage*, p. 172.

67   Kerry McSweeny, *Tennyson and Swinburne as Romantic Naturalists* (Toronto: University of Toronto Press, 1981), p. 63.

68   See R. Derek Wood, *Julia Margaret Cameron's Copyrighted Photographs* (London: privately published, May 1996), copy archived at the Royal Photographic Society, Bath, and online at www.midley.co.uk/cameron/cameron.pdf, entries numbered 91, 116, 224–7.

69   *Ibid.*

70   See *Musical Instruments of the World: An Illustrated Encyclopedia* (London: Paddington Press, 1976), pp. 164–7; Jean-Sebastien Laurenty, *Cordophones du Congo Belge et du Ruanda-Urundi*, 2 vols. (Tervuren, Belgium: Musée Royal du Congo belge, 1960), vol. 2, plates 17, 22; and *Musical Instruments from the Horniman Museum, London* (London: Inner London Educational Authority, 1970), pp. 67, 72–3. Many thanks to Dr David C. Hunter, Music Librarian at the Fine Arts Library of the University of Texas at Austin for his assistance in locating these instruments.

71   Rosenberg, *The Fall of Camelot*, pp. 93–5.

72   Smith, *Tennyson's 'Epic Drama'*, pp. 36–7.

73   David, *Rule Britannia*, p. 180.

74   Quoted in Jump, *Tennyson: The Critical Heritage*, p. 186.

75   Adams, 'Tennyson's Crimean War Poetry', pp. 417–20.

# 7

# North's gardens:
# redemption and the return to origins

## Leaving Freshwater

Virginia Woolf offered two reasons to explain why the Camerons left Freshwater in 1875. In her foreword to *Victorian Photographs of Famous Men and Fair Women* (1926), she described their decision to 'return to the East' as a combination of Charles's longing to live out the final days of his life in peace and warmth, surrounded by nature, and their shared desire to live near their sons in Ceylon, where they could reduce their cost of living and keep an eye on their estates. Once their preparations were made, they left Freshwater in October 1875. Woolf noted that their closest friends came to say goodbye at the port of Southampton:

> Two coffins preceded them on board packed with glass and china, in case coffins should be unprocurable in the East; the old philosopher with his bright fixed eyes and his beard 'dipt in moonlight' held in one hand his ivory staff and in the other Lady Tennyson's parting gift of a pink rose; while Mrs Cameron, 'grave and valiant', vociferated her final injunctions and controlled not only innumerable packages but a cow.[1]

In her satiric play, *Freshwater*, Woolf assigned the task of announcing their departure to Ceylon to 'Mary', one of the two housemaids, after which she imagined the following dialogue:

> **Mrs C.:** At last, the coffins have come.
> **Mr C.:** The coffins have come.
> **Mrs C.:** Let us pack our coffins and go.
> **Mr C.:** To the land of perpetual moon shine –
> **Mrs C.:** To the land where the sun never sets.
> **Mr C.:** I shan't want trousers in India –
> **Mrs C.:** No that's true. But I shall want wet plates – [2]

Woolf understood clearly that once she arrived in Ceylon, Cameron had no intention of abandoning photography. 'Within doors, Mrs Cameron still photographed', she wrote in *Victorian Photographs*, and then described in some detail how in 1877, the Camerons received a visit from a traveller from England, Marianne North, in the coastal town of Kalutara.

Woolf described Cameron's three-day effort to take photographs of Marianne North, which suggests that she was familiar with North's autobiography, *Recollections of a Happy Life* (1892), where North described her encounter with Cameron.[3] It is possible that Woolf knew of the photographs, although none are included in *Victorian Photographs*. Woolf also knew of North's history through her own personal biography: the Symonds frequently visited the Stephens, and it was North's sister, Catherine North Symonds, who edited *Recollections*. In the winter of 1889–90, when Virginia Woolf was only seven, Catherine's daughter, Madge, lived with the Stephen family in London, and apparently Madge left a lasting impression on the Stephen children.[4] Years later, Woolf used Kew Gardens, where the Marianne North Gallery is located, as the setting and title of her short story of 1919. When one of Woolf's characters says to his companion, 'Come along, Trissie; it's time we had our tea', it is to a building that housed 'little white tables, and waitresses' located near the Marianne North Gallery that they go.[5]

Marianne North achieved renown during her day as an accomplished botanical illustrator.[6] A self-sufficient woman of independent means, North devoted her early life to caring for her widowed father, learning to paint while travelling with him, and was encouraged in her botanical representations by Joseph Dalton Hooker, a family friend who was also the chief botanist at the Royal Botanic Gardens at Kew. When her father died, she found that she enjoyed travelling alone more so than in the company of others, and in 1876, embarked upon on a round-the-world trip, creating hundreds of paintings. By and large, these paintings are relatively small, designed for portability with most no larger that one by two feet, and are brilliantly coloured. Upon her return to England in 1877, she exhibited some five hundred of her paintings at the South Kensington Museum, garnering generally favourable reviews. In 1879, she exhibited her botanical paintings in Conduit Street, London, and then again, later that same year, she donated funds to erect a building to house her paintings in the grounds of the Royal Botanic Gardens at Kew. Three years later, 832 of these paintings were installed in the new Marianne North Gallery, where they remain today.

The meeting between North and Cameron produced several works by each artist, and some notable cross-fertilization in their styles, particularly when they represented a similar scene in each other's company. Before examining that influence, it is useful first to examine the narrative spaces occupied by North and Cameron, as each artist recorded her impressions both verbally, in letters (and in North's case, a diary), and in visual representations, producing paintings and photographs which expressed their own brand of visual conventions and strategies. In their written travel narratives, both women revealed their class awareness, describing superior attitudes toward the native populations they encountered.

Their observations are entitled and penetrating rather than withdrawn and recessive, however, denying a stereotype commonly attributed to British women travellers of this time, which Mary Louise Pratt has called 'the guilt of the sight'.[7] By contrast, both North and Cameron adopted a surveyor's active and possessive approach. Theirs is a penetration of broad scope that swallows up both the landscape and its inhabitants. These women, after all, were used to naming, framing, rearranging, and representing their world; they were not content to portray it passively.[8]

As the chief protagonist of their travels and agent of their independent artistic lives, they freely drew upon another privilege that characterizes their visual representations: at no time did they question their right to portray the subjects they chose. Although North's subjects were botanical, she also represented men and women of the colonies she visited, always in relation to a plant specimen or in a garden context. And although Cameron's subjects were people, it seems she focused solely on native islanders in her Ceylonese imagery, other than the portrait sessions she held with North. When the two worked in each other's company, both artists joined together elements of the picturesque and the primitive in a self-assured and confident manner. Their visual strategies framed their subjects to create narratives, in letters and diary entries, but also in paintings and photographs, where the picturesque and the primitive emerged as central motifs. These are evident, in part, in the ways that Cameron and North manipulated well-worn artistic conventions that portrayed foreign lands and their inhabitants as pure and unblemished by traces of industry or modern life, exotic relics that escaped both time and the progress of history. But we shall also examine how Cameron's and North's merging of the picturesque and the primitive in their narratives reveals their connection to British colonialism and, from their position in the world far from London, to the making of British national identity.

As they constructed their letters and diary entries as well as their works of art, Julia Margaret Cameron and Marianne North confronted their own narratives of home and displacement. The artists' objectifying gaze has frozen the native subjects depicted by both women; they frequently appear stiff and awkward, or stand unnaturally erect in an artificial manner. As subjects of Cameron's and North's gaze, they record the artist's own physical displacement from home. At the same time, these native subjects are never identified. Because they are nameless, they provide representational doubles or stand-ins for a 'primitive' and pre-industrial age, no longer depicting individuals but points of reference marking visual and cultural difference from Western norms. The colonized land and its people have been represented as subjects which are themselves dislocated and displaced, in part because they have been communicated through the multiple anxieties that characterize the expression of colonialism. Earlier, Cameron confronted East–West relationships in her portraits of Prince Alamayou and Captain Speedy. But because Cameron and North represented native subjects in Ceylon and disregarded the identities of the known individuals they depicted, their subjects have been transformed as a result. When the British artist represented the Ceylonese native islander, her subjects embodied the artist's internal conflicts, which demanded, on the one hand, that she support and endorse the colonial agenda, while on the other hand, that she repress uncomfortable and awkward social confrontations. North's encounters with Cameron in 1877 also make it possible to tell a redemptive story, as both artists dealt with their uncertainties by first articulating, and then undermining, an ideology of national salvation and deliverance, in which the present is redeemed by returning to a more authentic past, and one revealed through 'the return to origins': an eternally present and timeless worldview. North's meeting with Cameron at the edge of the Empire afforded them both an opportunity to create imagery affirming 'national greatness', especially when greatness was expressed as nation-building: from both North's and Cameron's point of view, Britain's colonial activities were redeemed when Ceylon was transformed from a land of 'primitive simplicity' into an economic and political force in 'British Asia'.

## 'Going home': the return to origins

How did the Camerons define 'home'? Julia Margaret Pattle lived her early years as a colonist, first in India, then in France, briefly in the Cape of Good Hope; then, after marrying Charles Cameron, she lived in India again, before coming to London and the Isle of Wight. Throughout this latter period, she stood ready to accompany Charles to Malta, back to India, possibly to Ceylon, even to the Ionian islands. Family income during these years also came from abroad: two large plantations on Ceylon, one called Dimbola, the other Rathoongodde, produced coffee, then tea; together, their combined holdings made the Camerons the largest private landowners on the island. After first settling in London and then on the Isle of Wight, Charles made frequent trips to conduct business on the island, and Julia Margaret remained in their Freshwater home. This period lasted fifteen years. While she often worried about her husband during these long trips, she had no doubt too that he was visiting something approaching an island paradise, having been assured that Ceylon was lush with a picturesque tropical growth that was punctuated by rushing mountain streams. The unmistakable psychological connection between home and 'home-away-from-home' was solidified by Julia Margaret in naming her Freshwater home 'Dimbola', after the Ceylonese plantation, and her picturesque sensibility of the land influenced markedly by her husband's numerous effusive letters. Yet she had no immediate wish to join him, nor to pick up the family and relocate to the colony. In order to persuade her otherwise, Charles named waterfalls for her, rebuilt the plantation's cabins to approach Western specifications, and drew pictures of a lush and welcoming landscape (Figure 7). Despite his ardent enticements, Julia Margaret never chose to accompany her husband or their sons to the island until October 1875.

When the time actually came for her to travel to Ceylon, Julia Margaret likened her journey to a kind of spiritual rebirth. Writing to her friend Lady Ritchie during her passage through the Suez Canal, Cameron asserted,

> O what good it does to one's soul to go forth! How it heals all the little frets and insect-stings of life, to feel the pulse of the large world and to count all men as one's brethren and to merge one's individual self in the thoughts of the mighty whole![9]

Feeling the 'pulse of the large world', counting 'all men as one's brethren': in 1875, Julia Margaret Cameron was 'going home'. As Marianna Torgovnick reminds us, 'the metaphor of finding a home or being at home, recurs over and over as a structuring pattern within [the discourses of] Western primitivism. Going primitive is trying to "go home" to a place that feels comfortable and balanced,' [for] "going home," like "going primitive," is inescapably a metaphor for the return to origins.'[10] In the act of the physical journey itself lies a search for deep psychological connections, even a universalizing impulse: '"Going home" involves only an individual journey – actual or imaginative – to join with a "universal" mankind in the primitive. There can be no homelessness then.'[11] The words primitive and primitivism are essential terms for this analysis, because they historically capture the narrative strategy that joins the myth of timeless origins with the evolutionary beliefs of the nineteenth century. Universalism is an important related concept – 'merging one's individual self in the thoughts of the mighty whole', as Cameron phrased it.

When the concept of 'going home' is located in representations of 'the primitive', the return to origins takes on an unforeseen magical ability to dissolve historical differences, 'creating an illusion of time and sense in which the primitive is both eternally past and eternally present. For the charm to work, the primitive must represent a common [Western] past so long gone that we find no traces of it in Western spaces.'[12] Primitivism is therefore eternally present if one has access to the spaces of primitive peoples. An anxious fear emerges as a result, requiring that any evidence of origins must be preserved against the possibility that they should disappear for all eternity, whether owing to indifference or to active destruction. In this respect, Cameron's photographs of the native inhabitants of the island and North's paintings of its fragile and disappearing flora help us situate their need to preserve the pure spaces of newly found primitivism in the midst of the encroaching colonial appropriation of the land and the new social laws established by the British to govern its people.

During her voyage to the island, Cameron anticipated her own well-being there using such terms, expecting to find in Ceylon not only a metaphorical connection of the island to the colonial centre, but also a spiritual connection to the 'universal primitive', especially when she expressed her sense of merging into the 'thoughts of the mighty whole'. When she finally arrived and established her new home, she found her anticipation confirmed, regarding Ceylon as England's 'Tropical sister'. After one year in Ceylon, she wrote:

> My first impressions have been modified – confirmed or effaced – My wonder for instance has been tamed but not my worship – The glorious beauty of the scenery – the primitive simplicity of the Inhabitants & the charms of the climate all make me love and admire Ceylon more and more. I do not think our severe Island of England at all recognizes the charms of her Tropical sister[.] They have only to be studied; for all the weak and fragile Inhabitants of our Northern Climes to flock here with the Instinct of the swallow and to find a sure redemption from every disease … combined with exquisite enjoyment: for dead indeed must be the soul who is not satisfied with Nature as here presented to the eye.[13]

Many of her Ceylonese photographs are not only inflected with her sense of native primitive simplicity and pure uncontaminated nature; they also express Cameron's conviction that a 'sure redemption' was made possible by returning to one's origins.

For Cameron, the natives were not only simple, as in child-like or uneducated, but also inherently incomplete in themselves. She framed many of her female subjects in such a way to represent them stereotypically as 'outside of history': pressed to the front of the picture plane, robed in flowing saris and jewelled arm-bands, removed from social interaction, and objectified in front of an abstract backdrop, they depict clichés of exotic and eternal beauty, idealized feminine symbolism (fecundity), and passive colonial subjects (Cox 1207 – Figure 46; and Cox 1209 – Figure 47).[14] In these examples, they also embody archaic mythological elements, especially when Cameron or North instructed them to hold a vase while modelling (Cox 1211). Traditional iconography associates vases of this kind with ancient water-carriers and could suggest the persistence of ancient traditions, but these are also props associated with immortal nymphs and river goddesses, items associated with timeless beauty. The outsider status, or 'exteriority of Orientalism'[15] is a paradox of the worldview expressed here, because the island girls are judged as culturally wanting from the outside but are also connected directly to the 'more advanced society' in evolutionary terms; in short, the two worlds are 'tethered' to each other.[16]

The representational strategy which equates the primitive and 'the return to origins' is therefore founded upon notions of universality and transcendence, as Torgovnick reminds us, because 'origins [must] transcend family, class, religion, or homeland', and all journeys which attempt to 'go home', to experience the primitive origins of mankind, are dependent upon a kind of reconciliation, even atonement, invoking the harmonious joining of the Westerner '[to] a "universal"

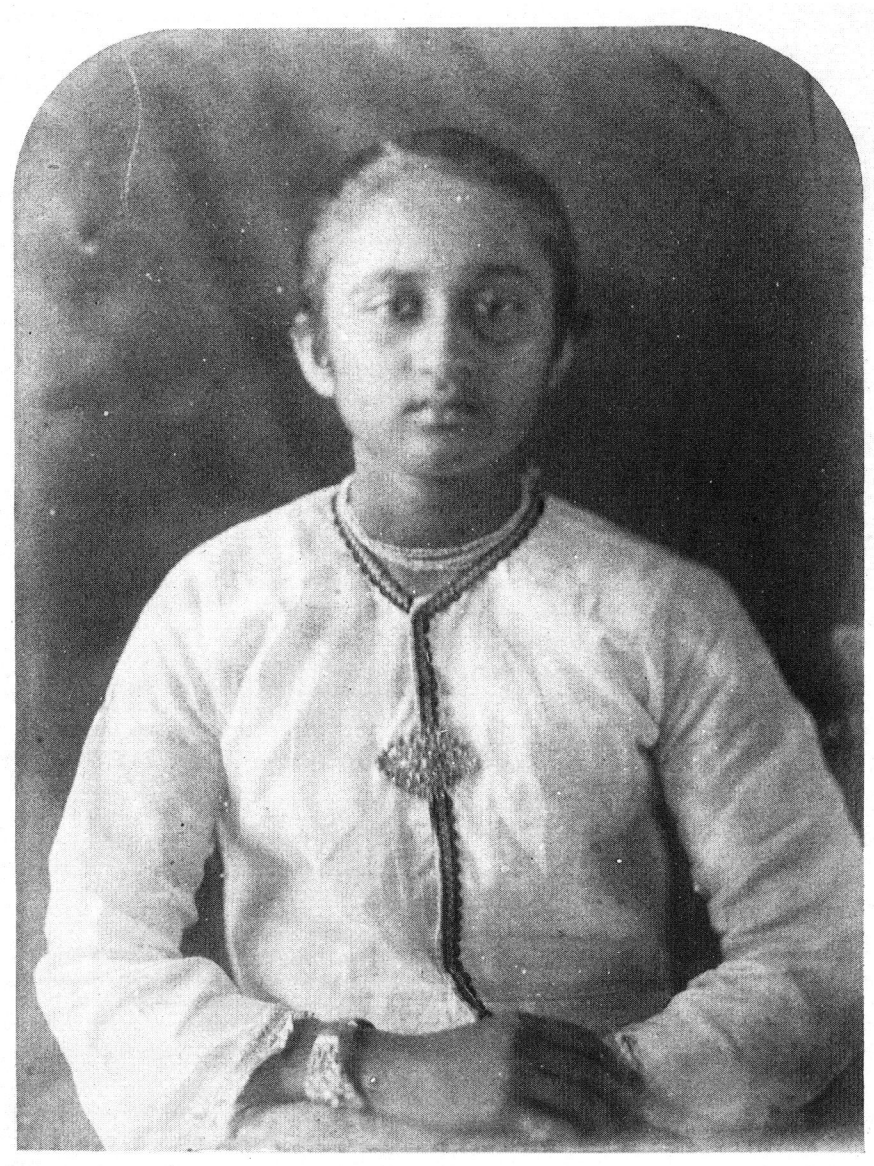

46        Julia Margaret Cameron, [*Girl, Ceylon*] (Cox 1207), c. 1875–79.
Albumen print, 25.2 x 18.8 cm.

mankind in the primitive'.[17] In a pair of telling photographs of an native island woman, Cameron appears to have effected a transformation into the universal and transcendent by creating a 'before and after' change, one made possible by altering her subject's pose and costume. In one image, a girl sits impassively before Cameron's lens, her hair pulled back behind her head, her chemise fastened to

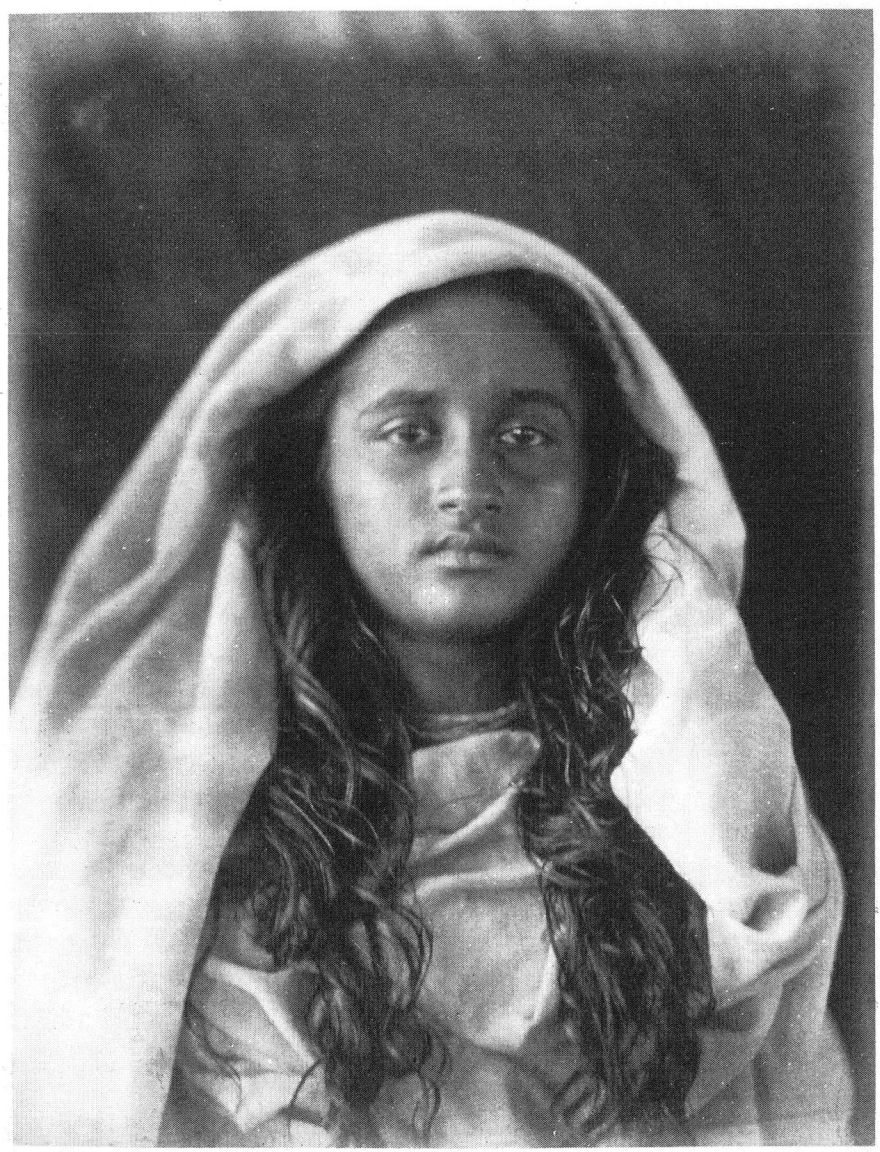

Julia Margaret Cameron, [*Young Woman, Ceylon*] (Cox 1209), c. 1875–79.          **47**
Albumen print, 24.5 x 18.3 cm.

the neckline and sleeves reaching each wrist (Figure 46). Jewellery is modestly
confined to a two-strand necklace, a bracelet, and a brooch. A second image
shows the same girl transformed (Figure 47): her long black hair is now loose,
appears wet, and cascades in long spirals in front of her on two sides; she now
wears a white cloak and fabric head covering, both deeply folded in an excess of

material; and while vestiges of her necklace remain, all other jewellery has been removed. The effect is one of effacement and abstraction: the explicit Western blouse has been replaced by an undefined Eastern drapery, less revealing than the fabric that also drapes Cameron's two models in her re-enactment of the Elgin Marbles pediment (Cox 1110); but more similar to the arrangement of holy draperies surrounding the Madonna, if we compare it to *La Madonna* (1867) (Cox 102), or *The Sphinx Madonna* (1864) (Cox 64), or a penitent Magdalene, as exemplified by an untitled photograph of 1869 (Cox 197). By removing evidence of the real world in her photograph of the Ceylonese girl, Cameron has removed traces of her identity, erasing family, class, and homeland; in short, she has 'universalized' her subject. While Cameron's authorship of these images have never been in doubt, they were never exhibited during her lifetime and their aesthetic value has been the source of much debate among art historians, although none have considered the act of reconciliation described here.[18]

At the same time, a different sort of message is also embedded in this imagery, one tied to the civilizing mission of colonialism, the stated purpose of which was to bring rational order to primitive societies in the form of modern governmental codes and civil procedures; sound forms of economic practice, educational policy, and labour regulations; and rational political structures. Both Charles and Julia Margaret were committed to spread this mission: years earlier, as a member of Thomas Macaulay's Commission overseeing the establishment of the judicial code in India, Charles Cameron had recommended to the British government that it was Britain's proper role and moral duty as a superior nation to venture into primitive lands to modernize the feudal social order they found and develop those institutions and political economies in the model established by advanced Western societies, with improved labour systems, upgraded communications and means of transportation, and advanced systems of law and education. With respect to Ceylon, Charles Cameron stated these ideas explicitly in a brief written in 1832 recommending judicial and governmental reforms to the colonial administration of the island:

> [T]he peculiar circumstances of Ceylon, both physical and moral, seem to point it out to the British Government as the fittest spot in our Eastern dominions in which to plant the germ of European civilization, whence we may not unreasonably hope that it will hereafter spread over the whole of those vast territories.[19]

As articulated by Charles Cameron and the Colonial Office, Ceylon was seen as emerging out of its infancy and developing toward Western norms, and for Julia Margaret, the 'primitivism of the island' was an unquestioned truth; both views were confirmed by prevailing Orientalist attitudes.[20] According to the theories informing this view, the 'origins of primitive man' could be found in 'primitive' cultures as remnants, relics, or cultural artefacts.

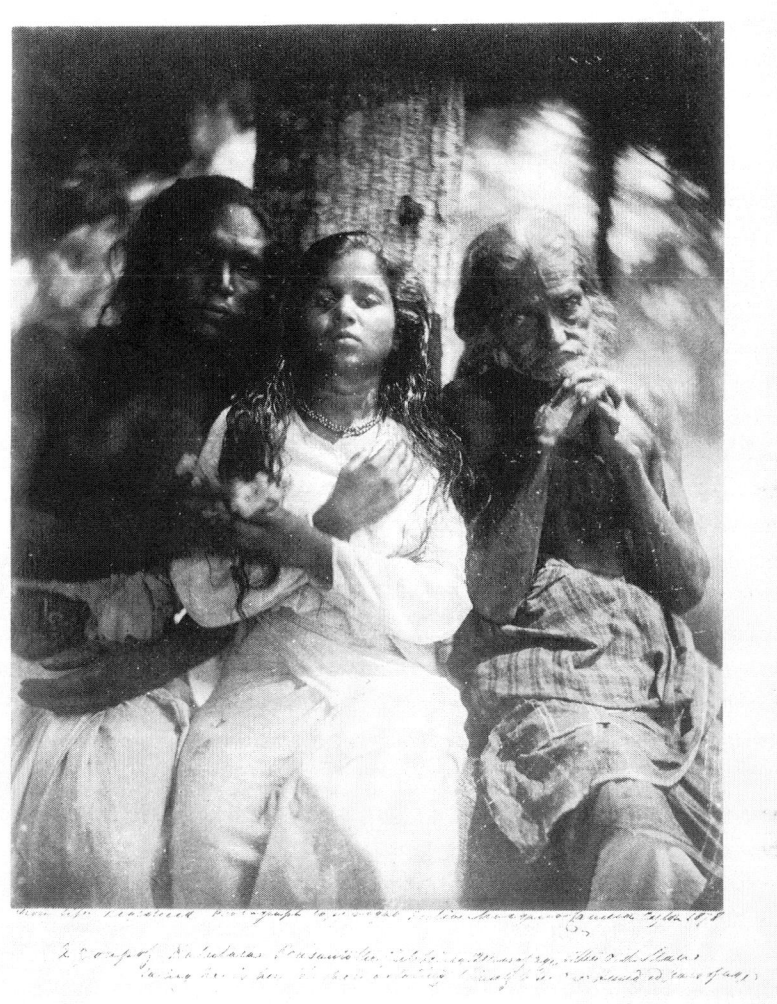

Julia Margaret Cameron, *A group of Kalutara peasants* (Cox 1216), 1878.        **48**
Albumen print, 34.3 x 27.2 cm.

In a telling photograph that seems to probe these cultural associations, Cameron depicted three generations of a native family group (Cox 1216; Figure 48) and labelled each print as if it were anthropological evidence for the persistence of the primitive in the present: beneath the print, she wrote: 'A group of Kalutara peasants, the girl being 12 years of age, the old man saying he is her father and stating himself to be 100 years of age'. On the reverse side of another print, in addition to these words, Cameron wrote, 'From Life Registered Photograph Copyright Julia Margaret Cameron Ceylon 1878'. In each image, three individuals are posed in front of a tree; its trunk provides a formal architecture to the group, as a young man and an old man flank a young girl in the centre. While the girl is fully clothed, the two men are naked to the waist. One image represents the group from head to knee; the other standing full-length. There is no doubt about Cameron's authorship here, nor her desire to reproduce this image for sale in accordance with the pattern she had established throughout her career; however, there is no corresponding entry in the copyright registers and no surviving record of her plans to exhibit the work publicly.

These photographs invite speculation into the subjects' line of progeny while simultaneously branding the group as emblematic of the persistence of primitivism. For example, the image contains markers of virility (fatherhood at age eighty-eight), fecundity (the girl aged twelve), tribal ancestry and unbroken familial lineage, and longevity, finding in each quality a primitive element or signifier that was uncomplicated and uninterrupted. In this regard, Cameron's text seems to reference the observations of British travel narratives written in the early 1800s about the sexuality and premature aging of the native population, where it was remarked that girls were routinely married by the age of twelve.[21] In both photographs of the three subjects, Cameron does not identify the second man by type (how is he related to the others, if at all?), but the implication is clear that he is part of the assembled group by some family connection. Because she has turned her subjects into symbols that stand for the native population as a whole, these subjects occupy a complicated narrative space that cannot be contained by the artist's verbal inscription alone.[22] She has situated this group in nature and recorded their family association as part of the natural world; at the same time, she has claimed this group of peasants as British colonial subjects, layering upon them cultural associations that emphasize their difference from Victorian practices while also pointing out their reality as part of the enduring situation that Britain encountered in the colonies, one that inherited such complex family associations as are depicted here, which were based on local tradition and customs demonstrably foreign to British conventions.

Charles Hay Cameron's work in 1832 establishing the judicial codes of Ceylon was instrumental in framing the new social structures that would become responsible for creating 'appropriate civil behaviour' in the colony. The ramifications of this so-called civilizing mission had a profound psychological impact, as Ashis Nandy has described. For example, the marked passivity, weakness, and immaturity of the three subjects in Cameron's image of the twelve-year-old girl with her hundred-year-old father could be taken as evidence of subservience and inferiority. Indeed, Cameron inscribed these factual and symbolic qualities in her own hand. For Nandy, British law and civil codes helped to foster an uncomfortable cultural consensus among the colonized men and women of 'British Asia', in which the political and psychological roles of dominance and submission were accepted mutually, by colonizers and colonized alike:

In such a culture, colonialism was not seen as an absolute evil. For the subjects, it was a product of one's own emasculation and defeat in legitimate power politics. For the rulers, colonial exploitation was an incidental and regrettable by-product of a philosophy of life that was in harmony with superior forms of political and economic organization.[23]

For Charles Cameron, it was Britain's role and moral duty as a superior nation to venture into primitive lands, like Ceylon, to transform the social apparatus and institutions of such societies into advanced civic and political structures. Because he was a follower of the Utilitarian Jeremy Bentham and member of the Political Economy Club in London, Charles Hay Cameron is often referred to as a 'social reformer', as his political views stressed the role of law and education in 'obtaining personal liberty for the native population', and in attaining 'civil equality and respect for the individual based on Christian principles', following the traditions of Bentham and John Stuart Mill. Charles Cameron was certainly devoted to the idea of fostering education in the colonies, especially the promotion of the teaching of English, following Macaulay's lead.[24] But in spite of the evident political context in which the Camerons functioned in Ceylon, contemporary historians have persistently claimed that social altruism, rather than any particular colonial agenda, motivated the Camerons; for Charles, they attribute benevolence and paternalism; for Julia Margaret, compassion and concern.[25] Letters and documents, however, reveal baser motives at work.

In his governmental role, Charles Cameron did support the creation of a strong judiciary in Ceylon, believing that the British paternalistic model would champion and protect the 'rights of inferiors', meaning those of low caste or who held few economic resources, so guarding against the possible exploitation of the native Ceylonese by others, spreading equality in relationship to the law as a social good. But in the jurist's view, it was also necessary to embed within the new governmental structures examples of moral lessons and civil responsibilities, especially in Ceylon:

> The truth is, that the administration of justice to [Ceylonese] natives is of far more importance than its administration to Europeans, because they are so much less disposed to do justice to each other voluntarily; and I know of no instrument so powerful for gradually inducing upon them habits of honesty and sincerity as a judicial establishment, by which fraud and falsehood may be exposed to the greatest possible risk of detection and punishment.[26]

New judicial institutions were therefore designed to contain elements of social engineering: a core value and implicit goal of the Colebrooke–Cameron reforms of 1832 effectively recommended that the legal apparatus produce positive civic outcomes that would lead to the exposure and punishment of fraud and abuse, resulting in an improved social order and a more honest citizenry. This process has been described by David Scott: 'What the rationality of colonial power is doing

[here] is inscribing a new authoritative game of justice into the colonized space, one which the colonized could accept or resist, but to whose rules they would have to respond.' To Scott, such instances of 'colonial governmentality' characterize the 'Benthamite principle of inducing desired effects on conduct by a careful and economic weighting of rewards and punishments'.[27] As Charles Cameron proposed, the European judicial model would act as a kind of 'overseeing eye' in its new incarnation in Ceylon, effectively replicating the authority and control that was associated with rational systems of court proceedings and due process. There, the 'eye of the court' itself could produce the same desired effects of Bentham's panopticon in producing docile subjects and inscribing the literal seat of power.[28] According to Charles Cameron:

> The juror performs his functions under the eye of an European judge, and of the European and Indian public, and in circumstances which almost preclude the possibility of bribery or intimidation … In such a situation [the native] has very little motive to do wrong, and he yet feels and learns to appreciate the consciousness of rectitude. The importance that he justly attaches to the office renders it agreeable to him; and he not only pays great attention to the proceedings, but for the most part takes an active part in them.[29]

As a result, Cameron's proposals empowered the judiciary to become yet another instrument of governmental rationality, the improved and 'reformed' institutions now able to establish 'a regulatory technique that would reach down to the very "motives" of the native and not only constrain or induce him to alter them but also encourage him to appreciate the alteration'.[30]

A related set of laws possessing similar incentives encouraged the spread of English in regional schools across the island. These laws originated with Macaulay, Cameron's former superior in India, conceived initially to create in colonial India 'a class of interpreters between us [the English colonists] and the millions whom we govern – a class of persons, Indians in blood and colour, but English in taste, in opinion, in morals and in intellect'.[31] This short statement captures the essence of the colonial project, and it was internalized by Charles Cameron: a decade or so after serving on the Council of India, when travelling in Ceylon solely to survey the health of his coffee plantations, Cameron helped to advance this cause in small but direct ways, as he himself reported in a letter to Julia Margaret in 1850 from Ceylon: 'I dismounted at Kikligosgodde to visit the school. There are 27 Kandyan boys in it. I heard five or six of them had english [sic] very nicely, and promised to give prizes to those who should make most progress. The schoolmaster is a colonial man of very respectable appearance.'[32] Years earlier, in 1823, when Colebrooke and Cameron were first charged with reforming the judicial and administrative codes of the island colony, the acquisition of English was mandated for those aspiring to administrative posts. As Colebrooke later observed in his recommendations, 'A competent knowledge of the English language should … be required in the principal native functionaries throughout the country. The prospect of future advancement to situations now exclusively held by Europeans will constitute a most powerful inducement with the natives of high caste to relinquish many absurd prejudices, and to qualify themselves for general employment.'[33] These inducements served Macaulay's goals well by helping to foster a native population that was easy to manage and govern, simply because it had been (or would soon become) at least partially assimilated.

By effecting such reforms in Ceylon, Charles Cameron also helped to accomplish at least two important tasks of the colonial project: on the one hand, the legal system was imposed as a benevolent and patriarchal act, meant to keep unsophisticated children from hurting themselves while keeping them in line and fostering a healthy respect for the legal system. At the same time, the high European values of honesty, sincerity, and fairness were imparted, protecting the unprotected and preventing exploitation of the weak by the powerful. According to G. C. Mendis, the historian of the Ceylonese legal reforms, the new laws helped to establish that 'the bond between Britain and Ceylon could be maintained not by retaining British ascendancy in Government but by sharing power with the people, by giving them offices of trust, maintaining good relations between Europeans and Ceylonese and imparting justice equally to all, both rich and poor'.[34]

Julia Margaret was also well aware of British activities in the colony to improve the living conditions of the native islanders. In 1877, she wrote to Sir William Gregory, the colony's Governor-General, giving her impressions about the new projects begun under his watch. By citing various improvements to the means of transportation, health care, education, and the organization of labour made possible by the government's investments in the colony, she appears to regard land-reclamation as if it were a benevolent force, a necessary precursor to spreading civilization:

> The Bridge is as it were a monument to the Power of Europe flinging its iron embrace over the noble River – and in its solidity and stability proving itself a benefit to all, thro' all time … The Hospital is half way completed & presents a grand face already, ensuring air & ventilation cleanliness & comfort … Opposite the Hospital the road is to be cleared of all huts & open to the delicious health-giving Sea and next there is to be a clean & good Market & just beyond this the Station is to be built, so that next year the rail may steam more & more of civilization towards us & around us – But the improvement in the Irrigation of the whole district is a real golden change which marks the present Kalutara from the past Kalutara – and thank God not only the lands & pastures of the natives are improved but their actual minds & mental pastures seem to be becoming irrigated, & watered with little rills of perception as to the *benefit* of labour.[35]

To Cameron, the railway helped to spread civilization by installing its structures and erecting its enduring symbols, the Bridge a symbol of the enduring Power of

Europe, the Station a figurative marker for civilization's walled gates. This new infrastructure, in turn, helped to improve native minds and open up in them a willingness to consider changes to their tradition and history, in particular, as we shall see, to their attitudes toward labour, especially as the conditions of work were being redefined by the British during the 1870s in Ceylon.

During this time, the island's native population appeared to accept changes to the institutions of law and education and the expansion of the railway without opposition. The apparent civil accord and broad acceptance of the new order was accomplished because the new regulatory system was effectively invisible, in spite of the addition of new hospitals, schools, markets, and railway stations to the physical landscape. If Charles Cameron's reforms reconfigured the instruments of power, they did not democratize those institutions. Instead, by enacting a complex governmental strategy that sought to control social life as much as to internalize new codes of conduct among the native population, the new laws actually re-inscribed those codes in a different form. According to David Scott, the recommendations of Colebrooke and Cameron created dramatic social transformations as a result, which 'signal the reconfiguration of colonial power, its redistribution and redeployment in relation to new targets, new forms of knowledge, and new technologies, and its production of new effects of order and subjectivity'.[36]

We have seen that Julia Margaret confronted the expansion of colonial power in her photography before: in her portraits of Edward John Eyre and Thomas Carlyle, she promoted the justness of Governor Eyre's cause as he defended himself against charges that he had abused power in Jamaica; in her portraits of Prince Alamayou and Captain Speedy and of colonial administrators and explorers who had infiltrated Eastern lands, she romanticized the danger of their adventures in the act of advancing British interests abroad. And she marked the key moments of 1860s British colonial activity in her photography by using literature and myth, allegory and fancy pictures, to embody contemporary political debates: in *Paul and Virginia*, she confronted questions of British ancestry and colonial immigration; in the *Maid of Athens*, the return of the Ionian islands to Greece; in *Spear or Spare*, the conflicts that arose when European powers converged in their efforts to influence political economies abroad; in *Maud*, the call for national rebirth by waging war against other world powers in the struggle for colonial expansion and dominance. How did Cameron's awareness of the colonial project in Ceylon manifest itself in her photography? Before answering this question, it is useful to examine the social landscape that Cameron inherited when she arrived on the island, prior to her rendezvous with North in Kalutara, and to provide some of North's impressions about the living conditions of the native islanders.

## Representing political economy: 'the natural world as picturesque'

Marianne North's first impressions of Ceylon were informed by her awareness of the island's coastal terrain and its buildings, the roads that described general commerce and the houses that contained its working population. She recorded the presence of the British in the colony, especially as found in its railways and its botanic garden. These impressions, as she noted them in her diary, were inflected often by her own painterly sensibilities, which joined together elements of the primitive and the picturesque. For example, reflecting upon her voyage up the island's coast from her first stop, the port of Galle, to the island's colonial heart and its largest city, Colombo, North wrote the following diary entry. In this account, she compared in her mind's eye a picture of Java that she had made there only a short time before to the mental sketch she was then forming in preparation for another picture she would soon create once she was settled in Colombo:

> The road was most interesting all the way, near the beautiful shore or through swamps full of pandanus and other strange plants, with perpetual villages. I much missed the neat mat and bamboo houses of Java. In Ceylon they were mud-hovels, and everything was less neat, the people lazier, but the little bullock-carts were very pretty. There were plenty of flowers, many of those I remembered having seen in Jamaica.
>
> Colombo is most unattractive, but cooler than Galle. All its houses seemed in process of being either blown up or pulled down. My hotel had 'temporary' actually printed on the bills.[37]

The Ceylonese photographic firm of Scowen and Company helped to feed widespread interest both in international tourism and in collecting picturesque vignettes of poverty-stricken areas of the colony by producing photographs for collection in albums. Street scenes produced for the mass market actually correspond well to North's experience.

For North, Ceylon was simply another stop on her world tour, and it seems natural that she compared one land that was new to her to another that she just visited recently. But in invoking the former Dutch colony of Java, North was specifically recalling Buitenzorg, the Royal Dutch Gardens located on the island, where she made several works immediately preceding her trip to Ceylon. In Ceylon, North's ultimate destination was Peradeniya, the Royal Botanic Garden of Ceylon, located near the mountaintop city of Kandy. North intended to paint the garden's plants during a stay lasting as long as several weeks.[38] By connecting together Java, Ceylon, and Jamaica in her diary, North was not randomly associating the qualities of different cultures or impoverished island colonies, but was instead comparing the specific colonial outposts where Britain's important botanical gardens had been established. North was able to reflect upon an apparent disjunction in which her immediate experience of the poverty and hardships of native life did not align with her experience of the comfort and abundance of the gardens, where she depicted the systematic, ordered, and planned cultivation of plants, flourishing undisturbed by the poverty outside the gardens' walls. For North, this formal connection operated as both the literal and ideological common thread that linked together Java, Ceylon, and Jamaica. In her writing, North regularly contrasted the ephemeral and the permanent, shuddering at the thought of 'temporary' housing and rickety means of transportation that characterized everyday life in the colony, calmed by the apparent enduring permanence and eternal qualities of the walled gardens that she was privileged to record, much like Cameron's assurance that a newly built iron bridge in Kalutara represented 'solidity and stability … thro' all time'.

Central to North's expeditions were the description, cataloguing, and recording of primitive plants. To contemporary botanists, these plants were considered 'primitive' not only because of their location on the globe, but also owing to their 'unusual' (called 'primitive') reproductive systems, their flamboyant and strange colours, and their apparent singularity or rarity in nature. One such example painted by North was the 'taliput' palm (no. 284 in the Marianne North Gallery; hereafter 'North 284'), which was said to flower only once, at full maturity and in a blaze of colour, and then die.[39] Other studies from Ceylon include paintings of stands of bamboo in the gardens at Peradeniya (North 218), Ceylonese pitcher plants (North 242), and an avenue of India rubber trees at Peradeniya (North 260). In choosing such diverse subjects, North marked their botanical importance not only by their brilliant colouring, unusual flowers, or interesting growth patterns; these plants were intriguing subjects of scientific investigation and possible economic use. Colonial gardens like Peradeniya were important to the British government. 'In colonial gardens we may discern a complex agenda', writes Richard Drayton:

> They were, like public gardens at home, symbols of wise government. But we may also see in them spaces to which Europeans might retreat from the strangeness of alien environments. They often encompassed areas of wilderness, making islands of the same forest plants which encircled the boundaries of civility. They were theatres in which exotic nature was, literally, put in its place in a European system. This spectacle of the inclusion of the strange within the familiar comforted the expatriates and impressed the locals … Indigenous nature, and aesthetic sense, were enclosed in an imported style.[40]

At Peradeniya, that 'imported style' included the regularized rows of cultivated plants (the avenue of rubber trees), the roads (and later the railroad) which brought travellers to and from the Garden's walls, connecting shoreline villages to the less-accessible inland hills, and the constructed vistas that were carefully placed in the Garden to create picturesque views. During the early part of the nineteenth century in India, for example, 'colonization by gardening' described British policy: new gardens were established wherever British garrisons and administrators were settled.[41] But paintings and drawings that depicted rare and unusual tropical plants also marked their fragility and called attention to their eventual disappearance under colonial expansion: as Sir Joseph Dalton Hooker, long-time Director of the Royal Botanic Gardens at Kew, wrote in the visitor's guide to the Marianne North Gallery, 'these [species,] though now accessible to travellers and familiar to readers of travels, are already disappearing or are doomed shortly to disappear before the axe and the forest fires, the plough and the flock, of the ever-advancing settler or colonist. Such scenes can never be renewed by nature, nor when once effaced can they be pictured to the mind's eye.'[42] To Hooker as well as North, the picturesque was under constant siege from external forces.

Charles Cameron's goal of 'planting the germ of western civilization' was literally established in Ceylon in 1822 when the Royal Botanic Garden at Peradeniya was established. The prehistory of Peradeniya dates to 1810, when the English Garden initially opened on a remodelled tract previously tended by the Dutch, on lands known formerly as 'Slave Island'. In its new incarnation, the Royal Botanic Garden was charged with collecting and describing the largely unknown plants of the island, continuing the eighteenth-century practice of Linnaean scientific classification, a well-established convention at Kew. As early as 1821, though, much of the Garden's 143 acres were planted with coffee plants and cinnamon trees, plants that were thought to hold economic potential for the island. On 20 September 1847, Kew's Museum of Economic Botany opened under the direction of Sir William Hooker, Joseph Hooker's father, with the intention to spread the use of plants in business and commerce. By mid-century, the Royal Botanic Garden in Ceylon followed William Hooker's lead and adopted the new practice of economic botany, or the cultivation of useful plants for their industrial exploitation and commercial profit.[43] 'Wise government' was expressed by the containment of wild nature and the controlled direction of its vast productivity toward industrial ends.

Seed and plant transfers were an important expression of the benefits of economic botany; we might even say seed transplantation was the world's first global trade where the colonial possessions of European nations were able to gain economic advantage through the successful cultivation of certain crops. The history of coffee provides a useful example. This plant was native to the highlands of Ethiopia, and introduced to India by Arab traders; the Dutch found it there and planted it in 1659 in Ceylon and in 1696 in Java. In 1706, a coffee plant was then transferred from Java to the Amsterdam Botanic Garden, from which its descendants were transported to Surinam in 1715, to French Guiana and Brazil in 1727, and to Martinique by way of the Jardin Royal de Paris in 1723.[44] In Ceylon, coffee flourished, at least initially: by 1850, the island's coffee exports were worth more than £500,000 annually; by 1860 that number tripled, and by 1870, increased 50 per cent more again.[45]

The story of cinchona in Ceylon tells a similar story, its importance tied directly to the spread of Britain's colonial empire. As early as 1841, quinine, the drug extracted from the bark of the cinchona plant, was recognized as an effective defence against the debilitating effects of malaria and other fevers. Quinine made possible new avenues of scientific, missionary, and economic exploration, especially in subtropical Africa. Yet Spain, which controlled the source of cinchona in the Andean highlands, restricted its extraction and kept its price high. As Richard Drayton has written, Britain, Holland, and France began a competitive race to secure the best varieties of cinchona for plantation in their Asian colonies in their desperate attempt to gain control of the plant: 'But the Dutch in Java stole the march: during 1853–4, Justus Charles Hasskarl, Superintendent of the Buiten-zorg garden [on Java], travelled to South America in disguise to collect seeds.' Kew responded in 1860, focusing 'the systematic collection of the best varieties of cinchona in South America, the germination of seed in British greenhouses, their transport to botanic gardens in British Asia, and introduction into planta-tions'. Joseph Hooker, who succeeded his father as Director at Kew, even enlisted his friend, the great naturalist Charles Darwin in the scheme, 'and Darwin wrote to the Superintendent of the Ceylon Botanic Garden to suggest a technique of artificial fertilization, noting that, "the growth of Cinchona is so important for mankind, that I am sure you will excuse me making this suggestion"'.[46] Hooker and Darwin had formed their initial alliance when Hooker defended Darwin's theory of evolution at the famous debate that took place in June 1860 in Oxford, best known as the clash between Thomas Huxley and Bishop Samuel Wilberforce. At that famous Oxford showdown, Hooker marshalled convincing arguments about the role of natural selection in the botanical world that apparently closed the debate, leaving Wilberforce uncharacteristically speechless.[47] Several years later, Cameron took portraits of both Hooker and Darwin (Cox 680, 645) and obtained copyright protection for these photographs in August 1868. In 1871, she photographed Wilberforce (Cox 830). If Cameron ever voiced an opinion on the debate, that record does not survive; nevertheless, she sent all of the portraits of these men to Colnaghi's for sale.

In part because of Darwin's persuasive intervention, the Director at Ceylon, George Henry Kendrick Thwaites, decided to plant the cinchona crop at Perad-eniya's satellite garden, Hakgalla.[48] But by 1878, owing to unfavourable weather, the cinchona crop was in distress, as Thwaites dutifully reported to Hooker: 'At Hakgalla the Cinchona plantation has suffered very severely from the unusually wet season. Nearly all the large trees, 20 or 30 feet high, and about 12 years old, are dying; the stock plants and about 300,000 cuttings have been killed. We hope to recover ourselves in time, and by opening fresh nurseries, there is every possi-bility of being able to meet the demand for plants.'[49] Cinchona apparently did not recover fully in Ceylon. However, in the early 1870s, Thwaites introduced the cultivation of tea to the island, an economic plan that proved auspicious. Three years later, Ceylon exported only twenty-three pounds of tea, but by 1895, the island exported seventy-four million pounds, 'representing about 40% of the tea consumed by Britain'.[50]

Economic botany was also defined by the transfer of useful plants from remote areas of the world, where a plant's cultivation was too expensive or labour intensive, to areas where labour was inexpensive and plentiful, thereby enhancing its profitability. The history of the rubber trees depicted by Marianne North illustrates how one such plant created its own kind of travel narrative as an economic force as well as its own kind of cultural capital. During the 1850s, Thomas Hancock in England and the Michelin firm in France determined that the Brazilian rubber tree produced a superior product as compared to other species of the tree. In 1876, the year of North's visit to Ceylon, Henry Wickham, aided by Tapuyo Indians, pirated seeds from Brazilian rubber plants out of the Amazon. They were transferred immediately to the Royal Botanic Gardens at Kew, where Joseph Hooker received them himself. From there, he sent them to botanical gardens in Calcutta, Singapore, and Ceylon, ostensibly to compare their growth patterns to other species of rubber tree transplanted to those lands earlier. When North visited Peradeniya in late 1876, she met with Director Thwaites of the Garden and, under his direction, made her first study of a stand of India rubber trees. To Thwaites, these trees were the Garden's chief asset (North 260).[51] These particular trees had been transplanted from Assam, in Northern India, and represented a rival to the Brazilian tree. Meanwhile, researchers at the Botanic Garden in Singapore devised a new method of gently tapping the Brazilian species to release the latex without killing the tree. In sharing this knowledge with administrators in Ceylon, therefore, Britain's colonial gardens effectively functioned as institutionally and politically connected economic research centres, supporting global efforts to promote the economic development of useful plants.[52]

North's painting of India rubber trees reveals two additional historical elements that are particular to the administration of the island colony under the British, and to Charles Cameron's legal and governmental efforts in particular, but which are not readily apparent in the imagery: the first is the situation that India rubber was then being considered a suitable replacement crop for coffee on British plantations throughout the island. Since the mid-1850s, in fact, Ceylonese coffee plants had been dying because of a fungus, an economic calamity that threatened many plantation owners, including the Camerons. The second is one of hidden conflict, represented by Britain's hostile views towards the native Sinhalese as indolent and obstructive labourers. Since the 1830s, Britain had supported plantation owners by importing Tamil coolies from southern India as a way to combat the labour problem, effectively repeating labour and immigration policies favoured by the Colonial Office that had backfired in both Mauritius and

Jamaica.[53] Concealed, then, by this magnificent stand of trees was the history of labour struggles between the island's native population and the British, which is unwittingly referred to in North's diary entry, as she described the extended view captured by two of her paintings representing the Garden's entrance:

> There was a noble avenue of India-rubber trees at the entrance to the great gardens, with their long tangled roots creeping over the outside of the ground, and huge supports growing down into it from their heavy branches. Every way I looked at those trees they were magnificent. Beyond them one came to groups of different sorts of palm-trees, with one giant 'taliput' in full flower. I settled myself to make a study of it, and of the six men with loaded clubs who were grinding down the stones in the roadway while they sang a kind of monotonous chant, at the end of each verse lifting up their clubs and letting them fall with a thud.[54]

The *Official Guide* to the Marianne North Gallery describes this painting of the 'taliput' palm in greater detail, paying critical attention to the role of the native men depicted (North 284): 'The road-makers in the foreground are working in the native fashion, singing a ballad and letting their rammers fall at the end of each verse only, with a long rest in between.'[55] The visitor is therefore advised of the apparent indolence of the road workers, noting that the 'long interval' between work and rest marked not only their 'native fashion', but also their fatigue, and perhaps too, their subtle resistance. At the same time, North has impressed upon the viewer the picturesque qualities of the scene: she has romanticized the workers' 'monotonous chant' as if it were a quaint ballad. It is also possible that Julia Margaret Cameron accompanied North to the Garden, using her camera to record native men standing erect and still in front of a similar stand of palm trees. Although there is no record that Cameron made such a visit, and there are no road-making clubs in the hands of the peasants in this photograph, this print exists in both positive and negative versions as part of a photographic album housed in the collection of the Royal Photographic Society. Although its attribution is uncertain, the date and location are consistent with North's visit to Peradeniya.[56] Much like North's painting, this photograph also depicts Ceylonese men dwarfed by their natural surroundings; they are still and reserved and as a result, fold into the landscape as a part of nature; rather than exerting command over it, the peasants become another example of the passive picturesque.

In North's painting of men in front of the taliput palm, the artist also depicted street workers with shovels, representing a chain gang at work. But in this painting and in the *Official Guide* to North's Gallery, these hard facts of the scene have been erased, replaced by a normalized description in which forced roadwork becomes classified as ordinary wage labour. However, North's painting actually captures one of the harshest chapters of the British colonial occupation of Ceylon, and one that involved Charles Cameron directly. In fact, together with Colebrooke, his fellow Commissioner, Cameron helped to institute the system of wage labour on the island, bringing British labour law and customs to a native economy that was still steeped in feudal allegiances to chieftains and kings, with the Sinhalese holding a non-proprietary attitude toward the fruits of the land. This ancient system was called *rajakariya*. When the British first took control of the island in 1798, compulsory roadwork was imposed under the *rajakariya* system, and workers received a daily allowance of rice in place of wages. In one form or another, compulsory roadwork was mandated as law under British occupation throughout the nineteenth century, and in 1832, when the Colebrooke–Cameron reforms took effect, minimal wages replaced compulsory labour. However, as the number of British plantations grew during the succeeding years, the need for more roads also increased, and in 1848, a new Road Ordinance was passed, requiring six days' labour from every native islander. Runaways were imprisoned, but then brought out to the roads once again to complete their work as part of chain gangs.[57] As North observed in her diary, they endured their captivity in song, rhythmically chanting amid short periods of rest as they crushed their stones. Cameron was undoubtedly aware of her husband's efforts to transform labour on the island; as she noted in her correspondence with the island's governor, Sir William Gregory, if the British colonial government improved the native islanders' living conditions and educated their minds, the native Sinhalese would come to appreciate the 'benefit' of wage labour.

## Portraits of ambivalence and redemption

Marianne North finally met Julia Margaret Cameron when she travelled from Peradeniya to Kalutara at the end of her visit to Ceylon. As documented by Cameron (Cox 1200), North made two paintings from the Camerons' land (North 240, 248), and in her diary, reflected upon their lifestyle:

> [The Cameron's] house stood on a small hill, jutting out into the great river which ran into the sea a quarter of a mile below the house … The walls of the rooms were covered with magnificent photographs; others were tumbling about the tables, chairs, and floors, with quantities of damp books, all untidy and picturesque; the lady herself with a lace veil on her head and flowing draperies.[58]

North spent several days there, making it possible to share several experiences with her host. At least one encounter occurred between a pedlar group and the two women, and the two artists produced very similar works, with three men displaying their wares while seated on the ground (Cox 1220). In her diary, North described a similar encounter from her preceding week in Peradeniya:

> [In the] morning at six I was at work on my sketch … and breakfasted in the old palace, when a party of Indian pedlars came and spread out their gorgeous shawls and other goods on the veranda. They made a fine foreground to the flowers and palm-trees beyond.[59]

Not surprisingly for the botanical illustrator, people take a back seat to plants in North's mind's eye. By contrast, in recording her pedlar group photographically, Cameron focused instead on the men and their goods, while North regarded the pedlars as minor subjects, blending them into the overall naturalistic composition of her painting.

North then described Mrs Cameron's efforts to photograph her as a subject, producing results that neither of them pronounced a success (Cox 1198, 1199). Speaking now as a photographic subject in front of Cameron's lens, North intriguingly wrote about witnessing how the photographer attempted to control both 'nature' and the picturesque by carefully arranging both her guest and her subject's backdrop, all in the name of trying to achieve some unrealized 'primitive' ideal, where the artificial pose would appear as somehow natural and uncomplicated:

> She dressed me up in flowing draperies of cashmere wool, let down my hair, and made me stand with spiky cocoa-nut branches running into my head, the noonday sun's rays dodging my eyes between the leaves as the slight breeze moved them, and told me to look perfectly natural (with a thermometer standing at 96°F)! Then she tried me with a background of breadfruit leaves and fruit, nailed flat against a window shutter, and told *them* to look natural, but both failed; and though she wasted twelve plates, and an enormous amount of trouble, it was all in vain.[60]

According to North, Cameron found her subject, a Western outsider, did not 'look perfectly natural' (or natural enough) before her lens or when posed in front of her symbols of tropical nature, the breadfruit leaves and fruit. It seems that in order for a believable representation of 'nature' to be recorded satisfactorily, Cameron required a native subject, one who was more convincingly portrayed as 'at home' in her primitive surroundings. Or perhaps Cameron thought the 'natural backdrop' surrounding North looked contrived and unnatural, or that her props (or even her model) appeared false and artificial. Either way, numerous contradictions complicate our understanding of this 'failure' that cost the photographer twelve ruined plates, particularly when the image is compared to other photographs Cameron made of native women around the same time.

In this imagery, native women stand robed in traditional saris or appear half-dressed, representing primeval fertility, on the one hand, or 'naturalized' essential women on the other, 'Madonnas of the tropics' (Figure 47). Cameron has not identified them with names or as Sinhalese or Tamil, although one collector appended the words 'Tamil Cooly women' on the reverse side of one print (Cox 1213). In earlier photographs depicting scenes of Tennyson's poetry, for example, or in portrait heads transformed into allegorical representations depicting the mythic attributes of muses or goddesses, Cameron did not hesitate to use props and costumes. In her photographs of non-European women in Ceylon, however, Cameron used the symbolic 'naturalism' of their surroundings, like the breadfruit

leaves and fruit, to help define them as native to Ceylon. By contrast, the 'unsuccessful image' of North becomes complicated as an uncomfortable hybrid, the
tropical surroundings working at odds with the woman's British identity. In the
photographs of native women, Cameron depicted the unadorned, uncomplicated,
and primitive East; whereas, in her portrait of North, she removed the Western-
ized Other outside her 'true context' and inserted her subject in the natural world
required of primitivism. The illusion broke down, because as Torgovnick reminds
us, the 'eternal present' of primitivism requires that native societies are denied a
historical past of their own. Indeed, during North's visit to Kalutara, Cameron
seemed preoccupied with artifice: in setting up yet another portrait of North, she
first re-costumed her subject to appear in a traditional Victorian full-length dress,
as opposed to the more practical clothes that North preferred, and then assembled her in front of an easel, pretending to paint a native boy holding a vase (Cox
1200), the kind of subject the painter would have never considered.

Cameron's apparent ambivalence toward her subjects certainly preceded
North's visit, but her Western visitor helped to complicate her conventional
attitudes towards nature and the picturesque. Throughout the different phases
of her photographic career, Cameron largely portrayed women in uncomplicated
and recognizable stereotypes; they epitomize Eastern exoticism, like the photographs in her Byron series; they portray Western ideas of goodness and holiness,
like her *Fruits of the Spirit* group; or they embody idealized elements of Victorian
femininity and moral duty, as in her illustrations of Tennyson's poetry. Ironically, however, in her final years as a photographer, Cameron could not create a
satisfactory image of Marianne North according to these well-worn strategies,
perhaps because their legitimacy had been called into question or the artificiality
of doing so in Ceylon made this iconography unconvincing.

Like her unsuccessful portrait of North, Cameron's photographs of native
women posed as if they were 'native Madonnas' are similarly unresolved. We
might take the example discussed earlier, in which the same young woman
appears first in a chemise with her hair pulled back, and then is posed in flowing
drapery with loose hair falling from a cloth headdress (Figure 47). This photograph is unable to portray 'the Madonna' convincingly in Western terms because
the subject's native appearance challenges Western norms and expectations. At
the same time, because of her subject's direct gaze back at the photographer,
she appears self-possessed; consequently, the photograph does not convincingly
represent a powerless individual, while at the same time, it fails as a stock image to
symbolize submissiveness under colonialism. Cameron's photographs of native
women and North's imagery of road workers mark the repeated confrontations
of these artists with themselves and others. Their imagery is complicated as a
result because these confrontations disclose the intermixture of fear and desire,
mimicry and difference, and obedience and independence that are present in

the encounters recorded by this imagery and which express the artists' constant struggle with their status as colonialist outsiders.[61] When conceived in these terms, both North's paintings and Cameron's photographs actually destabilize the narrative myths they supposedly represent: as a result, the mythic return to primitive origins, like the unquestioned superiority of colonialist power, is dramatically undermined by these photographs. They become instead another kind of hybrid work that expresses Cameron's ambivalence.

## Redemption at the edge of the Empire

The theoretical concept that joins the idea of 'going home' to the state of 'going primitive' was an important one for Georg Lukacs. In his *Theory of the Novel*, Lukacs wrote of 'transcendental homelessness', a condition particular to exile but also common to the long-distance traveller and the immigrant to colonial lands, where social separation, psychological displacement, and spatial dislocation contributed to the affliction. For Lukacs, transcendental homelessness was a restless and unsettled state of affairs, an inconsolable yearning for origins and home that was brought about by feelings of displacement. It may be difficult, if not impossible, to find evidence of displacement or yearning in a photograph, because visual representations generally do not lend themselves easily to express such psychological distress. But in an additional portrait of North in Kalutara, Cameron crystallized the competing and yet compatible allegories of displacement described by Lukacs. At the same time, she embedded in her portrait an invitation to those who might have viewed this image to speculate on the possibility of returning to one's origins and participate in the dream of claiming one's national inheritance.

Unlike the portraits described above, which portray North standing at an easel or facing the photographer, surrounded by nature, this particular portrait presents North seated at a table, glancing up from reading a book (Cox 1197; Figure 49). The immediate impression is commonplace and straightforward, with no overt expression of purpose or meaningful gesture, depicting no apparent confrontation with colonialism. But North is depicted holding a very particular book: Cameron's photograph shows North looking up from reading a section of George Eliot's novel, *Daniel Deronda*. This novel was published in instalments between February and September 1876. While the presence of the novel helps us date the image, it more importantly marks Cameron's connection to recent cultural events in English society and to her continuing personal interest in the literary work of George Eliot.[62] Moreover, Cameron's inclusion of an instalment section of *Daniel Deronda* also helps us transform the meaning of the book from a common desktop prop that might be used for any portrait into a resonant symbolic object because of the unquestionable significance of Eliot's

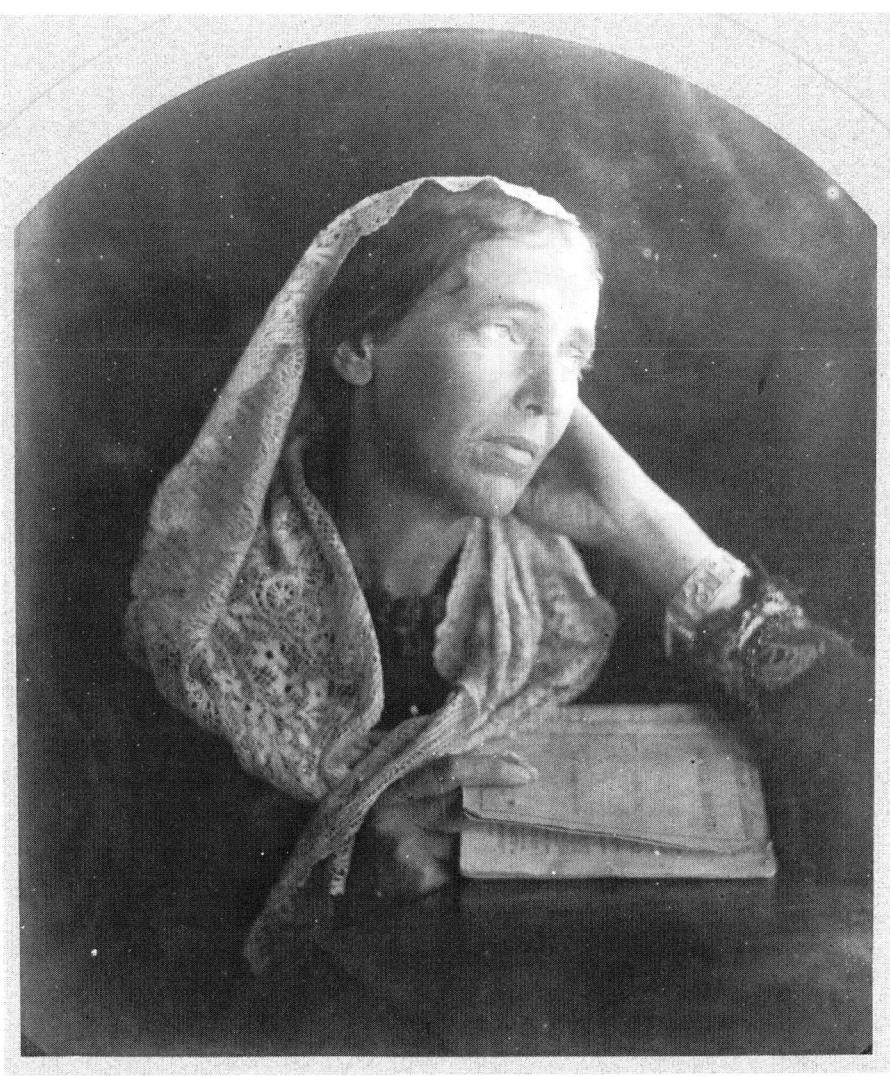

Julia Margaret Cameron, *Marianne North* (Cox 1197), 1877.    **49**
Albumen print, 28.3 x 23.3 cm.

literary work. The presence of *Daniel Deronda* metaphorically inscribes a sign of the British colonists' conflict in terms of the contemporary political debates embedded in the novel itself. In particular, Eliot's novel explored how nineteenth-century Victorians might actually embrace the search for a return to their origins to reclaim a 'lost' and foreign land.

Thematically, *Daniel Deronda* mines a similar terrain to the literary premise explored by Saint-Pierre in his novel *Paul and Virginia*. In these novels, Saint-Pierre and George Eliot depict the colonized lands as both extensions of 'home' *and* as alien lands, 'foreign' and inhospitable. Both authors portray the imperial centre as welcoming but also as hostile, as the political efforts to assimilate or segregate the colonial Other are portrayed as an accepted social goal, but one that is also resisted as well. Saint-Pierre, for example, acknowledges slavery as a fact of life on Mauritius; he makes a slave couple the childhood companions of Paul and Virginia. Similarly, in *Daniel Deronda*, Eliot's characters debate the aftermath of the 1865 uprisings in Jamaica, and she allows her character Grandcourt to declare, 'the Jamaican negro was a beastly sort of baptist Caliban'.[63] In each novel, the authors' protagonists discover their 'true' identity, which brings them into confronting their religion and ethnicity, and each major character contends with the newfound knowledge they have acquired by re-evaluating their relationships to their families and the larger society alike. Paul and Virginia, for example, come to learn they are not actually brother and sister, and Virginia learns the modern ways of French society; both facts bring about the end of their idyllic world. Similarly, upon learning of his Jewish identity, Deronda grows distant from Sir Hugo and Gwendolen and much closer to Mirah and Ezra. The settings and environment of both novels possess elements of the archaic and the modern, sometimes coexisting peacefully, often at odds. Finally, in both novels, the two authors' freshly enlightened protagonists are able to stake a new and informed claim to their true identities because they have come to terms with their past heritage as much as with their colonial selves. Self-awareness and independent will brings these characters into a reckoning with the past and the opportunity to determine their own future: the freshly awakened Virginia sees herself as an entitled European lady; she cannot return to Paul's natural but debased and now-desecrated world. Once Deronda is made aware of his own national heritage, the fact of his legal exclusion from political discourse and his religious isolation from society dislodges him bitterly from the security that once defined his world; in turn, he resolves to leave England for Palestine. From Kalutara, at the edge of the Empire in Ceylon, occupying lands she and her husband had acquired more than twenty-five years earlier, Julia Margaret Cameron found redemption herself in exploring once again the importance of these themes in her work.

In *Daniel Deronda*, Eliot confronts the return to origins directly. In the third chapter of the novel, for example, the author meditates on the nature of home and belonging, the satisfying and contented quality of feeling deep connections to home and family, and the negative consequences of being rootless in the world, both physically and spiritually. These interconnected themes are central to the novel; they describe the key hardships and principal source of internal conflict with which her two main characters, Gwendolen Harleth and Daniel Deronda, contend throughout the novel. Indeed, Eliot uses the very definition of home to link together the personal yearnings, life stories, and ultimate destinies of her characters:

Pity that Offendene was not the home of Miss Harleth's childhood, or endeared to her by family memories! A human life, I think, should be well rooted in some spot of a native land, where it may get the love of tender kinship for the face of earth, for the labours men go forth to, for the sounds and accents that haunt it, for whatever will give that early home a familiar unmistakable difference amidst the future widening of knowledge: a spot where the definiteness of early memories may be inwrought with affection, and kindly acquaintance with all neighbours, even to the dogs and donkeys, may spread not by sentimental effort and reflection, but as a sweet habit of the blood. At five years old, mortals are not prepared to be citizens of the world, to be stimulated by abstract nouns, to soar above preference into impartiality; and that prejudice in favour of milk with which we blindly begin, is a type of the way body and soul must get nourished at least for a time. The best introduction to astronomy is to think of the nightly heavens as a little lot of stars belonging to one's own homestead.[64]

Jean Sudrann has noted how in this passage Eliot deliberately asks her reader to reflect upon Romantic expressions of the universal, where all things are 'at home under the stars', where the heavens are a part of every person's homestead, and where universal truth binds people to each other in some meaningful but perhaps unknowable way.[65] Edward Said wrote that Eliot used the novel to represent 'a generalized condition of homelessness. Not only the Jews, but even the well-born Englishmen and women in the novel are portrayed as wandering and alienated beings ... Thus Eliot uses the plight of the Jews to make a universal statement about the nineteenth century's need for a home, given the spiritual and psychological rootlessness reflected in her characters' almost ontological physical restlessness.'[66]

In the novel, Daniel's Romantic search leads him to self-discovery, to a sense of purpose and civic obligation, and to recover his Jewish heritage, but his story is also one in which the character, who has lacked a true 'homestead' as the adopted child of Sir Hugo Malinger, resolves to create one of his own making. Moreover, Daniel is able to achieve true independence as an adult by reclaiming land that had been 'lost' in the past by ancestors unknown to him. By the end of the novel, Daniel's internal state of homelessness finds its corrective direction in his determination to leave England, the only 'homeland' he has ever known. Responding to a powerful and overwhelming urge to find redemption in a 'native land' that he has never even seen, Daniel resolves to establish a new Jewish homeland in 'the East'. In the final pages of *Daniel Deronda*, the character finds his destiny as the architect of a new nation, populated by those like him who are similarly exiled and homeless. A future homeland waits, he says:

I am going to the East to become better acquainted with the condition of my race in various countries there ... The idea that I am possessed with is that of restoring a political existence to my people, making them a nation again, giving them a national centre, such as the English have, though they too are scattered over the face of the globe.[67]

Once again, and somewhat ironically, the colonial agenda is implicitly taken as a suitable model for this redemptive act, as if it were the only available course of action that could heal the pain of homelessness or resolve the displacement and isolation that Daniel and his people have endured.

In Eliot's novel, Daniel Deronda's psychological redemption is accomplished through political means: the author elevates the British model of imperial expansion as an ideal model, portraying its interest in spreading English as a form of national identity and its belief in a spiritual connection to the universal as essential forces. Under this system, as imagined in *Daniel Deronda*, the colonies occupy solid and legitimate connections to the imperial centre; moreover, even at the remote edges of the Empire, the colonies secure their own identity by cultivating the idea that they occupy a mythic place of origins, a 'true' and universal homeland.[68] If Tennyson's *Idylls of the King* put forward the idea of re-establishing the earlier glories of an empire that had fallen in the past, *Daniel Deronda* advanced the idea of recovering that past, revitalizing the present, and laying the political foundations to establish a future of restored national strength because the newly expanded empire possessed a redeemed homeland.

Cameron's admiration for George Eliot found its most concrete expression in her photographic portrait of Marianne North looking up from reading *Daniel Deronda*. When she embarked on her journey to the East in 1875, Cameron expressed her enchantment in 'going forth' in harmony with 'the pulse of the large world'. She found her 'return to the East' both redemptive and revitalizing. North, too, represented botanical specimens that had been scattered, like seeds, throughout the world, and was able to reassemble them literally and metaphorically, reuniting them in her Gallery at Kew, an elegant stand-in for the visual coherence of the 'national centre'. On 21 January 1877, North left the Camerons and took a coach from Kalutara to Galle, and then boarded a French steamer to Aden, and arrived in Naples about one month later, slowly making her way back to England. In 1878, Cameron also returned to England one more time, and spent a month in London with her son Hardinge. Her brief return was all business.

## A lasting legacy in print

Before the Camerons departed for Ceylon in 1875, Julia Margaret signed two important commercial contracts, one with the publisher Henry S. King, and the other with the Autotype Company. The objective of both legal agreements was to disseminate her work widely and produce a financial return. Cameron's contract with King was written on 23 March 1875, specifying clearly that the publisher would represent Cameron on a commissioned basis for publishing both volumes of her *Illustrations to Tennyson's Idylls of the King and Other Poems*. For this privilege, Cameron paid King £100.[69] During the 1870s, a common type of publishing contract placed the entire financial risk on the author, rather than the publisher. In return for Cameron's fee, King pledged to provide printing, binding, and distribution, but additional fees would be charged for these services. In return, Cameron could use King's imprint on the title page. Leslie Howsam described how commissioned contracts of this time typically specified a publisher's fee of five guineas and then added a 10 per cent commission of all sales.[70] Cameron clearly assumed a greater financial burden than normal for the time.

In October 1877, Tennyson's publications were transferred, without his prior knowledge or approval, from Henry S. King to the imprint of C. Kegan Paul and Company, a source of great frustration to the poet.[71] Typically, publishers advertised their list in the back pages of their most popular publications as a kind of catalogue of available titles. One such advertisement, for example, was printed in the back pages of the 1878 edition of Henry Taylor's five-volume *Works*. In a 'List of C. Kegan Paul & Co.'s Publications', the item 'Tennyson's *Idylls of the King, and other Poems*, Illustrated by Julia Margaret Cameron. 2 vols.' is listed, each volume priced at £6 6s. Cameron's edition was evidently sold to Kegan Paul along with Tennyson's. But because Kegan Paul maintained the King imprint on many of his existing titles, Cameron's works sold after 1877 did not reflect the change in her publisher.

Records also show that Kegan Paul apparently spent additional funds to advertise Cameron's volumes: one entry of 30 June 1875 is marked for 'advertisements'; two additional entries, dated 30 June 1875 and 30 December 1876, are marked for 'catalogues'; and 'sundry' costs are recorded for March 1875 and 31 December 1878. Cameron also apparently received four copies of the first and second series of the published edition from the publisher. But it is unclear how sales fared for this publication: the only sale recorded on the printer's record is dated 20 April 1875, marked '1 copy hold in L'pool', probably a note to one of the publisher's distributors in Liverpool. For their part, Kegan Paul and Co. did not invest large expenditures to promote Cameron's title; the ledger shows no more than ten shillings and sixpence spent to advertise the volumes. Because most publishing contracts at the time lasted five years, the publisher's catalogue printed in 1878 mentioned above still indicated that Cameron maintained her contractual arrangement with Kegan Paul.

But some time between March 1875, when she signed with Henry S. King, and late October, when she departed for the last time to Ceylon, she apparently drew up another contract with the Autotype Company. The date must have been around 18 October 1875, since on this date she recorded for copyright protection 'Autotype copies' of the following portraits: Charles Darwin, Joseph Joachim, Alfred Tennyson, John Herschel, and George Frederick Watts.[72] All were based upon her earlier copyrighted work: autotypes were made by directly transferring Cameron's negatives into positive transparencies, from which multiple prints would be printed. These were ink-based carbon prints, produced by the most modern means of photomechanical reproduction at the time.

During this six-month period, Cameron was clearly concerned about the economics of her publishing venture and the arrangement she made with King. In 1874, for example, *prior* to settling her contract with King, she wrote that individual prints from *Idylls of the King* 'will also be sold singly at 16/- [sixteen shillings] each to those who prefer single copies'. Cameron calculated that the cost of the photographs, if purchased separately, 'would come to £10 8/- for the 13 pictures without the binding whereas the *book* is only six guineas'.[73] Clearly the purchase of the whole book would be more economical for readers. Of course, having put up £100 in her contract with King, it is also reasonable that she wanted to promote the unsold volumes over the individual prints as a way to recover her initial investment. When her contract migrated from King to Kegan Paul and Co., her publishing expectations also needed to change out of necessity: while the cost per volume remained the same at £6 6s, Kegan Paul took 25 per cent of that selling price as well as an additional 10 per cent commission of all sales, a steeper commission than the typical publishing contract described by Howsam.

At this time, therefore, it is likely that Cameron began to explore the viability of producing individual works through the Autotype Company, which at the time was the only London-based firm licensed to use Swan's carbon process. Carbon prints did not fade like albumen prints; in addition, one could remove slight imperfections from the original negatives and produce technically superior results. It is therefore likely that Cameron engaged the Autotype Company to print individual works from *Idylls of the King* during this time, perhaps on demand. The 1875 transfer of portraits of Darwin, Joachim, Tennyson, Herschel, and Watts, then, must have been an initial test before she agreed to transfer approximately seventy negative glass plates to the Autotype Company, which apparently occurred in 1878, very probably when she returned from Ceylon for her brief visit to London that year.[74] Like Tennyson, Cameron was simultaneously stepping forward and dancing backward with her publication of *Idylls of the King*. She made it possible for the public to buy individual carbon prints produced by the most advanced means of achieving unalterable photographs, yet she also produced her two volumes with hand-made albumen prints that risked fading and discoloration. By contracting with King and the Autotype Company during the same year, Cameron associated herself with the most modern means of photomechanical reproduction, yet she also attempted to retain control of her photographic legacy as long as possible prior to returning to Ceylon.

When Cameron registered her five autotype portraits for copyright protection in 1875, she made it possible to order extra copies of those prints from abroad. But she also made arrangements with the Autotype Company to print several photographs of her 'fancy subjects'. These include, among her literary illustrations: *Study of the Cenci* (Cox 409), *She Walks in Beauty* (Cox 172), and *King Lear allotting his Kingdom to his three daughters* (Cox 1141); among her mythological works, *Cupid's Pencil of Light* (Cox 895) and *Cupid* (Cox 902); and among her illustrations of Tennyson's poems, *'Call I Follow, I Follow, Let Me Die'* (Cox 257) and *'For I'm to be Queen of the May, Mother'* (Cox 1176). Since the business records of both the Autotype Company and her print dealer Colnaghi are no longer extant, it is not possible to identify all of the images that she assigned to autotype reproduction or to reconstruct the financial arrangements she made. Nevertheless, in 1876 while in Ceylon, she wrote to her son Hardinge in Kalutara from her own plantation, Cameron's Land, sending him 'one of my new Autotypes' and telling him: 'if you do not like this red chalk tone we will change them when I come to you'.[75] Given that the autotype portraits of Darwin, Joachim, Tennyson, Herschel, and Watts were all produced in a brown/black tone, the 'red chalk' print must have been of a different subject, perhaps one of the allegorical works noted above. Cameron also apparently enjoyed using autotypes to approximate the effect of sepia toning in her albumen prints: for example, in 1878, she wrote approvingly about the sepia effect she used for *The Kiss of Peace* (Cox 1129), noting on the reverse side of one photograph, 'This is a very splendid print so like a sepia painting that it is difficult to believe that it is genuine untouched photography.'[76]

As we have seen, Cameron returned to her older photographs in order to reprint them differently, to retitle the subject, to re-imagine the subject in a new composition, or to see what the effect of sepia or other toning might produce in the look of her prints. But her experiments with the Autotype Company preserved the earlier titles. Even if the size of the new prints was slightly reduced as compared to the original albumen prints and might have been produced in a different tint or shade of black or brown, Cameron's relationship with the Autotype Company was about reproduction and dissemination, not reinterpretation or deliberate changes in meaning.

Cameron died in Ceylon on 26 January 1879. During her lifetime she never acquired the financial gain that she had yearned for from her photography. It is not known whether she felt injured from her contract with King or upset with Kegan Paul, but there is no doubt she experienced what she called a 'fierce controversy' with the Autotype Company. Apparently she had made an initial investment of 'two guineas for each negative, consoling my self-reproach for this outlay by thinking that in selling each print for 7s. 6d. [seven shillings and sixpence] I should soon recover my expenses.'[77] But she had not read the contract carefully enough to contest the 40 per cent commission on each print that the Autotype Company charged, and the rashness of this unwise investment did not occur to her until far too late.

Some forty years after Cameron's death, her great-niece Virginia Woolf imagined why the Camerons decided to live their final days on the island. For

Woolf, it was as much the return to nature as it was a retreat from the avarice and falseness of the commercial world. Perhaps she knew of Cameron's bitter financial disappointments. Woolf's play *Freshwater* was intended to be a comedy, but in imagining the reasons behind their decision to leave England, Woolf brought forward an important kernel of truth in understanding their likely motivations:

> **Mr and Mrs C.:** We go to seek a land less corrupted by hypocrisy, where nature prevails. A land where the sun always shines. Where philosophers speak the truth. Where men are naked. Where women are beautiful. Where damsels dance among the currant bushes – It is time – It is time. We go; we go.[78]

## Notes

1 Virginia Woolf and Roger Fry, *Victorian Photographs of Famous Men and Fair Women* [1926] (London: Chatto and Windus, 1992), p. 19.

2 Virginia Woolf, *Freshwater: A Comedy* [1935], ed. Lucio P. Ruotolo (San Diego: Harcourt Brace Jovanovich, 1976), p. 45.

3 Marianne North, *Recollections of a Happy Life: Being the Autobiography of Marianne North*, ed. Mrs John Addington Symonds, 2 vols. (London: Macmillan, 1892).

4 Evelyn Haller, 'The Botanical Works of Marianne North (Painter, Writer, and Traveler). Edited by Absorption into Virginia Woolf's Writing', in *Woolf Editing / Editing Woolf: Selected Papers from the Eighteenth Annual Conference on Virginia Woolf, University of Denver, 19–22 June 2008*, ed. Eleanor McNees and Sara Veglahn (Clemson, SC: Clemson University Digital Press, 2008), p. 174.

5 Virginia Woolf, 'Kew Gardens', in *Monday or Tuesday* (New York: Harcourt, Brace and Company, 1921).

6 On the context of women as botanical illustrators, see Wilfred Blunt, *The Art of Botanical Illustration* (London: Collins, 1950), and Londa Schiebinger, 'Gender and Natural History', in N. Jardine, J. A. Secord, and E. C. Spary, eds., *Cultures of Natural History* (Cambridge: Cambridge University Press, 1996).

7 Mary Louise Pratt, *Imperial Eyes: Travel Writing and Transculturalism* (London: Routledge: 1992), p. 104.

8 Antonia Losano, 'A Preference for Vegetables: The Travel Writings and Botanical Art of Marianne North', *Women's Studies*, 26:5 (1997), 423–6.

9 Quoted in Anne Isabella Thackeray Ritchie, *From Friend to Friend* (London: John Murray, 1919), p. 34.

10 Marianna Torgovnick, *Gone Primitive: Savage Intellects, Modern Lives* (Chicago: University of Chicago Press, 1990), p. 185.

11 *Ibid.*, p. 187.

12 *Ibid.*, p. 186.

13 Quoted in Mike Weaver, *Whisper of the Muse: The Overstone Album and Other Photographs by Julia Margaret Cameron* (Malibu: J. Paul Getty Museum, 1986), p. 68.

14 Elizabeth J. Harris, *The Gaze of the Coloniser: British Views on Local Women in 19th Century Sri Lanka* (Colombo: Social Scientists' Association, 1994).

15 Edward W. Said, *Orientalism* (New York: Vintage, 1978), pp. 20–1.

16 Homi K. Bhabha, *The Location of Culture* (London and New York: Routledge, 1994), p. 44.

17 Torgovnick, *Gone Primitive*, p. 187.

18 See Joanne Lukitsh, '"Simply Pictures of Peasants": Artistry, Authorship, and Ideology in Julia Margaret Cameron's Photography in Sri Lanka, 1875–1879', *Yale Journal of Criticism*, 9:2

(1996), 283–308; Lori Cavagnaro, 'Julia Margaret Cameron: Focusing on the Orient', in Dave Oliphant, ed., *Gendered Territory: Photographs of Women by Julia Margaret Cameron* (Austin: Harry Ransom Humanities Research Center, University of Texas at Austin, 1996); Marie Czach, 'Some Thoughts on Cameron's Ceylonese Photographs', *Afterimage*, 1 (1973), 3.

19 Charles Hay Cameron, 'Report of Charles H. Cameron Esq. upon the Judicial Establishments and Procedure in Ceylon' [31 January 1832], in G. C. Mendis, ed., *The Colebrooke–Cameron Papers: Documents on British Colonial Policy in Ceylon, 1796–1833*, 2 vols. (London: Oxford University Press, 1956), vol. 1, p. 182.

20 See especially, V. G. Kiernan, *The Lords of Human Kind: Black Man, Yellow Man, and White Man in an Age of Empire* (Boston: Little, Brown, 1969), pp. 46–62, 76–8, 211–20; George D. Bearce, *British Attitudes Towards India, 1784–1858* (London: Oxford University Press, 1961); Henri Baudet, *Paradise on Earth: Some Thoughts on European Images of Non-European Man*, trans. Elizabeth Wentholt, [1965] (Westport, CT: Greenwood Press, 1976).

21 Robert Percival, *An Account of the Island of Ceylon* (London: C&R Baldwin, 1803), p. 181, quoted in Harris, *The Gaze of the Colonizer*, p. 13.

22 Bhabha, *The Location of Culture*, p. 145.

23 Ashis Nandy, *The Intimate Enemy: Loss and Recovery of Self under Colonialism* (New Delhi: Oxford University Press, 1983), p. 10.

24 Elmer H. Cutts, 'The Background of Macaulay's Minute', *American Historical Review*, 58:4 (1953), 824–53.

25 Weaver, *Whisper of the Muse*, p. 24; Bernard Semmel, 'The Philosophic Radicals and Colonialism', *Journal of Economic History*, 21:4 (1961), 513–25.

26 Mendis, *Colebrooke–Cameron Papers*, vol. 1, p. 136.

27 David Scott, 'Colonial Governmentality', *Social Text*, 43 (1995), 211–12.

28 Michel Foucault, *Discipline and Punish: The Birth of the Prison*, trans. Alan Sheridan (New York: Vintage, 1977).

29 Mendis, *Colebrooke–Cameron Papers*, vol. 1, pp. 146–7.

30 Scott, 'Colonial Governmentality', 213; Bhabha, *The Location of Culture*, pp. 70–1.

31 Hugh Tinker, 'Between Africa, Asia and Europe. Mauritius: Cultural Marginalism and Political Control', *African Affairs*, 76:304 (1977), 323.

32 Letter from Charles Hay Cameron to Julia Margaret Cameron, dated 11 December 1850, Cameron Papers, Getty Research Institute, Los Angeles, Box 1.

33 See Earl of Bathurst to J. T. Bigge and W. M. G. Colebrooke, 'Instructions to the Commissioners of Inquiry', and 'Report of Colebrooke upon the Administration', in Mendis, *Colebrooke–Cameron Papers*, pp. 6, 70.

34 Mendis, 'Introduction', in *Colebrooke–Cameron Papers*, p. xlii.

35 Quoted in Victoria C. Olsen, *From Life: Julia Margaret Cameron and Victorian Photography* (New York: Palgrave Macmillan, 2003), p. 255, original emphasis.

36 Scott, 'Colonial Governmentality', 213.

37 Marianne North, *A Vision of Eden: The Life and Work of Marianne North* (New York: Holt, Rinehart and Winston, 1980), p. 115.

38 In 'The Blue Guide', Roland Barthes wrote that Christianity fuelled Western tourism to the Holy Land, but economic ties connected to Britain's botanic gardens generate North's travels. Roland Barthes, 'The Blue Guide', *Mythologies*, trans. Annette Lavers (New York: Hill and Wang, 1972), pp. 74–7.

39 One is tempted to draw a parallel with popular fictional heroines, women who transgressed some moral or supposedly biological norm, to help explain the appeal of such exotic plant life to the popular culture of the time.

40 Richard Drayton, *Nature's Government: Science, Imperial Britain, and the 'Improvement' of the World* (New Haven: Yale University Press, 2000), p. 183.

41  Drayton cites, as examples, in the North: Agra, Cawnpore, Lucknow, Delhi, Meerut, Umbala and Simla; in the North-West Provinces, Kussowlie, Dugshai and Lahore; in the East, soldiers of the East India Company established a garden at Pegu; in the South, at Ootacamund. *Ibid.*, pp. 182–3.

42  J. D. Hooker, 'Preface to the first edition, 1 June 1882', Royal Gardens, Kew, *Official Guide to the North Gallery*, 5th edn (London: Her Majesty's Stationery Office,1892), p. iii.

43  See Lucile H. Brockway, *Science and Colonial Expansion: The Role of the British Royal Botanic Gardens* (New York: Academic Press, 1979).

44  *Ibid.*, p. 51; J. C. Willis, 'The Royal Botanic Gardens of Ceylon, and their History', *Annals of the Royal Botanic Gardens, Peradeniya*, 1 (1901–2), 1.

45  Drayton, *Nature's Government*, p. 195.

46  *Ibid.*, pp. 208–9.

47  Leonard Huxley, ed., *Life and Letters of Sir Joseph Dalton Hooker OM, GCSI.* 2 vols (London: John Murray, 1918), vol. 1, pp. 522–7 (letter to Darwin, 2 July 1860 and commentary).

48  Willis, 'The Royal Botanic Gardens of Ceylon', 8.

49  *Report on the Progress and Conditions of the Royal Gardens at Kew, during the year 1878* (London: George E. Eyre and William Spottiswoode, 1879), p. 9.

50  Drayton, *Nature's Government*, p. 249.

51  When he visited the Royal Botanic Garden at Peradeniya in 1875, Anthony Trollope also met Thwaites and saw the same stand of trees; to Trollope, it was 'a land of loveliness, surrounded by the most perfect scenery which the mind can imagine. If, as some say, Eden was in Ceylon, this must have been the spot.' Anthony Trollope, *The Tireless Traveler*, ed. Bradford Allen Booth (Berkeley: University of California Press, 1941), p. 60.

52  Brockway, *Science and Colonial Expansion*, pp. 156–8.

53  On the plantation system and importation of Tamil coolies, see Ananda Wickramasinghe and Donald C. Cameron, 'British Capital, Ceylonese Land, Indian Labour: The Imperialism and Colonialism of Evolution of Tea Plantations in Sri Lanka', paper presented at *Critical Management Studies Conference (Management and Organizational History)*, Cambridge, 4–6 July 2005; Patrick Peebles, *The Plantation Tamils of Ceylon* (London: Continuum International Publishing Group, 2001); Rachel Kurian, Jenny Bourne, and Hazel Waters, 'Plantation politics', *Race and Class*, 26:1 (1984), 83–95; Michael Webb Roberts, 'Indian Estate Labour in Ceylon During the Coffee Period (1830–1880)', *Indian Economic and Social History Review*, 3:2 (1966), 1–52.

54  North, *A Vision of Eden*, p. 118.

55  Royal Gardens, Kew, *Official Guide to the North Gallery*, no. 284, p. 42.

56  This image is housed in the former collection of the Royal Photographic Society under the accession number RPS 20583; it is mounted on an album page, and it is *not included* in Julian Cox and Colin Ford, eds., *Julia Margaret Cameron: The Complete Photographs* (Los Angeles: J. Paul Getty Trust, 2003).

57  See Jean Grossholtz, *Forging Capitalist Patriarchy: The Economic and Social Transformation of Feudal Sri Lanka and its Impact on Women* (Durham, NC: Duke University Press, 1984), pp. 63–5.

58  North, *A Vision of Eden*, pp. 118–19.

59  *Ibid.*

60  *Ibid.*, p. 119.

61  Bhabha, *The Location of Culture*, pp. 112–20. By analogy, Cameron's two untitled photographs of large groups of Ceylonese men and women (Cox 1221, 1222) have been called representations of apparent 'idle natives' or 'plantation workers' as scholars have unintentionally adopted a colonialist frame of reference. As photographs of large groups in an outdoor setting, these photographs are extraordinary in Cameron's *oeuvre*, and cannot be

easily categorized, as they are neither 'group portraits' nor 'landscapes'. However, recent analysis demonstrates these individuals are neither idle nor plantation workers, but more likely Buddhist pilgrims to the religious shrine of The Temple of the Tooth in Kandy, possibly gathering for the annual Perahara Festival. See Jeff Rosen, 'Cameron's Children of the Colonies', in Catherine de Zegher, ed., *Julia Margaret Cameron, 1815–2015* (exhibition catalogue) (Ghent: Museum voor Schone Kunsten, 2015), pp. 194–213.

62  Linda K. Hughes and Michael Lund, *The Victorian Serial* (Charlottesville: University of Virginia Press, 1991), p. 155. The connection between George Eliot and Julia Margaret Cameron has been made earlier, but only in terms of Eliot's apparent interest in photography and her use of William Henry Fox Talbot's home, Lacock Abbey, as a model for a building in the novel, and not in terms of the analysis of this image. Kathleen McCormack, 'George Eliot, Julia Cameron, and William Henry Fox Talbot: Photography and *Daniel Deronda*', *Word and Image*, 12:2 (1996), 175–9. In 1871, Cameron sent George Eliot several photographs, which were gratefully received. See *The George Eliot Letters*, ed. Gordon S. Haight, vol. 5 (New Haven: Yale University Press, 1955), p. 133.

63  George Eliot, *Daniel Deronda* (Ware: Wordsworth Editions, 1996), chapter 29, p. 272.

64  *Ibid.*, chapter 3, pp. 15–16.

65  Jean Sudrann, '*Daniel Deronda* and the Landscape of Exile', *English Literary History*, 37:3 (1970), 436.

66  Edward Said, 'Zionism from the Standpoint of its Victims', *Social Text*, 1 (1979), 18.

67  Eliot, *Daniel Deronda*, chapter 69, p. 669.

68  See Marc E. Wohlfarth, '*Daniel Deronda* and the Politics of Nationalism', *Nineteenth-Century Literature*, 53:2 (1988), 188–210; Monica Cohen, 'From Home to Homeland: The Bohemian in *Daniel Deronda*', *Studies in the Novel*, 30:3 (1998), 324–54.

69  Archives of C. Kegan Paul, Trench, Trubner and Co., vol. 2, pp. 333–4. Archives of this publishing firm, which absorbed Henry S. King's firm in 1877, are in the Rare Book Room of the Harry Ransom Humanities Research Center at the University of Texas at Austin. A guide to the microfilm is published as *Index of Authors and Titles of Kegan Paul, Trench, Trubner and Henry S. King, 1858–1912* (Bishop's Stortford: Chadwyck-Healey, 1974). A useful assessment of the importance of the archive to habits of reading and publishing in Victorian Britain is Leslie Howsam, 'Forgotten Victorians: Contracts with Authors in the Publication Books of Henry S. King and Kegan Paul, Trench, 1871–89', *Publishing History*, 34 (1993), 51–70. My commentary on Cameron's author's commission is drawn from the actual record cited above as interpreted through Howsam's more general observations about the implications of such a contract.

70  Howsam, 'Forgotton Victorians', 58.

71  Leslie Howsam, *Kegan Paul: A Victorian Imprint* (London: Kegan Paul International, 1998), pp. 37–8.

72  Public Record Office, Kew, COPY 1/31, 18 October 1875.

73  Quoted in Joanne Lukitsh, 'Julia Margaret Cameron's Photographic Illustrations to Alfred Tennyson's "The Idylls of the King"', *Arthurian Literature*, 7 (1987), 147, original emphasis.

74  Helmut Gernsheim, *Julia Margaret Cameron: Her Life and Photographic Work* (New York: Aperture, 1975), pp. 53–4.

75  Letter from Julia Margaret Cameron to Hardinge Hay Cameron, 3 August 1876, Cameron Papers, Getty Research Institute, Los Angeles Box 1 .

76  Cox and Ford, *Julia Margaret Cameron* , p. 459.

77  *Ibid.*

78  Woolf, *Freshwater: A Comedy*, p. 83.

# Conclusion

## Beauty, genius, fine art

Wilfred Ward, who grew up a neighbour to both the Camerons and the Tennysons in the 1860s, recalled that during his youth, 'Freshwater seethed with intellectual life. The Poet was, of course, the centre, and that remarkable woman, Mrs Cameron, was stage manager of what was, for us young people, a great drama.'[1] Anne Thackeray's recollections, William Allingham's diary, Emily Tennyson's letters, all support Ward's memory about the teeming cultural life surrounding Julia Margaret Cameron. For many years, however, the personal drama that Ward described threatened to define Cameron's photography by limiting discussion of her imagery to her personal activities – her maternal and domestic life, philanthropic undertakings, private devotions, and her relationship to her models – and these have been well researched and documented.[2] But this has also meant that her photographs have become largely separated from the ideas, religious controversies, literary criticism, philosophical positions, and political debates that drew together the village's artistic and intellectual society as well as the larger cultural milieu in London where her photographs acquired meaning.

After she received a camera from her daughter as a Christmas present in 1863, Julia Margaret Cameron was initially attracted to portraiture and to the 'fancy picture' because of her interest in portraying scenes of everyday life in Freshwater. But because of her interest in literature and fine art, her engagement with philosophy and religion, and her larger political awareness as a colonial landowner and spouse to a colonial official, she pursued allegory as a creative tool because of its ability to give multiple sensibilities and meanings to a photograph. This book has argued that Cameron's photographs were connected deeply to the complex intellectual and political world of which she was a part and that her ambitions to use photography to contribute to those cultural debates explain the choice of her subject matter in the 'fancy pictures'. Like the painters, graphic artists, and literary figures in her circle, Cameron chose familiar narratives from the Old and New Testament, from classical mythology, modern poetry, contemporary literature, and the popular illustrated press, and she employed allegory to embed latent or secondary meanings in her photographs. She trusted photography to communicate ideas that were vital to the formation of British national identity and she chose subjects that would allow her to embed moral lessons to strengthen the nation's character. She called these allegorical photographs 'fancy subjects' and over the course of a dozen years applied a discerning intellectual framework and deliberate artistic working method to assign specific titles to her imagery. She returned to these images over time, reconsidered older subjects and created new ones, and occasionally changed titles – and meanings – along the way. She treated her fancy subjects as serious investigations that explored stories of national origins and religious heritage; that destabilized the familiar references and iconography of Christian biblical tales; and that used ancient examples, like Anglo-Saxon legends and Hellenistic mythologies, to shed light and comment on contemporary political activities of the British state. She created coherent bodies of imagery that drew upon her evident familiarity with the poetry of Byron, Swinburne, and Tennyson and contended with the literary criticism of Taylor, Arnold, and Trollope. She confronted global political crises that erupted in the 1860s by creating photographs that commented upon Britain's return of the Ionian islands, insurrection in the Jamaican colony, and the war in Abyssinia; during the 1870s she made imagery with respect to the 'Eastern question' and Tennyson's *Idylls of the King*. And she was influenced by a wide range of contemporary popular art forms, including textiles, wall paper, and book illustrations of *Paul and Virginia*; engraved selections from period folios, like *Finden's Byron Beauties*; cartoons from *Punch* and line drawings from the *Illustrated London News*; and small *carte-de-visite* portraits and cabinet cards depicting in miniature the same famous subjects that she also photographed in her grand, imposing, and evocative style.

All of this is not to say that Cameron did not welcome sympathetic assessments of her photography that also praised her imagery using familiar descriptive language common to fine art appreciation, terms like genius, beauty, nobility, and poetry, for example. Rather, she was happy to participate in and promote such critical acclaim, desirous to be written into history at whatever cost, visible as a productive artist and not demeaned as the camera-toting socialite that even some of her contemporaries proclaimed. Cameron was unfailingly generous: she showered photographs on her benefactors and friends as gifts, calling her portraits noble and elevated, her Madonnas and children saturated in loveliness, her personifications of Greek heroines overwhelmed by feeling; in short, she regarded her work as thoughtful and important contributions to the world of fine art. Importantly, she engaged a London print dealer, Colnaghi's, to sell her photographs; she executed contracts to produce additional sales through Tennyson's publishers and the Autotype Company; and she participated in fine arts exhibitions internationally, exhibiting twenty-three photographs in 1870 at the ninth exhibition of the Société française de photographie.[3] Her personal letters to Sir Henry Cole, Director of the South Kensington Museum and a friend from the Holland Park circle, whom she photographed in 1865 (Cox 633), provide useful evidence of her artistic aspirations:

> [On beauty and the artistic value of her photography:] I have real pleasure in telling you that Mr Watts thinks my photograph of you 'extremely fine' … All yesty [yesterday] I took studies of Lady Elcho & Lord Elcho said they were the finest things ever done in Art![4]

> [On her ambitions to use photography to open eyes and change minds:] My late series of photographs … I intend should electrify you with delight and startle the world. I hope it is no vain imagination of mine to say that the like have never been produced & never can be surpassed! … Because these wonderful photographs should come out all at once & take the world by surprise![5]

> [On striving to achieve wide recognition beyond her immediate circle:] Thro[ugh] your generous loan of those two rooms [in the South Kensington Museum, which Cole let Cameron use as a portrait studio,] I am likely now to acquire fortune as well as fame.[6]

> [On the national importance of portraying 'men of genius' for posterity:] My last portrait of Alfred Tennyson (not yet published) which I think you will agree with me in feeling is a National Treasure of immense value – next to the living speaking man must ever stand this portrait of him, quite the most faithful & most noble Portrait of him existing.[7]

These fragments support the much larger idea that Cameron wanted to imbue her works with the abstract ideas of 'fine art': 'beauty' and 'fineness' in her portrait of Lady Elcho; 'the real and the ideal' in the *Fruits of the Spirit*; 'heroic genius' and 'noble sensibility' in her portraits of Tennyson, Carlyle, and Cole. But Cameron's practice was to create numerous photographs of her heroes and then turn those images into more complex allegorical compositions; as works of art, these allegories no more erase Cameron's admiration for her sitters than they remove her photographs from the commercial world of Colnaghi's gallery or extract the colonial context from the historical record. In general, these works were not admired by her critics, who were unable or unwilling to join together the twin strands of realistic portraiture and idealized allegory. Perhaps Cameron never accepted the distinction: in her one-woman exhibitions, in the albums she constructed for family and friends, and in her directions to Colnaghi and the Autotype Company, Cameron always displayed and produced the portraits and allegories together, considering them equal artistic contributions to her *oeuvre*.

In Cameron's personifications of *King David*, or *Hypatia*, or *Temperance*, abstract ideas take on human form. Allegorical representations like these rely upon viewers accepting that an artistic transformation has taken place when a recognized sitter has been inserted into a mythological tableau or biblical scene, or has been renamed and reframed in a different historical context. Because personifications in visual art rely upon narratives and ideas that are both abstract and exterior to their representation in visual form, their meaning is not dependent upon our knowing about the particular identity of the individuals who sat for those compositions. In fact, for many photographs we do not know the names of the children who posed as *Cupid*, for example; nor did Cameron record the identities of the two sitters who sat for the photographs called *Jephthah and His Daughter* (Cox 168; Figure 32) and *The Bride of Abydos* (Cox 1138). And it is not quite clear if Marie Spartali truly understood that she was going to personify both *Hypatia* (Figure 4) and the *Imperial Eleänore* (Figure 5) from the documentary evidence that survives about the portrait session that led to these photographs.

In photography, lighting, the point of focus and depth of field, and exposure time all contribute to the successful creation of a photographic negative. But as we have seen, *posing* is even more critical to photographs of human subjects, because, as Craig Owens insisted, 'the subject poses as an object *in order to be a subject*'.[8] Understanding the nature of this artistic transformation intuitively, Cameron described her photographs as being 'from life', the phrase carefully chosen to denote the objectification of her subjects by the camera *and* the liveliness and animation of her subjects in the composition. Today we speak conventionally of photography's ability to fix, capture, or seize a dynamic subject; during her time, Cameron used the word 'immortalized' to offer a similar connotation. William Allingham quoted her in his diary using this term: 'Carlyle refuses to give me a sitting, he says it's a kind of *Inferno*! The greatest men of the age (with strong emphasis), Sir John Herschel, Henry Taylor, Watts, say I have *immortalised* them – and these other men object!! What is one to do – Hm?'[9]

We have seen that for Cameron, photography was an act of appropriation. She posed her sitters, gave them costumes and jewellery to wear, set them up with others in *tableaux vivants*, and transformed them from sitters into artistic subjects. At this point, she assigned allegorical titles to her prints: she identified storylines and assigned personifications by means of a signifying caption, turning her sitters into expressions of desire, sympathy, or power; archetypes of national heroism and honour, or their anti-types; exemplars of moral behaviour and righteousness; even stereotypes of gendered Oriental passion. With each title, she created a formal construct whose meaning and references either commented upon or were modified by contemporary external events; these could be political, theoretical, or historical. With every retitling, reprinting in reverse, or change in format, when she re-envisioned the same subject at a later date or remade the subject in an arched frame or printed it in a different tint, she introduced a new interpretation for her audience to consider that could change the meaning of her photographs.

## Wise and foolish virgins

In 1864, when Cameron took up photography, *The Five Wise Virgins* (Cox 122) and *The Five Foolish Virgins* (Cox 123; Figure 2) were among her first subjects. As we have seen, her neighbour, Emily Tennyson, was confounded by her friend's efforts to use the new medium to pose modern young women in roles illustrating the biblical parable. Early critics were equally baffled, even derisive; one offered the following opinion: 'In the two pictures of "The Wise and Foolish Virgins" it is difficult to distinguish which are the "Wise" and which are the "Foolish", the same models being employed for, and looking equally foolish in, both pictures.'[10] But Cameron was undaunted; together with *The Fruits of the Spirit* and other photographs depicting the Madonna that were based on Renaissance paintings, she developed what she called a new 'theology' in photography.

In fact, she had not quite exhausted this subject in those two early photographs: ten years later, first in August and then again in December 1874, she returned to the Parable of the Ten Virgins to reinterpret the biblical allegory once again. As we have seen in Chapter 6, she illustrated Tennyson's poem *Guinevere* from *Idylls of the King* with a photograph depicting the Queen and the Little Novice, titling her photograph *The Little Novice with the Queen Guinevere in the Holy House at Almesbury* (Cox 1173; Figure 44). During this time, Cameron also depicted the foolish virgins from the biblical parable in two other closely related photographs for which she used the same title: *Have we not heard the Bridegroom is so sweet!* (Cox 1127 – Figure 50; Cox 1128); (officially listed as *Variant of Too Late! Too Late!*). This title refers to the point in Tennyson's poem when the young novice admonishes Guinevere for her sin against King Arthur in her lyric song, the one that contains the popular refrain, 'Too late, too late!' The title is also a direct reference to the biblical parable in the Gospel of Matthew 25:1–13.

Cameron's photograph of *The Little Novice* is almost didactic as she depicts the young nun scolding and preaching to the fallen queen and Guinevere as passive, reconciled to the burden of listening to what she experiences as the girl's annoying prattle. Both models are pressed closely to the picture plane in shallow focus. The head covering of each character – white for the novice, black for the queen – accentuate the differences in their attitude, dispositions, and outlook. Interestingly, both occupy the same amount of visual space in the composition, illustrating a kind of détente or equilibrium, one that is almost painful to watch if our sympathies lie with the queen. For Cameron's other title, *Have we not heard the Bridegroom is so sweet!*, she excerpted the phrase from the nun's song and made two distinct photographs, each one depicting the five foolish virgins in front of a locked gate, downcast and dejected at having been barred from entering. In both of the images titled *The Bridegroom*, the five women depicted in front of the ornamental gate appear disordered and confused, a great contrast to the simplicity, visual order, and

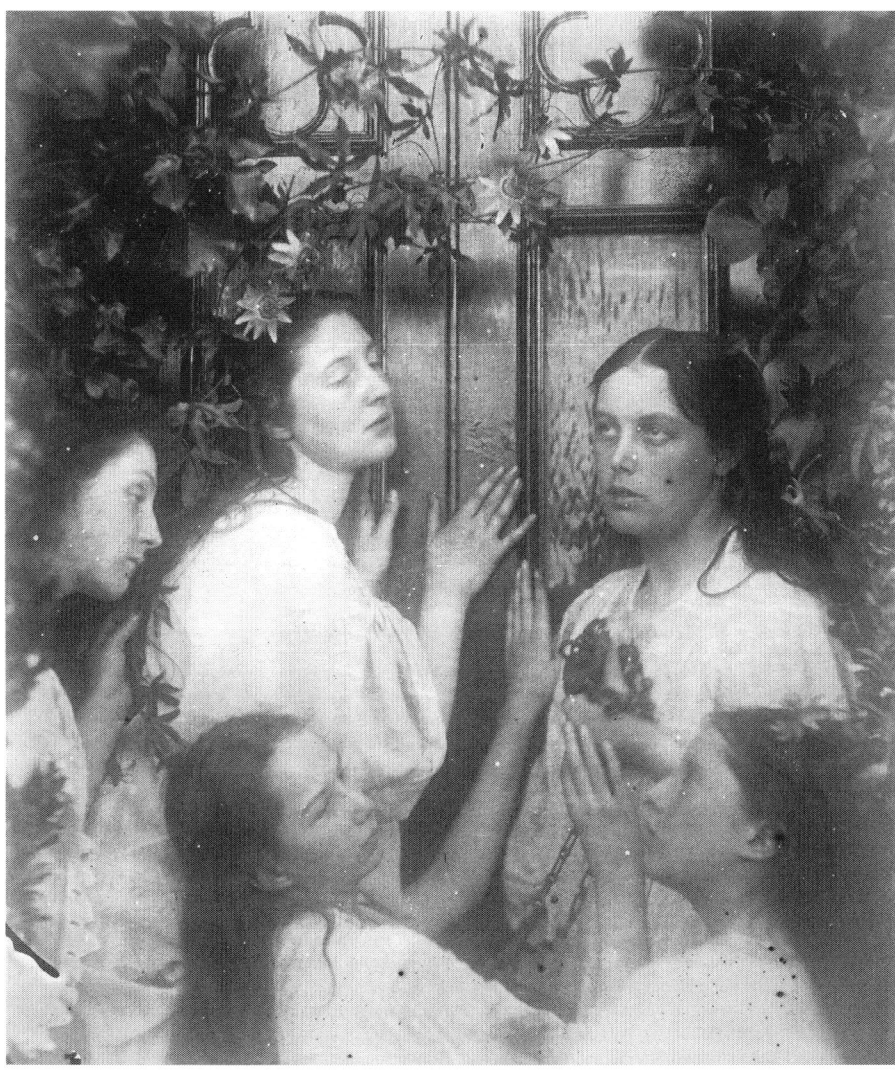

Julia Margaret Cameron, *Variant of Too Late! Too Late! [Have we not heard the*            **50**
*Bridegroom is so sweet!]* (Cox 1127), 1874. Albumen print, 32.8 x 27.5 cm.

symmetry that anchors *The Little Novice.* The five outcasts are portrayed sympathetically nevertheless in gestures of supplication and prayer.

Cameron produced all three of these photographs for wide distribution: she included *The Little Novice* in her published volume illustrating Tennyson's *Idylls of the King* and produced two different kinds of prints for the two compositions of *Have we not heard the Bridegroom is so sweet!* She selected one of these images (Cox 1128) to be printed by the Autotype Company and marked the other (Cox 1127; Figure 50) 'From Life Registered Photograph Copyright Julia Margaret Cameron

Aug 74' (although for that particular month in 1874, no official record exists for Cameron in the copyright registers).[11] It is unknown if Cameron made the two photographs of *The Bridegroom* as possible alternatives to *The Little Novice* in the making of her illustrated volumes of Tennyson's *Idylls*, or if she imagined some other purpose for these works.

What factors explain the staying power of this particular narrative for Cameron? In the biblical parable, ten virgins await a bridegroom as part of an Eastern marriage ceremony; their job is to greet the groom and escort him into the event. In biblical times, these rituals took place at night, which explains the need for oil lamps to guide the way. The five wise virgins are wise because they have prepared for the groom's arrival by filling their lamps with oil, while the five foolish virgins have not. While waiting for the bridegroom to appear, all ten virgins fall asleep because the bridegroom is unexpectedly late in coming to the ceremony. And all awaken upon his arrival, but only the wise virgins are ready to accompany the bridegroom, while the foolish virgins can only fumble about in the dark. They try to borrow oil from their much wiser sisters but cannot persuade them to lend them any. Reluctantly, they run off to find oil elsewhere. When they return, they find it is 'too late': the gate is locked, they have been excluded, the service has begun. As she did in 1864, Cameron portrayed the five foolish virgins looking forlorn because they have been excluded from the ceremony.

Since biblical times, the Parable of the Ten Virgins has been a staple in countless sermons, but in nineteenth-century England the allegory gained new currency, particularly in support of or in reaction to the orthodoxy of the Tractarian movement. The Parable may be traced to its early roots in the Church: ancient theologians like Augustine of Hippo and the medieval Anglo-Saxon abbot Ælfric, for example, wrote about the Parable in Matthew as an unmistakable allegory for the Last Judgement. Just as the Bridegroom comes unannounced and late to the ceremony, the monks taught, Christ can come at any time to judge all of mankind. In anticipation of that unpredictable moment, every person's soul must be prepared and stand watchful, ready to meet the Last Judgement. But Augustine and Ælfric also taught that it was essential that one lead a pure, ascetic, and penitent life in order to pave the way into heaven, and that only 'the foolish' would follow a different path. By Cameron's time, the Tractarian movement embraced this orthodox interpretation of the Parable. For example, Edward Pusey explained: '[Christ] will come as a thief in the night; and well will it be for those who have still their lamps burning, who have not forfeited the treasure of baptismal grace, who will be in a condition with trembling hope to go forth and meet their Saviour, relying on no merits of their own, but on His manifold and great mercies.'[12]

Low and Broad Church explanations of the Parable, by contrast, took several forms. But these sermons focused less on the mystical day of final judgement (especially as a transcendent or visionary experience) and more on the importance of leading a good and honourable life as a commonplace daily expression of ethical duty and moral obligation. Their interpretations evolved from the sermons of eighteenth-century evangelicals like George Whitefield, who compared the actions of the ten virgins to an individual's moral responsibilities. Whitefield's sermons introduced the Parable as a way to argue for enlightening 'the foolish' in order to give them wisdom, alerting them to their everyday responsibilities, preparing them to be vigilant. For Whitefield, the important analogical reference was not to the ultimate event of the Last Judgement but rather to the daily obligation to lead a moral life.[13] During the nineteenth century, Anglicans like Isaac Taylor directly criticized the asceticism, abstinence, and self-restraint that were advocated by early patristic fathers like John Chrysostom – which had been embraced by the Tractarians – and their portrayal of chastity and almsgiving as sure ways to be admitted into heaven.[14] The importance of teaching everyday morality was also embraced by the Archbishop of Dublin, Richard Chenevix Trench, who reinforced the lesson that the foolish virgins could not simply rely upon oil transferred to them from their more prepared sisters; he preached that moral preparedness was an individual's sole responsibility, a solemn duty that could not be reassigned or shared with another person: 'Every man must live by his own faith.'[15] Thomas Guthrie of the Free Church of Scotland went even further, using the Parable to urge his congregation to focus on the here-and-now rather than the hereafter, 'to make it all up with him who is willing to forgive all, and is now tarrying on the road to give you time to get oil, and go forth with joy to the cry, Behold, the Bridegroom cometh!'[16]

It is not known whether Cameron was aware of these particular sectarian differences, but we do know that she embraced rather than avoided theological controversies and that she engaged her closest friends and peers in discussing the merits of different positions. In Freshwater, as we have seen, Benjamin Jowett represented an unorthodox perspective about biblical interpretation that was opposed firmly by the local vicar, Reverend John Frederick Isaacson. Tennyson received Jowett as a friend, and also embraced another important cleric with whom he had been a close confidant since their student days at Cambridge, the Anglican priest William Henry Brookfield. Cameron met Brookfield during this period, most likely during one of Brookfield's regular visits to Tennyson. In 1864, she took his portrait (Cox 586) and included his photograph in albums she gave to Herschel and to Taylor. But also around this time, Cameron attended a church service in London with Anne Thackeray where Brookfield preached. The two apparently sought him out as an inspirational speaker. Thackeray recorded the event:

> Mrs Cameron led her way into the gallery and took up her place in front exactly facing the pulpit. When Mr Brookfield appeared climbing the pulpit stairs to deliver his sermon, his head was so near us that we could have almost touched it. Mrs Cameron chose this moment to lean forward and kiss her hand to him repeatedly.[17]

While we do not know what particular sermon Brookfield preached that day, his homily on the Parable of the Ten Virgins was popular enough to be reprinted in 1874, shortly after his death. In fact, many in Cameron's extended network of friends contributed to the memoir that Brookfield's widow assembled to honour his memory. This essay was included as the preface to a volume published in 1875 that reprinted his most popular sermons. The famous contributors to this tribute included Henry Taylor, James Spedding, FitzJames Stephen, A. W. Kinglake, Tennyson, and Carlyle. If Cameron did not own the book of sermons herself, she certainly would have discussed Brookfield's death, and contemplated his life's work, with friends like Tennyson and others in her immediate circle who knew him best.

In Brookfield's sermon on the Parable of the Ten Virgins, he expressed concern about the fate of the foolish virgins and by extension, to all those in his congregations who might now also be unprepared for the final judgement. He asked his listeners rhetorically: could a kind and compassionate god actually proclaim that it could ever be 'too late', and therefore risk denying the eternal life he promised from the unsuspecting, the unrepentant, or the unredeemed, especially if those individuals might seek redemption at the very last moment? As a way to illustrate this theological controversy with the aid of a modern poem, Brookfield quoted Tennyson's poem *Guinevere*, specifically calling attention to the song of the Little Novice to highlight the fateful moment and moral dilemma when 'repentance and the real wish for amendment have become impossible', and it then becomes 'too late. The door is shut.'

But Brookfield actually used this story to open the door to hope and compassion: his sermon contradicted official Church orthodoxy and introduced the prospect of last-minute deliverance: 'Once introduce the element of repentance and obedience, and there is no language large enough to express the comprehensiveness of the Divine mercy', wrote Brookfield. Such hopefulness can come to an individual even at the last possible moment, he says: 'if we feel with ourselves one single aspiration after a better and more spiritual life, accompanied by one single breath of prayer to cherish that aspiration into flame; if we retain one single spark of energy to leave that which is evil, and to do that which is good; if God gives us power this day to abandon one single sin and to give entertainment to one single grace – then with such persons it is not too late.'[18]

Tennyson, of course, was not obliged to uphold Church teachings in his poetry, and in *Guinevere*, he provided clues that affirm Brookfield's theological interpretation, finding that it was never 'too late' to lead a principled and moral life, even in spite of the effusive speech of the Little Novice. In fact, when Tennyson assigned the task of singing the refrain of the Parable of the Ten Virgins to the Little Novice, he did so as a way to undermine the nun's rebuke by indicating the young girl was an unreliable and inexperienced critic, too simple and unformed to understand precisely what she meant when she nattered 'too late, too late'. As Stephen Ahern has written, Tennyson made the Little Novice a naïf who 'sees the world in black and white, in terms of the inflexible categories of conventional morality'.[19] Accordingly, Cameron's photograph (Figure 44) is composed in stark black and white. But because of the girl's youth and innocence, Guinevere can only reply to her that 'outside "narrowing nunnery-walls"', moral judgements and virtuous decisions are not easily made and cannot be framed in absolutes; this is because the world, with 'all its lights / And shadows', is complex and uncertain, rather than unequivocal and universal (ll. 340–5).

In this poem, moreover, Tennyson denounced the severity and ruthlessness of the culture of chivalry and expressed contempt for an orthodox mind-set that could even conceive of excluding those who tried to redeem their moral failures, even with respect to Guinevere. In their final scene together, in fact, Guinevere receives Arthur's forgiveness. In response, the fallen queen releases herself from the utter despondency she felt from the song of the Little Novice and expresses immediate feelings of hopefulness and optimism for what remains of her future life: 'And blessed be the King, who hath forgiven / My wickedness to him, and left me hope / That in mine own heart I can live down sin / And be his mate hereafter in the heavens / before high God' (ll. 629–33). In clear opposition to the doctrines of the Roman Church, then, Tennyson's King Arthur grants forgiveness and hope as if he is a kind of British messiah. If we were to take Tennyson at his word, it would seem his sentiments about entry into heaven in *Idylls of the King* lie more closely with Brookfield's sense of compassion and generosity than with Pusey's unsympathetic warnings and harsh censure.

Julia Margaret Cameron's return to the Parable of the Wise and Foolish Virgins ten years after first illustrating the subject demonstrates her commitment to using allegorical subject matter as the abiding centre of her photography. Her long-standing interest in this particular story establishes her enthusiasm for exploring new visual strategies to illustrate the narrative and her embrace of controversial theological ideas in her imagery, connecting her photographs to the poetry of Tennyson and the sermons of Brookfield. Cameron's photographs of *The Little Novice* and *Have we not heard the Bridegroom is so sweet?* may express her own ambivalence, but these works also demonstrate her desire to represent multiple and conflicting interpretations of the same subject. Throughout her photographic career, her working methods supported this interest and gave voice to her intellectual engagement with these subjects, allowing her to continually re-evaluate her symbolic titles and even their compositions, even many years after first portraying an allegorical subject like *The Five Foolish Virgins*.

Cameron's enduring interest in compassion and redemption led her to the fancy picture, while her intellectual pursuits led her to allegory. Thematically, the two impulses fused together in photographs that depicted loneliness and isolation

(*Oenone, Daphne, Psyche*); the psychic pain of abandonment (*Beatrice, Christabel, Rosalba*); the human desire of yearning (*Sappho*; *The Imperial Eleänore*; *The Echo*); and the fragility of innocence (*Young Endymion*; *Young Astyanax*; *Paul and Virginia*). Cameron repeatedly portrayed the resilience of the human spirit and personified exemplars of moral strength and courage. She expressed these ideas photographically in religious imagery (*The Fruits of the Spirit, The Holy Family, The Shunamite Woman*); in Byron's heroines (*La Donna* [Julia] *at Her Devotions, Haidie, Zoë, Maid of Athens*); in historical characters reinterpreted by her literary contemporaries (*Hypatia, Balaustion, Boadicea, The Princess* [Ida], *Adriana*). And Cameron portrayed scenes expressing hope and optimism for the gift of reconciliation and redemption (*King David, Jephthah and His Daughter, She Walks in Beauty, Maud, The Little Novice with the Queen Guinevere, The Foolish Virgins*).

Cameron infused her fancy pictures with compassion and expressed sympathy with her human subjects. She was the first photographer in the medium's history to use allegory to depict narratives of moral relativism and conflict, to illustrate brave acts of female agency and independence, to represent the ambiguities of the colonial condition, and to use her imagery to teach moral lessons as a way to foster national identity and safeguard hope for the future.

## Notes

1 *Thackeray's Daughter*, ed. Hester Thackeray Fuller and Violet Hammersley (London: Guernsey Press, 1951), p. 113.

2 Mike Weaver agreed, writing: 'Too much attention has been given to the personal characteristics of this remarkable woman and her family, and too little to their intellectual background.' Mike Weaver, *Julia Margaret Cameron, 1815–1879* (Southampton: John Hansard Gallery, 1984), p. 89.

3 *Catalogues des expositions organisées par la Société française de photographie* (Paris: Editions Jean-Michel Place, 1985), 1870. Catalogue, p. 9.

4 Letter from Julia Margaret Cameron to Sir Henry Cole, 20 May 1865, collection of the Victoria and Albert Museum, London.

5 Letter from Julia Margaret Cameron to Sir Henry Cole, 21 February 1866, collection of the Victoria and Albert Museum, London.

6 Letter from Julia Margaret Cameron to Sir Henry Cole, 7 April 1868, collection of the Victoria and Albert Museum, London.

7 Letter from Julia Margaret Cameron to Sir Henry Cole, 12 June 1869, collection of the Victoria and Albert Museum, London.

8 Craig Owens, *Beyond Recognition: Representation, Power, and Culture* (Berkeley and Los Angeles: University of California Press, 1992), p. 215, original emphasis.

9 *William Allingham, A Diary*, ed. H. Allingham and D. Radford (London: Macmillan and Co., 1907), 10 June 1867, p. 153, original emphasis.

10 *The Photographic Journal*, 15 August 1865; quoted in Helmut Gernsheim, *Creative Photography* (New York: Bonanza, 1962), p. 84.

11 R. Derek Wood, ed., *Julia Margaret Cameron's Copyrighted Photographs* (London: privately published, May 1996), copy archived at the Royal Photographic Society, Bath, and online at: www.midley.co.uk/cameron/cameron.pdf

12  Edward Bouverie Pusey, *A Course of Sermons on Solemn Subjects: chiefly bearing on repentance and amendment of life, preached in St. Saviour's church, Leeds, during the week after its consecration* (Oxford: John Henry Parker, 1845), p. 79.

13  George Whitefield, 'The Wise and Foolish Virgins', in Robert Cochrane, ed., *The Treasury of British Eloquence* (Edinburgh: William P. Nimmo and Co., 1880), pp. 152–9.

14  Elizabeth A. Clark, 'Contested Bodies: Early Christian Asceticism and Nineteenth-Century Polemics', *Journal of Early Christian Studies*, 17:2 (2009), 281–307.

15  Richard Chenevix Trench, *Notes on the Parables of Our Lord*, 12th edn (New York: D. Appleton and Co., 1867), p. 212.

16  Thomas Guthrie, *The Parables Read in the Light of the Present Day* (New York: Robert Carter, 1874), p. 46.

17  *Thackeray's Daughter*, ed. Fuller and Hammersley, p. 111.

18  *Sermons by the late Rev. W. H. Brookfield*, ed. Mrs Brookfield (London: Smith, Elder, and Co., 1875), pp. 33, 35.

19  Stephen Ahern, 'Listening to Guinevere: Female Agency and the Politics of Chivalry in Tennyson's "Idylls"', *Studies in Philology*, 101:1 (2004), 102–3.

# Index